Emerging Communities:
Integrating Networked Information into Library Services

Papers presented at the 1993 Clinic on Library Applications
of Data Processing, April 4-6, 1993
Sponsored by
Graduate School of Library and Information Science
University of Illinois at Urbana-Champaign

Clinic on Library Applications
of Data Processing: 1993

Emerging Communities:
Integrating Networked Information into Library Services

Edited by
ANN P. BISHOP

Graduate School of Library and Information Science
University of Illinois at Urbana-Champaign

© 1994 by The Board of Trustees of the University of Illinois
ISBN 0-87845-094-7   ISSN 0069-4789

Printed in the United States of America
on acid-free paper

CONTENTS

Introduction

Wide area computer networks, such as those comprising the Internet, are providing teachers, students, researchers, businesspeople, the general public, and librarians with access to a growing array of information resources. They are also opening new channels for communication both within and beyond organizational boundaries, allowing librarians to develop new electronic communities with their colleagues and patrons. Electronic information resources and communication networks may facilitate, even transform, many aspects of library work. The push for libraries to get "on the net" is getting stronger as the costs of the technology fall, the number of network-accessible resources grows, staff and user expectations regarding network capabilities in the library rise, and librarians' familiarity with the benefits of networking broadens. As part of its current emphasis on the National Information Infrastructure (NII), the federal government has developed a number of policies that support the growth of the National Research and Education Network (NREN), the creation of digital libraries, and the use of electronic means for disseminating government information. The gradual introduction of networking workshops and formal coursework into schools of library and information science has begun to create a cadre of new entrants to the profession who have some familiarity with the latest networking technology and applications.

In spite of the factors that encourage libraries to make greater use of computer networks, we face a number of problems and issues related to the integration of networking into libraries and related settings, making the transition to a networked environment far from easy. Beyond the obvious problems of constrained financial resources, lack of expertise with networking technology, and the chaotic and unstable state of information resources on the network, other barriers also exist. Federal information policies related to networking, many people believe, favor private sector stakeholders and don't go far enough in their mandates to support the public interest and library participation in the NII. Perhaps most importantly, networked resources—by their nature—often necessitate a departure from the kinds of collections and services familiar to many librarians and library users. Little is known about the costs and benefits of networked information services or about how best to integrate them into library settings. This is true whether one approaches the equation from an economic or a social perspective or whether one focuses on the information professional, his or her institution, or the needs of patrons.

Thus, libraries are currently seeking models for providing network access, training network users, incorporating networked information into existing services and operations, and evaluating the impact of networked information on their operations. This situation led to "Emerging Communities: Integrating Networked Information into Library Services" being chosen as the theme of the 30th Annual Clinic on Library Applications of Data Processing. The conference, sponsored by the Graduate School of Library and Information Science of the University of Illinois at Urbana-Champaign, was held on April 4-6, 1993. It provided an opportunity for information professionals from a wide variety of settings to discuss their experiences and concerns related to computer networking, with over 25 speakers sharing their research, expertise, and insights with about 200 conference attendees. Conference topics included:

- the use of computer networks in public, school, academic, and special libraries to accomplish institutional goals, provide traditional and new services, and communicate with users;
- legal, economic, and policy issues related to the electronic dissemination of information;
- bibliographic control of networked information and the new generation of networked OPACs; and
- new roles for information professionals in the networked environment.

In addition, pre-conference workshops allowed participants to explore some aspects of networking in depth. Greg Newby and Brett Sutton (University of Illinois at Urbana-Champaign) provided a hands-on introduction to the basics of Internet use. Tracy LaQuey Parker (Cisco Systems, Inc.) and Philip Doty (University of Texas at Austin) discussed options and procedures for obtaining an Internet connection. Anne G. Lipow (Library Solutions Institute) presented principles and techniques for training staff and end-users in network use. Finally, a workshop led by F. W. Lancaster (University of Illinois at Urbana-Champaign) provided attendees with an opportunity to learn more about methods for assessing networking needs and impacts. This workshop included a panel of experts made up of librarians and system designers (conference speakers Pat Molholt, Pam Sandlian, and Hope N. Tillman), along with a sociologist noted for her ethnographic research into the behavior and habits of scientific communities (S. Leigh Star of the Department of Sociology at the University of Illinois at Urbana-Champaign).

The Clinic also included an evening of informal demonstrations of network tools and resources. Two new systems designed to encourage the development of network communities were highlighted. Joseph Hardin and Marc Andreessen (National Center for Supercomputing Applications at the University of Illinois) demonstrated NCSA Mosaic, a globally distributed hypermedia information system that allows users to browse the Internet and associated multimedia resources. Bruce Schatz (University of Illinois at Urbana-Champaign) presented the Worm Community System, a distributed, multifunctional digital library system used worldwide by members of a particular research community. And finally, a number of conference participants came prepared to "show and tell," demonstrating their institutions' OPACs, their favorite networked information resources, and networking tools they had developed. Another special feature was a "Meet the Authors" event: Tracy LaQuey Parker, Ed Krol, and Anne G. Lipow—authors of popular new Internet guides—were on hand to sign copies of their books and describe how they came to be written.

This volume represents the presentations delivered at the 1993 Clinic; the papers contained here range from edited transcripts of authors' remarks to more formal and lengthy papers. Linking libraries and local communities through networks was the focus of both the Clinic's keynote address by Tom Grundner and the first conference session. Grundner discussed the role of the National Public Telecomputing Network in the development of community computer networks called Free-Nets, describing their costs and benefits to the community and the potential role of NREN and other federal initiatives in relation to community-based computing. Cisler's paper presents a range of current models for community networks, places them within a historical framework, and speculates on the future of such networks, given changing technologies. Doman describes the Community Connections service at MAGGIE'S PLACE (the online catalog of the Pikes Peak Library District) and discusses its history and impact on the library. Erbes and Beechler-Rusch describe the outcomes—both positive and negative—of the Illinois Valley Library System's involvement with the Heartland Free-Net and present conclusions that are applicable to libraries connecting either to community networks or to the Internet itself. There is also a role for academic institutions in this realm. Ongoing efforts at Princeton University to use computer networking to forge links with the local community are discussed by Stokes. Princeton's approach is notable in its assumption that universities have a responsibility to use their networking resources in support of local communities; it is less unique in that campus libraries were not as involved in these activities as were campus computing organizations.

The second group of papers center on networked information and library catalogs. Dillon, Jul, and their colleagues at OCLC provide an overview of results from OCLC's Internet Resources project, which investigated the nature of electronic textual information available through remote Internet access and the practical and theoretical problems associated with creating MARC records for these resources. Drabenstott and Cochrane conducted an empirical investigation of online catalogs accessible over the Internet and discuss what they learned about the problems in subject searching that challenge users of these catalogs. Recognizing that the success of the electronic library will depend on distributed computing, storage, and retrieval standards that enable multiple user interfaces to multiple information stores, Troll examines the lessons learned by Carnegie Mellon University Libraries in building their library system. Her paper is of interest for its thoughtful exploration of theoretical issues as well as the practical guidance it offers. Charles Hildreth discusses advantages and problems associated with extending the online catalog to encompass "nontraditional" networked information resources.

Lynch presented a special address at the conference that examined possible roles for libraries in the new networked environment and draws insight from the history of mass media broadcasters and their relationship with advertisers and sponsors. His paper sketches provocative conclusions about legal and economic shifts due to networking and their potential implications: the breakdown of the current interlibrary loan system for access to networked resources, the great costs of electronic information, and attempts to market information directly to consumers, bypassing libraries entirely.

Many networking activities today focus on how electronic information and communication services can be employed to enhance learning and information access for children, and several conference papers explore this area. Sandlian asserts that the development of customized networked information for children is one step that serves to help them become sophisticated information users. Her paper outlines the conceptual and empirical foundations of the design of the Denver Public Library's Kid's Catalog (which is now available commercially) and provides valuable guidelines for the collection of the user-based data on information needs and behavior that should be incorporated in any system design project. Waugh and Levin provide an overview of their research into the nature and impact of educational interactions on computer networks and suggest instructional strategies that anyone involved in using networks for education can employ. CICNet's Pioneering Partners project is discussed by Hankins. The project was designed to foster the adoption of innovative technologies in primary and secondary schools and included instructional components as well as mechanisms designed to give participants some experience with the use of networks to communicate and exchange ideas. Hankins presents a candid assessment of the project's outcomes and offers some thoughts on the potential contributions of electronic networking applications to education.

One conference session was devoted to the use of networked information in special libraries and other settings. In their paper, Tillman and Ladner present the results of the empirical study of Internet training and use that they conducted among special librarians. Especially valuable to those trying to understand the real benefits of networking to librarians, and to predict where difficulties might arise, are the comments their survey elicited about how and why networks are used. Stam reports that museums have been slow to adopt electronic networking, and she analyzes the institutional characteristics that impede the more rapid and widespread adoption of networking in museums. Her discussion of networking barriers suggests that information science professionals have a role to play in making networked information more accessible and useful for a variety of audiences. Janet Vratny, an information scientist in the Apple Library, gave a presentation that focused on how networked information can be integrated into corporate libraries and also described her unique role as a participant in the development of new products intended to improve the delivery of networked information. We were unable to include the complete text of Vratny's presentation in this volume; an abstract is provided, and readers are invided to contact Vratny for more information.

Issues and initiatives in networking policy are gaining increasing attention as publishers, policymakers, and network service providers struggle to envision, create, and reap the benefits from the emerging global network. Peters provides an insider's description of current initiatives in the Clinton/Gore administration related to "information superhighways." He also discusses four constituencies (those anxious to secure networking's advantages for the research and education community, those interested in the implications of networking as a foundation for 21st-century life and enterprise, those contemplating how best to use global networking to create "a retail paradise for couch potatoes," and those who believe in the power of global networking to create a new social order) that have been instrumental in shaping how issues are defined and how public policies in the area of networking are formulated. Garrett explores the philosophical basis for emerging electronic communities. He examines the dynamic integration of evolving technologies, the transformation of thought and society, and ideas about democracy. Garrett addresses, thus, the critical questions of "What kind of world do we want?" and "What can and will we do to get it?" His paper offers readers a chance to pause and think about the broader implications of our increasing reliance on computer networks to transmit our thoughts and recorded knowledge. Love describes a range of specific federal activities related to the electronic dissemination of government information. His analysis allows him to discuss, with great force, critical issues such as who will own and control the information resources and systems created with federal funds, what types of value-added services federal agencies will be authorized to provide, how federal electronic information products and services will be priced and made accessible, and what the role of the average citizen will be in shaping federal information policies.

Several conference papers address the integration of computer networks into academic library services. Larsen describes the transition in academic libraries from using networks to supplement information resources to using networks to enable, more broadly, a range of scholarly activities. After describing current constraints facing academic libraries, he argues that networks are able to provide the demand-based, location- and time-independent access to resources that scholars demand and libraries must supply. In their separate papers, Garrison and Entlich present a wealth of specific information related to academic libraries and their attempts to integrate networked information into their services. Based largely on their participation in projects at Cornell University's Mann Library (a recognized leader in the adoption of new technologies), they offer excellent insights and guidance related to justifying, planning, implementing, managing, and assessing networked information services. Kovacs and Fleming offer guidance in another important area as they describe the range of humanities information resources currently available on the Internet. Frequently, it is science and technology disciplines that capture attention and support when new networked information services are considered. Kovacs and Fleming offer ample evidence that people in humanities disciplines are significant users of such new services as well, and they include some tips for offering Internet access at the reference desk.

The concluding set of papers in this volume deal with new roles for librarians in the world of networked information. Bruce Schatz describes the digital library—integrating biology data, archival literature, and informal material—that he designed for the community of molecular biologists who study the nematode worm. This networked system serves as a model for understanding both the technology and "sociology" of networked research communities. Its development allowed Schatz to identify roles that information professionals can play in the creation of digital libraries, where there is a critical need for people who can collect data, transform it into canonical format, and interconnect related items; understand how researchers want to interact with the knowledge they use; and design and build customized information systems. Molholt describes current efforts at Columbia University to develop a networked system that will better integrate the library into the curriculum by providing a student-centered electronic environment based on a knowledge model that links unique, local information resources with those established elsewhere in the world. Her discussion of project goals and potential problems and outcomes suggests both the need for librarians to participate in such efforts and the skills and characteristics that librarians should develop if they want to become active participants. The conference concluded with a paper by Watson and Hartman of Bradley University, who described how the vision of the wired university was brought to fruition on their campus. Their experiences lead them to conclude that important success factors for the survival of the academic library in the networked environment include involving the library and librarians in the sociopolitical matrix of the university and making proactive use of new technologies and services. The authors outline "real world" strategies for academic librarians seeking to take advantage of networked information, including teamwork, professional development, creating an explicit statement of expectations and making a commitment to quality service, and, perhaps most difficult, removing from the library staff those persons who are unable or unwilling to support the transition to the networked environment.

The purpose of this year's Clinic was not so much to provide an introduction to the latest and greatest networked information technology and tools; rather, we attempted to put together a program that would offer information professionals some guidance as they strive to make efficient and effective use of what is already available to them. We feel that the papers collected here do indeed provide, from a variety of perspectives, insights and information that will be valuable to librarians and others as they attempt to integrate networked information into their current operations. Taken together, the papers raise important issues related to the emergence of new electronic communities that we invite you to contemplate and help resolve.

The Graduate School of Library and Information Science is grateful for the support for the Clinic we received from the Coalition for Networked Information (CNI), CICNet, Data Research Associates, and, at the University of Illinois, the Institute of Government and Public Affairs and the MillerComm Committee. CNI's contribution, among other things, gave the School an opportunity for a new venture into the world of networked information; for the first time, conference papers were made available via Gopher and FTP so that the material could reach a wider audience, more quickly, than in the past.

ANN P. BISHOP
Editor

TOM GRUNDNER

President
National Public Telecomputing Network
Cleveland, Ohio

Seizing the Infosphere: An Alternative Vision for National Computer Networking*

INTRODUCTION

What I'd like to try to do this evening is cover a broad range of topics. I know that some of the people in the audience probably don't quite know what a community computer is, some do know and want to find out more, and some are actively involved in putting community computer systems together here in the Champaign-Urbana area or in other places.

So what I'd like to try to do first, so people don't get left out of the conversation, is to describe what community computer systems are and talk a little bit about how they work. I want to do that partially because there are people who need that introduction, but also because when I start talking about policy and so forth, I'd like you to think of those statements in the context of community computing. For that reason alone, I think we should cover a little bit of background.

The concept behind community computing is not particularly new. James Madison, I think, said it best when he wrote in an 1822 letter: "A popular government without popular information, or the means of acquiring it, is but a prologue to a farce or a tragedy; or, perhaps, both. Knowledge will forever govern ignorance; and a people who mean to be their own governors must arm themselves with the power which knowledge gives."

Now, when Madison wrote those words, he couldn't possibly have envisioned the kind of computerized information networks that we deal with today. Indeed, I doubt that he could have visualized the idea of radio or television, but he certainly knew what the printing press was about because that was the dominant medium of his day. He and his colleagues knew enough about it to be able to utilize that medium as an essential linchpin in the development of the American Revolution.

We've come a long way since those days. We have developed the radio. We have developed television. We have refined the print medium. And we have

*This paper is an edited transcript of the keynote address given at the Clinic.

integrated these media into a force that affects our daily lives. One of the points that I'd like to make tonight is the fact that what we're looking at now is literally the development of a fourth medium. We're talking about telecomputing systems. These things are not radio; they are not television; they are not print. Yet, they've got characteristics of all three, plus a whole lot of characteristics that are all their own. What we've been doing with community computing is trying to find a way to take this new medium, channel it, harness it, and find some way to make it work for the general public. That's the basic idea behind community computing.

HOW A FREE-NET WORKS

In a more direct sense, the way a Free-Net community computer system works is essentially this. A multiuser computer is established at a central location in a given city. These systems are, in turn, linked to the Internet. They are accessed by community members via regular voice-grade phone lines connected to modems. Community users include anyone in the community who can get access to a home computer, a school computer, or a library machine to dial in to the Free-Net and access the range and array of information and communication services that are available there.

One of the things that makes this concept a little bit different is the notion of system operators or "sysops." These are people from within the community who volunteer their time and effort to operate their little piece of the system. Yet, the net effect is a kind of collective whole that's greater than the sum of its parts. Sysops are doctors, lawyers, veterinarians, space scientists, hobbyists of all kinds—people from all walks of life who operate Free-Net SIGs, or Special Interest Groups—who receive information, ask questions, whatever. It's like a common fountain of information to which anybody can contribute, and from which anybody can draw. These community systems in turn are connected to the Internet (which we'll be talking about in some detail in a little while) which provides, basically, international connectivity. A person on any Free-Net can send electronic mail to any Internet location anywhere in the world. And, indeed, it's the way that we Free-Net administrators connect ourselves to our various affiliates.

Probably the easiest way to describe a community computer or a Free-Net system is to ask you to think of a continuum. At one end of the continuum, think of something like CompuServe, or GEnie, or Prodigy, or one of the other commercial services. At the other end of the continuum, think of something like a bulletin board system (BBS) that hobbyists would run in their basements or as a part of their organizations. What we're trying to do here is to occupy a new middle ground between those two extremes. Multiuser systems that have, hopefully, some of the power and sophistication of CompuServe or GEnie or Prodigy; yet, each system is locally owned, locally operated, and designed to wrap itself around the information needs of a given community.

NATIONAL PUBLIC TELECOMPUTING NETWORK (NPTN)

Now, what the National Public Telecomputing Network (NPTN) tries to do is to develop and support this growing network of community computer systems. We do that in three different ways. First of all, we do it by helping these systems to come online just as, for example, we're working with the Prairienet organizing committee here in the Champaign-Urbana area. Second, after the systems come online, we tie them together into a common organization, a common network. And the third thing that we try to do is to provide what we call "cybercasting services."

The word I wanted to use here was "broadcasting," but it has already been taken, so I had to invent another one—"cybercasting." Basically, it's the same service you find in radio or television networks. You might have, let's say, a local radio station here in Urbana and you might have your own radio talk show hosts or disk jockeys. But you might also be taking feeds from ABC Radio. Similarly, we have independent affiliates who operate their community computer systems, drawing upon local people, local information resources, and so forth. Then we try to supplement that with high-quality feeds from the network level—information services and features that supplement what they're able to do locally.

For example, we have a fully developed K-12 program called Academy One that can be put in when Prairienet starts up. In other words, on day one of Prairienet, there's going to be a very mature, fully developed program for the K-12 schools. We also have a program called the Teledemocracy program, in which we're trying to develop this medium as a way to bring people closer to the democratic process. We carry things like the full text of all U.S. Supreme Court decisions, within minutes of their release. This past election, we carried the full text of all of the position papers, press releases, fact sheets, etc., from the major candidates for the presidency. And these things stay online. So if you want to find out exactly what President Clinton promised during his campaign, you can log into any one of our systems and see exactly what was promised and when. These kinds of things are the sort of information features we try to keep flowing out to the affiliates.

BENEFITS OF COMMUNITY COMPUTING

In general, who benefits from all this? Basically, the entire range of people living in the community. First of all, the citizens of a given community benefit because they have access to information-age services that many people would not otherwise be able to afford or might not otherwise be able to obtain. These are people—both male and female—from all walks of life and all socioeconomic groups.

Elementary and secondary schools also benefit. Free-Nets give K-12 schools the opportunity to teach telecomputing, which, by and large, they've never really had a chance to do in the past. It's very difficult to go into a principal's office and say, "We'd like 30 CompuServe accounts because we want to teach kids about electronic mail and searching information bases." Free-Nets, on the other hand, can be used for exactly this purpose, but at a lower cost.

Government benefits because it's a new medium that allows people to communicate with their government and allows their government to communicate with their constituents in a whole new way.

Small- and medium-sized businesses also wind up benefiting from community computer systems. If you are a major corporation, you've got corporate electronic mail. You've got worldwide information resources. If you are a small- or medium-sized business, however, you can't afford that kind of thing. One of the things Free-Nets do is allow small- and medium-sized businesses to use electronic mail to keep in contact with their branch offices and suppliers and distributors and so forth.

The agricultural community benefits. Indeed, one of our areas of emphasis this year will be to reach out into the agricultural community by establishing these systems in county seats in rural areas throughout the United States. The basic model of a rural county in America is that it is big and square, it has a county seat somewhere in the middle, and it's a local phone call from anywhere in the county to the county seat. By placing just one of these systems in a county seat, you can suddenly bring information-age services to all of those rural consolidated schools, give farmers access to agricultural information and to the county agent, etc. And all of it can be done right now with existing technology.

Surprisingly, the telecommunications industry benefits. When you look at the demographics of who uses commercial telecomputing services in this country, what you're looking at is basically people with $65,000 to $70,000 a year household incomes, overwhelmingly white, male, upscale, well-educated, etc. Now, there's nothing wrong with those demographics, but if the telecommunications industry is going to survive, it has to find a way to penetrate the middle class with these kinds of services, just like the VCR industry did. And that's exactly what community computer systems do. They penetrate the heck out of the blue-collar neighborhoods of their urban areas. They penetrate the heck out of the lower socioeconomic areas and introduce this technology to a group of people who have never had the opportunity to get to it in the past.

Finally, community organizations will benefit. Because these systems are community driven, you now have a new voice for community organizations. On the Cleveland Free-Net, which is the system that I'm most familiar with, we have community organizations ranging from Alcoholics Anonymous to United Way—all using this new medium as a way of getting their message out, answering people's questions, getting people more involved with what their organizations are all about. The whole thing becomes a win-win situation for everybody.

I know that just talking about this stuff is not all that useful. Unless you are already a community computer system user, it's very difficult to envision. To help solve that problem, we developed a videotape about the Heartland Free-Net in Peoria that is intended to show you the kind of impact that community computing can have on a community. Now, Peoria is not the largest Free-Net. It doesn't have the most users. It doesn't have the most modems. It doesn't have the most services. But it *is* located in Peoria, and, as the saying goes, if it plays in Peoria . . . can Champaign-Urbana be far behind?

[VIDEOTAPE SHOWN HERE]

IMPLICATIONS OF COMMUNITY COMPUTING

When we were putting together the Free-Net tape, we spent a lot of time thinking about what it was going to be about and what kind of message we were trying to convey. I started thinking in terms of what should come across as the most important part. Who's the most important person on that tape? I've got to tell you that the most important person on the tape was not me. It was not the county commissioner. It was not the librarian—with apologies to all librarians here tonight. It wasn't even the schoolteacher. As far as I was concerned, the most important person on that tape was the guy who worked in the gas station—because if we can't find a way to bring the information age to people who work in gas stations, and who work in factories, and who work in other kinds of blue-collar jobs, then what the heck are we doing? What's all this about if we can't do that? If we can't find a way to bring these people into the information age, then, as far as I'm concerned, NPTN will have failed as an organization. And, as far as I'm concerned, you will have failed as librarians, as people who are a part of this information age in a big way. We've got to find a way to do this. We've got to find a way to do it in an economically sound way. We have to find a way to do it with equity.

What I can say is that it is NOT going to happen the way things are going now. I spend a lot of time going around giving talks in various places, at conventions and conferences and so forth, and one of the things that I see happening is what I refer to as the "balkanization of the information age." I go to conventions of librarians, and librarians are all talking about library networks and the great things that can be done with them. I'll give a talk at a convention of K-12 people, and everyone is talking about K-12 education networks. Or I'll talk to a group of government officials, and they are all talking about government information networks, and so forth.

We can't keep doing this, folks! We can't keep having all of these groups creating independent networks, all diving after the same minuscule amounts of funding. You wind up pitting K-12 versus librarians versus teledemocracy people versus health educators versus community computer types versus government information providers versus senior citizen networks versus rural networks versus urban networks, and on, and on, and on. We've got to find a way to have something with enough "conceptual bandwidth" to include everybody, as opposed to people elbowing each other out of the way trying to get to what very limited kinds of funds there are out there.

COMMUNITY COMPUTING AND THE NREN

A lot people have put a lot of hope in the development of the NREN, the National Research and Education Network, which is currently being considered in Washington. I'm not convinced that there is hope there, because nowhere in the development of the NREN legislation is anything being mentioned about the community—about making access available to the people who, after all, are paying for a large part of the NREN—the taxpayers. (You recall them?) The National Research and Education Network would not pass if it were just the NRN—the National Research Network. I don't think it would have gotten past Congress at all. I think the days of very expensive projects, like supercolliders, that are designed to benefit only a handful of scientists are pretty much over, at least for the time being.

The thing that makes the NREN work, that makes it sellable, is the E—the Education part of NREN, particularly when you start including K-12 schools in the mix. But, I'm wondering if even here the NREN makes a lot of sense. Look at it this way. Let's say you are working with a kid in a K-12 situation, or, for that matter, even in a college situation. This person, for four years, has had access to electronic mail and has telnetted all over the Internet and has had access to all these incredible information resources. OK. Now, on a given day, he graduates. After that, he or she comes back in and says, "Hi. I'd like to use my electronic mail account now. I've got something that I'd like to ftp from California." What do you say to him? You say, "No, you can't use it." He asks, "Why?" You say, "Because you are not a student anymore." He asks, "Then what was the point of training me on it in the first place?" A good question. Indeed, what's the point of training them on something like that if the day after they graduate they no longer have access to it because they are no longer students? It's like having mandatory driver's education in a world without automobiles. What is the point of creating a national education network that cuts you off the instant you graduate?

Is the NREN something that we should be developing? As it currently stands, I don't think so. But maybe it *would* make sense if parallel to the development of the NREN we were also developing community computer systems. Maybe the proper word here should not be NREN, maybe it should be NCON—the National Community Network—something that has enough conceptual bandwidth to include researchers, and K-12 educators, and librarians, and medical information people, and government information people.

FUNDING COMMUNITY COMPUTING

How are we going to do that? What mechanisms exist to do that? Right now there are none. There is no consistent mechanism to fund the development of community computer systems, as people who are developing Prairienet here are finding out. It is very difficult to get community systems funded because we don't fit anybody's existing priority. When you go to a corporation, or a foundation, or whatever, they look down the list of "things that they fund," and community computing just isn't on it. Consequently, you have a very difficult time trying to get the support you need to develop these systems and get them into place.

Is there a mechanism? Is there a model out there that we could use, that we could develop, perhaps, that would help us to draw up these systems? I think there is. Most of you are familiar with a really interesting corporation called the Corporation for Public Broadcasting. First of all, it's a nonprofit corporation that was created by federal law. It receives its core funding from Congress, but it's not a government agency. It has a board of directors that is appointed each year by the president of the United States. You can't have more than 50% of the board of CPB from any one political party. A very interesting kind of notion—a nonprofit corporation that is created by law and funded by government, but is not an agency of government. Maybe what we need to do, maybe the direction we should be going in, is to form the Corporation for Public Cybercasting. Why not? Think about it. What about the notion of creating an entity that will do for this medium what the Corporation for Public Broadcasting did for National Public Radio and public television. Does not this new and emerging medium deserve at least the same kind of consideration that was given to radio and television when they created CPB? I think it does. I think it's time for this. I think that if we plan to enter the information age in this country with any semblance of equity, I think this is the kind of thing that needs to be created.

What would such an entity do? First of all, a Corporation for Public Cybercasting would help to establish and operate free, public access computerized information and communications systems in cities and towns throughout the United States and it would link them together into a common national network via the NREN. This would supply initial and ongoing core funding for equipment and personnel costs—just as the CPB and NTIA, which is another agency, do for public television and for NPR. Second, it would develop and deliver across the network high-quality information services of national scope to supplement what each community is able to develop on its own— just as the CPB does now for PBS and NPR. Third, it would develop special programs to introduce telecomputing to the general public with special emphasis on K-12 students and teachers, senior citizens, handicapped, and minority populations. It would develop this medium with special regard to community service applications and government connectivity—just as the CPB does now (more or less) for PBS and NPR. Essentially it would be an analog, a parallel, to the Corporation for Public Broadcasting only its intent would be to develop telecomputing, to develop community computing in the cities and towns throughout this country.

What would that cost? That is going to be the first question that anybody asks in Washington, DC—how much is it going to cost and where are we going to get the money for it? What I see developing is basically a series of two-to-one grant proposals, whereby if you were putting up a system in a given area, you could receive core support up to a limit of $100,000 from the federal government . . . if and only if the state were to match it two-to-one and put up $50,000. The state puts up $50,000 if and only if the local city or county puts up $25,000. So it's a cascading series of two-to-one funding proposals. No one branch of government is tasked with the entire burden of putting together these systems.

With regard to special programs, these would be programs that would be developed and targeted towards special populations, such as K-12 or library programs, women and minority programs, etc. Again, the federal government would put up $50,000 if and only if the state puts up $25,000 if and only if the local area puts up $12,500 for the development of these programs on these systems. In effect, then, the total exposure that the federal government would have on a given system in a given city would be $150,000. The state's total exposure would be $75,000, and maximum local exposure would be $37,500. But the combined effect produces enough money to provide core funding in perpetuity to keep these systems going.

To put it into a little bit of a larger context, if the federal government wanted to put up community computer systems in 100 cities in the United

States—you can pick which ones you want: the 50 largest cities plus the 50 state capitals, maybe the 100 largest cities, maybe some mixture of urban and rural, whatever—a network of 100 cities would cost about $15 million. Now to you or me this is a healthy chunk of change, but in the grand scope of these kinds of programs, this is a tiny fraction of what the Corporation for Public Broadcasting receives each year. A tiny fraction.

For a similar scenario, let's use Ohio as an example. Ohio has basically seven major cities. The maximum exposure of the state of Ohio would be about $525,000 a year, but for that, you would be placing information-age services in the hands of over 50% of the population of the state. Locally, the city of Columbus (or Cleveland or whatever) would have to raise about $37,500. I think it would work. I genuinely think it would work.

THE FUTURE OF COMMUNITY COMPUTING

What I am worried about is the alternative. Where are we going to wind up if we *don't* do it? How exactly are we going to get information-age services into the hands of the people? Frankly, I don't know. I really don't. And this is not rocket science here, folks. I mean, we're not talking about technology that has yet to be developed. We're not talking about some huge effort to put a man on the moon. We're talking about technology that is here now, that is available now. Moreover, we've done this before.

Several generations ago in this country we put together a railroad system that stretched from one end of this country to the other, and, for the first time, this country was linked together from coast to coast. The sons and daughters of the people who put together that railway system put together the great public library systems in this country. The sons and daughters of those people put together the great radio networks. The sons and daughters of those people put together the great television networks.

What I'm saying is that maybe it's our turn! Maybe it's our turn to develop something for our children and our children's children as great as the legacy that's been left to us. A lot of people don't realize that 100 years ago there was no such thing as a free public library, at least in the sense that we know it today. They didn't exist. But we got to a point in this country where literacy got high enough and the cost of printing books got cheap enough that public libraries became feasible. We got to a point where people started coming together around a concept. They started coming together around a concept of free public access to the printed word. They not only came together, they came together in groups as small as a few people sitting around a kitchen table and in groups as large as this one. But they came together around that common idea and they made it happen.

What I'm suggesting to you is that we've gotten to the point in this country where computer literacy has gotten high enough and the cost of the equipment has gotten cheap enough, that we can now start looking at the similar development of free public access to computerized information and communications services. There are simply no barriers to that happening. The fortunate thing is that we still have a choice. We're at a point where we can choose to make this thing work—it is still something that's within our grasp. As individuals, you can talk about this kind of thing. You can write about it. You can think about it. You can, in a lot of ways, promote the idea that maybe we should have a way of opening the information age to everyone. You can come together in groups and start working towards the development of this Corporation for Public Cybercasting idea. We're going to start work on that coming up this spring. We need to develop some model legislation at both the federal level and the state level. And we need to start the process of getting this legislation passed, of getting something like the Corporation for Public Cybercasting, and the ideas it stands for, into place. It's in our hands now, or, more specifically, it's in *your* hands to make it all work.

STEVE CISLER

Senior Scientist
Apple Library
Apple Computer
Cupertino, California

Community Computer Networks: Building Electronic Greenbelts

INTRODUCTION

What are community networks? I am writing as a librarian and network user who has been involved in using telecommunications to communicate with other people and to provide information on a wide range of subjects. I have encouraged people in various towns and counties to use this technology to start and use networks that can strengthen the community. Many individuals, organizations, and institutions are becoming involved in these networks. Whether you are a technical expert, information professional, government official, businessperson, or interested citizen, there is a role for you to play in incubating, growing, maintaining, and using these systems.

A community network consists of one or more computers providing services to people using computers and terminals to gain access to those services and to each other. While many of these networks tie together geographically separated individuals linked by a common interest or profession (senior citizens, pilots, ecologists, librarians), this essay will not cover scholarly or affinity group networks. Other models and systems exist but have been described elsewhere (Rheingold, 1993). Instead, "community" will be used in the sense of a municipality, county, regional area, or Indian nation. The information contained in such networks as well as the relationships that form among the participants make up what I call an electronic greenbelt to reinforce and add value to the community. These communities do include a variety of other interest groups whose needs and interests transcend the geographic boundaries of the town, region, or state. The decisions these communities have made are similar, in some ways, to what happened with the spread of electrical networks a century ago.

THE PAST

As David Nye (1992) explains in *Electrifying America*, a great discussion took place in American society between 1890 and 1920 about the role of electricity, its benefits, how it should spread throughout the land, what standards should apply, and who should own or control the electrical plants once they were established. Nye, a Danish researcher, notes that in America each community has the right to grant charters and franchises to utilities, so the electrical infrastructure developed along two basic models: a power grid confined to a geographical area controlled by a local government or a system developed by private corporations whose operations usually crossed city and state boundaries. The latter entities were usually larger than the former. The consolidation of small private utilities produced an enormous production and distribution grid that was efficient but served the populace unequally. These systems produced more electricity than any other in the world, but there was little rural service or special considerations for large customers, and the public utilities commissions were influenced by the power of the holding companies and the publicity campaigns that they were able to mount. This difference between the electrified urban landscape and the underserved rural area contrasted with Europe and New Zealand where there was almost universal service. In America, the electrical networks were a business, whereas in Scandinavia, they were also seen as an instrument of social policy. In Europe, for example, electric streetcars were viewed as an essential service and were operated at a loss. In America, they were treated as a business.

As American businesses supplied or used electricity, changes were rapid. Samuel Insull, one of the great utility czars, found that streetcar companies needed electricity at a different time than the rest of his customers, so he could build a larger central power source, place it near the streetcar companies, and sell power to them for less than they could provide it for themselves. The trolley companies, in turn, built amusement parks at the end of their lines to encourage off-peak use of their lines, and a whole new industry of electric entertainment began to flourish. In Muncie, Indiana, movie theaters sprang up near the intersection of the trolley lines, and when the glass jar plant "electrified," eight men could produce as many jars as 210 men did in the old factory.

These development models—the past effects of new technologies on society, labor, the shape of the city, and its commerce—and the new forms of entertainment are being repeated now as we ponder the effects of computing technology, new entertainment and education media, and the restructuring of education and government to make use of the changing telecommunications infrastructure. What each group or city or region decides about its computing infrastructure, if they decide anything at all, will encompass variations on the models that worked or failed for previous systems such as the local phone system, the cable television companies, public transport, water treatment, or other social services such as schools, libraries, and museums. In many cases, one or more of these businesses or agencies will take the initiative and offer some of the network and information services that will be described in this paper.

THE PRESENT

Just as electrical systems began to transform urban and small-town America a century ago, community computer networks will do so in the 1990s. The present situation is that few people are aware of the concept of community computing networks, any more than people understood much at all about electricity in 1890. Most of the attention has been paid to national research networks such as the Internet and the commercial consumer services such as CompuServe, GEnie, or Prodigy or business services such as MCImail or Dialcom. On a local level, thousands of electronic bulletin boards have been started by dedicated individual hobbyists, small businesspeople, nonprofit organizations, corporations, federal agencies, other governments, and educational institutions. What is striking about many of these ventures is that each group is relatively unaware of the activities of the other groups. Database providers such as DIALOG and Mead Data stay out of the messaging business except for narrow uses; business mail systems are just beginning to make links to bulletin board networks, and the electronic bulletin board systems (BBSs) are just learning about the Internet. The Internet is going through an explosive growth process that has attracted new commercial and nonacademic users who are making new demands on the infrastructure and are in need of better security, more connectivity, and easier-to-use interfaces. However, many of these services and systems are starting to converge. Through the Internet, one can send mail to many large and small services and BBSs; DIALOG can be reached by Internet users, as can such commercial services as The WELL and Delphi. Some researchers are experimenting with audio and video transmissions on the Internet. Today's gimmicks may be tomorrow's services.

Some community networks are bulletin boards; others are based on large commercial services, and some are UNIX-based systems with connections to the Internet. These latter systems provide their users with an electronic on-ramp to a myriad of services all over the world that are not usually available outside of government laboratories, computer firms, and academic sites. Other systems have no connectivity outside of the town or area that they serve. Many unaffiliated users and former university students become interested in community networks for the connectivity to the Internet that some systems promise to provide.

Information and Services

What sorts of unique information and services are found on community networks? The key word is local. They provide electronic mail and discussion groups for local users. Local civic groups and local businesses provide information from the town or region in which the system is located, such as (and this list is not exhaustive): bus schedules; lifelong learning class schedules; job opportunities; city or county legislation and regulations; a calendar of events; school lunch menus; homework help lines, advice from local professionals and tradespeople (such as auto mechanics, lawyers, librarians, and law enforcement personnel); electronic catalogs for libraries; restaurant listings; tourist attractions; drafts of strategic plans; motor vehicle renewals; energy conservation aids; health information; an index to local newspapers; and reports from members of Congress who represent the area. There is a variety of activities besides electronic mail, searching databases, and reading text files. Some systems allow for real-time chat between users or interactive games or the sharing of sound and graphics files. In addition, most systems provide information of more general interest, such as world and national news, and discussion groups with participants from all over the United States and other countries as well. Very few systems provide the type of commercial transaction services that will be needed if files, services, and small info-nuggets are sold over these systems.

System Connections

What sorts of connections do these systems use? Every system allows local users to connect to the host computer(s) using a personal computer or public terminal and modem or, in some cases, a dedicated line or wide area network. Generally, each system has a bank of modems to handle multiple callers at one time at speeds of 300, 1200, 2400, 9600 or more bits per second. A few systems only have a couple of phone lines, while others have broadband Ethernet (nominally 10 million bits per second) connections for some users and dial-up for the rest. New systems such as the TeleCommUNITY Network in San Marcos, Texas, employ fiber optic links running at 45 million bits per second between a few school and training sites and offer two-way video, audio, and data networking for the participants. The goal of this effort is to move information, not people, and to involve more parts of the community than just the school systems. Many of these systems have terminals or personal computers in public places such as school classrooms, public libraries, laundromats, and government offices. Some systems are experimenting with new wireless radio networks as a way of providing less-expensive links between community information providers; the field trials of this technology are encouraging.

System Operation

Who starts and runs these systems? This is as varied as the services offered. Sometimes a computer enthusiast will start a BBS with one or two phone lines, invite other groups to disseminate their information on a dedicated part of the system, and then expand the service into a community information system. Other systems have been started by some part of a university. The Cleveland Free-Net began as an Apple II BBS under the wing of the Case Western Reserve University Medical School. Through publicity and effective fund-raising efforts by Dr. Tom Grundner and others in the community, it has grown to a large distributed UNIX system with dozens of dial-up lines and Internet connections for those users outside of the Cleveland calling area. Other key sponsors of such systems have included hospitals, local phone companies, nonprofit institutes, and specially formed not-for-profit corporations. In some places such as Chicago, Illinois, and San Jose, California, America Online has teamed up with the local newspaper to offer information services to the community as a new business. Much of the current activity has attracted a spectrum of local citizens from all parts of the community who think a citizen-run network sounds like a good idea and want to make it happen.

This can be difficult for many reasons. Community networks are new beasts with few people who know how they are conceived, what to feed them, and how to make them flourish and spread. There are at present three organizations that can provide some assistance for groups that don't know where to start. Heartland Free-Net in Peoria, Illinois, sells several packets of information and consulting time. The Center for Civic Networking in Charlestown, Massachusetts, works with groups planning such networks. Fees for their services are negotiable and can sometimes be included in funding requests. Tom Grundner's National Public Telecomputing Network (NPTN) is a nonprofit organization with some similarities to the Public Broadcasting System in that networks and users are solicited for support.

Funding

Where does funding come from? In some cases, these networks can be started with available hardware and software and local technical assistance, but sources for startup funds depend on the talents of the organizing group as well as the clarity of their vision for the future of their network. Obtaining funding has never been simple, nor is there one model that will work for every locale. Some systems are dependent on the owner/entrepreneur, the school, or the business; most depend on grants from foundations, computer firms, or local businesses; and a few have funds from local government. Many government institutions are severely constrained by taxpayer revolts, increasing overhead, budget cuts, and the current (1992-1993) recession, so few organizers expect that these systems will be started and supported by taxpayers alone. There are some whose funds come from the government, and others who depend on subscribers. Most depend upon a constantly changing group of partners, corporate angels, foundations, and user fees and donations to keep going. Steady funding is a serious problem even with outwardly popular and successful systems. In the online world, there are a number of services that everyone admits are useful and productive, but nobody has figured out an easy way to support them. Most community networks are hunting for stable support. Up to now, the users have not been willing to support these systems through substantial donations or fees.

COMMUNITY SYSTEMS

The following systems are representative of some of the more popular community systems. These may be called directly or reached by the Telnet function on the Internet. There are others that have no link to the Internet and are open to just the residents and property owners of the town.

HAWAII FYI

Hawaii INC was created in 1988 after the state House of Representatives Telecommunications Work Group issued a report exploring the business opportunities for telecommunications networks and gateways in Hawaii. The Capitol BBS, running on an IBM-XT, was used to gather data about the public's needs and interests for a larger system. I was able to gather information on HAWAII FYI while I was on vacation in Kona, Hawaii. The local library had a dedicated phone line to Honolulu and a terminal that could display the text files as well as the graphics files that use the format known at NAPLPS (North American Presentation Level Protocol Syntax). NAPLPS grew out of the Telidon program in Canada but never achieved the grand vision of penetrating to 50% of the households by 1990 (Godfrey & Chang, 1981). Discussions, sometimes very critical, about the shape and future of the HAWAII FYI system were available for people to read and print, even if they did not own a computer. The Kailua Kona library uses a Northern Telecom terminal that costs $350. Their dedicated line to the Honolulu central server comes out of the branch library budget. The HAWAII FYI service was opened in June 1991; by December 1991, usage increased from 127,000 minutes per month to 1,232,000 minutes per month.

The information provided by HAWAII FYI includes over 50 topics covering such diverse areas as legislative information services, job-related information, fish of Hawaii, tax information, and peace events.

HAWAII FYI has expanded its fee-based services to provide entertainment and Internet connectivity as an option to subscribers in 1993. Besides funds taken in from other information providers, the state provides about $500,000 annually to the not-for-profit corporation, making this the community system with the most financial support of any operating in North America.

Each year Hawaii INC sponsors a conference in Honolulu, comprised of speakers from the islands as well as visitors from the mainland. The diverse nature of the information providers and attendees makes it a model for other states that are thinking about building a state infrastructure. At the March 1993 conference, there were speakers from schools, satellite companies, the Maui supercomputer center, University of Hawaii, private firms offering services on HAWAII FYI, and Hawaiians interested in using the network for cultural preservation and language instruction.

National Capital FreeNet, Ottawa, Canada

The Free-Net model, started at Case Western Reserve University by Tom Grundner, has spread around North America and beyond. In fact, Free-Net has almost become a generic term for a community network, but it does apply to a UNIX-based system using the FreePort software developed by Grundner's team or other homebrew software from NPTN. Grundner says:

> The unifying factor is not software or hardware; it is conceptual in nature. All Free-Nets (1) are free to the user; (2) are primarily dedicated to the development of local information resources (supplemented by national-level feeds from NPTN); and (3) are dedicated to opening up the information age to as broad a spectrum of people as possible. That defines a "Free-Net" a lot more than mere software or hardware. (T. Grundner, personal communication, May 17, 1993)

The National Capital FreeNet (NCF) in Canada was started in November 1991 by George Frajkor and Jay Weston of the Carleton University School of Journalism. Besides receiving assistance from the university, they have received support from Gandalph Technologies, Sun Microsystems, 125 organizations, and more than 500 people who have given time and money. More than the developers of other systems, the organizers have stated their vision about the growth of Free-Nets in Canada, as evidenced by documents residing on the system:

> Because a Free-Net is run by the community and for the community, it helps to encourage and to revitalize community involvement. It creates a partnership, a shared responsibility between the community and existing social institutions for developing and providing timely information. Many people are recognizing that traditional ways of sustaining a community are no longer working well. They are beginning to accept the idea that greater voluntary donations of time and energy are required if their community is to be maintained. The information offered on a Free-Net is provided as a voluntary effort by private citizens and community agencies. A Free-Net thus offers new opportunities for citizens to become more involved in their community, and for groups, institutions and governments to become more visible and accessible. (National Capital FreeNet, 1993)

NCF uses the metaphor of an electronic city but allows for variation depending on the participating agencies and individuals in different locales. The top-level menu includes such options as Post Office; Public Discussion; Social Services, Health & Environment Centre; Libraries; and Special Interest Groups. Each item has one or more levels that provide access to discussions, documents, and listings of the information that each interest group or organization has agreed to provide. The degree of involvement by each volunteer determines the timeliness and accuracy of the information provided. Access is free to the citizens and, indeed, to anyone with Internet access or to modem users willing to pay the long-distance charges.

NCF is developing a "Community Free-Net Kit" containing software, training manuals, publicity tips, and system advice to bring any community in Canada online as efficiently as possible. They predict that there will be at least 100 Free-Nets in Canada by the year 2000. In some towns, the lack of personnel skilled in UNIX system administration will prove to be a hindrance to the effective operation of these complex hardware configurations. Talented volunteer help from distant university computer centers may get these systems up and running, but the day-to-day operations necessitate skilled on-site workers if the Free-Nets are going to be run as reliable networks that the local citizens depend on. Few novices or experienced users will tolerate constant service interruptions, mail that doesn't reach its destination, and the inability to easily transfer files without corruption.

There are Free-Nets operating or starting up in many areas of the United States; a partial list includes Tallahassee, Florida; Columbia, Missouri; Denver, Colorado; Buffalo, New York; Peoria, Illinois; and Youngstown, Ohio. The number continues to grow as the idea of community networks spreads.

Wellington (New Zealand) City Council's Community Computer Network

The Santa Monica (California) Public Electronic Network (PEN) was one of the first community systems supported by a local government. Its use of online discussion groups and databases of local information has generated an enormous amount of interest. The Wellington city council was partly inspired by Ken Phillips of Santa Monica and all the publicity surrounding the Santa Monica municipal PEN system.

Richard Naylor, a computer systems expert with the city council, has been instrumental in putting Wellington online and allowing a student in Amsterdam or Austin to read the city council minutes. In New Zealand, 65% of households have computers, and of those, 5% have modems. That is about 3,500 households in the Wellington area, but because the network is available as a Gopher hole (server) on the Internet, it is accessible at no charge to thousands of other users. Naylor started the New Zealand system about three years ago. For a time, the information system was merged with the city library system, but that configuration was seen as too radical, so it split. The development of the City Network continued, and today the public has access to a DEC VAX that has the USENET news system, VAX Notes (an old computer conferencing system), and files, including ordinances, images, and information about Wellington and New Zealand. At present, they have 500 to 600 users, mainly from the BBS community, and they are trying to extend access into the schools. Users have access to the Internet and to Telnet and File Transfer Protocol (FTP) without charge. Because of the speed of connections between New Zealand and the rest of the world, they try to limit local users' file transfers to New Zealand sites. New Zealand users can dial up using a modem as well. Gopher is an exciting application, freely available for nonprofit uses, which has been widely deployed by more than 1,300 academic sites around the world. Wellington is the first city to do so. There is client software available for various computers, and the server software is constantly being enhanced and updated by a team at the University of Minnesota and their collaborators around the world.

Big Sky Telegraph, Dillon, Montana

The Western Montana College of the University of Montana runs a multifaceted system that was started in 1988 by Frank and Regina Odasz, with help from the M.J. Murdock Charitable Trust and US WEST. In the early days, it provided access to teachers in one-room schools throughout rural Montana. The teachers took an online course in telecommunications and then used Big Sky for collaboration and other distance-learning experiences. Other groups such as the Montana Women for Economic Development began using the system to teach telecommunications basics to small groups of rural entrepreneurs. The library at Western Montana College has provided free ERIC searches and hardcopy library materials to remote users. The online community extends beyond Dillon, Montana, and is, in a sense, a model for other rural communities, mainly as a result of the evangelistic skills of Frank Odasz, whose writings and presentations have inspired many others interested in community networks. Odasz must, for the most part, depend on soft funding from various foundations. Though he requests a $50 subscriber fee from individuals interested in using the system, in reality, anyone can use the system at no charge. The lack of modems, poor phone lines in rural areas, and long-distance charges have limited growth. Big Sky runs on a UNIX-based 386 system using a home-grown amalgamation of BBS software assembled by Dave Hughes of Old Colorado Communications, and they now have full Internet connectivity as well as the ability to receive messages from UUCP and Fidonet systems. (Telnet to bigsky.dillon.mt.us for a trial run.)

Big Sky Telegraph has received a great deal of publicity and has attracted the attention and participation of Senator Conrad Burns of Montana as well as other politicians and writers. One of the more interesting studies of the effects of this community network is Willard Uncapher's (1991) *Rural Grassroots Telecommunication: Big Sky Telegraph and Its Community*. Uncapher studied the effects of Big Sky Telegraph in Dillon, as well as in Dell Valley and Wisdom, Montana, a small ranching community about 70 miles from Dillon, by interviewing teachers and other academics, ranchers, farmers, agricultural extension agents, forestry service officials, women, children, and people working in the service sector. The ranchers and farmers generally believed that support for education and telecommunications experiments would come out of their pockets, in the form of new taxes. Because there was so little opportunity for returning students, most were "exported" to other states to follow a new career. The community network was seen by this group as contributing to this outflow of young people. As these systems proliferate, they will be the subject of other theses and popular studies that will examine them in more depth than is possible in this brief survey.

SOCIAL ASPECTS AND NEW PROJECTS

Many writers, online enthusiasts, and researchers have commented on the promise of using the new communications technologies to reinforce communities, to invigorate the democratic process, and to redefine parts of society. Ithiel de Sola Pool's writings are particularly useful, and though he died in 1984, his works do not seem dated or out of sync with the events we are experiencing in the 1990s. In *Forecasting the Telephone*, Pool (1983, p. 50) describes how farmers in rural areas banded together to form telephone cooperatives, sometimes stringing wire on fence posts and even using barbed wire as a transport medium. He also describes an early use of the party line by farmers that seems to offer some advantages over the single household system that most of us use: at a specific time in the evening, after chores were done, the farmers would gather online, and one who subscribed to a newspaper or magazine would read to the others, some of whom could not read at all.

In *Technologies without Boundaries*, Pool (1990) discusses a number of profound changes including:

> The mass media revolution is being reversed; instead of identical messages being disseminated to millions of people, electronic technology permits the adaptation of electronic messages to the specialized or unique needs of individuals. (p. 8)

One of Pool's students was W. Russell Neuman, whose *The Future of the Mass Audience* influenced me greatly as I studied these community systems. It is a study of how the new technology and changing economics of mass media will influence public communications. In the introduction, Neuman (1991) observes:

> That would be something new indeed, a postindustrial society that would self-consciously use technology to return to smaller-scale institutions and a renewed commitment to the traditional norms of civic participation. (p. 1)

He cites the study by Tetsuro Tomita of Japan's Ministry of Posts and Telecommunication in 1980. Tomita plotted out personal and mass communications in terms of size of audience and response time, showing the gap between personal and mass media. This gap is being filled by such technologies as community-produced cable television, electronically filtered news, computer discussion groups, and, I would argue, community networks.

The origins of the data highway metaphor are not the speeches of Vice President Al Gore. It was used as early as 1970 when Ralph Smith, writing in *The Nation*, also coined the term "The Wired Nation":

> The nation provided large federal subsidies for a new interstate highway system to facilitate and modernize the flow of automotive traffic. . . . It should make a similar national commitment for an electronic highway system. (Smith, 1972, p. 83)

In the article and the book, Smith described how a variety of social objectives would be supported by the four kinds of broadband networks: telephone, cable, institutional, and community-owned. His vision convinced people at the Federal Communications Commission (FCC) to lower the regulatory barriers to the development of cable. What took place was a variety of interactive cable experiments in Europe, Japan, and the United States, which are described in *Wired Cities* (Dutton, Blumler, & Kraemer, 1987). This volume is a retrospective look at the uneven success of the technology trials and the lack of real revolution in the way cities were run, elections held, and issues decided. Even though it deals primarily with analog technology, it is highly recommended for those of us challenged by the changing state, local, and national telecommunications policies in the digital age.

Because, 20 years later, we have added powerful personal computers to the Wired Nation, many people believe it will somehow be different this time. Many libertarians and computer enthusiasts see the power being decentralized, with unlimited computer cycles available very cheaply and within the reach of most consumers. While the computer companies believe the intelligence will reside in the machine and its software, many communications companies, especially the telephone companies, are adding value by adding intelligence to the network. Groups such as librarians and educators feel that the intelligence should come from the users, moderators, and other intermediaries who will populate the networks, alongside the software agents slowly emerging from labs and companies. These developments and the spread of the national infrastructure will heavily influence the choices that cities and regions have as they establish community networks.

OTHER MODELS FOR COMMUNITY NETWORKS

The systems described earlier in the paper are not the only models. In Forsyth County, North Carolina, the library and other agencies dealing in information have formed the Forsyth County Information Authority. What emerges as a result of that innovative concept bears watching. Besides the spread of Free-Nets, Meta-Systems Design Group in Washington, DC, is negotiating with a number of municipalities to use Caucus computer conferencing software in new networks. Caucus is being used in the well-known Santa Monica (CA) Public Electronic Network and in one part of HAWAII FYI. Some planners have been looking at software developed in France for use on the Minitel system, and as noted previously when describing HAWAII FYI, there are some strong advocates for the use of NAPLPS to integrate text and vector graphics. Community Information Exchange, Inc. (CIX) is working with Cincinnati Bell on a community system similar to the Free-Nets.

There is a loose category of systems called pubnets or "grunge" networks. This is not a pejorative term. It means that the networks were assembled with low-cost materials, a lot of sweat equity, and innovative designs that made do with available materials. Little Garden in the San Francisco Bay area has 30 customers who use their services to hook subnetworks up to the Internet at dial-up phone line speeds as well as T1 speeds (approximately 1.5 million bits per second). M-Net and grex in Ann Arbor, Michigan, also offer low-cost solutions for people who do not need a lot of assistance and want access to electronic mail and USENET newsgroups at a very low cost. For several years Phil Eschallier (phil@jabber.ls.com) has maintained an ever-growing list of public access UNIX sites around the world. The January 1993 list included more than 130 sites, primarily in the United States but also in Europe and the Pacific Rim.

The interfaces for all of these systems can be improved, and while some believe that a command line interface is better because it is faster for some experienced users or because it builds character in the struggling novice user, most network managers want to make their systems as easy as possible to use. This usually means a graphic interface of some sort, but many systems must make do with hierarchical menus for beginners and experienced users alike. A serious issue is how many users are left behind when new interfaces are developed that will not work on underpowered, older computers or terminals. For some, the opposite is true: how the installed base of older machines can thwart technological progress because of an unwillingness or inability to upgrade equipment and software. Setting the bar too high when deciding on an interface and the platforms it will run on denies users the ability to use their old machines. Setting the bar too low and only providing a command line text interface will exclude users who have come to expect an online system that resembles the graphical user interface (GUI) they already use offline. The best systems will permit you to use the computer or interface of your choice. However, few developers have the resources to provide this sort of flexibility. America Online (AOL) has been collaborating with the *San Jose Mercury News,* the flagship of the Knight-Ridder chain of newspapers. With the readership (and advertising revenues) for many newspapers in decline, some newspapers are looking at new business models. Extending the newspaper business to users of online services is a natural, if difficult, move. The Merc, as the paper is known locally, has set up the Mercury Center on AOL that provides the full text of articles in the paper, a way of corresponding with columnists and editors, searchable classified ads, in addition to extra new material plus years of archived articles, using a fairly attractive and easy-to-use graphic interface. The service began in the spring of 1993, and the testing period for new users is still in effect. With 12 full-time staff plus the involvement of many of the print-based staffers, this new business bears watching. Users pay $9.95 per month and receive five hours of use (at 2400 bits per second access speed) in the monthly fee. Extra hours cost $3.50. Besides the Mercury Center, subscribers can use the other America Online departments and can subscribe to the *San Jose Mercury News* at a 45% discount. At this time, most of the information originates from the newspaper and its readers. There is some information for towns and suburbs of San Jose that can be accessed by browsing or by doing a text search, but these systems may never be more than an electronic extension to the newspaper and want ad services that account for so much of the revenue for publishing firms.

Some of these communities are starting their own systems. A group of five citizens in Mountain View, California, are planning a community system, and the nearby city of Cupertino is much further along. Cupertino City Net is a new effort by city officials, educators, and community participants, including computer companies in town, to allow residents access to community information and electronic mail for $20 per year. City hall plans to provide meeting agendas, minutes of meetings, and a city calendar. School district officials plan to post registration information and school board news. However, at the brainstorming sessions, it was clear that the participants want much more—but at a time when municipal budget constraints lead people to make statements such as, "City Net is a great idea and I support it—but not with the use of city funds" (Citywide, 1993). In this case, the person is Nick Szabo, the mayor of Cupertino, and if he is not convinced that public monies should be used to run such a system, there will be less willingness by schools and corporations to lend support.

Note that the Cupertino City Net is, at this time, a section of a larger BBS that also includes Small Business Administration information as well as items about other cities in the Silicon Valley. The software is FirstClass from SoftArc in Canada and runs on the Macintosh over modem or AppleShare local area networks. There are gateways available for other mail systems such as Fidonet, UUCP, and the Internet. Later in 1993, additional software will allow a FirstClass BBS to serve as an Internet host, along with gateways into relational databases. Another interesting feature of FirstClass is the ability to use foreign language fonts in messages, so text is no longer restricted to ASCII. For instance, Indian languages are used in the reservation network that the Zuni Middle School in Zuni, New Mexico, is designing. (The use of these networks for the purpose of cultural preservation is a topic for another paper.)

Res-Nova in Huntington Beach, California, is setting up a large system in Lansing, Michigan, using their Nova-Link Professional software. It offers a graphic interface for Windows and Macintosh users, has complete integration of TCP/IP protocols as an option, and can also communicate with UUCP and Fido networks. Res-Nova is also developing billing software for commercial applications.

With many sectors in education, society, business, and government pushing for broadband connections and communications pipes, the users who are teething on our text-based systems will demand and eventually receive information systems that can deliver reliable and secure transactional information, both sound and full-motion digital video, and high-resolution images for use in purchasing goods, making medical diagnoses, and for pure entertainment. It is unclear how the community networks of today, which have not found stable funding models yet, will meet the challenge to provide high-end technology. Commercial enterprises have the resources for well-supported trials of systems that can provide a wide range of services that they hope will bring people online and into the stores to buy new equipment to handle the sophisticated graphic interfaces.

With interest by commercial firms in these networks, what effects will underfunded grass roots efforts have over the next 10 years? If Apple, or Time-Warner, or America Online comes to your town, will there be a place for a strong voice and some control by local organizations rather than the "invisible hand" of market forces? If no group has already started a community network, the commercial firms will be able to write more of the ground rules and create a system designed primarily to achieve their business goals. This is less likely to occur if they offer services in an area where there is a healthy network with a broad range of volunteers and community expertise. Any system, commercial or otherwise, must meet the needs of many different users. If a commercial system can do that better, it will prevail. If the system is just strip-mining the disposable income of affluent telecommuters, it may not last as long as the more equitable network that meets the needs of more citizens for a wider range of uses. As new uses emerge, the network will grow and expand in functionality. If the network is viewed (or ignored) as the domain of a few groups of users or if the discussion sections are dominated by a handful of verbose contributors, broad public support is unlikely. The role of the commercial community, beyond that of marginally involved donors, has not developed yet. One system where they are planning for this is the Glendale, California, LNX network, which uses Coconut's software as a back-end. It is due online in August 1993 (contact Ruth Thompason at the Glendale Public Library for further information). Expect other new ventures from small and large entrepreneurs in various urban and suburban markets.

DESIGNING A SYSTEM FOR THE 1990s

What if there were government funding for five years to carry out the development, distribution, and support of software for a new community information system that could then be used across the country? The potential operators might be a school, an energetic individual, a library, a business, a local government, a hospital, a phone company, a consortium or cooperative, an information authority, a nonprofit organization, or an ad-hoc citizens group. Given the complexity of a full-featured community system, it is clear that this would be an expensive and management-intensive development project. Nevertheless, let us speculate how it might be used, and how it would benefit commercial and noncommercial enterprises.

The back-end system should run on various platforms: DOS, UNIX, Macintosh, as well as the future operating systems from NeXT, Microsoft, and Taligent. It should, therefore, be scalable (functioning on simple operating systems but able to migrate to more powerful ones), and it should be extensible (new components can be added to it for increased functionality). A system that handles text and binary files would later be adaptable to new input technologies and new sorts of information flow. For example, changes could be made to work with speech input and provision of full-motion video and other time-based data. People with low-end computers would have a basic level of access; those with more powerful and newer models could take advantage of more features.

The system should be easy to administer, with tasks and operating permissions easily delegated to people other than the system administrator. UNIX-based systems should be turnkey with no full-time UNIX wizard needed on site. Special care should be given to the design of utilities for local operators to reconfigure the system and its interfaces and for maintaining the accounts, including moving user directories from one kind of system to another. Users should have a similar ability to change their own client software, which should run on a variety of terminals, computers, hand-held devices, and workstations. Thought must be given to the installed base of older computers, but the power of the system cannot be crippled because of the meager capabilities of devices that cannot emulate a VT100 terminal.

The source code and the binaries for the systems and clients should be available through an organization such as Clearinghouse for Networked Information Discovery and Retrieval (CNIDR) or the National Center for Supercomputing Applications (NCSA) for the cost of distribution. Technical support would be provided within the five-year funding period. This is ample time to see whether or not these systems will take root and flourish in a variety of communities. While any group should be able to use it for any purpose, including adding value and resale or bundling with equipment, its no-cost availability in a more generic form from a clearinghouse will assure that many groups with many needs will be able to use it, enhance it, and experiment with it.

Some writers have envisioned even more complex systems. Looking years into the future, David Gelernter (1991), associate professor of computer science at Yale University, describes the framework for a system he calls *Mirror Worlds:*

> What *are* they?
> They are software models of some chunk of reality, some piece of the *real world* going on outside your window. Oceans of information pour endlessly into the model (through a vast maze of software pipes and hoses): so much information that *the model* can mimic *the reality's* every move, moment-by-moment.
> A Mirror World is some huge institution's moving, true-to-life mirror image trapped inside a computer—where you can see and grasp it whole. (p. 3)

In the first part of the book, he describes the richness of a community or institutional network where all activity is mapped to the computer; he explains the significance of many users having access to all this information and how it will affect relationships, business, elections, and public government. He argues that such a system would give us "whole-sightedness," the ability to see the whole operation, object, or community and thereby, presumably, make the right decisions when we wish to change or interact with the system. It seemed that many people would be tempted to interact more with the richly detailed computer model and not the community it represented.

Other experiments will combine existing forms of computer interaction to form a new class of infotainment networks. The Internet includes a variety of unsanctioned services such as Internet Relay Chat (IRC) and MUDs (Multi User Dimension, Multi User Dungeon, or Multiple User Dialog). A MUD is a construct that simulates a fictitious or fantasy world. Users wander about, conversing, examining the text simulations, and even constructing other areas or rooms. In some systems, volunteers have reconstructed textual versions of Disneyland, Oz, Narnia, and popular science fiction locales. The system at Mankato State University in Minnesota has integrated a Gopher service into the interactive role-playing aspect, so a player can visit the Gopher hole or even carry a Gopher "slate" during the MUD interactions. Visitors to the Gopher hole can receive real-time assistance from other participants who are more experienced. It is an idea that was suggested to the programmers by librarians. This unusual mixing of information and amusement is one of the current mutations that have appeared in the low-bandwidth text-based networks. The new forms of interaction and new vessels for holding and displaying information will continue to emerge, and some will not have real-world equivalents, but they should be used to enhance real-world participation.

CONCLUSION

Computers and community networks will change the way we do business, govern, and relate to one another. I support the idea that the computer systems we design are meant to facilitate and enhance the business or social relations we have with other people, not to supplant them. Keeping in mind that electronic networks can empower many who are on the fringes of our community because of age, handicap, physical appearance, or race, I recommend that any community network that is being designed or already exists not only include face-to-face meetings of the board and technical staff but also regular meetings or social events to involve the users and the volunteers and information providers. A community computing network must be integrated into the real-world community that it serves. This would hold true whether you are running a small electronic BBS, a large Free-Net, or a Mirror World in the year 2000.

REFERENCES

Citywide computer net in works. (1993, March 1). *San Jose Mercury News.*
Dutton, W. H.; Blumler, J. G.; & Kraemer, K. L. (Eds.). (1987). *Wired cities: Shaping the future of communications.* Boston, MA: G. K. Hall.
Gelernter, D. (1991). *Mirror worlds: Or the day software puts the universe in a shoebox . . . How it will happen and what it will mean.* New York: Oxford University Press.
Godfrey, D., & Chang, E. (1981). *The Teledon book.* Toronto: Porcepic Press.
National Capital FreeNet. (1993). The context of public access community networks (Electronic document posting, National Capital FreeNet).
Neuman, W. R. (1991). *The future of the mass audience.* Cambridge, England: Cambridge University Press.

Nye, D. E. (1992). *Electrifying America: Social meanings of a new technology, 1880-1940.* Cambridge, MA: MIT Press.

Pool, I. de S. (1983). *Forecasting the telephone: A retrospective technology assessment.* Norwood, NJ: Ablex.

Pool, I. de S. (1990). *Technologies without boundaries: On telecommunications in a global age.* Cambridge, MA: Harvard University Press.

Rheingold, H. (1993). *Virtual communities.* Reading, MA: Addison-Wesley.

Smith, R. L. (1970). The wired nation [Special issue]. *The Nation, 210*(19).

Smith, R. L. (1972). *The wired nation: Cable TV: The electronic communications highway.* New York: Harper & Row.

Uncapher, W. (1991). *Rural grassroots telecommunication: Big Sky Telegraph and its community.* Unpublished master's thesis, Annenberg School of Communications, University of Pennsylvania, Philadelphia. (Contact willard@well.sf.ca.us for an electronic copy.)

DAVID DOMAN

PAC Instruction Specialist
Pikes Peak Library District
Colorado Springs, Colorado

MAGGIE'S PLACE: Connecting with the Community at the Pikes Peak Library District

INTRODUCTION

The Pikes Peak Library District (PPLD) has long been known for providing access to community information through online databases. PPLD's patrons, both at terminals in the library's facilities and as remote users via dial-up lines, have had access to community information since 1978.

Today, there are 10 community information databases on the menu at PPLD: Agencies, Arts, Calendar, Child Care, Courses, Clubs, Local Authors, Local Documents, Senior Housing, and Social & Economic Indicators. Collectively, these databases are known as Community Connections. The Community Connections databases total more than 10,000 records and were accessed nearly 50,000 times in 1992 (a 10% increase over 1991 usage). Most of the Community Connections databases are also available for purchase in printed form. In most cases, the entire file may be purchased, or in other files, specific portions are printable.

HOW DID PIKES PEAK LIBRARY DISTRICT GET INTO THE ONLINE COMMUNITY INFORMATION BUSINESS?

PPLD's involvement in providing community information online began in 1976 with joint planning meetings with the Colorado Springs Junior League. Many of the ideas advanced in these meetings were incorporated in an effort put forth by a private, nonprofit, nonpolitical organization known as Citizen's Goals to establish a central, well-publicized, 24-hour information and referral service. The library's computer was a logical home for this much-needed service.

The first database available for online access resulting from this effort was CALL (Citizen's Action Line Limitless), which evolved into the present Agencies database. The information in the database was primarily about social service agencies, and volunteers from the Junior League provided most of the maintenance labor. Much of the information input initially came from an existing card file of community resources maintained by the library; other data came from United Way member agencies.

Although the Junior League phased out the volunteer program in 1979, PPLD was able to continue and expand the online community information program through the use of CETA-funded employees. In addition, a local events calendar was brought online in 1979, and a database of educational classes (Courses) was added during the same year.

In 1980 CETA funding was drastically cut, and PPLD moved several of the CETA employees into regular library positions. Several years passed before any additional databases were added, but in 1982 the Clubs file was brought online. The process for proposing and bringing up new online community information databases was also formulated during this time. Eventually PPLD's Information and Reference Committee would take the leadership role in evaluating proposed databases.

COMMUNITY INFORMATION DATABASES
AVAILABLE TODAY AT PPLD

Agencies (online since 1978)

The Agencies database (the continuation of the original CALL file) contained 671 records as of mid-March 1993. Information is available about vital community services, such as public and private social service agencies, crisis intervention agencies, and other information and referral services. The Agencies database also includes hot-line and emergency telephone numbers and information about elected and appointed state and local officials. Agencies in the database provide free, low-cost, or unique services, and information in each record indicates whether there is a fee and who qualifies for the services offered.

This database may be searched by using words indicative of the functions, services, or names of the agencies. Contact names, telephone numbers, hours of operation, and addresses are supplied. The Agencies database was accessed more than 7,000 times in 1992, and the first two months of 1993 show a 10% increase in weekly usage.

Arts (online since 1992)

The Arts database contained 1,735 records as of mid-March 1993. This database provides information on people and places involved in the arts, primarily in El Paso County, Colorado. It also includes detailed information about performing artists, performance places, visual artists, display spaces, and arts organizations.

The Arts database may be searched by using the name, functions, or services of an artist, space/place, or organization. This database permits a search by category (visual artists, performing artists, visual spaces, performance places, and arts organizations) as well.

Sources of information for the Arts database included paper files kept by a variety of arts organizations in Colorado Springs and several others with statewide scope. After the database was introduced to the public, artists and organizations not listed have been reported by artists and other interested people, and thus the Arts database continues to grow.

This database was available to the public online for only eight months of 1992 and was accessed 2,116 times. The first two months of 1993 show an 11% increase in average weekly usage.

Calendar (online since 1979)

The Calendar database contained 467 records as of mid-March 1993. Three main types of records are included in this database: (a) permanent records for annual events, (b) temporary records with more detail about this year's program for an upcoming annual event, and (c) temporary records for events occurring only once.

The information in the Calendar database is gathered in a variety of ways. Staff responsible for maintaining the database are in regular, direct contact with many representatives of venues where events take place. In addition, the local newspapers are a regular source for new events information, as are library patrons connected with the sponsors of events.

The Calendar database is also made available in printed format. Monthly or annual events calendars may be purchased. The Calendar database was accessed more than 6,000 times in 1992, and the first two months of 1993 show a 4% increase in average weekly usage.

Child Care Providers (online since 1984)

The Child Care Providers database contained 453 records as of mid-March 1993. This database was established to assist parents in locating, and making informed decisions about, child-care providers. Presently only providers licensed by the Social Services Department of El Paso County are included in the database.

Each entry in the database included the name of the provider, nearest major street intersection to the provider's location, telephone number, nearest school(s), days and hours of care (including overnights and weekends, if applicable), transportation availability, and a brief description of the provider's services. Such a broad array of information permits a variety of searches: by the name of the provider, by zip code, by school, by street name, and by a variety of words indicative of the services provided and age levels accepted by each provider.

The original entries for the Child Care Providers database came from card files maintained by the local Urban League and several neighborhood mothers' groups. As new providers are licensed, they are offered the opportunity to be listed in the database. Most wish to be listed and provide the information for the file. The Child Care Providers database was accessed more than 6,000 times in 1992, and the first two months of 1993 show no change in this rate of usage.

Clubs (online since 1982)

The Clubs database contained 926 records as of mid-March 1993. Information available in this database concerns civic, social, professional, and recreational clubs, as well as medical and emotional support groups. The record for each club provides a description of the club's function, meeting days and times, presiding officer, number of members, names of contact persons, and telephone numbers. This database may be searched by keywords describing the functions or interests of the club, the type of club (e.g., support group), acronym (e.g., NAACP), or the specific name of the club (e.g., Pikes Peak Genealogical Society).

The Clubs database began as a card file of local contact names and telephone numbers developed by a library staff member. This file, although valuable, was incomplete and not consistently maintained. Following the precedent of the Agencies and Calendar databases, the Club file was put online, and further sources of information were developed. Possibly the most valuable source of new club listings are the library patrons who use the database and naturally search for any club they belong to. If they don't find their club, these patrons frequently ask a library staff member how PPLD could possibly have overlooked it. The patron is asked to supply information about their club for the database. The technician assigned to the Clubs database also uses information from local newspapers (both daily and weekly), radio, and television.

Club entries are updated annually. The time for updating is built into each record and generally timed to come just after each club's election of officers. The Clubs database was accessed more than 10,000 times in 1992, making this the most frequently accessed of the Community Connections databases. The first two months of 1993 show a 12% increase in average weekly usage.

Courses (online since 1979)

The Courses database contained 1,975 records as of mid-March 1993. There are two primary types of records: (a) individual courses, workshops, seminars, and forums offered in the Pikes Peak region; and (b) profiles of institutions or organizations offering courses.

Each record of an individual course includes the name of the course, the school or organization offering the course, the address and telephone numbers for enrollment information, dates, times and length of the course, cost of the course, and other miscellaneous information. Profile records include the name of the school/organization, addresses and telephone numbers, and keywords for the types of courses offered.

This database began with the information contained in the files of the Consortium for Coordinating Education for Adults, a local community group that ceased to function because of lack of funding. PPLD combined these files with the course listings already known to the library and put the information online.

The information in this file is gathered in a variety of ways. Two of the larger institutions that list courses in the database (University of Colorado at Colorado Springs and Pikes Peak Community College) supply PPLD with computer tapes of all their offerings on a regular basis. Other institutions supply paper copy for each session. More than 50 different sources provide course listings for the database. The technician responsible for maintaining the Courses database has also established contacts at a number of the institutions. In addition, the local news media occasionally provide information on new course offerings. The Courses database was accessed approximately 4,000 times in 1992; the first two months of 1993 show no change in average weekly usage.

Local Authors (online since 1986)

The Local Authors database contained 164 records as of mid-March 1993. This database provides current information on authors who live and work in the Pikes Peak region. Each record includes the author's name, the genre or subject of work, a list of publications, biographical information, and an indication of availability as a speaker.

This database may be searched by the name of a particular author or by subject words (to find a list of local authors that write on that subject). Searching on the word "yes" will generate a list of all the local authors who are available to speak to seminars, club meetings, etc.

The Local Authors database began with a mass mailing of questionnaires to all the writers that PPLD knew about. The appearance of the database led to library patrons suggesting additional authors missed by the first mailing. The Local Authors database was accessed more than 1,500 times in 1992, and the first two months of 1993 show a 21% increase in average weekly usage.

Local Documents (online since 1986)

The Local Documents database contained 3,674 records as of mid-March 1993. This database provides access to documents written by city and county government departments, citizens groups, and developers. Each record includes the name of the issuing agency, the date the document was issued, the title of the document, an abstract of the document, and keywords for the subject(s) of the document.

This database also resulted from the efforts of Citizen's Goals. Although some city and county agencies were routinely sending documents to the library, many were not. Funding from Citizen's Goals permitted the expansion of the document collection and the addition of computer capacity to handle the increased number of documents. The Pikes Peak Area Council of Governments donated its library of documents to PPLD to enrich the Local Documents collection. Today, PPLD routinely receives copies of new local documents and adds them to this database. The Local Documents database was accessed more than 7,500 time in 1992, and the first two months of 1993 show a 6% increase in average weekly usage.

Senior Housing (online since 1988)

The Senior Housing database contained 84 records as of mid-March 1993. This database provides access to housing facility information for those 55 or older. Each record includes the name of the facility, address, telephone numbers, price range, admission requirements/restrictions, services offered, and amenities provided. The database may be searched by zip code, street, name of the facility, or by keywords describing services or amenities.

The original entries in this database came to PPLD as the result of a joint project of PPLD and the Area Agency on Aging. Cooperation between the two agencies continues. This database was accessed approximately 800 times in 1992, and the first two months of 1993 show no change in this rate of usage.

Social and Economic Indicators (online since 1988)

The Social and Economic Indicators database contained 396 records as of mid-March 1993. This database was established to provide a single source for existing statistics that had previously appeared in a number of formats and in a wide range of sources. This database was constructed from scratch, not from previously existing source files. Each record includes statistical information, keywords for the subject(s) of the record, and the source or sources of the information. Most of these data concern the Pikes Peak region and Colorado, but some statistics include comparisons with other parts of the United States. This database covers such diverse subjects as climate, residential and commercial construction, vital statistics, education, and numerous others.

Social and Economic Indicators may be searched by keyword(s), by source (e.g., 1990 Census or Colorado Springs *Gazette-Telegraph*), or by the words in the title of the record (e.g., Population—Municipalities). The Social and Economic Indicators database was accessed nearly 4,500 times in 1992, and the first two months of 1993 show a 30% increase in average weekly usage.

IMPACT ON STAFFING LEVELS AND ASSIGNMENTS

Maintaining the Community Connections databases at Pikes Peak Library District involves a variety of tasks and staff members to perform them. Presently, each of the databases is assigned an information technician/librarian team responsible for maintenance, development, and promotion. Each information technician assigned to a database devotes approximately 25% of her time to this task. The supervising librarians spend approximately 10% of their time on database-related activities.

The information technician is responsible for adding and deleting records from the database, gathering the information for updating records (some databases are updated annually, others at various intervals), and surveying local sources for leads to additional entries. The supervising librarian is responsible for broader decisions about the content of the database, determining what reports will be generated from the database, speaking to groups involved in the database, making new contacts regarding the database, and a variety of other supervisory tasks. Occasionally, the supervising librarian may also be called upon to input data.

THE FUTURE OF COMMUNITY INFORMATION ONLINE AT PPLD

At the time of this writing, the Pikes Peak Library District is proposing another giant step forward in providing community information. PPLD and the Pikes Peak United Way are considering the joint creation of an Information and Referral Center, housed in the downtown library facility, that would extend the community information concept further. This Community Intake Center would build on the existing Community Connections databases and add client referral to the appropriate agency. Both walk-in and telephone clients would be welcome. PPLD would provide the facility, the staff, and the expertise in using the Community Connections databases; the United Way would work with PPLD to improve agency listings and insure that services are accurately listed in the database. Application has been made for grant funding to begin the program.

CONCLUSION

The Pikes Peak Library District is well known throughout the world as a leader in providing community information online. Library staff from many countries have visited PPLD to see the Community Connections in action, and PPLD is understandably proud of the success of the program. The high rate of use of the databases (five accesses per record in the databases) indicates that they fill a need in the community, and without a doubt, the future will surely see a continuation of this commitment to Community Connections.

BILL ERBES

Internet Coordinator
Illinois Valley Library System
Pekin, Illinois

YVONNE BEECHLER-RUSCH

Blind and Physically Handicapped Consultant
DuPage Library System
Geneva, Illinois

Integrating Free-Net into Library Services

HEARTLAND FREE-NET

The Heartland Free-Net is a totally community-based, automated network that has been developed by Peoria-area businesspeople, lawyers, and scholars. The system permits users to search the Heartland Free-Net system and to enter questions or responses through modem-equipped microcomputers. Communicating via electronic mail, users exchange information on various topics, view and contribute to community bulletin boards and forums, seek and provide current information on local government and business developments, and make referrals to social service agencies. For a time, users were also able to search listings of the Illinois Job Service and to post questions at the Library Reference Desk, a module designed to handle not only bibliographic questions but also any questions that did not seem to fit anyplace else within the system.

The Heartland Free-Net was originally funded by agencies throughout the Peoria area, including the following: Advanced Information Systems, Inc.; Ameritech; Becker Bros., Inc.; the Bielfeldt Foundation; Bradley University; Caterpillar, Inc.; Computerland of Peoria; FOA—Illinois; Heyl, Royster, Voelker, & Allen, P.C.; IBM; the Illinois State Bar Association; the Peoria Journal Star; and Proctor Community Hospital. The Heartland Free-Net service is provided free of charge to the people of the greater Peoria area.

Individuals can visit the system, or they can become registered users. Visitors can read any item on the system. Registered users have the special privilege of sending mail to and receiving mail from any other registered user, and they can pose questions to the EIPs (Expert Information Providers). Questions are posed anonymously. There is no charge to become a registered user; the process involves filling out a brief form used for demographic analysis.

The stated purpose of the Heartland Free-Net is to enrich the quality of life and enhance the image of central Illinois. Further, the system seeks to provide an educational forum for those living in the region and contribute to the area's economic life. The actual contents of the Heartland Free-Net are changing constantly. New modules are added and seldom-used modules are deleted, and the administration of the Heartland Free-Net is willing to consider ideas from any source for system enhancement.

Heartland Free-Net users are also able to link to other Free-Net systems through limited access to the Internet. Users may link to Free-Nets in Cleveland and Youngstown, Ohio, and to the Cornell University Electronic Information Source. All of the above is accomplished through a simple menu system. Advanced users may also use the Internet to link to electronic mailboxes nationwide.

"NOT ALONE, BUT TOGETHER" PROJECT

Project Goals

The Illinois State Library *Task Force on Rural Library Services Report* (1989) stated that:

> Rural libraries should be committed to providing the same level of service as urban libraries. Two levels of library service, one for urban residents and a second less complete level for rural residents, cannot be justified. All libraries should strive to provide equal access to information through available local, state, and national networks. A minimum level of service is the right of all Illinois citizens served by tax-supported libraries whether in rural or urban settings. (p. 6)

Further, the report notes that:

> Rural libraries should take the lead in organizing networks of locally operating information providers, such as chambers of commerce, cooperative extension services, farm bureaus, social service agencies, and education institutions. The Illinois State Library and the library systems should take leadership roles in setting up model pilot projects for facilitating this cooperation and dialogue. (p. 6)

The "Not Alone, but Together" project, also known as P.A.T.H. (Public Access to the Heartland Free-Net), was a model pilot project designed to organize and coordinate not only local information providers but also those information providers in other communities, rural and urban, that may not have previously even known of each other's existence. The project was a technologically innovative yet cost-effective approach to meeting those needs identified by the Rural Library Services Task Force. Further, and also in strict accordance with the *Task Force on Rural Library Services Report*, the project was designed to not only "improve access to information through the use of new technologies," but also, for many of the participants, to make such access possible for the first time (p. 6).

The project was aimed specifically at improving local library service through an automated approach to the provision of information. As designed, the project permitted not only immediate access to information for citizens at all levels of the socioeconomic scale, but it also allowed an in-depth analysis of how a shared, public access automated retrieval system could work in tandem with local public libraries to encourage economic development, coordinated cooperative development, and overall library development. The project was an innovative approach to meeting the need, stated so many times by so many agencies, of equalizing access to information for the citizens of rural and urban communities.

Implementation

Without question, the most difficult aspect of the project was the limited time available for implementation. "Not Alone, but Together" should have been spread over two years, with the first year devoted to hardware installation and Free-Net training. The second year could then have been used to actually test the efficacy of the system as a library tool, as well as the impact of an automated community-based information retrieval system on libraries, particularly in rural areas.

Delays in receiving signed contracts from the Illinois State Library delayed the actual equipment purchase until October 1990. Once the equipment was in hand and installation began, it was discovered that the installation of 28 computer systems required far more time and labor than anticipated. The primary problem was with telecommunications equipment; many libraries simply were not equipped with the appropriate telephone lines to provide a modem link. When such situations were encountered, installation was delayed until appropriate action could be taken by the telephone companies involved.

The installation of phone lines and the resolution of various telephone line problems were further complicated by the several telephone companies involved. It was often a problem just figuring out who to call for assistance. Often, phone company representatives were themselves unsure as to how to resolve the problems this project presented. Further, libraries confronted with line installations faced an unanticipated financial burden. Appropriations of funds often required board action and thus entailed further delays; therefore, some libraries were unable to begin participation until November or later.

Training

System training, in most cases, took place on the same day as installation. The Heartland Free-Net is a remarkably user-friendly system, and very little training is required. Still, the project director held a training session for staff at each participating library. Throughout the installation and training period, all involved seemed satisfied and comfortable. No calls were received requesting further training (though that offer was made to all participants). Still, when the project was evaluated by an independent research team from Bradley University, several librarians commented that they felt inadequately trained and therefore were reluctant to use or publicize the system.

Software Problems

Early on, a number of software problems were discovered. It had been decided to provide each participant with software that, when the user typed the word *path*, would automatically dial in to the Heartland Free-Net. Further, the software would perform only that function. Significant reprogramming would be necessary for a user to modify the software to allow access to other remote databases, an act that was intentionally discouraged as it would incur unanticipated telecommunications charges for P.A.T.H. Again, the time factor worked against successful implementation of the software—there was insufficient time for testing and debugging prior to distribution. There also was not enough time to complete the programming to allow automatic statistical retrieval; all usage statistics had to be retrieved and compiled manually. A further software complication arose with the availability of "Letters from Home," a service of the General Electric GEnie network to allow users to send electronic mail to soldiers in the Persian Gulf. To enable that link, all of the software had to be rewritten and redistributed. Again, there was not sufficient time for testing, and numerous problems arose with incompatibility.

All of the above problems could have been eased with a full-time, rather than a half-time, project director. Though Yvonne Beechler-Rusch put in far more hours than her contract stipulated (all for no additional compensation), she was still unable to keep up with the myriad of software problems or to consistently respond to problems in a timely manner. To make matters worse, the individual who wrote the original software seemed to lose interest in the project and was not forthcoming with solutions or advice. In the final months of the project, a budget amendment was written to hire more help. That action eased problems considerably.

Free-Net Procedural Problems

The Free-Net software was the cause of some procedural difficulty. Essentially, the Free-Net is designed to disconnect a user after 30 minutes of use. This feature is extremely important to librarians paying per-minute long-distance fees. Unfortunately, that feature proved to be unreliable, and upon receipt of monthly telephone bills, several libraries discovered fees for hundreds of minutes. Some telephone companies were cooperative in deleting those charges; others were not.

Another significant problem arose with the Heartland Free-Net's own procedures. The Heartland Free-Net advertises a 48-hour response time for questions posed by users; however, such is not always the case. Oftentimes many days go by before an answer is posted, and in far too many cases, no response is ever posted. Another problem involved the texts of historical documents available through the Heartland Free-Net, which were retrieved primarily by students. One library discovered early in the project that the text of one document was in fact an abridged version with no warning to that effect. This oversight was not acceptable to many librarians, and the discovery made the entire module suspect.

It should be noted that throughout the project the Free-Net organization was very cooperative and eager to provide assistance. It would have been helpful, however, to have protocols more firmly established from the very start. It was not always clear whose area of responsibility was being called into play when problems arose. The Heartland Free-Net executive director was responsive to these concerns and, as the project progressed, worked with Illinois Valley Library System personnel to establish better lines of communication to avoid misunderstandings.

On various occasions throughout the grant period, unannounced visits were made to participating libraries. The most common observation, and the most disturbing, was that computers usually were not turned on to display the P.A.T.H. welcome screen. Further, publicity materials and P.A.T.H. brochures were frequently not on display. It may be that better in-house publicity would have resulted in heavier use of the system. This problem, too, may have been alleviated through a full-time project director, one with the time to make more frequent site visits and to offer more one-on-one support and encouragement.

As noted earlier, shortly after the United States became involved with Operation Desert Shield, the General Electric Corporation instituted a program whereby computer users could send electronic mail to service personnel in Saudi Arabia. The program created monumental confusion for P.A.T.H. participants as it was publicized locally as an element of the Heartland Free-Net. In fact, it had nothing to do with the Free-Net. The instructions for accessing "Letters from Home" were printed in a Free-Net module, but that was the extent of the relationship between the two programs. Librarians and library patrons were led to believe that they could access "Letters from Home" through the Free-Net, and their inability to do so often resulted in frustration and anger. The P.A.T.H. software was hurriedly rewritten and redistributed to allow access to "Letters from Home," and the untested nature of that software often led to unanticipated problems. Other problems developed because the "Letters from Home" project was heavily used nationwide and was often inaccessible. Patrons would try over and over to connect but would meet with a busy signal each time. The program also had a habit of disconnecting in mid-use for no apparent reason, and the editing function simply did not work. Adding to the frustrations of all, because "Letters from Home" was handled entirely by General Electric, with no local modification possible, the project director was unable to respond to users' problems.

Publicity

Although "Letters from Home" created many problems and demanded many hours of time from the project director, the project also generated tremendous publicity for the Heartland Free-Net and for the P.A.T.H. project. It received extensive radio, television, and newspaper coverage; it brought scores of people to participating libraries; and beyond the confines of the grant project, it gave participating libraries an opportunity to respond to a national crisis in a very real, very positive way.

Publicity for a project of the magnitude of "Not Alone, but Together" is quite difficult, and much time was devoted to that aspect of the project. A packet of publicity materials generated throughout the project has been filed with the Illinois State Library. The project director created sample press releases and provided them to each participant. Though very few invitations were received, both the project director and the grant coordinator were available to speak to local groups and community organizations about the project. The executive director of the Heartland Free-Net was also available for speaking engagements. Posters were created and distributed to each library participant, and several radio interviews were given. Television news carried the "Letters from Home" story, which was repeated on several newscasts. Participating libraries were supplied with brochures about the project, and those brochures were also distributed to community organizations throughout the Illinois Valley Library System.

During the project period, the Heartland Free-Net was the subject of a documentary videotape produced by the Ameritech Corporation. The P.A.T.H. project was very briefly mentioned in that tape.

Finally, a radio commercial was prepared for broadcast on the two Peoria radio stations with the highest listening audience. In addition, 10,000 placemats advertising the project were printed and distributed to restaurants in communities where participating libraries were located, and six billboards concerning the project were designed and exhibited. It should be noted that the primary cost of the billboards was donated by Adams Outdoor Advertising of Peoria, Illinois.

As with other aspects of the project, publicity required far more time than was available. A full-time project director might have been able to spend more time both publicizing the project from the system standpoint and working with individual participants to assist them with local publicity efforts.

IMPLICATIONS FOR LIBRARIES

The "Not Alone, but Together" project represents a significant step forward for automation and networking within the Illinois Valley Library System. As a direct result of this project, 28 public library sites are equipped with computers, printers, and modems. Further, wiring and telecommunications links in each library have been installed or modified to allow simple access to virtually any remote database. Library staff have also been trained in the use of telecommunications equipment, and it seems likely that any initial apprehension has been overcome. As a by-product of the project, the Heartland Free-Net has registered hundreds of new users and received enormous amounts of free publicity.

Perhaps of greatest importance, the participating libraries have been, and continue to be, capable of providing a unique and valuable library service. The P.A.T.H. project was originally conceived in response to the feeling that although the Heartland Free-Net is a very worthwhile endeavor, it runs the risk of being elitist; that is, those most in need of the information provided by the Heartland Free-Net may very well not have computers and modems in their homes. There was a strong feeling at the Illinois Valley Library System that public access needed to be provided to the system and that public libraries were the best vehicle to provide that access. As a result of this project, patrons can walk into virtually any public library in the Illinois Valley Library System and access the Heartland Free-Net anonymously and free of charge. (At the conclusion of the project, only two libraries, the Pekin Public Library and the Kewanee Public Library, decided to discontinue the service.)

Accomplishments have been tremendous, but they have occurred primarily in the realm of physical infrastructure improvements. The computers have been installed, training has been completed, and patrons have grown accustomed to using the system. What has not been resolved are the philosophical and experimental aspects of the project. As noted in the original grant application: "As Heartland Free-Net becomes available, and as the systems it will engender nationally also become available, it is imperative that libraries respond and participate. Those libraries that ignore this logical step in automation may expect to see their roles as information providers eroded and eventually supplanted." The veracity of that statement has not been tested through the "Not Alone, but Together" project. More time and study are required, and that continued study is currently taking place. An article about the Free-Net P.A.T.H., by Bryn Geffert (1993), recently appeared in an issue of *Public Libraries*. That article continues an evaluation of the project from the perspective of someone not directly involved in the P.A.T.H. project. It offers many observations, often highly critical, that are not noted here.

There seem to be two levels at which the Heartland Free-Net can be viewed in libraries. It can be seen as a viable information tool, a link both to community functions and expert information providers. The other level is essentially that of entertainment, an electronic mailbox and forum used, to a great extent, by teenagers sharing nonsense. An examination of the teen forum, for example, reveals hundreds and hundreds of messages that have no purpose other than entertainment. Often, the messages are virtually unintelligible gibberish. Faced with ever-increasing costs of telecommunications and storage, librarians must wonder if such is an effective and efficient use of tax dollars.

There was, throughout the project, little feedback from participants. Calls were received by the project director only if there were equipment malfunctions or if there was confusion about reimbursement or some particular element of the Free-Net. In fact, for a project of this scope and size, there were remarkably few calls to report problems. At the same time, however, it seems that most library participants simply installed the computers and gave the patrons access. The participants then seem to have stepped back and let the project take its course. There were no reports of any librarians at participating institutions actually attempting to use the Free-Net as a reference tool. There were no attempts to establish the Free-Net in lieu of any print material, and there were no suggestions for system enhancements. Essentially, there seems to have been no particular interest on the part of the participants to do anything more than have the computer available; that is, to fulfill their individual requirements, with no attempts at creative use.

This observation is not derogatory. At no time either before or after the project began were the librarians led to believe that experimentation was expected. In fact, it was not. Experimentation was to be the province of the grant coordinator and the project director. As noted throughout this paper, however, there simply was no time for extensive experimentation.

CONCLUSION

The effects of the "Not Alone, but Together" project are significant and will be long lasting. Much experimentation and development remain to be done, and it is hoped that the Illinois Valley Library System and the Heartland Free-Net will maintain close ties. It is further hoped that this project will lead to even more experimentation with the networking of small, rural libraries, especially with the Internet.

REFERENCES

Geffert, B. (1993). Community networks in libraries: A case study of the Freenet P.A.T.H. *Public Libraries, 32*(2), 91-96.
Illinois State Library. Task Force on Rural Library Services. (1989). *Task Force on Rural Library Services report*. Springfield, IL: Illinois State Library.

VELGA B. STOKES

Assistant Manager
Computing and Information Technology Information Centers
Princeton University
Princeton, New Jersey

Linking Academic Systems with the Community: Current Activities at Princeton

INTRODUCTION

The fabled ivory towers of our storied past have crumbled, deservedly, I think, into dust. Today's colleges and universities are involved citizens in the lives of their communities. The institution as a whole and its individual members participate in community activities and support community needs. In Princeton, New Jersey, Princeton University too is viewed as having an important role in the surrounding community.

To set the scene, let me provide a few brief facts, as listed in the university's publication *A Princeton Profile:*

> Chartered in 1746 as the College of New Jersey, Princeton was British North America's fourth college. First located in Elizabeth, then in Newark, the College moved to Princeton (approximately 55 miles from New York City and 45 miles from Philadelphia) in 1756.
>
> The College was officially renamed Princeton University in 1896; the Graduate School was established in 1901.
>
> Fully coeducational since 1969, Princeton enrolls about 6,200 students (4,550 undergraduates and 1,650 graduate students).
>
> Today, Princeton's main campus consists of more than 5.5 million square feet of space in 135 buildings on 600 acres. The University's nearby James Forrestal Campus consists of a million square feet of space in four building complexes on 340 acres.
>
> The Borough and Township of Princeton in New Jersey's Mercer County have a combined population of 30,000. The University employs about 4,660 people, including approximately 900 faculty members. It is the largest private employer in Mercer County.

Though not a public institution, Princeton has always been very involved in the community. By virtue of its location in a relatively small community, Princeton is a major employer and, unavoidably, an influential resident. To support our community relations efforts, we have an Office of State and Regional Affairs that maintains contacts and works on issues of common interest with our local borough and township communities, as well as with the state government and regional area groups. In addition to the centralized community contacts, many groups and individuals within the university work with the local community in a wide variety of ways. The Office of Computing and Information Technology attempts to play a part too, and it is that connection to the community that this paper will discuss first.

OFFICE OF COMPUTING AND INFORMATION TECHNOLOGY

Princeton's present Office of Computing and Information Technology came into being six years ago, in October 1986, when Ira Fuchs was appointed to the newly established position of Vice President for Computing and Information Technology. CIT, as it has come to be known, provides support to the entire university community, for both administrative and academic work, without infringing on the academic mission of the Department of Computer Science. As part of its computing-related responsibilities, CIT provides IBM mainframe-, UNIX-, PC-, and Mac-based computing resources; a campus network that reaches all buildings on the main campus and several off-campus sites; access to both BITNET and the Internet; and dial-out capability to other networks. Our support services include hardware installation and repair, consulting, documentation, training, local area network maintenance, programming, and software and hardware testing—a fairly full array of services designed to meet the university's needs. (Just for completeness, I will note that a number of noncomputing-related university services are also provided by CIT, for example, the telephone system, printing and mailing, campus video, the language lab.)

Before CIT, some similar functions were performed by an entity called the Computer Center, which named not only a building but also the staff within it. Our efforts to link to the community go back to the time of the Computer Center, when the Computer Center Education Series presented classes on computing topics. The topics of interest in those days were things like keypunching and Fortran and assembly language programming; the classes were open to all, and members of the community were frequent attendees. The classes were scheduled in the evening, after normal working hours, and we often found that university neighbors outnumbered university staff in the classes.

Our transformation from the "Computer Center" to "Computing and Information Technology" coincided with the computing revolution that removed computing from the esoteric realm of assembly language programmers running jobs on mysterious mainframes and placed it in the hands—and job descriptions—of nearly everyone on campus. As the university's computing needs changed, the jobs of the computing support staff changed, and some aspects of our interaction with the community changed as well.

The old, casual, all-welcome evening computing classes were among the first to undergo a change. With computing now part of everyone's job description, CIT staff had to focus their educational efforts on the suddenly greatly expanded needs of the rest of the university to learn how to use word processing, spreadsheets, and databases. Our evening lectures became daytime hands-on workshops, and the demand among university staff for this training was so high that workshops were limited to university faculty, staff, and students. Some non-hands-on lectures continued to be given and were open to all, but they too frequently focused on more specifically university job-related tasks—administering Novell networks, for example—and were thus of less interest to the general community.

We do, however, participate with other university departments in sponsoring special lectures on computing topics by well-known "players" in the computing field, both academic and commercial, and we have had good community interest in a number of these events in recent years.

Several computing "users' groups" flourish on the Princeton campus, most with the lively involvement of both university staff and local community members. While CIT provides no financial assistance to the activities of the groups, the cooperation of our staff and townspeople in an activity of common interest benefits us all.

We host visits from community groups and from conference groups meeting in the Princeton area. Businesspeople are interested in everything from general computing topics to very specific items related to their field, and when appropriate, we try to put them in touch with university academic departments and resources.

In addition to striving to maintain personal contact, our community outreach efforts focus on facilitating access to electronic communication and information sharing.

PRINCETON NEWS NETWORK

Since 1989, CIT staff have maintained a campus-wide information system (CWIS) called PNN, the Princeton News Network. Most, but importantly not all, of the information provided by PNN is Princeton University information covering campus events and activities, office and department listings, curriculum and course information, library information, university policies and procedures, and university employment listings. PNN is available in a public, non-logged-on format to anyone who can access the system, while dial-in access to the public version is also available. Some items of information, for example campus addresses, are not available on public PNN for legal reasons, nor is printing, but all other PNN information is available to anyone.

One of the main menu categories in PNN is "Travel and Visitor Information." Among the documents available—and these are among our important nonuniversity documents—are train schedules to New York, airport transportation schedules, airline toll-free telephone numbers, and directions for traveling to Princeton. For community members and visitors (and no doubt university members as well), the online version of the university's publication *Campus: A Guide to Princeton University* provides information about the university and its facilities, as well as a history of the town.

Among the most widely read items on PNN is the university's events calendar. The calendar is compiled for the university's newsletter, the *Princeton Weekly Bulletin* (the PWB for short), which is published weekly when classes are in session; its calendar is the closest thing we have to a complete university events calendar. Whenever the calendar is published, an electronic version is sent to PNN and posted there. Usually the electronic calendar is available at least a day before paper copies have reached their destinations. The PWB is available in paper form at the Princeton community public library, and at least once every semester free copies are sent to addresses in the community (paid subscriptions are also available). For those community members who can reach the university network, the electronic calendar provides quickly and easily accessed information about university events. Most university events are open to the public, and community attendance is encouraged; the PWB calendar clearly marks those events that are not open to the public, as well as those events—concerts and football games, for example—that require the purchase of tickets. In addition to the weekly university calendar, PNN includes weekly and semester calendars from a variety of other university departments and organizations. For example, the Woodrow Wilson School of Public and International Affairs, which sponsors many lectures on topics of public interest, publishes a calendar of its events for the semester. The monthly schedules for the drama, music, and dance programs at our McCarter Theatre are also available.

The community newspapers that serve Princeton, New Jersey, do not appear daily. One is published as a weekly; the other appears twice a week. The university's newsletter appears weekly, except during summer recess and university break periods. As a result, the timeliness of PNN is much appreciated by readers who can use the system to see announcements of changes and cancellations that occur after paper publications have gone to press.

The local community (as well as the university community) is also an interested reader of the university's employment listing. Like the calendar, this listing of available jobs also appears in printed form in the PWB. The PNN version, however, is usually more current, since it does not have to meet the week-ahead deadline of the printed publication. It also includes all jobs available (the printed version, if space is tight, omits older job listings), and it provides more complete job descriptions than can be accommodated in the printed version. In addition, while the PWB version appears only when the newsletter is published (only once for all the summer months, for example), the PNN version is updated every week and is an especially valuable resource for community members interested in jobs at the university.

FUTURE DEVELOPMENTS

While we feel that PNN has been an extremely useful system for both the university community and the broader Princeton community, we are now actively engaged in moving toward a more global CWIS that is based, for the present, on the implementation of appropriate Gopher clients and servers. As this paper is being written, work on the project has just begun, and I expect that notable changes will occur by the time the paper is published. Several guiding principles have already been established, however, and they are worth mentioning in the context of this discussion.

It is our intent to continue making our CWIS freely and widely accessible, so that those who have been able to read information on PNN will continue to be able to do so via any vehicle selected as the technology evolves. The information currently provided in PNN will continue to be included in our new CWIS, which is at present Gopher-based. We also plan to encourage other university departments and groups to establish their own Gopher servers, so that a broader range of university information can be made available to all. We are holding discussions, for example, with the university's Office of Publications/Communications, to see how we might facilitate inclusion of a greater number of university publications in Gopher. And of course Gopher's ability to reach online information resources around the world will extend access globally.

Another resource that is currently widely used, the university library's online catalog, with records of all library acquisitions since 1980, is available without logged-on access, as are a number of other university library-provided indexes and catalogs. For example, anyone can look at the Center for Research Libraries catalog; the Princeton data library catalog; the Early American imprints catalog; the monthly catalog of U.S. government publications; current serials about Latin America, Spain, and Portugal; and Princeton University manuscripts, archives, and special collections.

In addition, the library is experimenting with a "gateway" implementation that would provide access not only to the catalogs and indexes, but also to other library resources, including the circulation database to allow networked users to check whether a specific book is in the library or out on loan. As our plans for the transition to Gopher mature, we hope to include the library's gateway in Gopher, thus making it even more widely available to both the university and the local community.

With the expansion of online information resources, Princeton is facing the paradoxical need to limit access to some of the resources. I have mentioned that we already deny access to campus phone book information on public PNN; as we move to Gopher, limitations on this information must continue. It may be possible, for example, to provide office telephone numbers for staff or e-mail address information for everyone, but student dorm address and phone number information can be available only to identified (that is, logged-in with university accounts and passwords) members of the university community. Other kinds of information are restricted by contractual agreements: we make Clarinet news available only to the university community, and, similarly, several library indexes are contractually restricted to the university community. And, of course, an overriding security consideration is the National Science Foundation's prohibition on anonymous access to the Internet, so that our implementation of access to online information resources must be strictly controlled to allow, for the public, "read only" access, without the ability to "do" anything else. With PNN, for example, anonymous users cannot print information, save it in a file, or send it to anyone else—any of these actions would require an opening in the tightly closed "box" that public PNN runs in, and would endanger system security.

K-12 OUTREACH

A second major community outreach area involves the local schools. The university supports K-12 education in a variety of ways; some of the more visible include presenting Outstanding Teacher awards every year at our commencement, hosting conferences for teachers, sponsoring essay contests among area schools, and allowing high school student participation in university classes.

CIT frequently hosts visits by classes ranging from first graders to high schoolers. Even first graders, of course, are now experienced with computers (many in the Princeton community say they have computers at home), and they enjoy our demonstrations of exchanging e-mail with colleagues in California, and making artistic masterpieces with MacDraw, and going home with an instant newsletter describing their visit—complete with a digitized photograph of the visitors. High schoolers have a different interest, and frequently want to hear about what careers are available in the computing field. We cheerfully devote time to such visits because we feel that familiarity with computing is essential to the future of all those in school today; the responses of our visitors indicate students are increasingly exposed to and comfortable with computers—and they are pleased to learn more about what computers can do.

Our summers frequently include some more formal school contact efforts, with seminars sponsored by various organizations and agencies as well as special summer classes for small student groups.

The most recent of our information-sharing projects has been our work to provide Internet access to the Princeton Regional Schools (PRS). Begun in response to National Science Foundation efforts to broaden the availability of databases on the network not only to colleges but also to elementary and high schools, the project has been encouraged by the Vice President for Computing and Information Technology, Ira Fuchs, and has been supported by a variety of CIT groups working cooperatively with an enthusiastic group from the PRS system. JvNCnet, at the time a part of CIT and now an independent network service provider, had connected several school districts in New Jersey and Connecticut, and was instrumental in providing the network connection for PRS. CIT's Network Systems group was involved in establishing the connection. Our Advanced Applications and Technology group provided space on one of their machines and set up special disks and folders for teachers and students to make Internet access and resource use quick and easy.

When the PRS project was first suggested, some CIT staff expected that contact with the university community would be the goal of the teachers and students. In practice, however, we have found that teachers and students at all levels are most interested in communicating with their peers. For this reason, the access to e-mail provided by the project is a major benefit for the schools. Teachers discuss issues of common interest with other teachers; students find electronic pen pals in distant schools.

In response to our better understanding of what the PRS project participants really wanted to do, CIT staff provided software and instruction enabling teachers to easily access Netnews—focusing on the K-12 discussion groups of particular interest to them. The instructions also identified "Interesting Places" (Rutgers University Info, for example, and the Library of Congress), as well as the Princeton information in PNN and the wide world of information that becomes accessible with Gopher.

The coordinator of the PRS project praises CIT assistance especially for getting teachers started with the right software and pointing them toward some of the more interesting materials available over the network. Our making e-mail accounts available on one of our machines until PRS had appropriate equipment in-house has also earned the gratitude of those involved in the project. At present, teachers and students are actively using Internet resources on 35 new Macintosh systems received as a grant from the state; a recent workshop for staff on using the Internet included 30 teachers but unfortunately was not able to accommodate many more who wanted to attend. PRS now has a Gopher, FTP server, SMTP mail service, and may have a Chat server. The mail server handles more than 100 active accounts including those belonging to teachers and students, with more added weekly.

Several CIT staff are still actively working with PRS. Discussions are being held about the establishment of a Gopher users' group that would include both university and PRS members.

A couple of unexpected developments have followed our work with the PRS project: a Princeton University student is writing her senior thesis on the use of the Internet as a K-12 learning tool, and the Educational Testing Service (ETS), a locally situated but internationally known institution, has become interested in what PRS is doing. In addition, PRS is still researching possible grant funding to expand Internet access to homework centers that are being set up around town. Thus, while the project has made significant progress in the course of less than a year, it is still in the beginning stages when we consider possible future enhancement and expansion. We at CIT will do what we can to aid its growth and development.

CONCLUSION

As we consider the variety of our community contact efforts, we see that our intended goal is always the sharing of information. For centuries, information was stored in isolated treasure houses—frequently those mythic ivory towers of academe. The keepers of the treasure allowed access to very few. We are now at the very edge of a new age that is using technology to build information roads and bridges and to open doors (on sometimes rusty hinges) to make the information that is gathered and safeguarded by the few available to all. Our efforts now represent the first small steps along the paths that will widen into new information highways. We cannot yet foresee the new landscape that will result from the electronic web that has begun to cover the world. But we know that the present is the result of past revolutions, and this beginning technological revolution in information sharing will shape the future as forcefully as the printed word and television have shaped the present.

MARTIN DILLON

Director

ERIK JUL

Communications Manager

MARK BURGE

Research Assistant

CAROL HICKEY

Research Assistant

OCLC Online Computer Library Center, Inc.
Office of Research
Dublin, Ohio

The OCLC Internet Resources Project: Toward Providing Library Services for Computer-Mediated Communication

INTRODUCTION

Locating, accessing, and using information resources on the Internet, a global computer network of networks, can be difficult, time-consuming, and sometimes impossible. In this new and rapidly expanding electronic environment, network users have unprecedented access to information and computing resources. However, the development and implementation of systematic methods of describing and accessing information lag behind deployment of the Internet itself. Network users' ability to share information surpasses by far their ability to discover information on the Internet. Traditional library services such as cataloging have yet to find widespread application in this emerging environment.

Funded by the U.S. Department of Education, Library Programs, the OCLC Internet Resources project investigated the nature of electronic textual information accessible via the Internet. This empirical study also explored the practical and theoretical problems associated with providing traditional library services for electronic text in a wide area network environment. This report presents the findings and recommendations arising from the project, as well as suggested areas for further study.

OBJECTIVES

The primary objectives of this project were, first, to provide an empirical analysis of textual information on the Internet; second, to test the suitability of current cataloging rules and record formats governing the creation of machine-readable cataloging records; and, third, to develop recommendations that would assist the efforts of standards bodies and others interested in systematically cataloging or otherwise describing and providing access to electronic information objects available through remote network access.

METHODS

Project methods included, first, locating, collecting, and analyzing a sample of textual information objects derived from sources accessible via the Internet; second, developing and testing a taxonomy of electronic information based on the sample; and, third, conducting a cataloging experiment to identify and analyze problems associated with cataloging and providing appropriate levels of access to this information.

REFERENCE SOURCES

The early focus of the project was to collect sample text documents from Internet sources. In fall 1991, when the project was initiated, few resources existed to describe or assist access to Internet resources. Primary source materials initially available to project staff included Barron (1992), Frey and Adams (1991), Malkin and Marine (1992), National Science Foundation (1989), Krol (1989), LaQuey (1990), Quarterman (1990), and St. George and Larsen (1991). A now-defunct, manually maintained list of Internet File Transfer Protocol (FTP) sites also provided initial direction. The "Request for Comments" series of documents, which form the official Internet documentation sanctioned by the Internet Activities Board, also provided valuable initial direction. In the year of the study, print and electronic guides, directories, and other reference materials proliferated, and general discussion of the Internet moved from government, technical, or trade publications to the popular press.

Not surprisingly, much of the information about Internet resources is published, at least originally, in electronic form for distribution across the network. For the novice network user and those without Internet access, this is a hindrance to knowledge and a source of frustration. In recognition of this problem, several quality users' guides have been published recently in traditional book form (see, e.g., Kehoe, 1993; Krol, 1992; and Marine, 1992).

In addition to print and electronic reference tools, project staff used an array of systems specifically designed to assist the discovery and access of Internet resources. These electronic aids included WAIS (Wide Area Information Servers) by Thinking Machines Corporation, Gopher by the University of Minnesota, archie by McGill University, HYTELNET by Peter Scott, and electronic conferences (Kovacs, 1991; Strangelove, Okerson, & Kovacs, 1992).

WAIS is a distributed search and retrieval system using a client/server model and the draft Z39.50 standard for bibliographic retrieval (see Kahle & Medlar, 1991; Lincoln, 1992a, 1992b; and Nickerson, 1992). Gopher is a client/server protocol for distributed information systems (see Alberti, Anklesaria, Lindner, McCahill, & Torrey, 1992). The archie system facilitates information discovery and access by creating a searchable database of file and directory information obtained from FTP host computers (see Deutsch, 1992). HYTELNET provides hypertext access to lists of Internet resources and facilitates logging on to the remote resource (see Scott, 1992). These methods were augmented by electronic mail and online browsing.

ANALYSIS OF FTP SITES

The TCP/IP (Transmission Control Protocol/Internet Protocol) protocol suite provides FTP, allowing the transfer of electronic files among remote computers. Using FTP, system administrators can designate computers as anonymous FTP servers, that is, computers allowing anonymous FTP access to a store of files.

A feature of this protocol allows users to log on to remote computers on which they do not have an account as an "anonymous" user. Users can traverse the computer's file structure, display directory and file names, and initiate the transfer of files from or to the remote site. FTP prevents users from accessing other portions of the computer's file system.

FTP accounts for a significant portion of network traffic (46% of characters carried by the network as compared to 18% for electronic mail, 6% for Telnet, and 29% for other traffic). Internet traffic statistics derive from various sources and represent a snapshot of network development at a particular point in time (see Lottor, 1992, and network statistics provided by the Merit Network, Inc., available by FTP NIC.MERIT.EDU; directory: nsfnet/statistics; file: history.netcount). For this reason, project staff undertook a detailed analysis of FTP sites.

Method

Investigation of electronic documents was undertaken through manual collection and analysis and through computer-assisted statistical analyses and automated categorization. Each of these methods is described in the following sections.

File Collection and Analysis

The early focus of the project was to collect sample text documents from Internet sources. Project staff used an array of resources to discover the whereabouts of electronic text, including printed books, journal articles, and newsletters; online electronic publications and lists; information discovery tools such as WAIS, Gopher, and archie; hypertext programs; electronic conferences; electronic mail; and online browsing.

Project staff sought to categorize and quantify the information available via FTP sites automatically. This investigation was facilitated by data collected by the archie service, developed by Peter Deutsch and Alan Emtage of McGill University. The archie service is an early entry into the field of wide area information discovery. In short, the archie service has developed software that attempts to discover anonymous FTP sites and their contents. The software initiates an anonymous FTP logon at Internet host sites, cycling through the entire list of sites approximately once every 30 days. If the anonymous FTP logon is successful, the software executes a listing of the FTP site's directories, thus obtaining a list of every available file at the site. The file names extracted from the FTP sites are stored in a file and mounted in a searchable database. Users of the archie service can search the database for file names, and the system will provide the Internet address for sites containing files whose names match the user's query.

The archie service is a ready source of information about FTP sites and provides data that served as a starting point for generating a statistical snapshot of Internet resources. The file containing the list of FTP sites and their holdings is itself available via FTP, and project staff obtained it to extract a database for processing and analysis. The database includes a listing of FTP sites, paths, names, and file sizes, along with several other pieces of informaiton about each site.

To discover trends in the growth of FTP sites, we created and analyzed this database periodically. This sampling revealed rapid growth in the number of FTP sites during the time of this study, the number of files available at these sites, and the amount of data stored on magnetic disk. From January 1992 to August 1992, the number of sites grew from 829 to 1,044, a 25.93% increase; the number of files grew from 2,089,544 to 3,059,689, a 46.43% increase; and the size increased from 101.02 Gbytes to 165.05 Gbytes, a 63.38% increase.

To begin to get a sense of the makeup of these FTP sites, we selected 20 sites at random for closer analysis (Table 1). This sample clearly shows a wide range of profiles by every measure, including the number of files at a site (from 12 to 38,440), the amount of data stored (from 104,969 to 913,679,044 bytes), the largest file (from 45,056 to 28,437,472 bytes), and the average file size (8,747 to 2,530,930 bytes). The distribution of data among the sample sites is uneven; for example, the site csam.lbl.gov has only 57 files, yet it contains the largest file in the sample (28,437,472 bytes) and has the largest average file size (2,530,930 bytes). In contrast, the largest site in the sample, lth.se, has both the most files (38,440) and the most storage (913,679,044 bytes) but a comparatively low average file size (23,768).

The 20 largest FTP sites are shown in Table 2. At the time of our sampling, the largest FTP site on the Internet in terms of total files and total storage was src.doc.ic.ac.uk; the largest file, "db.pag" (1,846,821,888 bytes), was also at this site. These 20 largest sites, or 2% of Internet FTP sites, account for 57% of the available files and 38% of the storage, again revealing the disproportionate distribution of data and the significant contribution made by several large sites.

Directories, Paths, and File Names

Collectively, the Internet's anonymous FTP sites may be viewed as an archive or "library" of electronic information. Project staff investigated the methods

TABLE 1
SURVEY OF 20 SAMPLE FTP SITES BY NUMBER OF FILES

Site Name	No. Files	Total Bytes	Largest File (Bytes)	Average File (Bytes)
lth.se	38,440	913,679,044	13,344,768	23,768
research.att.com	9,102	257,800,968	8,752,643	28,323
archive.cis.ohio-state.edu	8.843	669,287,526	7,287,625	75,685
merit.edu	1,696	147,797,681	2,546,131	87,144
ftp.cica.indiana.edu	1,475	167,161,346	2,052,422	113,329
hubcap.clemson.edu	726	75,764,452	5,455,054	104,358
a.cs.uiuc.edu	459	65,460,295	6,097,773	142,615
turbo.bio.net	390	16,851,476	750,368	43,208
boombox.micro.umn.edu	382	36,239,511	2,047,933	94,867
dsl.cis.upenn.edu	134	6,102,098	816,261	45,538
gem.stack.urc.tue.nl	142	13,309,519	1,081,976	93,729
okeeffe.cs.berkeley.edu	115	18,078,337	3,853,003	157,202
nic.mr.net	124	9,552,240	1,854,848	77,034
watcgl.waterloo.edu	124	3,352,867	1,033,077	27,039
shemp.cs.ucla.edu	58	8,393,452	1,696,416	144,714
csam.lbl.gov	57	144,263,025	28,437,472	2,530,930
paul.rutgers.edu	19	1,638,718	602,699	86,248
suna.osc.edu	18	1,574,391	342,822	87,466
uop.uop.edu	16	4,174,683	784,987	260,917
jhname.hcf.jhu.edu	12	104,969	45,056	8,747

currently used to classify, describe, and facilitate the location of and access to information at these sites.

Apart from the FTP site names, other indicators of the type and location of information available at the site include the directory names, path names (a hierarchical series of directory names), and the individual file names. Minimally, any particular file will have a file name, directory name, and site name associated with it. Each of these names may provide meaningful information about the nature and contents of a file. In aggregate, these names may produce a cogent hierarchy of descriptors or they may be unintelligible to anyone but the creator of the directory/path/file-name structure.

The directory and path names provide description and location information for the files contained at the FTP site. On average, a typical file has fewer than three (2.47) associated content/location indicators, including the file name itself (Table 3). This indicates that the average hierarchical file structure is rather shallow and may provide inadequate descriptive information. (The depth of a hierarchical file structure does not affect the utility of location information.)

Readme and Index Files

FTP sites may contain text files that provide additional descriptive information about the contents of the site, a particular directory, or particular files. These informational files are often named "readme," "index," or some variation thereof in combination with other characters. The value of these informational files can vary greatly depending on the completeness, clarity, and currency of the descriptive information provided.

TABLE 2
20 LARGEST FTP SITES BY NUMBER OF FILES*

Site Name	No. Files	Total Bytes	Largest File	Average File
src.doc.ic.ac.uk	170,966	7,923,289,150	1,846,821,888**	46,344
wuarchive.wustl.edu	147,173	6,039,051,548	30,121,209	41,033
capella.eetech.mcgill.ca	131,262	5,199,556,552	30,121,209	39,612
mcsun.eu.net	109,483	1,065,088,972	12,082,830	9,728
isfs.kuis.kyoto-u.ac.jp	76,880	4,022,047,707	24,169,327	52,315
ucs.edu	67,288	289,291,834	12,886,016	4,299
gatekeeper.dec.com	67,100	4,279,830,040	44,877,484	63,782
toklab.ics.osaka-u.ac.jp	65,135	2,237,389,271	25,518,080	34,350
ftp.uu.net	59,508	2,689,716,008	10,573,106	45,199
plaza.aarnet.edu.au	54,046	3,677,983,744	30,121,209	68,052
athene.uni-paderborn.de	49,418	2,486,320,000	11,534,336	50,312
stis.nsf.gov	40,792	102,695,505	5,124,940	2,517
emx.cc.utexas.edu	40,550	478,590,134	4,841,472	11,802
erratic.bradley.edu	38,687	987,391,765	5,458,229	25,522
ipcl.rrzn.uni-hannover.de	38,511	1,291,990,465	33,144,095	33,548
lth.se	38,440	913,679,044	13,344,768	23,768
faui43.informatik. uni-erlangen.de	35,091	2,214,839,896	12,881,920	63,117
cs.ubc.ca	33,744	1,460,556,438	20,200,637	43,283
arp.anu.edu.au	32,142	126,915,618	2,803,093	3,948
rusmvl.rus.uni-stuttgart.de	28,963	1,573,641,267	46,097,964	54,332

* The top 20 Internet sites account for 57% of the available files and 38% of the storage.
** Largest file at Internet FTP site: /ic.doc/whois/db.pag.

TABLE 3
DIRECTORIES AT FTP SITES

Sites	1,044.00
Files	3,059,689.00
Directories	192,446.00
File/directory (avg.)	15.90
Directories/site (avg.)	184.34
Top-level directories	4,861.00
Top-level directories/site (avg.)	4.66
Maximum directory nodes*	20.00
Average directory nodes/file*	2.47

* Number of nodes in directory path including file name (std 1.26).

Project staff examined the frequency of these auxiliary informational files in a 20-site sample. Based on this sample, there is one readme file for every 3.5 directories and one index file for every 7 directories. By extrapolation, there is one readme file for every 55.65 files and one index file for every 111.3 files. Thus, despite the potential utility of these files, they occur infrequently.

TYPES OF FILES AT FTP SITES

Acquiring a statistical overview of FTP sites is useful and straightforward; determining the contents of FTP sites is more difficult and, for the average user, more necessary. Project staff sought to determine the composition of the aggregate FTP sites using automated methods. The chief and most readily available guides to the nature and contents of files at FTP sites are the directory and file names. Drawing from the 20-site sample, project staff compiled a list of all path names (the complete hierarchical path for each file in the data set), which were then counted and sorted by frequency. (A directory name was counted each time it occurred in a path for a file. For example, many FTP sites organize publicly accessible files hierarchically under the top-level directory "pub." Thus, while the /pub directory may have the most associated files, it likely occurs only once in file hierarchy at any given site.) The directory names in this sample set are highly idiosyncratic but nevertheless representative of the type of information provided by hierarchical naming structures.

To assess the correlation between directory names and file types, project staff created a list of the top 500 directory names drawn from a data set of 1,044 FTP sites. This list was manually reviewed, a subset of "meaningful" directory names was derived, and major categories of file types were established. Project staff obtained sample files from selected FTP sites containing key directory names in the file hierarchy. The files were examined, and correlation between file types and directory names was noted. This process was repeated, and the list of directory names was refined.

The list of directory names served as the basis for a dictionary of regular expressions (rules allowing the matching of various combinations of upper- and lowercase characters, variant spellings, and partial character strings). This process was repeated to refine the dictionary. Using the data dictionary, project staff developed software to parse directory path names, thus enabling automated classification of files.

Summary Analyses

Two random samples of 20 FTP sites were extracted from the total then available from the archie listings file. The data were then parsed, yielding the classification and statistical analyses shown in Figure 1. The percentage of file types for the two samples was very similar, giving a measure of confidence in the algorithm.

The rules for categorizing files were changed based on an analysis of the results of the two 20-site samples, and the categories were adjusted. The final categories were as follows: system code—software, including operating system software, associated with the administration of a computer system; source code—software programs and applications or their components; news—archives of newsgroups and discussion lists arising from group electronic mail transactions; text—files containing or intended to produce, in conjunction with other software applications, a textual document; PC (personal computer)—software applications identifiable as intended for use on personal computing systems; data—raw information, often numerical; images—representations of visual objects, to be used in conjunction with image-viewing software; games—software applications primarily used for entertainment; executable—compiled files directly executable by a user or an associated software application. The file categorization program was run against all 1,044 sites. The results of this analysis appear in Figure 2.

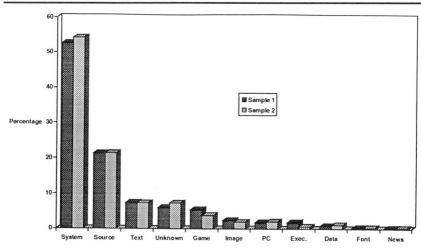

Figure 1. Comparative analyses of two 20-site samples

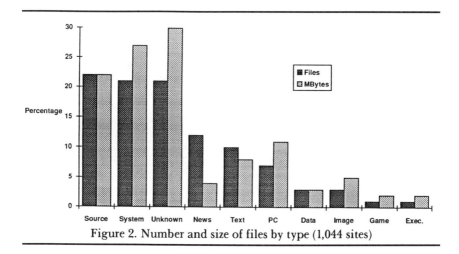

Figure 2. Number and size of files by type (1,044 sites)

CATALOGING EXPERIMENT

Having obtained a statistical overview of FTP sites and their contents, project staff sought to discover the problems, both theoretical and applied, associated with creating and using machine-readable cataloging records for remotely accessible electronic information objects.

Current MARC (MAchine-Readable Cataloging) records enable the creation, exchange, and subsequent use of machine-readable descriptive cataloging data for a wide spectrum of media, including books, serials, audiovisual materials, maps, musical scores, realia, and computer files. However, the applicability of the MARC cataloging model to the types of electronic information existing on the Internet was unknown. A systematic experiment was devised to ascertain, first, difficulties encountered by cataloging librarians in determining bibliographic data based on an examination of electronic information objects and, second, deficiencies in either the USMARC format for computer files or the *Anglo-American Cataloguing Rules*, second edition, revised (*AACR2R*) (Gorman & Winkler, 1988).

Assumptions

In conjunction with an advisory panel of MARC format and cataloging experts, project staff made the following assumptions when designing the cataloging experiment:

1. The current USMARC Computer Files Format and *AACR2R*, chapter 9, Computer Files, are adequate for creating descriptive cataloging records for electronic file resources on the Internet.
2. Electronic file resources on the Internet contain sufficient data elements for creation of minimal level cataloging records.
3. Catalog records can provide essential access information for electronic file resources on the Internet by incorporating selected fields from the USMARC Format for Holdings and Locations.

Methods

The hypotheses were tested by cataloging librarians who attempted to create catalog records for actual electronic information objects obtained from Internet sources. Project staff assembled a collection of computer files for this experiment using manual and automated methods to minimize bias and ensure a heterogeneous mix. The collection contained 300 files representative of files found on the Internet. The test collection focused on text files, which account for approximately 10% of files on the Internet but which comprise slightly more than half of the files in the test collection. The text files include electronic books, journals, newsletters, poetry, essays, lyrics, guides, lists, papers, reports, legislation, and a range of informal, unpublished materials including USENET newsgroup archives.

The remainder of the test collection consists of various types of software and data files such as source code, programs, games, images, and font files. These files are present in the collection in roughly the same proportions as they exist on the Internet, as determined by our earlier sampling; thus, source files predominated.

Items were not selected for inclusion in the test collection based on their merit as candidates for cataloging. The experiment was intended to test whether the files *could* be cataloged, not whether they *should* be cataloged.

To ensure sufficiently rigorous testing and to minimize difficulties encountered by any single cataloger, each computer file was to be cataloged by three different catalogers.

The 300 experimental files were numbered 001 to 300 and randomly sorted into 10 groups of 30 files each. This process was repeated to yield 30 groups of 30 files; each file occurring in 3 different randomly sorted groups. If each file were cataloged, this would yield 900 catalog records (3 × 300).

For each computer file in the experimental collection, project staff created an ancillary information file, numbered 001 to 300, which was available to participants in the experiment. The information files contained data related to associated computer files such as the size of the file in bytes, the original file name, the source from which project staff obtained the file, and additional information for use by project staff only. It was thought that this basic information about the file would generally be available to catalogers. Moreover, it was necessary to provide the file names, which had been changed to facilitate management of the experiment.

Requirements for Participation

Participants for the cataloging experiment were solicited via a Call for Participants, which was posted to several electronic conferences. Project staff made every effort to ensure widespread opportunity for participation. Responses were received from librarians throughout the world, including Australia, New Zealand, and Hong Kong. The published requirements for participation are given below:

1. MLS degree or equivalent, experience cataloging computer files, and a working knowledge of both the USMARC Format for Computer Files and the applicable cataloging rules (*AACR2R*, chapter 9).
2. Willingness to catalog 30 computer files within the three-week time frame of the experiment from May 11-29, 1992.
3. Internet access, although a limited number of non-Internet sites will be selected, if possible.
4. A word-processing system that can produce ASCII text files.

Participation was not limited to OCLC-member libraries, and online access to OCLC was not required.

Thirty-seven librarians responded to the call. Thirty individuals or teams were selected as primary participants; the remainder were considered auxiliary participants. On average, the 30 primary participants had three years' experience cataloging computer files, although experience ranged from one to 12 years.

Experimental Procedures

Participants were provided with guidelines and instructions. Insofar as possible, all communications and file exchanges related to the experiment took place via the Internet. (The Internet facilitated all administrative aspects of this experiment, including collecting and distributing files for cataloging, distributing ancillary documents, and receiving catalog records created by project participants.) This communication medium was augmented, when necessary, by phone, fax, and U.S. mail.

Each participant was assigned an identification number from 01 to 30 (auxiliary participants were indicated by the letter "a," e.g., 01a). The identification number corresponded to a similarly numbered set of 30 randomly generated sets of 30 numbers from 001 to 300. Using FTP, each participant was to obtain the appropriate set of numbers from an OCLC computer.

Each number in the set corresponded to a similarly numbered computer file to be cataloged. The computer files were named 001 to 300, with the file extension .obj (for "object"), and each associated information file was named 001 to 300, with the extension .info (for "information").

Participants were instructed to retrieve the assigned object and information files from an OCLC computer using FTP. Project staff provided a record template. The record template contained the valid fixed-field mnemonics and variable-field tags for the Computer Files format, with the addition of field 852 from the USMARC Format for Holdings and Locations. Participants were to complete the record using whatever cataloging aids were available to them and submit the completed record to OCLC, again using FTP.

In addition, participants were requested to complete a log file for each item cataloged and to record in this file the number of the object file and the time required for cataloging. Optionally, participants could record comments, suggestions, or problems related to the object, the cataloging rules, or the MARC format.

Experimental Results and Analysis

Of the 300 electronic files in the test collection, one or more bibliographic records were created for 291 (97%). For these objects, a total of 714 (79.4%) records were created; 650 (72%) log files were created for 291 objects.

The bibliographic records created were analyzed automatically and manually. Automated methods determined the occurrence of a particular field, the length of the field, and the degree of similarity among identical fields when more than one record was created for a single object. Any interpretation of results, however, must include the following overarching factors:

1. Although the participants had experience cataloging computer files, they generally lacked experience cataloging electronic files of the sort included in the experimental collection.
2. Some participants lacked experience cataloging serial materials.
3. The participants were unfamiliar with some of the experiment's guidelines, particularly those relating to location, access, and acquisition information, or the suggested guidelines provided inadequate direction or instruction.
4. In some cases, technical problems confounded the cataloging task.

Despite these limitations, the results of this experiment reflect a substantial amount of empirical data provided by competent and experienced professionals. Summary conclusions are presented in the following sections.

Fixed Fields

With the exception of date fields, fixed-field data consist of single-character codes. Records exhibited a high degree of similarity among these fields with the exception of "country," "dates," and "encoding level." Despite the likelihood that fixed-field elements will be coded similarly, the number of fixed fields included in the records ranged widely. This indicates that catalogers disagreed as to whether a field should be included in the record.

The "dates" field, while present in most records, exhibited dissimilarity among records for the same object, which may indicate difficulty in determining dates related to computer files.

Variable Fields—Authors and Titles

Variable fields, due in part to the longer text strings they contain, exhibit greater dissimilarity among records for the same object. Two key fields, 100 (Main Entry Heading, Personal Name) and 245 (Title Statement), exhibited the most similarity; however, records do indicate some difficulty determining or recording the authors and titles of computer files. Some records did not contain a 245 field, which is a required field in a bibliographic record. Minimally, every record should have a title field, which may contain the file name itself (*AACR2R*, 9.1B3).

For the 100 field, when two or more catalogers recorded a personal name as a main entry heading, the similarity of the entries was high. However, often one or more records for the same object would not contain a 100 field, although it had been supplied by at least one cataloger. In addition, the overall occurrence of 100 fields was low, appearing in only 18% of all records. This may indicate that this information is lacking or difficult to identify in the information objects.

Notes Fields

Not surprisingly, notes fields were thought to be valuable, occurring in 78% of all records, but the contents of the fields varied greatly. Much of the information provided in the 5XX fields related to subscription or acquisition information, which assumes even greater importance in an electronic, networked environment. The low similarity score may indicate the need for additional fields or subfields to record information now relegated to notes fields.

Location and Access

Two fields could meet the need for expressing location, access, and acquisition information and thereby lessen the reliance upon free-text notes fields: 037 (Subscription Address) and 85X (Electronic Location and Access). With format integration, field 037 will subsume field 265 (Source for Acquisition). This field could record subscription information and instructions, which is particularly important for electronic serial publications. A new 85X field, modeled after the existing 852 field (Location/Call Number) could provide coded location and access information. (For this experiment, field 852 was used for electronic access.)

For acquisition and electronic location and access information, accurate coding of this information is essential. However, coding problems were evident in both the 037 and the 852 fields among records for the same object. In addition, electronic location and access information occurred in only slightly more than half the records. To be effective, all records should contain location and access information for remotely accessed electronic files.

RECOMMENDATIONS

The findings of this project reveal aspects of electronic information objects available via the Internet, provide a taxonomy of file types available via FTP, and, through repeated application under test conditions, provide a substantive body of data on the suitability of conventional methods for providing bibliographic description and access for Internet information objects.

Clearly, the Internet is a rapidly growing environment that facilitates and encourages the creation and dissemination of electronic information objects. As network access broadens, data storage costs drop, and bandwidth increases, the problems of discovering, accessing, and using information on the Internet will likely compound in the absence of additional information management tools and services.

Experimental methods and systems such as WAIS, Gopher, and archie begin to address the problems of network information management; continued research and development of these and other systems are warranted at this early stage of network development and deployment.

To date, remote access, electronic information objects and network information management systems are not well integrated within existing library infrastructures. The reasons for this are many, among them: lack of Internet connection, lack of awareness of electronic information, perceived lack of value of electronic information objects, and the difficulty of locating, accessing, and using electronic information.

Libraries must continue to provide value-added services to the nation's growing body of electronic information objects, systems, and services. While aspects of this electronic information collection—mutability, lack of fixity in a medium, remote accessibility—require adjustments in procedures for cataloging description and access, they do not argue for the abandonment of existing methods. To the contrary, the value of the nation's existing infrastructure of libraries, library systems, and local, regional, and national union catalogs must be leveraged for the information needs of the future.

Libraries stand ready today to begin or to continue the process of providing bibliographic control for remotely accessed information objects. The value of information on the Internet varies widely, and its usefulness is often best determined by the individual user. However, even as not all print materials are collected by all libraries, neither should all electronic files be cataloged. Experience gained in the course of this project indicates that the body of formal, published information is actually rather small when compared with the amount of information available.

As with print and other media, libraries can continue to provide the value-added service of selecting materials for description and access, or inclusion in a collection, whether it be local or remote and dispersed.

As a practical starting point, libraries could create bibliographic records for electronic information objects produced by the faculty or staff of their home institutions. By creating such records, complete with location and access information, libraries help assure broad awareness and access to the work products of the institution. When contributed to a searchable union catalog, these records become widely available.

As a second step, libraries could create records for materials requested and obtained on behalf of patrons, if such records do not already exist. Following the bibliometric wisdom that the best indicator of a subsequent use of an object is an initial use, libraries could contribute to a growing catalog of resources, regardless of whether the library chooses to obtain the file for local holdings.

From this reasoning and the experience gained through this project, the following recommendations are offered:

1. Implement the creation of MARC records for remotely accessible electronic information objects.
2. Monitor the use effectiveness of records created for providing description and access information.
3. Extend cataloging rules and formats to include interactive network systems and services.

To achieve recommendation 3, further examination of the nature of electronic information systems and services is warranted.

The proposals put forward herein do not address all outstanding problems. For example, while electronic description and access are clearly needed, methods of assuring immutable location and access indicators would extend the value of bibliographic records.

LIBRARIES AND THE INTERNET

The Internet facilitates unprecedented connectivity among users and the dissemination of electronic information as never before possible. By every measure, whether you consider the number and types of information objects, the speed of their transmission, or the worldwide breadth of their distribution, computing technologies and high-speed, wide area networks have changed radically the ways in which information is created, stored, and disseminated.

While underlying information technologies have undergone recent and rapid change, the need to preserve and organize information for efficient access, the types of services historically provided by libraries and information professionals, remains an age-old constant.

With the deployment of a new national information infrastructure, such as the National Research and Education Network, a chief concern should be the integration of the Internet and the existing (and enormous) infrastructure of the nation's libraries, library systems, and local and union catalogs. Using existing record formats and cataloging rules, modified as necessary, libraries can begin immediately to provide improved description and access for an important segment of electronic information objects available via the Internet.

Because many libraries participate in national union catalogs, and because the Internet provides widespread access to individual libraries' catalogs, these catalog records created for remotely accessed electronic files would be widely, and immediately, available to information users worldwide. Using existing library systems in this way adds value to the electronic information objects (through improved description and access information) and adds value to the Internet itself by leveraging for the benefit of all users the familiar information services provided by our nation's libraries.

ACKNOWLEDGMENTS

The OCLC Office of Research gratefully acknowledges the support of the U.S. Department of Education, Office of Educational Research and Improvement, Library Programs, and the contributions of the following, without whose help this project would not have been possible: Glee Cady, Diane Kovacs, Ann Okerson, and Peggy Seiden. Special thanks to our Internet Resources Cataloging Experiment Advisory Committee—Priscilla Caplan, Rebecca Guenther, William W. Jones, Jr., Nancy B. Olson, and Glenn Patton— and to the many volunteer participants in the experimental cataloging portion of this project. Special thanks to Peter Deutsch and Alan Emtage for providing access to the archie listings database.

REFERENCES

Alberti, B.; Anklesaria, F.; Lindner, P.; McCahill, M.; & Torrey, D. (1992). *The Internet Gopher protocol: A distributed document search and retrieval protocol.* University of Minnesota, Microcomputer and Workstation Networks Center (ftp boombox.micro.umn.edu; directory: pub/gopher/gopher_ protocol; file: protocol.txt).

Barron, B. (1992). *UNT's accessing on-line bibliographic databases.* University of North Texas (ftp ftp.unt.edu; directory: library; file: libraries.txt (ASCII) or libraries.wp5 (binary for WordPerfect 5.1 file).

Deutsch, P. (1992). Resource discovery in an Internet environment—The archie approach. *Electronic Networking: Research, Applications and Policy, 2*(1), 45-51.

Frey, D., & Adams, R. (1991). *!%@@:: A directory of electronic mail addressing and networks.* Sebastopol, CA: O'Reilly.

Gorman, M., & Winkler, P. W. (1988). *Anglo-American cataloguing rules* (rev. 2nd ed.). Chicago, IL: American Library Association.

Kahle, B., & Medlar, A. (1991). An information system for corporate users: Wide area information servers. *Online, 15*(5), 56-60.

Kehoe, B. P. (1993). *Zen and the art of the Internet: A beginner's guide* (2nd ed.). Englewood Cliffs, NJ: PTR Prentice Hall.

Kovacs, D. K. (1991). *Directory of scholarly electronic conferences.* (ftp ksuvxa.kent.edu; directory: library; files: acadlist.file1, acadlist.file2, acadlist.file3, acadlist.file4, acadlist.file5, acadlist.file6, acadlist.file7).

Krol, E. (1989). *Hitchhikers guide to the Internet.* Network Working Group Request for Comments 1118. (ftp nis.nsf.net; directory: /documents/rfc; file: rfc1118.txt).

Krol, E. (1992). *The whole Internet: User's guide & catalog.* Sebastopol, CA: O'Reilly.

LaQuey, T. L. (Ed.). (1990). *The user's directory of computer networks.* Bedford, MA: Digital Press.

Lincoln, B. (1992a). *Wide Area Information Servers (WAIS) bibliography.* Menlo Park, CA: Thinking Machines Corp. (ftp quake.think.com; directory: pub/wais; file: bibliography.txt).

Lincoln, B. (1992b). Wide Area Information Servers (WAIS) bibliography. *Information Standards Quarterly, 4*(3), 13-15.

Lottor, M. (1992). *Internet growth (1981-1991).* Network Working Group Request for Comments 1296 (ftp nis.nsf.net; directory: /documents/rfc; file: rfc1296.txt).

Malkin, G., & Marine, A. (1992). *FYI on questions and answers: Answers to commonly asked "New Internet User" Questions.* Networking Working Group Request for Comments 1325 (ftp nis.nsf.net; directory: /documents/rfc; file: rfc1325.txt).

Marine, A. (Ed.). (1992). *Internet: Getting started.* Menlo Park, CA: SRI International.

National Science Foundation. Network Service Center. (1989). *Internet resource guide.* Cambridge, MA: BBN Systems and Technologies Corporation (ftp nnsc.nsf.net; directory resource-guide).

Nickerson, G. (1992). Getting to know Wide Area Information Servers. *Computers in Libraries, 12*(9), 53-55.

Quarterman, J. S. (1990). *The matrix: Computer networks and conferencing systems worldwide.* Bedford, MA: Digital Press.

Scott, P. (1992). HYTELNET as software for accessing the Internet: A personal perspective on the development of HYTELNET. *Electronic Networking: Research, Applications and Policy, 2*(1), 38-44.

St. George, A., & Larsen, R. (1991). *Internet-accessible library catalogs & databases.* Albuquerque, NM: University of New Mexico. (e-mail list-serv@unmvm.bitnet; message: GET LIBRARY PACKAGE.)

Strangelove, M.; Okerson, A.; & Kovacs, D. (1992). *Directory of electronic journals, newsletters and academic discussion lists* (2nd ed.). Washington, DC: Association of Research Libraries.

KAREN M. DRABENSTOTT

Associate Professor
School of Information and Library Studies
University of Michigan
Ann Arbor, Michigan

PAULINE A. COCHRANE

Visiting Professor
Graduate School of Library and Information Science
University of Illinois at Urbana-Champaign

Improvements Needed for Better Subject Access to Library Catalogs via the Internet

INTRODUCTION

It would appear from all we have heard and read that Internet access to library catalogs is at best a mixed blessing. It will be difficult if not impossible for Internet access to improve online catalog use unless the catalogs are each improved on site. That at least is our contention, and a group gathered at ALA Midwinter, January 11-12, 1991, agreed that the picture is not rosy. In the proceedings of their deliberations entitled *Think Tank on the Present and Future of the Online Catalog,* the group concluded that "the number of apparent search failures, or of search results that fall far short of what a knowledgeable and experienced searcher could uncover given the same search quest, is appalling" (Hodges, 1991, p. 106).

Another gloomy report for Internet users of catalogs around the world is a 1991 survey of subject access to academic library catalogs in Great Britain (Crawford, Thom, & Powles, 1992). The Glasgow group found that almost half the online catalogs studied had no separate subject searching option based on subject terms.

Charles Hildreth, in his landmark study on online catalogs, laid out the obstacles systems designers had put in place along the online catalog access path (Hildreth, 1982, p. 114). Although his figure is 10 years old, we can easily see how catalog access via the Internet can *complicate but not improve* access because many catalogs still contain the following obstacles:

1. nonuniform input/display terminal devices;
2. differing search and retrieval functions;
3. differing command entry techniques;

4. differing database access points;
5. irregular entry vocabulary;
6. differing index construction;
7. differing system-to-user dialogue;
8. differing results display, manipulation, and interpretation.

Instead of being a stairway to a retrieval goal as Hildreth presents it, online library catalogs (and other information retrieval databases on the Internet, we might add) present an obstacle course which Ed Krol (1992) in *The Whole Internet: User's Guide & Catalog* has aptly called "Stalking the Wild Resource." Krol thinks that "friends, network news and mailing lists, and the Archie, Gopher, WAIS, and World-Wide Web services . . . [will help you] find the resource of your dreams" (p. 279). We are not so optimistic. The rest of this paper documents why optimism is in short supply. We are not usually so pessimistic, but until the library and information professions confront these obstacles head on and become determined to correct them across the board, the Internet will be no more than direct access to the Library of Babel. We will end this paper with some messages to the systems designers of online library catalogs and Internet services like WAIS (Wide Area Information Servers) and Gopher. But first let's consider the users and uses of online catalogs via the Internet.

USERS AND USES OF INTERNET-ACCESSIBLE ONLINE CATALOGS

To the authors' knowledge, no research singles out remote users who connect to online catalogs through the Internet and discusses their characteristics, behavior, and needs separately from other remote users. The closest is a study of the University of California's (UC) MELVYL online union catalog. It separates respondents to an online questionnaire into two categories for UC-affiliated and non-UC-affiliated remote users. Respondents' non-UC affiliation does not necessarily mean they are accessing MELVYL through the Internet. Such respondents could have connected to MELVYL through a phone line, local area network, or one of many wide area networks besides the Internet. However, the MELVYL researchers admit that remote MELVYL users access "the system through more than 460 uniquely identifiable networks, most of them employing the Internet as their main highway" (Ferl & Millsap, 1992, p. 285).

The MELVYL study notes a gradual increase in the percentage of "find" commands issued by remote MELVYL users from 1988 (9%) to 1991 (25%) (Ferl & Millsap, 1992, p. 285). Of the 1,317 completed online questionnaires, 34.5% were submitted by non-UC-affiliated respondents. Another 30.7% of non-UC users are outside California, and 6.5% of them are outside the United States. Large percentages of non-UC users are librarians (28.4%), faculty (15.1%), and the general public (14.6%). High percentages of remote users report that they need no help connecting to MELVYL or searching MELVYL, and that they do not use on-screen help.

In a follow-up study, the MELVYL researchers examined the transaction logs of user activity accompanying completed questionnaires to determine what types of indexes non-UC users accessed and what searching difficulties they encountered (Millsap & Ferl, 1993). Of the 616 search sessions conducted by non-UC users in the full MELVYL online catalog, 60% of sessions included a search of the title index, 46% included a search of the author index, and 30% included a search of the subject index. For searches conducted in the 10-year MELVYL online catalog, the percentage of search sessions that included a search of the subject index is higher (48%) than the full MELVYL catalog. The MELVYL researchers describe frequently occurring errors connected with constructing commands, spelling, finding the right subject search terms, and retrieving high numbers of records or none at all. Although they give several examples of search sessions containing many errors in which users did not call for some on-screen help, the researchers recommend that online catalogs need more on-screen help, a computer initiated/guided mode, and more heuristics—"design elements that guide or lead the user toward the discovery of desired information" (Millsap & Ferl, 1993, p. 336).

An informal study of nonconsortium patron use of the TRIPOD online catalog at Swarthmore College reports that 470 patrons used the Internet to search TRIPOD during a seven-week period in fall 1992 (Sowards, 1992). Internet users of TRIPOD came from 78 different Internet sites with two sites representing 50% of their Internet activity. The number of Internet users ranged from 59 to 77 over the seven-week period but did not show any appreciable increase from week to week. Interestingly, Internet use followed the same patterns as use on campus and in campus libraries; that is, use is higher on weekdays than on weekends, and peak times are the same as for campus users.

We can also learn about users and uses of online catalogs on the Internet from studies of remote users like Kalin's (1991b) research on users of Pennsylvania State University's (PSU) LIAS online catalog. She places them into one of three categories: dial-access users, users connecting through the university's network, or users accessing terminals in PSU libraries. Dial-access and network users were more likely than in-library users to enter known-item searches for author names. Her findings about known-item searches are echoed by a study of remote users of the ILLINET online catalog who are "over 30% more likely to search the OPAC by author or title than are system users as a whole" (Sloan, 1991, p. 136).

In the LIAS study in Pennsylvania, the percentage of searches that failed due to errors ranged between 8% and 13% for the three groups. This finding contrasts with Sloan's study, which reports more error messages for remote than in-library ILLINET users (Sloan, 1986, p. LC4). In her studies of collection failure, Kalin (1991a, 1991b) finds that 21.4% of dial-access users' searches fail because the library does not have the requested material.

Other published accounts address remote users, but they are not based on research findings. Several papers discuss Internet capabilities and resources and offer reasons why individuals would want to search online catalogs through the Internet:

1. To find material that may not be available through the local library (Raeder & Andrews, 1990, p. 16; Engel, 1991, p. 153; Engle, 1991, p. 8; Kalin, 1991a, p. 198). (To obtain such material more traditionally, the user would have to submit citations to interlibrary loan staff or travel to the institution themselves.)

2. To access cataloging records through additional access points that the local library's online catalog may not feature (Engel, 1991, p. 153; Engle, 1991, p. 8).
3. To take advantage of searching capabilities absent in a local catalog (Kalin, 1991a, p. 198).

Library staff search online catalogs on the Internet for the reasons mentioned above and for additional ones:

1. To evaluate online catalogs for purchase (Raeder & Andrews, 1990, p. 16; Kalin, 1991a, p. 198).
2. To determine how other online catalog systems operate in the course of profiling one's own system (Raeder & Andrews, 1990, p. 16; Engle, 1991, p. 8).
3. To answer specific reference questions (Engel, 1991, p. 154; Engle, 1991, p. 8).
4. To develop and assess collections (Raeder & Andrews, 1990, p. 16; Kalin, 1991a, p. 198).
5. To obtain cataloging copy (Kalin, 1991a, p. 198).

TODAY'S SCENARIO OF SUBJECT SEARCHING

Today's users of Internet-accessible online catalogs are pioneers in every sense of the word. Although they may be frequent searchers of their local online catalog, they are likely to search Internet-accessible online catalogs with unfamiliar interfaces, different subject searching capabilities, and cataloging records in formats unlike those of the local catalog. All the obstacles Hildreth recorded—plus one more—are there in a variety of guises. Subject searching on the Internet is truly as Krol described—stalking the wild resource. At Lund University, for example, the popularity of WAIS, campus-wide information systems (CWIS), and the Internet Gopher is growing steadily because connectivity is good, but "they all suffer from a lack of consistent structure of the information offerings as well as good tools for finding relevant information sources" (Ardo & Koch, 1993, p. 207).

Determining Which Online Catalog to Search

Having mastered the equipment and telecommunications software to connect to a computer across the network, the next step for our adventurous pioneer user is to determine the domain name of a remote computer that features an online catalog. General books on Internet use, e.g., Krol's (1992) *The Whole Internet* and Kehoe's (1993) *Zen and the Art of the Internet,* describe how users can access the electronic directories of Internet-accessible online catalogs produced by Billy Barron (1992) and Art St. George and Ron Larsen (1992). Their directories give domain names and detail the sign-on procedures to hundreds of Internet-accessible online catalogs in the United States and abroad.

Entries in directories of Internet-accessible online catalogs are generally restricted to sign-on procedures and hours of availability; however, a few describe unique characteristics of a particular library's collection. To identify unique collections or subject areas before connecting to an online catalog, users could consult traditional printed sources such as the *American Library Directory* (1991) or *Subject Collections* (Ash & Miller, 1985), but who has either of those handy while searching?

Up to the late 1980s, a blank screen was not an unusual greeting to remote users of online library catalogs. Fortunate were users who had printed user guides to these catalogs, because without them users had to guess at command names, search and display options, and help capabilities. Today we are seeing an increasing number of online catalogs greet users with introductory screen(s) that include information on how to exit the system and how to get help, and a definition of paragraph labels corresponding to valid search options.

The remote user of Internet-accessible library catalogs faces a bewildering variety of user-system interfaces. There are subtle differences even among online catalogs that libraries purchase from the same vendor. For example, the labels for search options may differ and options associated with one catalog may be absent in another. We are a long way from the uniformity that would come with the adoption of Z39.58-1992.

At the time of Hildreth's analysis of the first online catalogs, there were so few operational online catalogs that one could classify all of their interfaces. Today this would be a monumental task owing to the hundreds of online catalogs available through the Internet. Based on our experiences with many of these catalogs, we see a trend toward the design and development of interfaces under the computer initiated/guided classification. To demonstrate this claim, let us look at the responses of two online catalogs—MIRLYN, the NOTIS-based online catalog at the University of Michigan (Figure 1), and URSUS, the Innovative Interfaces catalog at the University of Maine (Figure 2)—to the display of the first screen of a two-screen cataloging record.

At the bottom of the screen, both catalogs give prompts to tell the user possible next actions. Action names are different (e.g., IND to browse the subject headings index in MIRLYN and R or RETURN to browse the subject headings index in URSUS); however, many of the same possible next actions in MIRLYN are also possible in URSUS and vice versa. Ten years ago, few, if any, online catalogs displayed prompts or gave suggestions to users about possible next actions. The only problem now is that each online catalog has an array of synonyms for the same functions or commands.

Now that systems give users guidance as to their next action, this does not mean that users will always choose the one or two prompted actions that will further their search in a fruitful way. Users could also choose the wrong action because they have confused the action for a similarly worded action in another system. Generally, we feel the trend toward computer initiated/ guided interfaces is good news for users of Internet-accessible online catalogs. These interfaces have freed users from the burden of memorizing commands or consulting a printed user guide to find desired commands, but a better solution would be a common command language for all Internet-accessible catalogs. The Think Tank on the future of the online catalog came to this same conclusion (Van Pulis, 1991).

```
Search Request: S=ANOREXIA NERVOSA         UM Online Catalog
BOOK - Record 57 of 73 Entries Found              Brief View
-------------------------------------------------------------
Author:        Brumberg, Joan Jacobs.

Title:         Fasting girls : the emergence of anorexia
               nervosa as a modern disease

Published:     Cambridge, Mass. : Harvard University Press,
               1988.

SUBJECT HEADINGS (Library of Congress; use s=):
               Anorexia nervosa--History.
               Anorexia nervosa--Social aspects.
               Teenage girls--Diseases--History.

SUBJECT HEADINGS (Medical; use sm=):
               Anorexia Nervosa--history.
               Socioeconomic Factors.
----------------------------------------- + Page 1 of 2  ----
STArt over    LONg view               <F8>  FORward page
HELp          INDex                    <F6>  NEXt record
OTHer options GUIde                    <F5>  PREvious record

NEXT COMMAND:
```

Figure 1. MIRLYN screen with next-action prompts

```
You searched for the SUBJECT: anorexia nervosa         URSUS

AUTHOR      Brumberg, Joan Jacobs.
TITLE       Fasting girls : the emergence of anorexia nervosa
            as a modern disease.
PUBLISHER   Cambridge, Mass. : Harvard University Press, 1988.
PHYS DESCR  366 p. : ill. ; 24 cm.
NOTE        Bibliography: p. [275]-350.
            Includes index.
SUBJECT     Anorexia nervosa --History
            Anorexia nervosa --Social aspects.
  _____
 |    LOCATION      CALL NO.             STATUS           |
 | > BCL Stacks   RC552.A5 B785 1988   DUE 06-12-89 BILLED|
 | > POR Stacks   RC552 .A5 B785 1988  AVAILABLE          |
 | > AUG Stacks   RC552.A5B785 1988    DUE 03-01093       |
 | > FAR Stacks   RC552.A5 B785 1988   AVAILABLE          |
 | > LEW Stacks   RC552.A5 B785 1988   AVAILABLE          |
 |____ 7 volumes/copies to view - Press I to see more of them __|

V > Find specific VOLUME/COPY     B > BACKWARD browse
M > MORE BIBLIOGRAPHIC Record      N > NEW Search
R > RETURN to Browsing            A > ANOTHER Search by SUBJECT
F > FORWARD browse                O > OTHER options
Choose one (V,M,R,F,B,N,A,I,Z,S,P,G,T,O)
```

Figure 2. URSUS screen with next-action prompts

Searching for Subjects in Internet-Accessible Library Catalogs

To demonstrate the great variety of subject searching approaches in operational online catalogs, the authors searched almost all the unique online catalogs listed in *Internet-Accessible Library Catalogs & Databases* dated May 21, 1992, except for those requiring tn-3270 emulation (St. George & Larsen, 1992). This represents 27 different systems in 100 different institutions. Thirteen systems are unique to a particular library. Fourteen systems are available for purchase from a vendor. Table 1, in outline form, describes the many different subject searching approaches these catalogs offer and gives some examples of how users enter their queries using these approaches. The authors used information in help screens as much as possible to determine how a particular subject search approach handled their queries. In the absence of such information, the authors entered a set of queries repeatedly and compared results to determine what was going on.

TABLE 1

OUTLINE OF SUBJECT SEARCHING APPROACHES IN
OPERATIONAL ONLINE CATALOGS

---

1. Alphabetical approaches: results in a list of subject headings in the alphabetical neighborhood of the user-entered term
    a. Finds matches of exact and/or longer subject headings; includes names and subjects; no backward/forward browsing to the beginning (a) or end (z) of the file.
        ●Examples: browse subject [term]*
                s=[term]
                find su [term]
    b. Finds matches of exact and/or longer subject headings; includes names and subjects; unlimited forward browsing to the end (z) of the file.
        ●Examples: s=[term]
                s [term]
    c. Default response regardless of extent of match; includes names and subjects; unlimited backward/forward browsing to the beginning (a) or end (z) of the file.
        ●Examples: sub/[term]
                br su [term]
                f s [term]
                choose SUBJECT; enter term(s) separated by spaces;
                    hit CTRL-W
                s=[term]
    d. Finds matches of exact and/or longer subject headings; limited to subjects only; no backward/forward browsing to the beginning (a) or end (z) of the file.
        ●Example: fi su [term]
    e. Finds matches of exact and/or longer subject headings; limited to personal names only; no backward/forward browsing to the beginning (a) or end (z) of the file.
        ●Example: fi pn [term]
2. Keyword-in-heading approaches: results in a list of subject headings bearing word(s) in the user-entered term
    a. Finds subject headings in which the words of the user-entered term are adjacent to one another
        ●Examples: f su [term1 term2]†
                su [term1 term2]
    b. Finds subject headings bearing the word(s) in the user-entered term
        ●Examples: s=[term1 term2]
                sws/[term1] [term2]
                bro su [term1 term2]
                f su [term1] and [term2]
                su [term1] and [term2]

3. Keyword in record approaches: retrieves records bearing the word(s) in the user-entered term

   a. Title keyword search; if more than one term entered, the system performs an implied Boolean "and" combination

      •Examples: find ti [term1 term2]

               choose TITLE; enter terms separated by spaces;

                  hit CTRL-K

               find kti [term1 term2]

               tws/[term1 term2]

               t=[term1 term2]

               fin tw [term1 term2]

               f ti [term1] and [term2]

               tt [term1 term2]

   b. Finds the word(s) of the user-entered term in single subject headings

      •Examples: fin su [term1 term2]

               f s [term1 term2]

   c. Finds the word(s) of the user-entered term in subject heading fields

      •Examples: find su [term1 term2]

               fi su [term1] and [term2]

               find ksh [term1 term2]

               s=[term1].su. and [term2].su.

               st [term1 term2]

   d. Finds the word(s) of the user-entered term in subject-bearing fields

      •Examples: w [term1 term2]

               find top [term1 term2]

               find kw [term1 term2]

               te [term1 term2]

   e. Finds the word(s) of the user-entered term in all fields

      •Examples: k=[term1] and [term2]

               find gen [term1 term2]

               fin [term1] and [term2]

---

*[term] represents a one- or multiple-word query.

†[term1] and [term2] represent single words of a two-word query.

The outline demonstrates the wide variety of subject searching approaches in operational online catalogs. Basic approaches are the alphabetical, keyword-in-heading, and keyword-in-record searches. There are several different implementations of these three basic approaches.

The outline also shows that command names for the same approaches are different from catalog to catalog. Furthermore, a command that initiates a particular search approach in one system might perform a totally different approach in another system. Had the authors tagged the examples by system, one would realize that a subtle change in the syntax of a search statement produces an entirely different result. For example, the statements "f su [term1 term2]" and "f su [term1] and [term2]" are valid in one particular system; the first statement finds subject headings in which the words of the user-entered term are adjacent to one another (2a), and the second statement performs the same operation but disregards word adjacency (2b).

Within a particular approach, the outline does not show differences between catalogs that arise due to differences in indexing. This is another serious obstacle to retrieval that Hildreth noted in the early historical development of online catalogs. We can speculate that such differences exist not only between different "brands" of catalogs but between different implementations of the same catalog "brand" at different institutions. This could mislead a user into thinking that a query resulting in zero retrievals means that the institution does not own the desired item, when, in fact, the fields and subfields indexed for the particular subject search option chosen by the user do not include the one(s) that would have produced the desired result.

Many of the 100 online catalogs we examined to prepare the outline in Table 1 feature subject searching approaches that are not publicized in introductory screens. For example, the introductory screen of Michigan's MIRLYN system offers the alphabetical approach (s=[term]) and keyword-in-record approach (k=[term1] and [term2]). It also has a title keyword search (k=[term1].ti. and [term2].ti.) and keyword search of subject heading fields (k=[term1].su. and [term2].su.). To find out about these searches, users must read online documentation available through the system's help capability. Judging from our knowledge of how seldom users access help capabilities (Slack, 1991), we can speculate that users probably do not know about these subject search approaches. Even if they knew about these approaches, would users know which approach would provide the most useful results for their subject query?

Studying transaction logs, we see that some users enter their queries using *every* approach—even approaches for author searches. For example, a user might enter the query "guatemala weddings" using all the search options that the system provides on its introductory screen even if some of them (e.g., "a=guatemala weddings" for an author search) do not look logical. Perhaps such actions indicate users' attempts to determine for themselves which of the catalog's several search options will yield the most useful results.

TOOLS FOR IMPROVING SUBJECT
SEARCHING ON THE INTERNET

We recommend four tools to improve subject searching on Internet-accessible library catalogs. These tools would help those users whose failed subject searches of the local catalog are the impetus for their searches of online catalogs on the Internet.

Tool #1. Search Trees

The designers of the OKAPI experimental online catalog in the United Kingdom first defined search trees as "a set of paths with branches or choices, which enables the system to carry out the most sensible search function at each stage of the search" (Mitev, Venner, & Walker, 1985, p. 94). Search trees were also developed and reported in a recent empirical study of the subject terms that users enter into online catalogs (Drabenstott & Vizine-Goetz, 1990). These latter search trees emphasize subject headings because the vast majority of cataloging records created by American libraries are assigned subject headings based on the Library of Congress Subject Headings (LCSH) (O'Neill & Aluri, 1979, p. 5).

Search trees invoke searching approaches that look for matches of user queries in subject heading fields of cataloging records before enlisting keyword search approaches that look for matches in title fields or in a combination of title and subject heading fields.

Some online catalogs have subject searching routines that resemble search trees. For example, the online catalog of the University of Illinois at Urbana-Champaign responds to user queries for subjects with keyword searches of assigned subject headings. When users terminate searches, the system prompts them to continue and gives the results of a title keyword search (Hildreth, 1989, pp. 86-87). The Illinois online catalog always performs keyword searches of subject heading fields before title keyword searches because the former consumes fewer system resources than the latter.

Search trees require that online catalogs feature a wide range of subject searching functionality: (a) exact approach, (b) alphabetical approach, (c) keyword-in-heading approaches for searching main headings and subdivided headings, and (d) keyword-in-record approaches for searching titles, subject heading fields, and all subject-bearing fields of cataloging records (Drabenstott & Vizine-Goetz, 1990). Integrated into exact, alphabetical, and keyword-in-main-heading approaches are references and notes from the machine-readable Library of Congress Subject Headings (LCSH-mr) to increase the catalog's entry vocabulary and give users ideas for synonyms and related terms for the subject queries they enter. Search trees also require systems to prompt users to indicate whether their queries contain personal names because search trees for subject searches for personal names are different from search trees for subject searches generally.

Within the context of searching online catalogs through the Internet, search trees have three important benefits:

1. Search trees place the responsibility of determining which approach produces useful results on the system.
2. Except for singling out queries bearing personal names from queries for subject generally, search trees do not require users to enter commands associated with a particular subject searching approach.
3. Search trees guarantee a comprehensive search of the online catalog's database.

Tool #2. An Online Directory of Collection Strengths of Internet-Accessible Library Collections

Of the hundreds of online catalogs accessible through the Internet, how do searchers select the online catalog that will satisfy their information needs? In the absence of solid research findings about such searchers, we can only speculate about their selection methods. Searchers, no doubt, would prefer searching online catalogs with interfaces that are familiar to them. To accomplish this, at the University of Michigan, for example, users enlist the library's Gopher client that has an option to search the text of Billy Barron's online catalog directory for keywords. Since the university's MIRLYN online catalog is based on the NOTIS system, users could enter the keyword "notis" to retrieve a list of NOTIS-based online catalogs, then use the Gopher to connect to these systems. Would that be the best way to get to other collections stronger than those at the University of Michigan in the user's subject area? We don't know. Another approach might be what is now offered by the SIRSI Corporation's Retrieval Interface Manager (RIM) that can be programmed to make other online catalogs look and perform like SIRSI's Unicorn-based online catalog (Johnson, 1990). But here again the user must know which are the collections that are stronger than the library being searched.

At the present time, electronic tools like Gopher and WAIS are limited in their ability to pinpoint a particular online catalog that would satisfy users' subject queries. No one has as yet mounted on the Internet the electronic version of the printed subject indexes to library collections such as the *American Library Directory* or *Subject Collections*, but DIALOG offers online searching to the former at a cost of $75 per connect hour and $.40 per record displayed or printed.

Featuring a directory/database of collection strengths and special collections could be an intermediary service to libraries when they allow access to their online catalogs through the Internet. Users could then start their searches in this database and then be switched to the online catalog(s) with the greatest potential for their subject interests. We can look to the Research Libraries Group's Conspectus-Online as a model of documenting collection strengths (Ferguson, Grant, & Rutstein, 1988). The Library of Congress Classification (LCC) serves as a subject outline for librarians to rate the strength of their existing collection and current collecting intensity. Librarians can search the Conspectus-Online on the RLIN (Research Libraries Information Network) by subject, LCC class, collection level, participating institution, and other criteria.

LCC outlines and Dewey Decimal Classification (DDC) summaries could serve as the framework for such a directory, or we could revive and use the Broad System of Ordering developed several years ago (Coates, Lloyd, & Simandl, 1978). Some people have also suggested using LCSH, but in its present state this would be a little unwieldy (Lynch & Preston, 1992).

Tool #3. Aids to "Find This Record or Similar Records"

Nearly all online catalogs have a capability for exporting cataloging records in USMARC (United States Machine-Readable Cataloging) format. This capability might not be available to public catalog users, but it is probably in the staff mode that library staff enlist to search the catalog. This capability should be extended to public users. When users find cataloging records of interest in a library catalog that they are searching through the Internet, they should be able to download these records to their hard or floppy disk. A computer program resident on the user's microcomputer could then manipulate the downloaded records to "find the actual records or similar records" in the local online catalog by creating search statements using the tagged USMARC data in the downloaded records. Such a function might also be in the locally available Gopher client. When users reconnect to the local online catalog, the program would formulate search statements to search and find the same or similar cataloging records in the local catalog.

Let's say that the system is unable to find the same record in the local catalog. It could use data in several fields—author, classification number, subject headings, title—to find similar records. One approach could feature searches of the author fields. If too many records are retrieved, the system could limit retrievals using the first two or three digits of DDC numbers or letter(s) of LCC numbers. If the original records come with DDC numbers and LCC is used locally, the system could consult the subject headings on the originating records and use the LCC numbers printed with the same subject headings in LCSH-mr. Another approach could feature searches of the subject heading fields. If too few records are retrieved, the system could consult LCSH-mr to find related terms for the main headings in the record and formulate subject searches using the related terms and subdivisions from the subject headings in the original record. Many more scenarios are possible including ones that involve the user in related term selection.

Tool #4. Common Command Language for Every Internet-Accessible Library Catalog or Bibliographic Database

We have all heard of developments like Z39.50, but how many know about Z39.58-1992 or ISO 8777 (Common command language, 1992)? This later standard could remove one of Hildreth's obstacles (Hildreth, 1982, p. 114) from every catalog on the Internet and would meet a requirement of the ideal catalog that was described by the Think Tank at an RASD/ALA session in 1991 (Van Pulis, 1991). Attention to it is important because it will help services like WAIS or Gopher and the various library catalog command languages become one common command language for the itinerant and remote user. Consideration of either the U.S. or International standard would help with several problems that Internet library catalog users experience, namely, "now that I'm into this system, how do I view previously displayed data, how do I print results remotely, how do I review my search, and last but not least, how do I end a session?" The command names in the Z39.58-1992 standard covering these situations are BACK, PRINT, REVIEW, and STOP. Other command names in the standard are CHOOSE, DEFINE, DELETE, DISPLAY, EXPLAIN, FIND, HELP, MORE, RELATE, SAME, SCAN, SET, SEE, SORT, and START. The standard also includes several command operators (AND, NOT, OR, DESC, GT, LT, NE, GE, LE, ALL), symbols, and punctuation (for character masking, expressing a range of values, separators, and restoration marks). The ISO 8777 differs in only a few respects, so a truly international standard that conforms to an American standard is at hand. It must be remembered that this would be a minimum set of common commands, and system designers could have functions and commands that go beyond the minimum, but in the Internet collection of "wild resources," the adoption of such a common command language could help tame the environment.

SUMMARY AND CONCLUSION

This paper focuses on general difficulties that challenge users of Internet-accessible online catalogs and specific ones connected with subject searching.

Solid research findings on reasons why people search Internet-accessible online catalogs are very much needed. Future research studies could be designed along the lines of the MELVYL study that features an online questionnaire and logs system user responses. The MELVYL studies reveal that remote usage of online catalogs represents a significant component of system usage. In view of this finding, it is important for librarians and systems staff to gain a better understanding of remote users and use this knowledge to build efficient and useful tools to improve their searches of online catalogs on the Internet. Even before such a study of Internet users of online catalogs, the authors recommend four tools to improve subject searching on the Internet because of the known failed subject searches in local catalogs.

Maybe, just maybe, this conference will serve as the catalyst to form public opinion about this issue. Daniel Yankelovich, one of America's premier pollsters (according to Al Cole [1993] in *Modern Maturity*), said that the formation of public opinion on important issues resembles a biological process, evolving slowly through clearly defined stages: "1, Dawning awareness; 2, Sense of urgency; 3, Discovery of choices; 4, Wishful thinking; 5, Weighing choices; 6, Intellectual stand; and 7, Responsible judgment" (p. 10). Regarding improvements in online catalogs, we think we are now at stage 4, wishful thinking, where we hope that WAIS, Gopher, and other "front-ends" will improve access to the information in library catalogs. Maybe, we can move on to stage 5 and weigh some of the choices suggested by us and others at this conference.

REFERENCES

American library directory, 1991-92 (44th ed.). (1991). New Providence, NJ: Bowker.

Ardo, A., & Koch, T. (1993). Wide-Area Information Server (WAIS) as the hub of an electronic library service at Lund University. In A. H. Helal & J. W. Weiss (Eds.), *Opportunity 2000: Understanding and serving users in an electronic library* (15th International Essen Symposium) (pp. 199-210). Essen: Universitätsbibliothek Essen. (e-mail: anders@dit.lth.se)

Ash, L., & Miller, W. G. (Comps.). (1985). *Subject collections: A guide to special book collections and subject emphases as reported by university, college, public, and special libraries and museums in the United States and Canada* (6th ed.). New York: Bowker.

Barron, B. (1992). *UNT's accessing on-line bibliographic databases.* University of North Texas (ftp ftp.unt.edu; directory: library; file: libraries.txt (ASCII) or libraries.wp5 (binary for WordPerfect 5.1 file).

Coates, E.; Lloyd, G.; & Simandl, D. (Comps.). (1978). *BSO: Broad System of Ordering: Schedule and index* (3rd rev.). (FID Publication 564). The Hague, Netherlands: Fédération Internationale de Documentation (FID).

Cole, A. (1993, February-March). Birth of a notion. *Modern Maturity,* pp. 9-10.

Common command language for on-line interactive information retrieval. Z39.58-1992. (1992). Available from: Transaction Publishers, Dept. NISO 92, Rutgers University, New Brunswick, NJ 08903. 30pp. $35.00. (Includes ISO 8777 in the appendix.)

Crawford. J. C.; Thom, L. C.; & Powles, J. A. (1992). *A survey of subject access to academic library catalogues in Great Britain: A report to the British Library Research and Development Department.* Glasgow: Glasgow Polytechnic.

Drabenstott, K. M., & Vizine-Goetz, D. (1990). Search trees for subject searching in online catalogs. *Library Hi Tech, 8*(3), 7-20.

Engel, G. (1991). User instruction for access to catalogs and databases on the Internet. *Cataloging & Classification Quarterly, 13*(3/4), 141-156.

Engle, M. E. (1991). Electronic paths to resource sharing: Widening opportunities through the Internet. *Reference Services Review, 19*(4), 7-12.

Ferguson, A. W.; Grant, J.; & Rutstein, J. S. (1988). The RLG conspectus: Its uses and benefits. *College and Research Libraries, 49*(3), 197-206.

Ferl, T. E., & Millsap. L. (1992). Remote use of the University of California MELVYL library system: An online survey. *Information Technology and Libraries, 11*(3), 285-303.

Hildreth, C. R. (1982). *Online public access catalogs: The user interface.* Dublin, OH: OCLC.

Hildreth, C. R. (1989). *Intelligent interfaces and retrieval methods for subject searching in bibliographic retrieval systems.* (Advances in Library Information Technology 2). Washington, DC: Cataloging Distribution Service, Library of Congress.

Hodges, T. (1991). Library education: Impact of OPACs and their kin. In N. Van Pulis (Ed.), *Think tank on the present and future of the online catalog: Proceedings* (pp. 97-126). Chicago, IL: Reference and Adult Services Division, American Library Association.

Johnson, S. W. (1990). SIRSI's RIM: More than a gateway. *Information Retrieval & Library Automation, 26*(6), 1-3.

Kalin, S. W. (1991a). Support services for remote users of online public access catalogs, *RQ, 31*(2), 197-213.

Kalin S. W. (1991b). The searching behavior of remote users: A study of one online public access catalog (OPAC). In J.-M. Griffiths (Ed.), *Systems people understand* (Proceedings of the 54th ASIS Annual Meeting) (Vol. 28, pp. 178-185). Medford, NJ: Learned Information.

Kehoe, B. P. (1993). *Zen and the art of the Internet: A beginner's guide* (2nd ed.). Englewood Cliffs, NJ: PTR Prentice Hall.

Krol, E. (1992). *The whole Internet: User's guide & catalog.* Sebastopol, CA: O'Reilly.

Lynch, C. A., & Preston, C. M. (1992). Describing and classifying networked information resources. *Electronic Networking, 2*(1), 13-23.

Millsap, L., & Ferl, T. E. (1993). Search patterns of remote users: An analysis of OPAC transaction logs. *Information Technology and Libraries, 12*(3), 321-343.

Mitev, N.; Venner, G.; & Walker, S. (1985). *Designing an online public access catalog* (Library and Information Research Report 39). London: British Library.

O'Neill, E. T., & Aluri, R. (1979). *Subject heading patterns in OCLC monographic records* (OCLC Research Report No. OCLC/RDD/RR-79/1). Columbus, OH: OCLC.

Raeder, A. W., & Andrews, K. L. (1990). Searching library catalogs on the Internet: A survey. *Database Searcher, 6*(7), 16-31.

Slack, F. (1991). Subject searching on OPACs: Problems and help provision. *Vine, 83*(August), 4-9.

Sloan, B. G. (1986). High tech/low profile: Automation & the "invisible" patron. *Library Journal, 111*(18), LC4, LC6.

Sloan, B. G. (1991). Remote access: Design implications for the online catalog. *Cataloging & Classification Quarterly, 13*(3/4), 133-140.

Sowards, S. (1992, November). Internet use of TRIPOD from outside the Consortium. Memorandum. Swarthmore College, McCabe Library.

St. George, A., & Larsen, R. (1992). *Internet-accessible library catalogs & databases.* Albuquerque, NM: University of New Mexico. (e-mail listserv@umnvma.bitnet; message: get library package)

Van Pulis, N. (Ed.). (1991). *Think tank on the present and future of the outline catalog: Proceedings.* Chicago, IL: Reference and Adult Services Division, American Library Association.

CHARLES R. HILDRETH

Chief Consultant
READ Ltd.
Seattle, Washington

Extending the Online Catalog:
The Point of Diminishing Returns

INTRODUCTION

This paper discusses online public access catalog (OPAC) models and milestones. The journey of the networked online catalog has clearly departed from its early, first-generation manifestation as a stand-alone, local "card catalog online" and continues at an alarming pace in its evolution to some fuzzily conceived expanded, transformed entity we may humbly refer to for now as the library catalog information system. What this future information management and retrieval system will be like is not entirely clear, which makes it the topic of much speculation and wishful thinking. Its parameters and features may be decided by, nay, even driven by, new, emergent technologies, or, hopefully, its form and function will be guided by the knowledge attained from a vast body of research and experience with online catalogs and their users.

Technology defines the possible—what can be done with available resources. Technology sets no intrinsic limits on itself and has no magical power to articulate its ideal future. On the other hand, advances in technology may add the spark of innovation to the application of acquired knowledge in the design of new and improved information systems. As we stand on the threshold of an exciting era of expanded information access and delivery, there is another danger equal, perhaps, to the uncritical adoption of new technologies. The danger I speak of is the danger of uncritical devotion to outmoded models (forms, if you like) and long-standing ways of doing things. (I am tempted to coin the phrase, "bibliographic nostalgia," but I shall restrain myself.) Furthermore, the gloss of new technologies may disguise the fact that underneath things remain pretty much the same as they always were.

Let me bring to mind imagery from a not-so-long-ago era in library history. It is a personal recollection of a "hard" reality, far distant, it would seem, from those virtual realms we hear so much about these days. Thirty years ago, while an undergraduate student at Ohio State University, when I went to the main library on campus to look up materials, I accessed the massive public card catalog to locate needed books or bound periodicals. If successful at the card catalog, I then went to a designated "workstation," which supplied small pencils and slips of paper. For each book I desired, I wrote down on one of these slips its author, title, and call number. I then took these slips to the circulation counter where a clerk confirmed that they contained sufficient data and sent them via pneumatic tubes to "stack runners." You see, the stacks with their organized shelves of books were closed to ordinary folk like undergraduate students (unless one was employed by the library as a stack runner). Bookshelf browsing, as a means of discovering works of interest, was not permitted. In this closed-stack retrieval system, you had to know precisely what you wanted and identify it in the card catalog before it could be retrieved by a stack runner from the bowels of the library warehouse.

The central question I want to pose today is this: By providing network access to our conventional online catalogs using advanced access tools, such as Telnet, Gopher, Z39.50 protocols, Wide Area Information Servers (WAIS), and World Wide Web (WWW)—that is, opening the doors to a vast number of online "libraries without walls"—are we not at the same time "closing the stacks" and eliminating the opportunity for a variety of kinds of meaningful browsing—browsing that often leads to the discovery of previously unknown items of interest? I consider personal interaction with an organized collection of published materials to be a rewarding activity, and I think providing this opportunity should be a service priority of most libraries. As we shift our priorities from building and maintaining physical collections to the provision of electronic access to document collections, are we not in danger of eliminating a qualitative experience and closing the stacks once again? Perhaps today's network access technologies like WAIS and Z39.50 are the digital versions of human stack runners and book retrievers.

THE DEVELOPMENT OF OPAC MODELS AND APPROACHES

OPAC Access Models

Figure 1 presents a framework for understanding 15 years of OPAC history and the significance of recent developments. Two access models informed and motivated the design of the first OPACs. One track of development reflected attempts to emulate the familiar card catalog. Another track adopted the model familiar to online database searchers of commercial search services like DIALOG and BRS. Second-generation OPACs, with their multiple access points, search approaches, and user-friendly display formats, represent the marriage of these two access models.

From the earliest days of second-generation OPACs, the challenge that confronted system developers was to combine the ease of use (or at least, familiarity) of the card catalog with the powerful search capabilities available to trained online database searchers. This task has not been easy, but significant progress has been made.

Recent developments with OPACs, including the advent of the networked OPAC, must be kept in proper perspective. Progress has been made along some, but not all, dimensions. Improvements to the user interface have made second-generation OPACs more usable for the untrained user, and new graphical user interface (GUI) techniques like windows and point-and-click buttons hold the promise of rendering the search process both more intuitive and more direct.

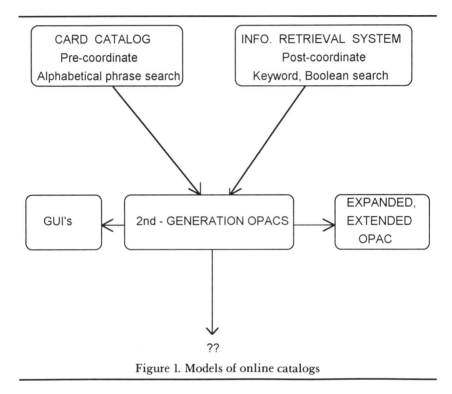

Figure 1. Models of online catalogs

In less than five years, escalating demand and professional ingenuity have resulted in the expanded, extended OPAC. Second-generation OPACs are being expanded in information content and coverage almost daily, and access to and from these OPACs has been extended to vast numbers of remote users through network technologies. Why, you may ask, is not this expanded, extended OPAC advanced enough to qualify for the distinction of a third-generation OPAC? I shall address this question in a moment.

Online Catalog Perspectives

At about the time second-generation functionality was becoming the operational standard for installed online catalogs in the mid-1980s, librarians and system planners had already begun to expand and extend the traditional access boundaries of these library catalogs. These developments have enriched and enlivened the debate about the proper role, content, and functions of the online catalog. In this continuing debate, several perspectives on this evolving library access system can be identified. The online catalog may be viewed as

- the expanded bibliographic database,
- a sophisticated computerized search and retrieval system,
- a "gateway" to other online catalogs and electronic resources,
- an integrated component of a multifunction "scholar's workstation."

These new perspectives on the library catalog represent the nature and extent of the rising expectations for expanded online catalog data content, access, and functionality. Furthermore, these perspectives are being integrated in our emerging vision of future library information systems, a vision that hopefully will guide the design of these systems.

The E³OPAC

There has been some confusion in the literature of late as to whether the emerging online catalog is the "expanded" or the "extended" online catalog. Some writers view these terms as synonymous and use them interchangeably, while others use them to explain related but different developments. For example, Potter (1989) identifies three complementary "expansion" paths along which online library systems will proceed: (a) more indexes to more sets of collections and more online reference databases; (b) the gradual inclusion of more full text of journal articles and, possibly, books; and (c) "greater connectivity from online library systems to other systems, including other library systems, commercial services, bibliographic utilities, local networks, CD-ROM servers, and other information providers in the community" (p. 104). Mischo and Cole (1992) put it this way: "Recently, the idea of the 'extended' OPAC has been introduced to describe online catalogs containing specific functional or data extensions. Extended third generation catalogs typically provide value-added access beyond the conventional OPAC by providing expanded entry points, augmented information resources, access to locally mounted and/or remote periodical index databases, and gateway functions to local, regional, and national telecommunication networks" (p. 38).

I have introduced the notion of the E³OPAC as a vehicle for elucidating these concepts: the E³OPAC would have *enhanced* functionality and usability; its indexing, record data content, and collection coverage would be *expanded* to make it a "full-collection" access tool; and its access would be *extended* (through linkages, networks, and gateways) to include the collections and resources of other libraries and information centers.

Progress along the road to the E³OPAC may be tracked on a three-dimensional scale, as illustrated in Figure 2. One can redefine or reprioritize the axis values, but such a scale is useful for identifying where progress may be lagging and also for comparisons of different systems. Third-generation systems are defined primarily by their advanced interface search functionality. It is along this dimension that OPAC progress seems to be stalled. It is important to understand why this is the case.

Third-Generation Online Catalogs

I have outlined a general framework for classifying online catalogs into first-, second-, or third-generation systems, each generation having its distinguishing features and functions (Hildreth, 1989). Innovative design work on the user-system interface, including GUIs, has made many of the second-generation online catalogs far easier to use than the conventional, dial-up commercial database search systems after which they were modeled. Third-generation online catalogs are not yet generally available in the mainstream

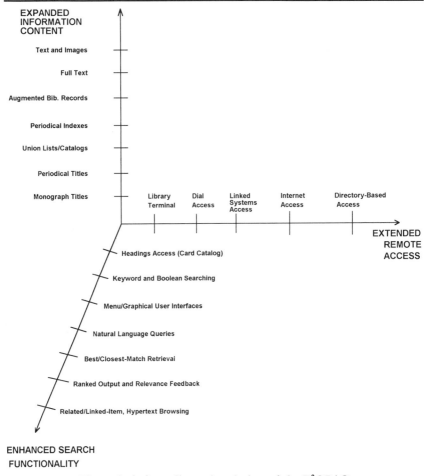

Figure 2. A three-dimensional view of the E³OPAC

library system marketplace. Only a few of these more advanced catalogs have been developed, primarily as prototype or demonstration systems. These systems incorporate many of the listed search, matching, and interactive display techniques developed and tested over the past 25 years by information retrieval system researchers. The major functional improvements that will define the next generation of online catalogs are listed below. Third-generation OPACs will include second-generation functionality plus the following features:

- Natural Language Query Expressions (In your own language, what it is you are looking for)
- Automatic Term Conversion/Matching Aids (Spelling correction, Soundex, intelligent stemming, synonym tables, etc.)

- Closest, Best-Match Retrieval (Unlike Boolean queries, doesn't require exact match to be retrieved as possibly relevant; matching documents are weighted for ranking)
- Ranked Retrieval Output (Many ranking criteria: most likely to be relevant first, most recent, most cited, most circulated, etc.)
- Relevance Feedback Methods ("Give me more like this one." "What else do you have on this topic?" "This book is not at all what I want!")
- Hypertext, Related-Record Searching and Browsing
- Integration of Keyword, Controlled Vocabulary, and Classification-Based Search Approaches
- Expanded Coverage and Scope (The "full-collection access tool")

There are many ways of describing and classifying these features, and progress will almost certainly occur in incremental steps, but the third-generation online catalog will be a wholly new kind of retrieval system because it will be based on much more representative models of actual user information-seeking behaviors.

The Scholar's Workstation

The model of the E³OPAC is being extended further—some might say, replaced—by the recent development of microcomputer-based personal or "scholar's" information workstations. The emergence of several important information technologies has provided researchers and system developers the tools needed to support not only the expanded, extended online catalog, but also this further development of powerful, multipurpose, information workstations. These technologies include powerful microcomputer workstations, optical and advanced magnetic disk storage media, computer graphics and imaging technologies, sophisticated document retrieval and management software, and widespread national and institutional high-speed computer communication networks, gateway, and linking facilities.

The early applications of these technologies center around the development of personal information systems or "scholar's workstations" linked via local networks to both nearby and remote computing and information resources. The workstation is typically implemented on a microcomputer platform that employs a variety of special-purpose software modules to enhance user access to the online catalog and other local and remote information resources. The workstation may be viewed as the center of a client-server access system model that includes a distributed retrieval network of databases on local and remote file servers, with the user interface, gateway, and other "client" software residing on the microcomputer workstation. The University of Illinois's implementation of this model is illustrated in Figure 3 (adapted from Mischo & Cole, 1992). In this architecture, the information databases may be contained in a variety of storage media and may reside at various locations. Search interface software is used to provide a unified access environment for the end-user.

Some have described this scenario as the "one-stop, self-service information station." Others call it the "electronic library without walls." Mischo and Cole (1992) point out that:

> From a single workstation, a user will be able to: 1. perform a literature search using the major periodical index databases; 2. identify, retrieve, and read the full text of journal articles, book chapters, etc.; 3. send results to

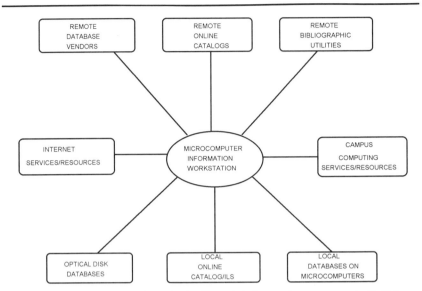

Figure 3. Workstation-based distributed information access via LANs, gateways, and wide area networks

electronic mailboxes and personal databases as desired; 4. use scholarly software residing on the workstation or provide a gateway to a remote computing facility (such as a supercomputer) for data analysis or preparation; and 5. capture and display the results of the work using the multimedia capabilities of the workstation to prepare presentation materials for the classroom or publication. (p. 43)

With the proper communications software installed, these workstations can provide access to the expanded, extended catalog from within libraries, as well as other locations such as work offices and homes. Some predict that most online catalog searches in the future will be performed on nonlibrary workstations.

SUBJECT SEARCHING IN OPACs

In the use of conventional information retrieval systems and second-generation OPACs, we are faced with the paradox of information retrieval: the need to describe that which you do not know in order to find it. You see, this is because these systems are *query-oriented* retrieval systems. Query-oriented retrieval systems require the matching of queries and representations of documents or text. The specifications provided in the query must be satisfied to some extent by any document representations that would make up the retrieval or "results" set. Thus, in a query-oriented retrieval system, one must have a pretty good idea of what one is looking for; what one needs to satisfy the information need, the "object of one's interest"; *and* one must be able to describe that object linguistically, at least partially, in a way that can be "understood" by the system. There is good reason to question whether or not this search and retrieval paradigm reflects the way most information seeking is actually carried out by individuals.

For purposes of analysis, I have classified OPAC subject searching approaches as either "querying" or "browsing," which are discussed below.

I. QUERYING
    A. Phrase Matching
       (Text strings or controlled vocabulary)
    B. Keyword Matching
       (Discrete words, with Boolean or proximity formulations)

**Query search requirements: Search aim/criteria known and can be expressed with relative precision and completeness

II. BROWSING
    A. Pre-sequenced, linear, inflexible
       (Typically, lists of index terms, headings, descriptors, or brief titles)
    B. Nonlinear, multidirectional, flexible
       ("navigation," "chain," "bridge," "relational," "hypertext," "serendipitous" browsing)

**Browse search requirements: Search aim/criteria not specific, not known, and/or cannot be expressed in appropriate query/indexing language

Query Searching

There are two kinds of query searching: phrase matching and keyword matching. A query consists of a term or terms (e.g., a character, number, word or words, or a phrase) and the specification, sometimes called the query "formulation," which defines how the component term(s) of the query are to be interpreted or related for matching purposes (e.g., word truncation, Boolean combinations, word adjacency). The matching function of an online catalog is the mechanism through which the retrieval software makes a comparison between index terms that represent documents and query terms to effect retrieval. The matching criteria are specified through the query by the user or applied automatically by the system. Query searching of either kind (often called just "searching," to distinguish it from an online catalog's browse mode) utilizes an exact matching function on the part of the system, regardless of the manner in which the matching criteria are specified.

In this all-or-nothing approach, documents (bibliographic records in online catalogs) will be retrieved in response to a search only if an exact match of the query is found. The query may consist of a pre-coordinated phrase (with or without truncation) or a post-coordinated Boolean expression of keywords. In either case, the query search matching requirements are precise and rigid. The process is purely mechanistic. The burden is on the searcher to enter terms that will match the entry (index) terms in the database and to specify appropriate proximity or term relationship logic. Bates (1986) criticizes this predominant approach to subject searching for requiring a "perfect 'pinpoint' match" on the one best term (p. 373). No match means no retrieval, as viewers of empty online catalog screens witness too often. The search may fail (i.e., not identify relevant documents that are in the collection) unless the searcher knows or guesses the exact way the term (word or phrase) appears in the subject index.

In keyword, Boolean queries, the system's matching mechanism makes a binary (yes/no) split of the database into bibliographic records that conform exactly to the requirements of the query, and all the rest. Only the former are retrieved as "hits." Partial or "closest" matching operations are generally not supported in second-generation online catalogs and conventional retrieval systems.

Query searching is an appropriate, useful search option when the aim of the search is specific, when the searcher knows precisely what he or she wants, and when this request can be expressed in the language of the database. Even in subject searching for books or articles on a topic, the searcher may know his or her topic exactly and may be able to express it in the language of the system (e.g., the assigned subject headings or descriptors).

Browse Searching

Browsing in online catalogs can take many forms. Typically, the system displays ordered lists of terms, descriptors, or brief bibliographic records for scanning by the searcher. Lists of index terms are usually presented in alphabetical order. The arrangement of brief citation records may be according to date, and some systems support short record browsing in shelf-list order. Usually the only "navigation" option for browsers is to go backward or forward through the list in a constrained, linear manner. Cross-references, if included, represent a way of jumping out of the sequence and over to related areas of the database. Hypertext operations, which permit navigation throughout the database's network of related terms and records, and the dynamic definition of "related areas and interests," have not been implemented in second-generation online catalogs. Conventional browsing assumes a vocabulary aim on the part of the searcher. It assists in identifying the correct form of a term and any related terms. Other forms of browsing, rare in today's online catalogs, support related record or document discovery through nonlinear explorations of the database.

Browse searching is the most useful and preferred approach when the search aim is not specific (regarding, for example, discipline or topic, type of publication, level of treatment, perspective, etc.), the desired results are not precisely known in advance, or the correct terms for representing the user's query (which may be vague) are not known at the outset. One or more of these circumstances may be present in most subject searching activities.

Current Status of Subject Searching

Most of today's operational information retrieval systems and second-generation online catalogs use exact match retrieval techniques, featuring keyword, Boolean, proximity, and string searching. Search field specification, truncation, and/or wild card searching is usually supported as well. These exact match techniques require that the specifications of the query (e.g., the search terms and their specified logical or textual relationships) be satisfied precisely by any and all document representations that would make up the retrieval set.

Although the object of widescale criticism by researchers and many librarians, exact match searching remains the paradigm for operational online information retrieval, CD-ROM, and online catalog systems. There is much discussion and debate in the research literature regarding the reasons for this situation and why it continues. Two explanatory factors should be mentioned in brief: first, some techniques have been employed by system designers that relax the constraints of exact match searching, for example, stemming of query or index terms and the provision of "wild card" searching; and, second, the conventional Boolean, post-coordinate search approach is preferred by professional searchers of online databases because its precision and flexibility permit them to express an information need accurately. In other words, it can be plausibly argued that Boolean propositions provide the flexibility and finesse to represent fine aspects of a user's information with great precision. Researchers and designers have given database searchers post-coordinate searching tools that are both powerful and flexible for constructing expressions of users' information needs.

Designers of second-generation online catalogs implemented this model in the 1980s largely because it was the model incorporated by the major commercial online search services and because it was preferred by the librarians who had become the trained, experienced users of those services. Willett (1988) points to the inertia factor: "Boolean systems have been with us for many years now and there is a natural disinclination on the part of both users and system providers to develop new techniques" (p. 11).

After end-users' difficulties with Boolean query systems began to be widely reported and discussed, some online catalog designers implemented various techniques aimed at reducing the difficulties associated with formulating and entering complex queries. For example, menus were provided for command selection, and users of these system interfaces had only to enter search terms and optionally specify a type of search or field to be the target of the search. The online catalog software then "constructed" the query and supplied the Boolean or proximity operator to coordinate the terms entered by the user. The default or "implicit" operator used to specify the relationship between the search terms could, in many cases, be changed by system managers if they felt it was necessary to change the logic of the relationship between search terms. For example, changing the system-supplied implicit operator "between" search terms from adjacency to the Boolean "AND" would likely broaden the search and usually yield a larger results set or reduce the number of no match, "no hit" search failures. This change was found to be necessary when users began to complain of not being able to find titles of books they knew were in the collection, and consultation with transaction logs confirmed the problem. Searchers typically remember and enter two or three significant words in a title, rather than the complete title or precise order of words in the title.

Explicit and Implicit Online Catalogs

With or without these "user-friendly" techniques, most online catalogs in operation are still Boolean query or string-matching, exact match retrieval systems. One might refer to these two kinds of second-generation online catalogs as "explicit" and "implicit" exact match systems. In implicit online catalogs, the query formulation requirements placed upon the user are greatly reduced or removed altogether. In the former case, the searcher is required to enter a term or terms that represent his information need and, perhaps, specify a type of search or search field by selecting it from a menu or by using a simplified command language (e.g., FIND TITLE medieval art). The system then supplies the combinatorial logic which specifies a relationship between the terms to be assumed and acted upon in the matching operation. Implicit truncation, for example, might also be applied to the terms such that a match could occur on both "medieval" and "medievalist," or "art" and "artists."

Such implicit online catalogs leave the user entirely in the dark about the term combinatorial logic, truncation (if any), and matching functions they automatically employ. As a consequence, most searchers will not have a clue as to why some searches fail to retrieve any documents, or why other searches retrieve large numbers of nonrelevant documents. Thus, they have no information feedback to aid in the modification or reformulation of their search queries for a second or third try. Even if they guess that the online catalog they are using searches on "medieval art" as a unitary string of contiguous characters, these implicit online catalogs generally do not provide the means for a searcher to respecify the request as, for example, "medieval AND art."

Another category of implicit online catalogs includes those that remove the requirement to formulate and enter a query altogether. Using these online catalogs, the searcher may optionally select a type of search from a menu (e.g., author, title, subject, etc.) or proceed directly to a display of index terms or brief document titles usually presented in an alphabetically ordered list. (Some online catalogs display title lists in class number order.) Markey (1989) calls this approach "alphabetical searching." This approach closely mimics the way searchers access and scan document records in the earlier manual card catalogs. Searchers choose a location in the displayed alphabetical list (or drawer of cards) of "headings" terms as an entry point to the database, then scan nearby terms or the bibliographic records filed under them. In the online catalog, a selection of a single term from the list (terms can be keywords extracted from text or pre-coordinated phrases from a controlled subject vocabulary) will typically call up a display of all bibliographic records associated with the selected term. These usually abbreviated document "title" records may, in turn, be scanned for further selection, fuller display, and assessment.

This list scanning and selection approach to searching, found in many online catalogs, is often named the "BROWSE" mode or searching option. The only search approach offered in a few online catalogs, in most second-generation online catalogs this approach is offered as a search option, along with a keyword, Boolean search option (explicit in some, implicit in others). Thus it is that we have identified three types of operational online catalogs: (a) explicit, exact match systems (usually Boolean and string searching systems); (b) implicit Boolean exact match systems (in which the system software defines the term relationships); and (c) "browse" online catalogs that feature alphabetical searching of index terms or citation lists.

The "browse" online catalogs make the least demands on the searcher with regard to the process of query formulation and entry. The searcher merely scans a list, selects a term from the list (rather than entering one of his own), then sees what document records are retrieved. The searcher may have a term or terms in mind, of course, then consults the system's lists to find it or one like it in some sense and thus suitable for searching. When a term has been selected, the system carries out the "built-in" matching and retrieval operations. Such browse online catalogs may still be classified in the category of exact match systems.

In all three types of operational online catalogs—and most are mixed, hybrid systems—effective subject searching requires the user to express his need for information in a form or terminology acceptable to the system. This means that users must not only specify their need in advance, but think about what sort of documents will satisfy their need, and *also* translate these concepts into the terms used in the indexing vocabulary of the system. These terms may then be used in a formal query, if the particular system requires one, or sought for in an alphabetical list displayed for this purpose. The system then takes the query or selected term and applies a matching function to determine which records are to be retrieved for display and evaluation by the user.

Larson (1991) explains that the process of query formulation or term selection from lists required in conventional information retrieval systems and online catalogs "involves *predicting* which terms in the indexing language of the system have been used to index the documents that the user would want to retrieve" (p. 5). He goes on to state that evidence indicates that online catalog users do not conceive of subject searching in this way, and that when required to, they usually do not do a very good job of predicting or guessing the terms used to index the desired or potentially useful documents. Some of the guessing required may be reduced in systems that permit or require searchers to scan lists of index or thesaurus terms to identify search terms. However, in large online databases, the length of these lists, or the complex structure of lists such as thesauri, may place an unreasonable burden on the untrained, infrequent user.

BROWSING AS AN INFORMATION-SEEKING METHOD

Browsing is not one but many kinds of activities, any one of which may be observed in actual searching behavior. All information retrieval systems, including online catalogs, support some form of browsing. In traditional, query-oriented systems, browsing plays a subordinate, supporting role in assisting with the formulation or modification of a query that is to be matched exactly or partially with document representations. This probably explains why some people view browsing as a secondary activity and not as real searching. Some forms of browsing are quite different from this and may serve as the *primary* information-seeking method used by most people in real-life searching situations. In light of this, some researchers have suggested that a browsing paradigm for searching replace the query-matching paradigm in the design of information retrieval systems. Before commenting further on this point of view, it will be well to examine more closely the concept and types of browsing.

The Concept of Browsing

A browse is an edible in the eyes of a young animal. It may be a tender twig, leaf, or shoot of a plant that is fit and easy to eat. These delicacies must be sought for and are the object of selective review, that is, browsing. Browsing takes place in a patch of interest and is characterized as tentative nibbling, at least at the start. Human browsing activity has many connotations. In the context of information seeking and library use activities, probably the most visible and commonly understood browsing activity is the behavior of roaming among the shelves of a library or bookstore to scan materials of potential interest or utility. Books and other materials are casually perused in order to decide what we want to buy or borrow, if anything at all. Librarians have long recognized that users who come into the library enjoy browsing among the shelves, and thus they make special efforts to display groups of related books of potential interest in noticeable, easy-to-browse ways. Research studies of library users confirm this experience and show further that many library browsers prefer to browse the organized materials on the shelves than search and browse in the library catalog (Hyman, 1971; Hancock-Beaulieu, 1989).

From our ordinary experiences, we recognize that both the focus of our browsing interests and the strength of our motivation to discover relevant items vary from time to time. When browsing, we may employ a variety of techniques ranging from the casual and undirected to the planned and systematic. As Marchionini (1987) explains, "These techniques are dependent on the object sought, individual searcher characteristics, the purpose of the search, and the setting and context for conducting the search. The objective of browsing may be well-defined (e.g., a particular antique chair to match a desk), or ill-defined (e.g., an interesting wall hanging for a favorite room)" (pp. 69-70). In the latter category, I prefer the example of a tourist on the last day of an island holiday searching about for a souvenir suitable as a memento of the trip.

Browsing can thus be viewed as a family of information-seeking activities. As Herner (1970) concludes, browsing is not one but many things:

> It is sometimes a purely random, unstructured, and undirected activity. Other times it is closely directed and structured, where, although the final sources or media may not be known, the desired product or goal is clear. Then again, specified media and sources may be browsed or consulted on a regular basis, not necessarily to produce answers to concrete queries, but because it is highly probable they contain items of interest. (p. 414)

Browsing Aids

This brief reflection on the varieties of browsing activities is useful because it invites us to expand our traditional understanding of browsing. Browsing may be more or less planned and directed, or it may proceed from an information need or interest that is more or less well defined at the start. In addition, browsing may be carried out in a variety of information media, packages, and bibliographic tools, both manual and online. Many of these media and tools have been systematically designed and structured to facilitate browsing. They employ structural, semantic, and navigational aids for this purpose. The library itself can be such a tool if its collection of materials is stored and maintained in any way other than a random manner. When direct access to the shelves is permitted, the arrangement of books on the shelves according to a subject scheme or some other classification (e.g., author, genre) facilitates browsing by library users.

A book or periodical journal is typically organized and structured to promote browsing. Such devices as the tables of contents, indexes, prefaces or introductions, and lists of references both encourage and enhance browsing. Whatever the user's level, specificity, or area of interest, such devices permit the easy and convenient gathering and perusal of information needed to make preliminary decisions about the relevance or potential usefulness of the documents.

Various forms of library catalogs, and indexing and abstracting publications or services, manual or online, incorporate devices and features that permit browsing of one kind or another. These sources utilize structure, recognition, and navigation devices to assist and guide the user looking about for items of interest or pointers to such items. Browsing is essentially visual and depends more on recognition than on recall or a priori formulations of need. A good browsing tool, source, or system exploits the human ability to recognize items of interest, a cognitive ability that is faster and easier than juggling concepts to specify a need and describing relevant items in advance (Card, Moran, & Newell, 1983).

Searching or Browsing?

Marchionini (1987) discusses three primary reasons why people browse:

> First, they browse because they cannot or have not defined their search objective; they have what Belkin, Oddy, and Brooks have called anomalous states of knowledge (1982). . . .
> Second, people browse because it takes less cognitive load to browse than it does to plan and conduct an analytical, optimized search. . . .
> Third, people browse because the information system supports and encourages browsing. . . . Particular information sources like encyclopedias invite browsing by supplying indexes, outlines, section headings, tables and graphs, which help users quickly filter information. (p. 70)

Searchers often have difficulty defining and expressing their information needs. The database structure and vocabulary requirements of the search system may be unknown to the searcher. For such searchers, looking is more inviting than formulating. Browsing is inherently active and engaging, and many users seem to prefer action and encounter to reflection and analysis. It could be said that good browsing systems and sources attract such users, but there are not enough good online browsing systems in operation to justify this claim at this time.

Reflection on the reasons and circumstances in which people browse should yield a new understanding of the importance of this activity. These insights should inform the design of information retrieval systems and lead to improved browsing capabilities in these systems. In the past, browsing has often been viewed as a secondary or supplemental search strategy or technique to primary, query-oriented, directed, structured searching. Bates (1989) suggests that there may still be a "lingering tendency in information science to see browsing *in contrast* to directed searching, to see it as a casual, don't-know-what-I-want behavior that one engages in separately from 'regular' searching" (p. 414).

Searching by browsing is a natural, preferred searching technique for many people, especially when they are engaged in "general purposive" information seeking. Ellis's (1989) research on the information-seeking behavior of social scientists shows that various forms of browsing are a standard component of their research and "keeping aware" activities. He recommends that browsing of a variety of types of information that supplement the standard bibliographic record be provided in online retrieval systems. Liebscher and Marchionini's (1988) research has demonstrated that browsing can be as effective in its results as structured, query-oriented Boolean searching for novice searchers of full-text documents. Marchionini (1987) argues that because of the massive amounts of poorly organized information available in electronic form, browsing is even more important in electronic environments than in traditional environments like those presented by open-access libraries.

There are a variety of information-seeking needs, aims, and strategies that would seem to require searching by semidirected exploration, recognition, and discovery, in a word—browsing—rather than searching by explicit query formulation-matching operations, whether aided or not by relevance feedback, query expansion techniques. Thus, it seems self-evident that users would greatly benefit from the development of computer-based information systems that support and encourage searching and exploration of electronic information resources via browsing or "berrypicking" (Bates, 1989).

Designers of information retrieval systems and online catalogs must expand their knowledge of the browsing requirements of searchers and provide capabilities and search options in their systems that will support these requirements. Most information retrieval systems support some aspects of browsing, but most still implement the paradigm of direct, query-matching retrieval. Browsing also provides a suitable paradigm for information system design and, perhaps, an even more representative one, given the many varieties of information needs and searching behavior.

CONCLUSION

Hundreds of OPACs can now be accessed with relative ease via the Internet, either by telnetting to an OPAC's network address or by selecting one from a Gopher directory menu. Almost all of these OPACs can be characterized as second-generation, query-oriented online catalog retrieval systems. They have very limited relevance feedback, query refinement, and browsing capabilities. As such, they place intrinsic limits on the potential of new network-based access and search technologies, like the Z39.50 protocol, to provide more effective and more appropriate search environments for many kinds of search needs and behavior.

The Z39.50 NISO standard search and retrieval protocol, and its International Standards Organization counterpart standards, ISO 10162 and ISO 10163, conform to the query-oriented paradigm embedded in so many second-generation online catalogs. These specifications have recently achieved draft international standard (DIS) status. The search and retrieval protocol is designed to function as an application-level (layer 7) protocol within the Open Systems Interconnection (OSI) protocol suite for the connection and interfunctioning of different computer systems. Among other things, the ISO search and retrieval protocol specifies a canonical search format through which searches can be transmitted from one computer (the "client") to another (the "server"). This format consists of a series of predicates linked by Boolean operators such as OR and AND; the predicates are composed of field names, relational attributes, and values (for example, AUTHOR—lastname value; or TITLE—keyword-of value). Both the field names and relational attributes are selected from a predefined and registered (i.e., officially sanctioned) attribute set that forms part of the context of a connection between a "client" computer and a "server" computer. The current "working set" of attributes represent fields in MARC or MARC-like bibliographic records.

Although some uniformity will be introduced in the searching of networked online catalogs when Z39.50 and the ISO search and retrieval protocols are available for use (conforming software must be developed and installed on hosts and/or network servers), limited search and browse functionality will be supported by the standard approach, and no assistance to the user having search problems during a session will be provided by the new protocol-based search interaction. For example, this approach will not inform the user why a search resulted in no matches. The search can be repeated with new attributes and/or values, but it will be transmitted and processed in the same predefined and rigid manner. The assistance of a friendly local user interface will be excluded from this process.

WAIS, a distributed database retrieval system also based on the client-server model, provides a rudimentary kind of weighted-term/document retrieval from indexed databases on the Internet. WAIS displays retrieved documents in ranked order, with those documents most likely to be relevant to the query listed first, and WAIS offers some opportunity for relevance feedback on retrieved documents so that the search can be refined and extended. WAIS is an application of the probabilistic theory of information retrieval promoted for many years by researchers as a better alternative to conventional Boolean retrieval systems. However, WAIS is still a query-oriented approach that provides only limited, rather linear browsing capabilities.

A fundamental shortcoming of the client-server approach is that any client, no matter how usable, is limited by what the server search and retrieval "engine" can do.

The first network access technology with promise for inveterate browsers is the World Wide Web (WWW or W3). WWW supports hypertext retrieval and browsing among selected, specially organized databases on the network. Through the multiple linking of related data entities, textual units, or entire documents, the hypertext approach offers the user a network of alternate paths for self-directed, nonlinear browsing and exploration of bibliographic and other document spaces. At this time, there are few if any hypertext OPACs accessible via the Internet.

To end on an optimistic note, there is good reason to expect that these new network access and retrieval technologies will have an impact on OPAC vendors and developers, motivating at least some of them to venture beyond second-generation functionality. The Internet is marvelously hospitable to innovators, and it is a wonderfully public and influential medium.

REFERENCES

Bates, M. J. (1986). Subject access in online catalogs: A design model. *Journal of the American Society for Information Science, 37*(6), 357-376.

Bates, M. J. (1989). The design of browsing and berrypicking techniques for the online search interface. *Online Review, 13*(5), 407-423.

Card, S. K.; Moran, T. P.; & Newell, A. (1983). *The psychology of human-computer interaction.* Hillsdale, NJ: Lawrence Erlbaum.

Ellis, D. (1989). A behavioural model for information retrieval system design. *Journal of Information Science, 15*(4/5), 237-247.

Hancock-Beaulieu, M. (1989). Subject searching behaviour at the library catalogue and at the shelves: Evaluating the impact of an online public access catalogue. Doctoral dissertation, City University, London.

Herner, S. (1970). Browsing. In A. Kent & H. Lancour, *Encyclopedia of library and information science* (Vol. 3, pp. 408-415). New York: Marcel Dekker.

Hildreth, C. R. (1989). *Intelligent interfaces and retrieval methods for subject searching in bibliographic retrieval systems.* Washington, DC: Cataloging Distribution Services, Library of Congress.

Hyman, R. J. (1971). Access to library collections: Summary of a documentary and opinion survey on the direct shelf approach and browsing. *Library Resources & Technical Services, 15*(4), 479-491.

Larson, R. R. (1991). Classification clustering, probabilistic information retrieval and the online catalog. Prepublication typescript.

Liebscher, P., & Marchionini, G. (1988). Browse and analytical search strategies in a full-text CD-ROM encyclopedia. *School Library Media Quarterly, 16*(4), 223-233.

Marchionini, G. (1987). An invitation to browse: Designing full-text systems for novice users. *Canadian Journal of Information Science, 12*(3/4), 69-79.

Markey, K. (1989). Alphabetical searching in an online catalog. *Journal of Academic Librarianship, 14*(6), 353-360.

Mischo, W. H., & Cole, T. W. (1992). The Illinois extended OPAC: Library Information Workstation design and development. In M. Ra (Ed.), *Advances in online public access catalogs* (Vol. 1, pp. 38-57). New York: Meckler.

Potter, W. G. (1989). Expanding the online catalog. *Information Technology and Libraries, 8*(2), 99-104.

Willett, P. (Ed.). (1988). *Document retrieval systems: Vol. 3. Foundations of information science.* London: Taylor Graham.

DENISE A. TROLL

Research Manager, Library Automation
Hunt Library
Carnegie Mellon University
Pittsburgh, Pennsylvania

Designing the Gateway Interface: Tips and Techniques from Carnegie Mellon's Experience

THE GATEWAY INTERFACE

What, exactly, is an "interface" and why does the electronic library need more than one of them? The etymology of the term can be traced back to the Greek *prosopon*, meaning a face that is facing another face in a living, mutual relationship. In ancient Greece, an interface was a third state of being, an ontological reality achieved through communication. Similarly, some modern scholars, for example, Marshall McLuhan (1962), Walter Ong (1982), and Michael Heim (1987), define "interface" as a technological environment that slowly transforms perception and cognition and eventually induces a new state of being, a new consciousness of self and world.

Computer users learn to experience and participate in the world in a digital way through encounters at the interface. The software and hardware they use shape their digital experience and their expectations about the interface. For example, Macintosh users expect to use a mouse to select menu options, click buttons, and navigate with a scroll bar; they don't expect to type commands or examine files without starting an application. UNIX workstation users may or may not expect to use a mouse; they do expect to type commands and examine files without starting an application. Computers are not neutral tools. They are driven by ideology. Users interiorize the ideology of their desktop computer. The successful electronic library will give users the "look and feel" and power of their desktop computer so that they can learn the application quickly, focus on the information, and share the information across applications and services (e.g., cutting, pasting, filing, and printing).

What, then, is a "gateway" interface? In the domain of information retrieval, a gateway interface essentially provides access to one or more databases in addition to the online public access catalog (OPAC). The definition may be finessed from a narrow or broad perspective. From the narrow perspective, a gateway provides access to multiple databases that are managed by one group or organization. Though the databases may be created from local or commercially licensed data and reside on the same or different retrieval servers using the same or different retrieval software, there is only one information store, that is, one information store "owner," designer, controller, negotiator. From the broad perspective, a gateway provides access to multiple databases that are managed by multiple groups or organizations. Some databases may be locally loaded and managed; others are available over the network from other sites and managers. In this model, there are multiple information stores. The design implications and ontological ramifications of a gateway interface depend on which definition of gateway is invoked. For example, if all of the databases are locally loaded and maintained using the same database-building and retrieval software, then search syntax and retrieval protocols are easily specified and controlled. However, if databases are loaded and maintained at different sites using different software, then search syntax and retrieval protocols require rigorous standards and experimentation to achieve interoperability. In both scenarios, authentication and protection may be necessary to meet database licensing agreements. Search syntax, retrieval protocols, and authentication and protection affect user interface design and functionality.

This paper examines five lessons in interface design learned by Carnegie Mellon University Libraries in building Library Information System II (LIS):

1. Be prepared: User interface design is difficult and time-consuming.
2. Be informed: Distributed retrieval has implications for user interface design.
3. Be smart: User interface design specifications save time and aggravation.
4. Be flexible: User interfaces need to be tested and revised.
5. Beware: Politics and egos can disrupt user interface design.

THE LIBRARY INFORMATION SYSTEM (LIS)

Some background information will provide a context for the lessons to be discussed. LIS is a distributed retrieval system of clients and servers that implements the narrow definition of a gateway interface. It currently provides access to 14 databases in one information store managed by the University Libraries. Developments are underway for LIS to provide access to multiple information stores managed by other groups on campus and by groups at remote sites.

In January 1992, LIS replaced the mainframe retrieval system operated by the Carnegie Mellon University Libraries since 1986. LIS has two client user interfaces: a Motif interface for UNIX workstations running X Windows, and a command-line ASCII interface for other machines. The command-line interface is called the VT100 interface, though it emulates many terminal types. Long-term plans include a Macintosh interface and a MS Windows interface. The LIS retrieval servers are four DECstation 5000s. Databases are built on a separate machine, then moved to the retrieval servers. Databases were initially built on a VAX 6420, but the VAX was replaced in 1993 with a DEC Alpha Flamingo to greatly increase the speed of database building. The database-building and retrieval software used in LIS is Newton, which was developed by the Online Computer Library Center (OCLC). Newton is optimized for Boolean retrieval and large databases. Experiments have begun with a second retrieval engine, Ful/Text from Fulcrum, to provide smaller databases and easy-to-use database-building tools for individuals and groups outside of the University Libraries. Plans are for Ful/Text to facilitate the provision of multiple information stores at Carnegie Mellon and a truly campus-wide information system accessed through the LIS clients.

The protocol that enables LIS clients to "talk" to LIS servers is Z39.50 layered on TCP/IP (Transmission Control Protocol/Internet Protocol). Z39.50 specifies a Boolean query language and general search and present (display) services. The released version of LIS uses version one of Z39.50, which is predominantly site defined and therefore not robust enough to support interoperability across sites. Version two of the standard is being implemented now, with an eye towards changes coming with version three—changes that will render the standard robust enough to begin experiments in interoperability. Authentication in LIS, required by database licensing agreements, is based on Kerberos, developed at the Massachusetts Institute of Technology (MIT). Access control is provided by Transarc's PTS (Protection Server). The names, addresses, and structures of the databases are provided using the Andrew File System (AFS). However, by winter 1993, a reference server will provide database information and access control. The reference server will "talk" to both clients and (retrieval) servers and pass information dynamically upon request. It is being developed at Carnegie Mellon in preparation for retrieval from multiple information stores.

LESSON 1
Be Prepared: Interface Design is Difficult and Time-Consuming

Interface design is not for the squeamish. Read and apply the literature, but don't expect to get it right the first time. Don't expect to get it perfect—ever.

A survey of user interface programming conducted by Brad A. Myers and Mary Beth Rosson (1992) revealed that the average time spent on an interface (independent of the project application, country, or host computer system) was 45% during the design phase of the project, 50% during the implementation phase, and 37% during the maintenance phase. Use of a programming toolkit increased the percentage to around 60%. Many of the most difficult problems reported in the survey related to the design of the user interface rather than to its implementation. For example, finding appropriate test subjects, assessing user needs and expectations, accommodating both novice and expert users, understanding and conforming to style guidelines, achieving consistency (particularly across developers), selecting colors and fonts, and providing online help were raised as serious design problems (p. 201). Serious implementation issues included achieving acceptable performance and portability, finding and fixing bugs, getting enough memory, and communicating among different components of the interface and between the interface and the underlying application.

Carnegie Mellon University Libraries' experience matches the results of this survey with few exceptions. Designing, implementing, and maintaining the LIS Motif and VT100 user interfaces took more time and were more difficult than anticipated when work began in 1989. Porting the user interfaces to multiple platforms (e.g., DECstations and Sun Sparcstations) was problematic, but tracking bugs and prioritizing bug fixes across interfaces, platforms, and versions of the software are ongoing management headaches. The design problems revolve not so much around testing but around the negotiations required to interpret research results, generate an improved design, and allocate resources to implement the design. Details about the University Libraries' design problems and process are provided throughout this paper. The remainder of this lesson focuses on general design problems and solutions that can be learned from the literature and how they match University Libraries' experience.

Computer Technology and Literate Habits

Admittedly this is not the place to review the entire body of literature on interface design, but mention must be made of key works and areas for concern. Edward R. Tufte's remarkable books *Envisioning Information* (1990) and *The Visual Display of Quantitative Information* (1983) shed considerable light on what visual excellence is, why it is important, and universal principles for achieving it. Tufte's pamphlet on user interface design (1989) and an article published in the *Bulletin of the American Society for Information Science* (1992) pinpoint four serious design problems related to the current state of computer technology and the literate habits of human beings. The following discussion is organized around Tufte's four points with related research introduced to confirm and elaborate them.

1. Resolution

According to Tufte (1992), the primary problem in user interface design is the burden placed on visual memory by the low resolution of the computer screen. In comparison with a printed book or map, a computer screen conveys very little information. The information density is so poor that user interfaces must break information—and therefore information processing—into small pieces that must be viewed or done in sequence. The cognitive processing required to keep the sequence coherent impairs the user's ability to contrast, compare, or make a choice. The constant context-switching required by menus, dialog boxes, error and status messages, etc., impairs the user's ability to concentrate.

Tufte (1989) describes two ways to lighten the burden placed on visual memory by poor screen resolution: first, reduce the noise; second, improve the signal. To reduce the noise, provide clean, sharp, precise interfaces free of unnecessary elements. Bruce Tognazzini (1992) explains that anomalies or unnecessary elements in the interface are sources of noise in the communications channel between the computer and the human. He warns: "Be wary of interface elements that detract from or overwhelm the content regions of your application" (p. 196). This is Tufte's (1989) second solution to the memory problem: improve the signal by making the organizing grid implicit or transparent. Devote more space to the data than to the data container so that users can focus on the information rather than on the design and mechanics of the interface.

2. Typography and Icons

Tufte's (1992) second problem with today's user interfaces is the design of the typography and icons. He calls for standards of quality book typography to insure the readability of electronic documents, and for typographic and artistic skills to be applied in icon design, along with a careful consideration of vocabulary, cultural context, and computer functionality. According to Tognazzini (1992), people want multiple channels of information using both words and pictures.

3. Interaction

Design elements that work well alone do not always work well together: "a complexity of marks generates an exponential complexity of shapes" (Tufte, 1992, p. 16). The result can be dancing gray spots or vibrating black lines that distract or even irritate the user. Furthermore, "Visual clutter [can result] from prison grids of window frames, empty paths, and rectangles and blocks" (Tufte, 1992, p. 16). Tufte's solution: reduce the noise and the contrast between figure and ground.

The arrangement of information and features on the screen determines what (if anything) interacts and what users will find (easy) to do. Clutter will distract the user and interfere with concentration. According to Tognazzini (1992), "Any element that does not communicate information that the user may need right now is superfluous" (p. 136). Bring to the foreground frequently used features on menus and buttons while nesting less frequently used features in dialog boxes. Put popular options at the top of lists. Display cursors prominently. Open dialog boxes over the button or menu used to request them, where the mouse is likely to be. "Close targets are faster to acquire than far ones: Keeping everything but menu bars and other edge-hugging items close to the area of interest saves the user time" (Tognazzini, 1992, p. 206).

4. Color

One way to reduce the contrast between figure and ground is with color. Color is one of the most powerful agents available for depicting complex information. Be careful, though: like all design features, colors can interact and produce jarring effects. Tufte (1992) recommends following cartographic principles for the use of color. For example, use colors found in nature like light grays, blues, and yellows. Background colors and colors in inactive windows should be muted or grayed. Foreground colors and active windows should be lighter and brighter. Strong colors can be used for emphasis.

In Preparation for Electronic Document Delivery Services

In addition to the general research on interface design and human factors, those involved in electronic library development projects should become familiar with the research on reading and writing online. Years ago OPACs spearheaded an ongoing movement into bibliographic databases, but the new trend is to talk about delivering full-text documents to the user's desktop. Readability is more of an issue when the electronic library goes beyond ASCII bibliographic records and abstracts and dares to confront users with an ASCII version of *Alice in Wonderland* or a bitmapped "page image" version of an academic journal. Library and computer ideologies are mixing and mingling at the interface, creating a new digital experience that is rattling print-literate habits. The technology is upping the ante on the ontology.

Research by Wilfred Hansen and Christina Haas confirms Tufte's analysis of the memory problems related to the low information density of the computer screen. In studies of reading and writing online, Hansen and Haas (1988) discovered that the amount of information that can be seen at a glance (the "page size") determines the context for viewing and understanding the information. If the amount is small, readers must move ("page") frequently to view an entire document. Moving takes time, burdens short-term memory, and interferes with concentration, comprehension, and recall. Hansen and Haas conclude that four design features can facilitate reading and writing online:

1. Sufficient "page" size—comparable to a printed page (Tufte's despair over breaking information into a sequence of bits).
2. Legibility—font, spacing, contrast, sharpness, flicker, antialiasing, and resolution (Tufte's attention to typography).
3. Responsiveness—"page" quickly, easily, flexibly (Tufte's focus on the data rather than the mechanics of the data container).
4. Tangibility—provide spatial cues to facilitate context and recall; provide cues that users can manipulate, for example, bookmarks and annotations (Tufte's concern for the burden on visual memory).

Hansen and Haas (1988) argue that these features boost the user's confidence and facilitate learning the interface and the information.

The implication seems to be that a workstation interface is preferable to a terminal interface for full-text documents. However, research done at Bellcore on the SuperBook and MiteyBook full-text document browsers indicates that providing interactive contextual views like dynamic tables of contents and tailored text displays can compensate for the loss of context derived from the limited screen space and poor resolution of today's computer monitors (e.g., Egan, Remde, & Landauer et al., 1989; Egan, Remde, & Gomez et al., 1989).

A Note about Consistency

Efforts to support the user's visual memory and provide a sense of context are efforts to put the user in control. The user's sense of control derives from consistency in the interface. Tognazzini (1992) explains that control "arises from neither tyranny nor anarchy but from the freedom of a supportive environment constructed of reasonable and consistent rules" (p. 225). Having said that, one must know when to break the rules. "The most important consistency of all is consistency with the user's expectations" (p. 250). "Consistency with the Guidelines should be maintained unless a new solution is demonstrably and vastly superior" (p. 41). In other words, follow style guides as much as possible, but when the guidelines conflict with user needs and expectations, break the rules.

Experience with LIS

Carnegie Mellon University Libraries' experience with LIS matches the literature. The poor resolution of today's computer monitors, the limited screen space of different machines, and the distance between the computer screen and the computer user (almost twice the distance between book and reader) necessitate breaking information into pieces. Readability problems are not particularly striking with bibliographic databases, where records are relatively short, but they increase with full-text databases that deliver lengthy documents to the desktop.

Given the heterogeneous computing environment at Carnegie Mellon and limited resources, all primary information displays in LIS are in ASCII format (e.g., the list of result sets, list of titles retrieved, and bibliographic records). LIS also has several full-text ASCII databases. Figures 1 and 2 show the Motif and VT100 LIS Records windows displaying the same (full-text) article from the *Academic American Encyclopedia.* VT100 LIS is limited to displaying 24 lines by 80 characters of ASCII text. In the current interface, 9 of those 24 lines are used for on-screen instructions, prompts, and system messages. Consequently users see very little of an encyclopedia article at one time. If users have a larger monitor, they can resize VT100 LIS windows to take advantage of the screen space and see more of the article at a glance. To reduce the noise, improve the signal, and enable users who cannot resize the window to see more information at a glance, a future release of VT100 LIS will enable users to hide and display the six lines of instructions at the bottom of the screen with a keystroke.

Motif LIS, in contrast, runs on UNIX workstations, which have more screen space and capabilities than terminals or terminal emulators. Therefore, Motif LIS can display not only more information at once than VT100 LIS, but multiple views and formats of information at once. For example, VT100 LIS must display either the list of titles retrieved in a search or a bibliographic or full-text record; it cannot display both at once. Motif LIS, however, combines these displays in one window and enables users to reallocate space between the list and the record (see Figure 1). The entire Records window can be allocated to the record, in which case the amount of information displayed is comparable to a printed page. The combination Motif Records window was the result of prototype testing in September 1990.

Though ASCII text can be displayed on any machine, it lacks the visual-spatial cues that facilitate reading longer documents. Users may have few problems reading a bibliographic record in ASCII format, but many problems reading a technical report or a novel in ASCII format because they easily lose track of where they are and where they've been. The trend for document delivery services to provide documents in bitmapped "page image" format (where the image sent to the user's screen or printer is identical to the original print publication) escalates problems with screen resolution and typography. Some typefaces scan better than others. Some scanners do a better job than others. Regardless of the dots per inch (dpi) at which a page is scanned, the dots per inch of the display monitor affects readability.

In cooperative experiments with selected publishers, Carnegie Mellon University Libraries scanned journal pages at 400 dpi for display on a 72-dpi workstation monitor. Usability tests in spring 1992 revealed that the quality of the images and the prototype image user interface were inadequate for general release to campus. Research subjects wanted to see a whole page on the screen and have the text be legible at a distance of 16 to 24 inches. Though the size of a UNIX workstation monitor makes it possible to display an entire page on the screen, it is not possible to insure readability at the requisite distance.

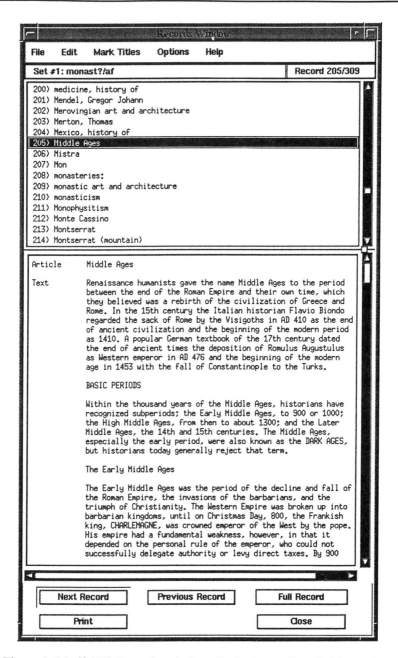

Figure 1. Motif LIS Records window displaying a list of titles and an encyclopedia article

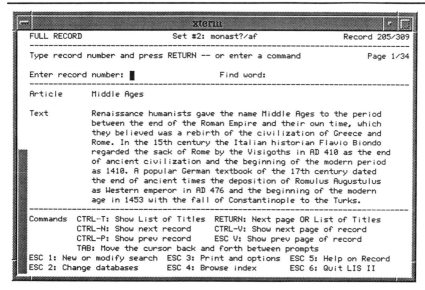

Figure 2. VT100 LIS Records window displaying an encyclopedia article

The fonts and typefaces of printed journals were designed for print technology, which has a higher resolution and can assume a shorter distance between document and reader. Though the prototype image user interface provided several levels of zoom for users to enlarge and shrink the page, they were not comfortable when the text was large enough to read at a distance of 16 to 24 inches—they couldn't see enough of the page to keep track of where they were on the page. They preferred to keep the entire page visible (the text small) and move their faces closer to the screen. Users also lost track of where they were in the document because the prototype interface provided no visual-spatial contextual cues for the entire document. Detailed user interface design specifications were prepared following the prototype testing of the image user interface (see lesson 3).

While the new image user interface is being implemented, the University Libraries are finalizing agreements with vendors and publishers to acquire a substantial body of journal information in page image and ASCII formats. Plans are for LIS to provide image document delivery services in selected subject areas by spring of 1994. Work has begun on tailored text displays and dynamic tables of contents. The prototype image user interface included interactive tables of contents generated using optical character recognition (OCR) software and manual touchup. Development is underway on recognition software that will distinguish text from graphics on a page image and enable users to move from one graphic to the next or one section heading to the next in an image document.

LIS interfaces currently have no icons. VT100 LIS provides instructions in ASCII text at the bottom of each screen or display. Motif LIS provides features on buttons and menus. Icons require a graphic artist, and the development team does not include a graphic artist, but more importantly, icons require considerable attention to cultural context. The international student population at Carnegie Mellon complicates the design of appropriate icons.

Space constraints make composing on-screen instructions or selecting the proper textual label for a menu or button difficult. Vocabulary problems also arise from the synonymy and polysemy of the language. A vocabulary must be found for features and displays that quickly conveys to users an accurate conceptual model of online information retrieval. Unfortunately, it is not easy to determine when information retrieval requires a technical vocabulary and when a technical vocabulary is needless jargon. For example, is "record" an unnecessary technical term? Is "browse" best used to denote the feature for examining database indexes to select search terms or for stepping through a hierarchical directory to find a document? Do users need to know the differences between "fields" and "indexes" or can information retrieval blur the distinction without inducing a cognitive model of information retrieval that interferes with retrieval and usability? What is "full text?" Is it searchable text? A picture of text? Text and graphics? Hypertext? Hypermedia? Experience at Carnegie Mellon indicates that information retrieval is a sophisticated business and that users need to learn certain fundamental concepts and strategies to be proficient with the technology. Interface design should bring these concepts and strategies to the fore, and vocabulary should be tested (see lesson 4).

Motif buttons present several additional problems. First, in the current implementation, they don't resize. The University Libraries want to provide some Motif LIS workstations with large fonts suitable for the visually impaired. Motif menus resize appropriately when the font is enlarged, but Motif buttons do not. Enlarging the font makes button labels no longer fit on the buttons. Second, buttons occupy considerable screen space. User protocols indicate that they may clutter and complicate the interface and distract the user rather than simply highlight heavily used features. Using Tufte's terms, too much space may be devoted to the data container rather than to the data. Future research and design work will determine whether Motif LIS should continue to use buttons or eliminate some or all of them. With the aid of a graphic artist, the buttons could be transformed into icons.

Though the additional screen space provided by UNIX workstations enables Motif LIS to display more information at a time and thus helps readers concentrate, comprehend, and recall the information, the additional space also introduces problems. More space is available to be cluttered with more views and formats of information. Figure 3 shows the three primary Motif LIS windows open at once. The Search window is on the upper left, the Browse window is on the lower left, and the Records window is on the right. When document delivery services are provided in image format, there will also be a Document window overlaid on the screen. The heavy contrast of black and white space all over the screen creates vibrating lines and dancing gray spots. Again, part of the problem is the quality of the monitor. Though the Motif toolkit supports the "look and feel" of three-dimensional space using subtle variations in color, the typical workstation monitor on campus is 72-dpi monochrome. The subtle variations in color and the three-dimensionality of Motif are lost in the dithering

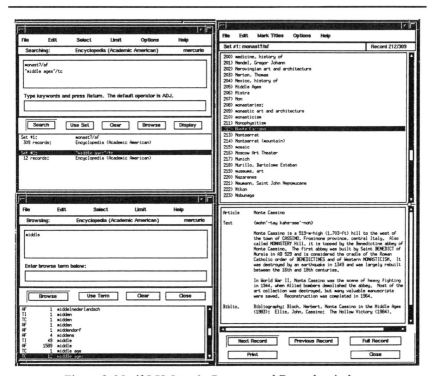

Figure 3. Motif LIS Search, Browse, and Records windows

of pixels. Indeed, depending on the monitor, lines surrounding default buttons in Motif LIS may or may not be visible. (See Figure 3.) Better monitors, preferably color monitors, will enable the University Libraries to provide better user interfaces, with active windows and information foregrounded by lighter, brighter colors and higher contrast, and background or related information subdued to be less distracting.

LESSON 2
Be Informed: Distributed Retrieval Has Implications for User Interface Design

The implications don't always mesh nicely with user needs and expectations or library resources. Try to negotiate the best compromise between the long-term vision of interoperability with other retrieval systems and short-term needs, resources, and schedules.

One of the advantages of distributed computing is that it affords multiple user interfaces. Satisfying user needs and expectations in a multivendor world means providing multiple user interfaces. Needless to say, designing, implementing, testing, supporting, and maintaining multiple user interfaces is more work than dealing with one user interface. The requisite labor and design problems increase exponentially.

In addition to the sheer number of interfaces to be designed, implemented, and maintained, and the complications that arise from practical considerations like resources and schedules, each component in the distributed architecture has implications for interface design and functionality. For example, each component generates error messages. The messages are typically written by different programmers using different technical vocabularies. The language is typically foreign to users, and the information provided is typically insufficient for them to know how to resolve the problem. In Figure 4, for example, the client, the retrieval server, the reference server, the retrieval protocol (Z39.50), and the parsers that translate user syntax into Z39.50 syntax into Newton syntax and back again may generate error messages. A good interface will trap all of the messages coming from the different architectural components and convert them into something more helpful for users. To this end, the University Libraries conducted a study of error messages in May 1991. The result was a user-friendly LIS vocabulary and a model for error messages: one sentence explaining the problem, followed by a blank line, followed by one sentence explaining how to solve the problem. The vocabulary has been implemented in both Motif and VT100 LIS, but to date only Motif LIS error messages follow the model. VT100 LIS currently provides only one line for error messages. Longer messages will require redrawing the screen and may introduce performance problems.

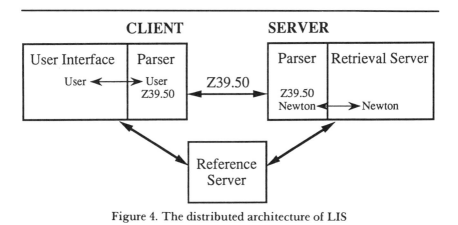

Figure 4. The distributed architecture of LIS

Clifford A. Lynch (1991) explains that the separation of user interfaces from the underlying retrieval application introduces certain problems. The success of distributed retrieval hinges on a retrieval protocol standard between clients and servers. The hope is that Z39.50 will become robust enough to sustain retrieval from multiple information stores. Currently, however, clients need to know certain information about servers that Z39.50 does not address.

For example, Z39.50 assumes that clients already know the names and addresses of the servers; the "explain" service in Z39.50 version 3 will provide information about databases on known servers. If clients do not know the names and addresses of servers, Z39.50 cannot help them. Similarly, servers may have information that users want, but Z39.50 version 2 has no way to communicate it to the client. For example, a server may know how records are sorted or ranked or why a search retrieved large or zero results, but Z39.50 version 2 has no way to communicate this information to the client.

Carnegie Mellon is developing a reference server to handle information not covered by Z39.50. In communication with a client, the reference server will dynamically pass database names, addresses, record formats (e.g., MARC, ASCII), search attributes (e.g., relational predicates and defined fields), display formats (i.e., what fields or data element set names), and error and diagnostic message formats. In communication with a retrieval server, the reference server will dynamically pass access control information (i.e., the list of databases that the user is allowed to see). The reference server is being tested now for release in LIS in December 1993.

Even when different components of the distributed architecture have similar ideologies, there may be problems because the ideologies conflict with user needs and expectations. For example, early versions of Z39.50 supported only the presentation of a single (overall) result set for a query, no intermediate results. This made it impossible for Z39.50 compliant applications to indicate which term(s) in a query retrieved zero records and thus caused the entire query to fail. Similarly, the Newton retrieval software creates a single result set for a query. It does not enable users to search across databases and retrieve and manipulate (e.g., sort) one result set; Newton creates a result set for each database, and each result set must be manipulated separately.

LESSON 3
Be Smart: User Interface Design Specifications
Save Time and Aggravation

Prepare detailed user interface design specifications based on research and peer review. Make sure that the specs take into consideration human factors as well as budget, scheduling, personnel, and technological factors. Implement the specs.

Who should be involved in interface design, and how does development proceed from design to implementation? Tufte (1992) argues that user interfaces should be designed by a single guiding intelligence because of the danger of distracting interactions among elements designed by different people: "User interface design decisions cannot be made one-at-a-time. Local optimization of design will never yield satisfactory global outcomes; perfecting many little separate pieces and then putting them all together will produce cluttered and fussy screens" (p. 16). Tognazzini (1992) seems to disagree: "The most successful designs result from a team approach where people with differing backgrounds and strengths are equally empowered to affect the final design" (p. 57). Experience in the University Libraries indicates that both men are right—that the design process requires both the participation of people with different insights and priorities and the expertise and commitment of one person whose task is to incorporate these insights and priorities into an interface that meets user needs and expectations without introducing distracting interactions.

According to Tognazzini (1992), the design model should reflect the user's needs and expectations, not the limitations of the hardware, the toolkit, or the programmer. This is the ideal. However, in Carnegie Mellon's experience, interface design is inseparable from the budget, schedule, personnel, and technology available for the project.

In the beginning, LIS programmers worked without documented user interface design specifications. Detailed design discussions were held. Some decisions were made. Some decisions were avoided. Then programmers went back to their offices and generated code. Over the years, significant problems arose from misinterpretations of needed features and functionality, from unforeseen design issues that were not discussed by the group but handled in isolation by different programmers, and from inconsistencies and incompatibilities in code written by different programmers. The current procedure in the University Libraries is to involve many people in design discussions and research, but to have one person design and document a unified vision of the interface.

In the two major design projects undertaken in 1992, the Research Manager for Library Automation (the author of this paper) conducted the research, participated in the discussions, and documented the design in great detail. I worked closely with the programmers and project leaders to understand the nuances and implications of each design element and the context in which we worked. I submitted a comprehensive draft of the user interface specifications for peer review and discussion. In keeping with Tufte's (1989) directive—"Specifications should be given by example, by detailed illustration, not by words alone"—the drafts included pictures of every window, menu, dialog box, and information display. Provisions were made for providing error messages and online help at a later date. Comments were gathered and used to revise the specifications. The final specifications were submitted to the project leaders and distributed to the programmers for implementation. The initial design and specification process took approximately six months for the basic Macintosh LIS interface and the new Motif LIS interface for document delivery in page image format. (The prototype image user interface was produced without design specifications.) Now if programmers encounter a problem or situation not addressed in the design specs, they are required to discuss it with the group rather than implement their vision in isolation.

It is not enough to document design specifications. Programmers must implement the specs. This is easier said than done (see lesson 5).

LESSON 4
Be Flexible: User Interfaces Need to be Tested and Revised

Test to save time. Time is money. Test to increase quality. Quality is defined by the user, not the developer. Test every component of the interface. Test multiple times using multiple methods. Test multiple groups of real users. Then revise accordingly—within reason and resources.

The goal of software development is to get the best quality for the lowest cost. The fact of the matter is that user perceptions can only be discovered by testing. "Guessing does no good" (Tognazzini, 1992, p. 37). Quality software is the product of testing and revision. Contrary to popular belief, testing can be cheap and easy to do. "It can even save you money—lots of it" (Tognazzini, 1992, p. 79). Jakob Nielsen's (1989) research on cost-effective usability testing determined that the cost could be reduced by 50% if mirrors, video cameras, and research assistants were eliminated. Testing often reveals serious problems where no problems were expected, and no problems where fatal flaws were expected.

Development groups should understand the trade-offs they are making when they decide on a research method. Research by Karat, Campbell, and Fiegel (1992) indicates that empirical testing is more cost-effective than cognitive walkthroughs regardless of the application being tested. Empirical tests require the same or less time to identify problems as individual and team walkthroughs, though they require more time to prepare materials, administer sessions, and analyze the data. Empirical tests identify a larger number of problems than walkthroughs and a significant number of severe problems overlooked by walkthroughs. Team walkthroughs are more productive than individual walkthroughs. Karat, Campbell, and Fiegel (1992) recommend the use of walkthroughs early in a project or when resources are severely limited, but encourage the use of empirical tests at key points in the development cycle "where coverage of the interface and identification of all significant problems is essential" (p. 403).

Tognazzini (1992) recommends beginning a project with field analysis of the audience and scenarios of use. Who are the users? How do they differ from one another? What kind of experience do they have? What are their goals? What tasks do they need to perform? What sources and features do they need? What information will they (want to) retrieve or generate? After a design is implemented, use "think aloud" protocols and intuitive observation to discover where users get frustrated because their needs and expectations are not met.

Carnegie Mellon University Libraries conduct feasibility and usability tests before and after designing and implementing an interface. Focus groups or surveys are carefully conducted to determine what people want and expect in information retrieval before design meetings are held or specifications are documented. Development team members contribute to the design of the interfaces and the test instruments by sharing their insights, priorities, and concerns at formal meetings and informal gatherings (e.g., in the staff lounge over coffee or pizza). After a design is implemented, every component of the user interface is tested—both the data container (e.g., the buttons, menus, and prompts) and the data or information presented within that container (e.g., the list of result sets, the list of titles retrieved, the bibliographic records, and full-text documents). Multiple research methods are used, including paper designs, prototypes, surveys, protocol analysis, and intuitive observation. Approximately four to six formal studies are done each year, along with several informal studies. A formal study typically takes a couple of months to design the test instruments, run the subjects, analyze the data, and prepare the report.

Each LIS interface is tested multiple times before it is released to campus. Typically two sets of protocols are run. The first set identifies serious problems and leads to a new design. A month or so later, when the new design is implemented, a second set of protocols identifies lesser problems and leads to minor changes (e.g., vocabulary). Then the software is released to campus. Usage monitoring of the released software will eventually lead to changes in the interface. Efforts are currently underway to build usage models from the transaction logs and design a process for using the models to guide development of the interfaces.

Tests are always conducted with multiple groups of real users, for example, librarians, faculty, graduate students, and undergraduate students. A minimum of six subjects are tested from each group. Depending on the study, subjects may self-select or be randomly chosen. Development team members sometimes participate in the testing process as research subjects.

After testing, then what? According to Karat, Campbell, and Fiegel (1992), "The identification of usability problems is not an end in itself. Rather, it is a means towards eliminating problems and improving the interface" (p. 403). The goal is to revise and improve the interface based on the research results. However, caution is in order: changes to the interface should be disciplined and relatively infrequent. Users need consistency and stability. They do not need interfaces that appear to change randomly. According to Tognazzini (1992), "If it ain't broke real bad, don't fix it" (p. 153).

Carnegie Mellon University Libraries' revision process—like the design process—evolved over time. In the beginning, when development proceeded without design specifications, research was conducted and changes were made in a closely coupled yet undisciplined cycle. Programmers changed the user interfaces in reaction to empirical research results that matched their experience or in reaction to indignant user comments posted on electronic bulletin boards or overheard on the stairs. The result was clutter, inconsistency, confused users, and bewildered management—not to mention a frustrated researcher. Concerted efforts were made in 1992 to integrate the revision process with the research and design process. Changes are more holistic, now, in that they are approached conceptually and contextually—in terms of the budget, schedule, personnel, and technology—rather than helter-skelter.

A relatively new approach is to devote considerable time and planning to the presentation of research results. Experience indicated that the significance of the research results was often overlooked because the results were presented quickly at the end of a meeting that had already run overtime, and to an audience that was not necessarily interested in the results. The new method carefully selects the time, place, and audience. For example, initial usage models were presented to the Library Professional Council rather than to the development team. The presentation lasted almost an hour. Empirical data and anecdotes will be included in future presentations along with carefully designed text and graphics. The goal is to engage everyone in the audience, to move them to understand and appreciate the problems that users encounter, and to invite their participation in interpreting the data and solving the problems.

LESSON 5
Beware: Politics and Egos Can Disrupt User Interface Design

Researchers can be zealots. Programmers can be mules. Managers can be bigots. Nobody's perfect. Love one another and what you do or get out of the business.

A development team is a group of people with different strengths and weaknesses who are more or less dedicated to the same goals. Working closely together to solve difficult problems in an environment constricted by limited resources inevitably creates tensions and trade-offs. The sense of camaraderie among the group affects the quality of life in the workplace and the quality of the work. Everyone on the team has the potential to facilitate or disrupt the development process.

Experience at Carnegie Mellon indicates that development team members are likely to exhibit certain shortcomings that can be overcome by good communication. For example, researchers and user advocates can be zealots lacking in diplomacy. They need to be made aware of the "big picture" of the development project, given a "reality check" of constraints in addition to human factors that affect the design and implementation of the software. Researchers seem to be more easily swayed by empirical data than anecdotal evidence, so concrete information about budgets, personnel, schedules, etc., will help them make informed (realistic) design decisions and specifications. Programmers tend to read programming manuals, not style guides. They can be stubborn and reticent. They need to be drawn into design discussions to explain how the technology (e.g., the programming toolkit) shapes the design, and to learn how human factors (e.g., the resolution of the human eye) affect usability and customer satisfaction. Programmers seem to be more easily swayed by anecdotal evidence and direct confrontations with users than by empirical data. Managers can be temporarily motivated by budget concerns or inflexible deadlines or power struggles among the group. They need to adjudicate conflicting needs and priorities based on a thorough understanding of all facets and forces in the project, which means that team members must bring their expertise and concerns to the table.

Management must somehow orchestrate communication among members of the development group in such a way that requisite information is shared, informed decisions are rendered, and slow-and-steady progress is made toward the goal. In the University Libraries, team members communicate in person and by using electronic mail and bulletin boards. Constant and open communication is encouraged by the peripatetic management style of the project leaders. Regular meetings are held and everyone is invited to voice their issues, concerns, priorities, and constraints. There is no excuse for not being heard or taken into consideration. In addition to constantly encouraging dialogue among team members, management also works to create an atmosphere of caring and good will. For example, pizza delivery, coffee and donuts, jokes, and Library

Automation sweatshirts are standard practice for the development team. The most recent sweatshirt says: "Library Automation on patrol. Trust us. We're professionals."

The solution to the problems of politics and egos is to love what you do and to love the people with whom and for whom you do it. This researcher prays for charity—to be charitable to users and colleagues. I reiterate, with Andrew Carnegie: "My heart is in the work." I recommend reading the book *Love and Profit* by James A. Autry (1991). "Research and development" really means "negotiate and compromise." It means "grow and learn." It leads to a Zen experience wherein you know that the team has done good work, that users have some of what they need, and that you can do better—given the time and resources. I hope to contribute to the design of digital experiences that express the full plenitude of human beings, not the agenda of a privileged few. And I hope to do this in such a way that my colleagues appreciate and enjoy my presence on the team.

REFERENCES

Autry, J. A. (1991). *Love and profit: The art of caring leadership.* New York: Morrow.

Egan, D. E.; Remde, J. R.; Gomez, L. M.; Landauer, T. K.; Eberhardt, J.; & Lochbaum, C. C. (1989). Formative design-evaluation of SuperBook. *ACM Transactions on Information Systems, 7*(1), 30-57.

Egan, D. E.; Remde, J. R.; Landauer, T. K.; Lochbaum, C. C.; & Gomez, L. M. (1989, May). Behavioral evaluation and analysis of a hypertext browser [Special issue]. *SIGCHI Bulletin,* pp. 205-210.

Hansen, W. J., & Haas, C. (1988). Reading and writing with computers: A framework for explaining differences in performance. *Communications of the ACM, 31*(9), 1080-1089.

Heim, M. (1987). *Electric language: A philosophical study of word processing.* New Haven: Yale University Press.

Karat, C. M.; Campbell, R.; & Fiegel, T. (1992). Comparison of empirical testing and walkthrough methods in user interface evaluation. In P. Bauersfeld, J. Bennett, & G. Lynch (Eds.), *Striking a balance: CHI '92 conference proceedings* (ACM Conference on Human Factors in Computing Systems, 3-7 May 1992) (pp. 397-404). Monterey, CA: Association for Computing Machinery; Reading, MA: Addison-Wesley.

Lynch, C. A. (1991). The client-server model in information retrieval. In M. Dillon (Ed.), *Interfaces for information retrieval and online systems: The state of the art* (pp. 301-318). New York: Greenwood Press.

McLuhan, M. (1962). *The Gutenberg galaxy: The making of typographic man.* Toronto: University of Toronto Press.

Myers, B. A., & Rosson, M. B. (1992). Survey on user interface programming. In P. Bauersfeld, J. Bennett, & G. Lynch (Eds.), *Striking a balance: CHI '92 conference proceedings* (ACM Conference on Human Factors in Computing Systems, 3-7 May 1992) (pp. 195-202). Monterey, CA: Association for Computing Machinery; Reading, MA: Addison-Wesley.

Nielsen, J. (1989). Usability engineering at a discount. In G. Salvendy & M. J. Smith (Eds.), *Designing and using human computer interfaces and knowledge-based systems* (pp. 394-401). Amsterdam: Elsevier.

Ong, W. J. (1982). *Orality and literacy: The technologizing of the word.* London: Methuen.

Tognazzini, B. (1992). *Tog on interface.* Reading, MA: Addison-Wesley.

Tufte, E. R. (1983). *The visual display of quantitative information.* Cheshire, CT: Graphics Press.

Tufte, E. R. (1989). *Visual design of the user interface.* Armonk, NY: IBM.
Tufte, E. R. (1990). *Envisioning information.* Cheshire, CT: Graphics Press.
Tufte, E. R. (1992). The user interface: The point of competition. *Bulletin of the American Society for Information Science, 18*(5), 15-17.

CLIFFORD A. LYNCH

Director, Library Automation
Office of the President
University of California
Oakland, California

The Roles of Libraries in Access to Networked Information: Cautionary Tales from the Era of Broadcasting*

THE DEVELOPMENT OF THE NREN: THE SEARCH FOR HISTORICAL PRECEDENT

The development of the Internet and the implementation of the National Research and Education Network (NREN) program are massive, intellectually inspiring enterprises. They represent a great adventure into a largely uncharted future. And, as we look beyond the NREN towards the National Information Infrastructure (NII) program now under discussion at the federal government level, we face the challenges, the promises, and the threats of networked communication and information access that is now reaching beyond the research and education communities to the broader population of the United States. Indeed, as we increasingly recognize that the Internet is a global rather than a national effort, we must consider the worldwide impact of these technologies. We have opportunities to create new industries and to change how we do business as a nation, how we educate children, and how we inform our citizenry.

In the absence of other guidance, it is natural to seek analogies with past technology shifts of an equally massive nature. The lessons of history can, we hope, guide our policy and planning and offer models and experiences that can inform our debates and our decisions.

I have several problems with the current search for analogies in the past. First, those seeking parallels almost always characterize the Internet and its future progeny as infrastructure. While there is an element of truth in this—certainly the Internet is an enabling infrastructure for communication and the formation of communities, for teaching and learning, for access to information,

---

*This paper is loosely based on a talk given at the Clinic. After the humbling experience of reading the transcript of the actual presentation at the meeting so kindly obtained by Ann Bishop, the order of topics has been substantially revised, and parts of the talk have been expanded, while other topics already well-covered in the literature have been largely omitted. At the same time, I have endeavored to retain the informal style of a talk.

and for the conduct of commerce—I believe that this is a limiting view. The infrastructure perspective suggests parallels with the development of railroads, highways, the power grid, and the telephone system. True, the development of these infrastructures enabled massive social and cultural changes. But most of the changes happened *outside* of the infrastructure in social, commercial, political, and other realms. I don't know how to say this more clearly.

The viewpoint I want to present here is that the Internet forms a new medium for communication and the distribution of information. It is a new carrier of *content* in a way that highways, railroads, and power grids never carried content, and in which traditional person-to-person telephony has never, by its nature, been able to support directly the distribution of content. (Ironically, some of the early telephony pioneers did believe that the telephone would be a form of mass media, where people would use party lines to get news and entertainment. Obviously, with a few exceptions like the time and weather numbers and the developments in 900 number services over the past decade, this didn't develop.) None of the infrastructure systems discussed as possible models for the Internet served as actual carriers for media content. But I believe that there is a truly interesting parallel that can be drawn between the Internet and the development of radio and television as broadcast media earlier in this century. While these media brought along an infrastructure of radio and television receivers and broadcasting stations, the really central issues had to do with the development and control of content carried by the media and not the deployment and management of the infrastructure. Similarly, I think that it is useful to focus on networked information as *part* of the content of the new networked medium, as distinct from the network as simply infrastructure. What makes the distinction between medium and infrastructure particularly complex in the networked environment is that the Internet mixes media (information distribution channels) and communications in a novel way, giving rise to hybrid forms such as interactive media. It's difficult, and probably misleading, to try to separate the media elements from the interactive communications elements.

I can't possibly explore the full implications of this parallel here. The development of the mass broadcast media, and issues such as the role of government regulation and the private sector in this development, are enormously complex and have merited extensive study already. I recommend particularly the book *Technologies of Freedom* and other works of the late Ithiel de Sola Pool (1983) as a broad look at some of these issues.

One of the concerns of this meeting is the changing roles of libraries in the networked information environment. Recast in the context we are discussing, we might restate this as the role of libraries in managing and providing access to the content of the new medium represented by the Internet and the new world of networked information. I want to focus on the relationship of libraries to content in this new medium, but I do want to view this question broadly, in the context of public libraries as well as academic research libraries. I believe that in discussing library roles in the networked information environment, we are often too parochial in our almost exclusive focus on academic research libraries. Given that the Internet was initially created to serve the academic and research communities, it is natural that this group of libraries would be the first to explore the question of library roles and services in a networked environment, and natural that they would be a primary focus of our interest. Thus, our thinking and experience is most mature in the research library context. To my mind, the issues are simplest for research libraries (although this view may simply reflect how immature my thinking is outside of the research community). Research libraries are relatively well-funded; they serve fairly well-defined user communities; and they have fairly well-defined missions. Perhaps most importantly, they have a close mission connection with the research and education communities that are today embracing information technology, networking, and networked information on a large scale. Indeed, aggressive adoption of these technologies is part of the strategic plan for most of the organizations that support research libraries. But few of these factors are valid for a typical public library. As we look beyond the NREN towards the proposed NII, we must include the realities of the public and the public libraries.

One of our collective obsessions in our examination of historical analogs to the Internet is the allocation of operating (access) costs and the support of investment in infrastructure. In the broadcast media, the infrastructure investment was almost entirely private. (Except that in some philosophical sense the government did enable and subsidize the development of this infrastructure by making available and licensing parts of the electromagnetic spectrum—a public resource—for broadcasting; and it did set up the Federal Communications Commission (FCC) to manage use of this resource. Today, the proposals to auction spectrum are making this public sector investment more tangible.)

You may not like the results—the "vast wasteland" as former FCC commissioner Newton Minnow has characterized it—but the fact remains that few public funds were invested in developing this broadcast infrastructure. Corporations and the consumers paid for the infrastructure. Consumers invested in infrastructure—purchasing TVs and radios—because they wanted access to the content of the new media. Who created this content? To some extent, corporations that wanted the public to invest in infrastructure created the content. In many cases, the same corporations sold receivers and ran networks, particularly in the early days. But other forces played a role as well. Interestingly, advertisers played, and continue to play, a pivotal role in making the content of the broadcast media (and indeed, even the mass market print media) available to the public on acceptable financial (access cost) terms. I believe that advertisers or, to use a broader, yet more accurate term, "sponsors," may play an unexpectedly large role in enabling the networked information environment for the general public.

Libraries exploring and evaluating possible roles in this new environment can draw insight from the history of the relationship between sponsors and advertising agencies on one side and broadcasters (media operators) on the other. Within the context of the networked environment as a *medium*, I will stress the potential role of content sponsors. I believe that in the new networked environment we will see bizarre organizational role shifts. As existing organizations try to survive and to define viable new roles in this environment, some libraries will assume some of the characteristics of broadcasters and commercial service providers; at the same time, new commercial or quasi-commercial interests will compete intensely with traditional libraries for patrons.

DILEMMAS FACING LIBRARIES IN AN
ELECTRONIC INFORMATION ENVIRONMENT

Let us assume that users will finance their connections to the developing networked environment: they will purchase the necessary computers and network connections, most probably at a flat monthly rate under the Internet model. Current experience supports this assumption. And the parallels here to services such as cable television are interesting: one invests in equipment (a television, a radio receiver) and obtains content for free or perhaps at a rather nominal monthly charge (for cable connection or premium services such as HBO). All evidence suggests that most users do not want to pay for information transactionally, or they don't want to pay much (i.e., they will pay for small amounts transactionally, "pay-per-view," or by subscription for a newspaper or popular magazine; but they will not pay $1,000 a year for a journal subscription or $200 an hour to search online databases).

So what is the information content that these new network citizens will enjoy? What is the library's role in providing this content? One attractive and comforting (but, unfortunately, probably totally wrong) picture of the future has libraries continuing to act as purchasing collectives which acquire riches of the new era (scholarly, electronic information; new electronic resources for education and reference; and information in captivating, vivid new multimedia formats) and make them freely available to the public. Looking to the current Internet and the roles that libraries are assuming in this environment will show just how unlikely this picture of the future is. Consider these barriers (which will be examined in more detail):

- As major publishers go electronic, the electronic information is usually priced higher than the original print information—sometimes by one to two orders of magnitude. The new multimedia information resources that we anticipate will be enabled by the networked environment are enormously costly to produce. Their economics are akin to producing feature films or television shows. Most libraries simply cannot afford to acquire much of this material.
- Because of the changing legal framework for acquisition of electronic materials, libraries that can afford to purchase such materials often cannot share them with other libraries. Each library's collection is increasingly limited to what it can afford to purchase directly.
- As a matter of principle, most libraries remain unwilling to pass even part of the charges for use of electronic materials directly to patrons, and most patrons are probably unwilling to pay very much, at least outside of corporate special library settings.

On the Internet, there are strong cultural biases against paying for information, and their roots are complex. There has always been information on the network that has been restricted to specific user communities; but until recently the Acceptable Use Policies (AUPs) that governed much of the Internet and its predecessor networks largely forbade general fee-based information.

Most network users don't view themselves as paying for use of the network; their costs are absorbed in overhead of the institution in which they work. If access is free, information should also be free. And because there was no fee-based information on the network until recently, network users never needed to consider whether they might be willing to pay for information of value—in terms of timeliness, accuracy, or distillation—rather than simply sifting through masses of free information of questionable quality.

These biases convinced people to use primarily "public" information that has been made available by libraries, universities, and government agencies, or has simply been placed on the network for general access by individuals (for example, archives of free or shareware computer software). New types of information are appearing, such as Michael Hart's Project Gutenberg, an initiative which is providing electronic access to old, out-of-copyright information. The quality and utility of such information will be covered later in this discussion; but it should be noted that this is a heavily used class of information on the Internet. Many publishers do not regard the network as an attractive vehicle for marketing access to their high-value information because they fear that the perception of the quality of their information will be degraded. And many well-established publishers (in the broadest sense of content providers) are doing well enough financially with their existing marketing channels that they have little incentive to venture into new, untested marketplaces that don't promise large profits but do threaten these providers with a loss of control over distribution channels. (We should recognize that as a group, large, well-established content providers are generally rather conservative; their economic basis affords them that philosophy. Consider, for example, the very negative reaction from major music rights holders to the recent proposal by the IBM/Blockbuster Video consortium for digital distribution of musical material with creation of audio CDs on demand at point of sale.)

Libraries have done quite well as purchasing collectives and access providers to printed information. Operating under the copyright law and the doctrine of first sale, they have built a national and international interlibrary loan system that allows a patron at any library extraordinary access to the print literature. They have pushed the copyright envelope by delivering copies of journal articles through this system, to the growing discomfort of publishers, and now are even using new technologies such as facsimile and Ariel (network fax) to expedite delivery of copies of this material to patrons. But libraries have largely abdicated any meaningful role in providing access to existing broadcast electronic media, even though broadcast media content often has a much higher general public impact than print publications.

The evolution to electronic information foretells the demise of the interlibrary loan system. Information providers are not selling electronic information to libraries; they are licensing it. And licenses permit the library to make the information available only to specific, limited user communities, for specific purposes and in specific ways, for limited periods of time. Provision for use of electronic materials via interlibrary loan, for example, does not appear in a typical license agreement.

I believe that content providers view the transition to electronic information as an opportunity to restructure their relationships with libraries. Now they are even attempting to apply the license model to printed materials and traditional audiovisual materials, not just to electronic materials. Some information providers are unwilling to sell (or sometimes even license under any type of acceptable terms) materials of all types to libraries. Outside of the scholarly publishing marketplace, where libraries pay almost all the bills, and sales to individuals are a relatively small, secondary marketplace (even with highly discounted individual rates for journals subscriptions), information providers apparently do not regard libraries as an important marketplace and would prefer to deal exclusively with the end-user marketplace. There are different values underlying this market: in the scholarly publishing marketplace, there is general acceptance of the belief that long-term access to the scholarly record must be ensured. This has been a traditional responsibility of the library community, and one that the publishers acknowledge. In more consumer-oriented information markets, archiving is not generally acknowledged as an issue.

Outside of the academic and research communities, most libraries have little to offer to the networked environment except for information that is made available for them to redistribute without restriction. Such information might come from government agencies. Much of it, however, is likely to come from new sources—sponsors. In this context, where libraries are heavily involved in redistributing and providing access to information that is either free or rather inexpensive because it is sponsored/subsidized, how does the library add value through its involvement in the information distribution cycle? Partly by facilitating access and helping users find what they want, and partly by providing the access technology itself for use by patrons who cannot afford their own. But, as information technology and network access become increasingly ubiquitous, I believe that this will be a question that will continue to haunt many libraries: how many libraries today justify their existence in part by offering access to TV and radio broadcasting to their patrons?

Within the academic environment, one can speculate about brave scenarios where universities take back control of the information and knowledge that their communities create and make it widely available (although I do not believe that this will happen, generally). In such situations, it is likely that parent institutions would assign the responsibilities for managing and accessing these knowledge bases to their libraries, thus providing these libraries with an inventory of valuable electronic content. But public libraries are not part of organizations or communities that create much information, other than public information at a local, state, regional, and federal level. So local information (which will be relatively unique) will be of primarily local interest, and government information at the federal level will be offered by a wide range of providers across the network and thus will not represent a very unique offering by any local library. This is not to say that libraries of all types will not have a public presence on the networks. If nothing else, they will continue to make their online catalogs of their print holdings available, and public libraries will move into community information, service bulletin boards, and databases. Perhaps libraries of all types will serve as mediators and facilitators for various electronic communication and conferencing vehicles for their communities. But this is not the same as providing access to large amounts of electronic information.

FREE, PUBLIC, AND SPONSORED INFORMATION

Whenever information is offered for free (or, indeed, even for what seems to be an unrealistically low cost), it is reasonable to ask: Why? Where did it come from? Who is offering it?

Sometimes the answers are fairly simple: government agencies are required by law to make certain public information available to the public for free or at low cost, or they may choose to make such information available as part of their basic agency mission. (There is a major public policy debate currently taking place at the federal and the state levels about what government information really should be made available, to whom, and at what cost. This debate is important to libraries and to the population at large in the networked information age.) An academic may distribute free reprints of a paper simply to get the ideas out to a wider audience. Corporate or nonprofit institutions (e.g., political parties, major corporations, ecological groups, and educational institutions) may share their institutional views with the public, either by directly preparing and distributing material or via advertising or sponsored programs. Such free information often, and naturally, represents the distributor's point of view. If we agree with it, we usually call it a public service; if we don't, we label it propaganda or crank material. Basically, sponsorship for the distribution of the material usually comes from the authoring institution (the information provider). There is already a lot of this on the network: product literature, technical notes, position papers, and the like. The scope of topics that will be addressed by this class of information will be defined by the interests of the sponsoring institution. Certainly, it won't address the full range of people's interests.

There is a new, ambiguous class of "free" information appearing on the Internet. This is information that is offered by various individuals and groups for the general good or general interest, often as resource information. Sometimes it's inaccurate. Sometimes it becomes obsolete. Sometimes it represents an individual's not necessarily well-considered or well-expressed thoughts, intended to provoke discussion and reaction. Sometimes it's excerpts from another source taken out of context or even inaccurately quoted. This information is often published without a commitment of responsibility; often it is made available as a one-time (perhaps honestly altruistic) action, with little or no commitment to ensure its validity or to keep it current. In the current economy of free information on the networks, these are important resources, but they must be viewed with constant awareness and caution.

A different source of funding for free or inexpensive information exists in the traditional mass media environments (newspapers and popular magazines and radio and television broadcasting): sponsorship. In the print media, consumers usually pay some fraction of the costs while advertisers subsidize the rest. Newspapers would cost several dollars an issue if they did not accept advertising. Some free print publications are entirely advertiser supported. The general public may be generally unaware of the amount of price subsidy in print media that is provided by advertising and the subsequent influence that advertisers may exert on their editorial contents.

We usually don't pay for radio or television broadcasts, which are totally supported by sponsors. In broadcast media, models of fee-based access to content came very late, which was not, in my view, entirely because of a lack of enabling technology. Content is so much more costly to create in the broadcast environment than in the print world that relationships become much more complex.

The history of the relationships between sponsors, advertising agencies, and the networks during the development of radio and television is interesting. Readers wishing more information might enjoy *The Mirror Makers: A History* of *American Advertising and Its Creators* by Stephen Fox (1984). In the early days, most shows had a single sponsor, and many of them were developed by the advertising agencies on behalf of the sponsor; the broadcasters simply sold airtime without control of content. A considerable battle ensued which led to a new model in which the broadcasters developed programs and then marketed them to the sponsors and their agencies, allowing them to purchase advertising time. Even after the broadcast operators gained control of content creation, many shows had sole sponsors. Thus, while initially sponsors (or the advertising agencies working for them) created the content, and thus shaped it completely after the transition, they continued to have a great deal of control over the content by virtue of being the "buyer" of the program. Obviously, as multiple sponsorship became the norm and broadcasters became more sophisticated about designing content to reach various types of audiences, the influence of sponsors on direct content waned. But it is still real.

Unlike the radio and television broadcast channels, computer networks can support a basically infinite amount of programming. One wonders, as more sponsored material appears, if we will see independent producers and broadcasters develop content which is then sold to sponsors. Carl Malamud's Internet Talk Radio project is one of the few examples we have today of sponsored content on the Internet, though "sponsorship" here conforms more to the public television model of underwriters than to the model of purchasers of advertising time as part of the talk radio programming. Certainly, Malamud's model is one of content production independent of sponsors. Or will sponsors themselves return to the old model of creating content primarily as a vehicle for advertising products? Advertising might be directly embedded in the programming, as was done with some of the early radio shows ("The Chesterfield Hour" characters made dozens of specific references to Chesterfield cigarettes!), or might be more indirect, in what we now view as more traditional advertising messages surrounding content that does not contain explicit advertising.

The influence of sponsors and advertising agencies on the content of mass media has been of great concern for decades and has been studied in depth by a number of authors. One excellent study is *The Media Monopoly* by Ben Bagdikian (1990). There are many aspects to this problem, including:

- Inability to get controversial materials sponsored and thus made available to the public. Many sponsors prefer to avoid controversial shows. Offsetting this concern, of course, is the fact that controversy often attracts interest, and controversial shows may be a way to reach a large audience.
- Direct meddling in content. A show may give a bad review of a product from a vendor who is a sponsor, who then discontinues its advertising, and thereby program support. News coverage of lawsuits against advertisers may be strongly discouraged. The move away from sole sponsorship, however, has limited the impact of such a withdrawal of support. But the recent formation of huge conglomerates with massive advertising budgets has led to new concerns in this area, as has the acquisition of broadcasters by those conglomerates.

- Indirect shaping of content coverage. This is a more subtle issue. A newspaper that relies primarily on local stores for advertising may not run a series explaining why mail order is a more cost-effective way to purchase products.

There is a final question that merits attention in the discussion of sponsorship of mass media: Exactly what is being sponsored? In the print context, an advertiser pays for inclusion of advertising content with a print publication such as a newspaper. The revenue from the advertising allows the publisher to sell the newspaper at a low cost. A library can purchase the periodical at the subsidized cost and make it available to library patrons or even to other libraries through interlibrary loan.

In the broadcast environment, the issues are more complex. Essentially, the advertiser is purchasing airtime scheduled in a specific relationship to specific programs, which economically enables the network to broadcast the programs. But the programs can also be rebroadcast with other advertising. Often, today, purchasers of advertising airtime are really interested in the viewer demographics of the airtime they are buying, rather than the content of the sponsored programs, subject only to the caveat that the content not offend their customers. If anything, the advertisers can be viewed as subsidizing a performance of the content, rather than the publication of that content in the way that a library might capture and subsequently make available a program to its user community. Ironically, libraries probably cannot legally capture the performance of the advertising itself and make it available to patrons as part of the overall cultural record without specific permission. In this sense, sponsorship of material distributed over the Internet may offer sponsors many more options—a continuum between a print-like publication model and a performance subsidy that is similar to broadcast advertising practice. By sponsoring material that is placed in libraries under license, a sponsor might be able to gain the analog of airtime for an unlimited number of performances within the term of a license (for example, a year or two). One can imagine an entrepreneur creating products like "the consumer health information database" and signing up sponsors to subsidize its placement in public libraries in exchange for including advertising for their products.

ADVERTISING AND SPONSORSHIP IN A
NETWORKED INFORMATION ENVIRONMENT

Certainly, one can view the Internet as a media channel waiting to be filled with content, and with a "viewer" base that is hungry for such content. In this sense, it should be an attractive environment for sponsored content. But we cannot assume that the frameworks and practices that work in the print and broadcast mass media will succeed in the new networked information environment. The unlimited number of "channels" and the ability to narrowcast to individuals or small groups, the interactive nature of the media, and the ability of the medium to reach a national or international user base, thus allowing inexpensive aggregation of relatively large numbers of people with specialized interests for the benefit of service or information providers (or advertisers), will also alter the nature and economics of advertising and sponsorship.

If, for the moment, we equate sponsorship with advertising (and I will argue that sponsorship may come to have other, perhaps more substantive, benefits in a networked environment), then we must recognize that the usual purpose of advertising is to reach the maximum number of target viewers at minimum cost. Advertising is expensive and adds substantially to the costs of many products. In the network environment, it may be possible to link sponsorship much more closely to content that engages precisely defined target audiences. Mass media are just that—they reach the masses, and, unless one is advertising very broad-based consumer products (which is often simply image or name recognition rather than product information advertising), they are inefficient. Even broad-based consumer articles such as cars are inefficiently advertised through mass media. Most viewers buy cars only occasionally; most of the time they just ignore the advertising. How much more effective would it be if people interested in purchasing cars could simply subscribe to an electronic distribution list, receive material as long as they were interested, and then unsubscribe when they were no longer interested? This is but one argument suggesting that in the networked information environment there may be far fewer advertising dollars to support traditional broadcast-type media content, and that advertising price/performance for products may improve dramatically, at least in situations where advertising is trying to "inform" customers rather than just promote brand name recognition. *Future Shop: How New Technologies Will Change the Way We Shop and What We Buy* by Snider and Ziporyn (1992) offers a much more extensive exploration of these themes.

Advertisers will face other concerns in the networked environment. How easy will it be for a viewer to filter out advertising content? In broadcast media, this has always been inconvenient for the viewer, even when using a VCR and fastforwarding through advertisements in TV programs. If this could be simply accomplished by an automated filter, it seems likely that investing in traditional mass media advertising as part of networked information content would be unappealing to many advertisers. And, based on the experience of public television, it is unclear that simply receiving a recognition in the opening panel of a networked resource will sell many products.

A final issue is the increasing emphasis on the value inherent in the development of lists of interested purchasers of certain types of products. This is well understood in areas such as the mail-order catalog industry, and is increasingly being emphasized as retailers, particularly large chains, move into more precise point-of-sale technology. For example, bookstores may give you a modest discount if you join their book clubs; this simply means you fill out a form with some demographic information and receive a card with a member number. From that point, however, the store can build a detailed database of the books that you purchase, which is of sufficient value to them that they are willing to discount their prices. Similarly, grocery stores are now delighted to let you pay by credit card, and the credit card companies are also mining their databases of purchasing patterns in more sophisticated ways.

The networked environment seems to be an ideal context in which to extend this sort of point-of-sale compilation. It supports very narrow interest publications and distribution lists. One can easily offer free software or other information in exchange for demographic information or for the identities of those who want to participate in the free offer. An advertiser or sponsor might make information available just to build up these sorts of profiles of potential buyers for other products. Unlike the mass media, in the networked environment it's often easy to find out who is looking at your sponsored content or at your information. Here, perhaps, is a new justification for sponsorship: to acquire and possibly resell information about people's interests.

CONCLUSION: LIBRARIES AND THEIR COMPETITORS ON THE NETWORK

It should be clear from the above arguments that libraries that are not in a position to act as purchasing collectives for well-focused and well-funded user communities face a difficult time in the networked environment, at least in providing information in electronic form. We've identified a number of problems already:

- Breakdown of the interlibrary loan system as a way of providing access to electronic information,
- High costs of electronic information,
- Attempts to bypass libraries and market this information directly to consumers.

Some argument has been made that libraries may obtain certain types of sponsored content that they can make available to their user communities in electronic form. Yet their role as providers of access to this type of information will weaken as information technology and network access becomes more prevalent; it will be easier and easier for the developers and sponsors of this type of information to reach library patrons directly.

Libraries will also be uncomfortable with pressures to collect demographic information, and perhaps even individual user identities, as a condition of being able to make the information available. Of course, if they stand on principle and refuse, any number of commercial information suppliers will have no such reservations.

There is a final factor at work as we move into the networked environment. Networks dissolve geographic distance which has always been the strongest link between public libraries and their user communities. As we move into the networked environment, we may be moving into an age of increased specialization by information providers, including the libraries. The economics work: it is possible for anyone in the United States, and indeed in much of the world, interested in a specialized topic to use the network to reach some central organization that offers information on this topic. And this may set the stage for new organizations that compete with libraries by mixing access to information, services, and products, as well as to communications mechanisms, for specific communities of interest rather than geographically defined communities.

Consider collectors—of stamps, coins, antiques, or even model airplanes. A good public library may have a few reference books of interest to such a collector. An interested collector probably subscribes to one or two magazines or newspapers, as much to look at the advertising as to read the articles. Perhaps the local library subscribes to a few of these magazines. The collector may also attend meetings to chat with other collectors and to transact business with dealers. In the network environment, one could combine a buy/sell bulletin board, reference sources, various communications tools, online magazines, and everything else (except for face-to-face social and business interaction) that could be desired by even the most avid collector in a given area. In this situation, it is likely that the service operator would want to create significant electronic content and perhaps even partially subsidize access to it to attract collectors to other services. Advertisers would also want to subsidize content access to some extent, just as they subsidize magazines for collectors through their advertising today. It is difficult to see how a library could match the attraction of the combination of information access and services that these new electronic environments can offer, even if it were willing to invest in acquiring the electronic reference content for its user community. In areas where people are willing to spend money, specialist services on the network will quickly supplant the limited services offered by general-purpose libraries.

I do not want to suggest that libraries will go away. But general-purpose public libraries are, to my mind, severely threatened and constrained in scope by many aspects of the evolving networked information environment, particularly if they continue to avoid, as a matter of policy, fee-for-service offerings and refuse to act as brokers acquiring information for patrons at cost. They will continue to serve a number of roles: providing access to at least some electronic information, particularly for those who do not have the information technology, the access, or the skills to obtain and use this electronic information directly (a slowly but steadily diminishing group). They will still offer a place where an information seeker can obtain personal help from a specialist in locating, navigating, and obtaining information, to the extent that libraries can continue to offer these services. They will continue to be places that teach literacy and information-seeking skills. They will play an essential role in providing access to government and other free information, and perhaps to some information that is made publicly available through sponsored funding. And, of course, they will continue to provide access to their print collections, which will continue to grow.

But libraries may play a limited role in providing access to networked information outside of scholarly and scientific settings, where the libraries are still the sponsors to a great extent. This is perhaps the key lesson in the parallels with the history of the broadcast media, where libraries play an extremely limited role in making the content of these media accessible or in organizing and preserving their content. It is commercial sponsors, rather than libraries, that make this media content available to the public at a price the public is willing to pay, and that largely set the terms for what is available for viewing.

Consider the shifting models of information and the roles that libraries play in funding and providing access to information in its various forms. Libraries played a role in financing traditional book publishing: creating content was relatively cheap, and libraries purchased a fair amount of the product. They were able to make these books available to their patrons and could share them through interlibrary loan. This is the model that has been projected with scientific and scholarly information. Though the costs have gotten out of hand in recent years, this is still the model we follow. Here, libraries are actually the primary funders. Print mass media (a relatively recent development in the history of publishing) is mostly subsidized by advertisers and by readers. Libraries get involved mainly in its preservation as part of the cultural and historical record rather than by providing access to it when it's new (few people go to the library to read the daily newspaper). But, because the information was in print form, libraries could still acquire, house, and share it. Broadcast content has become very expensive. It is paid for mostly by advertisers. Libraries cannot afford to acquire it, in general, since it is "performed" under advertiser subsidy rather than sold. And under the legal regimes governing performance, the ability of libraries to capture and replay these performances is highly restricted. The goal of those paying for broadcast content is to reach consumers. They don't need the libraries' help. Indeed, they make the content "freely available" themselves. Libraries have been cut out of the loop as initial access providers, much as they have been with mass print media, but because of the different legal framework (and, frankly, because most libraries seem to be rather uncomfortable with broadcast media on a number of levels and certainly have not, generally, aggressively pursued a role for themselves), they have little to do with ensuring continued access to the content of broadcast media.

Electronic information is taking on strange new shapes; it is a mix of content, communications, and services. It is not clear to libraries what part of the new kind of information is properly part of their responsibility. And again, networked information comes under a legal and marketplace framework that does not facilitate a role for libraries in providing access to it. It is expensive to produce, and since libraries will not be the primary funders for the creation of much of this information, they are likely to play a small role in offering access to it, unless they can convince those who are financing its creation that they can add value by furthering the objectives of the financiers.

REFERENCES

Bagdikian, B. H. (1990). *The media monopoly*. Boston, MA: Beacon Press.
Fox, S. R. (1984). *The mirror makers: A history of American advertising and its creators*. New York: Morrow.
Pool, I. de S. (1983). *Technologies of freedom*. Cambridge, MA: Belknap Press.
Snider, J., & Ziporyn, T. D. (1992). *Future shop: How new technologies will change the way we shop and what we buy*. New York: St. Martin's Press.

PAMELA SANDLIAN

Children's Library Manager
Denver Public Library
Denver, Colorado

The Kid's Catalog Project: Customizing Networked Information

CHILDREN AND NETWORKED INFORMATION

Why customize networked information for children? After all, children are more computer literate than adults. While adults often refuse to touch a computer, children will walk right up to one, compelled to explore, play, and see what makes it tick. Unfortunately, information that children find through a variety of online catalogs and databases is often overwhelming, complicated, irrelevant to their needs, and presented in a complex display that is difficult to read. Sorting out this overwhelming display of text, complicated by myriad screens of directions and indecipherable help, library locations, codes, call numbers, and subject headings, is difficult for adults and overwhelming for children. Customers who are experienced enough to know what a call number is have difficulty locating material once they have deciphered the bibliographic record. While the goal of most customers is to identify an accurate source of information and then locate the material on the shelf, finding the item on the online catalog is often the most difficult part of the process.

Organizing this explosion of information is a Herculean task. Helping people decipher the information puzzle is complicated, time-consuming, and labor-intensive. The clues to solving the puzzle are often so complex that professional librarians, with years of experience, have difficulty locating information and answering reference questions. This task becomes more significant when we recognize the vital necessity that children become sophisticated information users in order to succeed in the 21st century. The traditional library tour with a review of the Dewey Decimal Classification system no longer suffices as a means for teaching children how to use the library. The networked information available in libraries, homes, and schools is not only technically difficult to acquire, but a dull source compared to other media. A generation of children who have grown up with sophisticated computer games complete with 32-bit color graphics, not to mention painless ease of access to information and recreation via the television, are not satisfied with the text-based online catalog. Creating customized information for children that incorporates appealing color and graphics sets up a successful relationship between the child, the library, and the computer. It acknowledges the importance of children's information needs while at the same time creating a package that excites them. Customizing networked information is a step towards helping children become sophisticated information users.

A beginning solution to this information conundrum is the Kid's Catalog. Developed by a team from the Denver Public Library and CARL (Colorado Alliance of Research Libraries) Systems, Inc., this Macintosh and PC software product interfaces with online library catalogs. This paper outlines the theoretical planning and research foundations of this library project.

FOCUS GROUPS

The project started with input gained from children in a series of five focus groups during the summer of 1990 at the Denver Public Library. Children and their parents told us they had difficulty understanding how to use the library. Children rarely asked for assistance from staff; in fact, they asked if we could make the librarians shorter (i.e., they would feel more at ease asking a peer for help). They wanted an environment that was friendlier, more accessible, more comfortable. The children asked that fiction be organized by subject, instead of by author. They wanted information in other formats besides books. The online catalog system, CARL, was difficult for children to decipher. They had difficulty spelling, typing fast enough to avoid the built-in time allotment limitations to searches, and formulating the right words to initiate a search. The successful searches indiscriminately provided hundreds of titles, both juvenile and adult, relevant and irrelevant. Once this display of materials was available, children had difficulty deciding which books held the most promise for their query. After a great deal of thought about children's information needs, it became apparent that the online catalog had to better reflect the information use and skill levels of children.

The results of these focus groups provided valuable information for the planning of the new Denver Public Library, scheduled to open in 1995. Every element of library service to children was examined in an effort to repackage the Children's Library. As the library staff and architects set out to design a library that would work better for children, the development of a children's catalog became a vital component of providing improved library service to children (Sandlian & Walters, 1991). With the technological advances available to us today, the online catalog showed potential for developments far beyond an "automated card catalog." The opportunity to add value to the online public access catalog (OPAC) by rethinking the display of information and the design of the screen was an intriguing challenge. The possibility for integrating graphics, sound, and video as part of the information displayed in the online catalog was limited only by production time, imagination, and cost. To not only assist children in their information searches but also to entice them to explore information became a goal of the Kid's Catalog. Producing an "expert system" to help children become independent users of the online catalog and the library took hold as a project for the Denver Public Library.

Given the charge of the library to explore these ideas, I pursued funding and began putting together a team to accomplish the project. After receiving an Apple Library of Tomorrow Grant, which supplied the requisite equipment, Denver Public Library staff began working with CARL Systems, Inc., to build the next-generation library catalog. Paula Busey, Tom Doerr, John Duanne, and I became the collaborators in the development of "Kid's Catalog." Combining the knowledge of librarians and computer specialists was a unique approach to software development.

PRELIMINARY RESEARCH

Research began with an investigation of literature involving children and online catalogs. Although there is limited work in this area, a number of researchers greatly influenced and confirmed our original theories. Walter and Borgman's (1991) science catalog project at UCLA prompted HyperCard training and provided a design platform that was investigated, simulated, then completely redesigned. Edmonds and associates' research with children's use of online catalogs convinced us that catalogs should be designed to assist children in their use of the library (Edmonds, Moore, & Blacom, 1990). Kuhlthau (1988) reinforced our understanding of cognitive levels and the abilities of children and presented the idea that library services should be mindful of these abilities. Solomon's (1991) OPAC research with children provided a basis for conducting our own research with children.

CHILDREN'S RESEARCH STUDY

Funding through an LSCA grant provided resources to conduct research with children at three local elementary schools: Mission Viejo, a suburban elementary school in the Cherry Creek School District, and Park Hill and Edison Elementary, both urban Denver public schools. The purpose of the research was, first, to identify children's online catalog "breakdowns" (i.e., problems and failures) and, later, to evaluate the Kid's Catalog in relation to these breakdowns. This paper reports preliminary findings, particularly on the success of the Kid's Catalog.

The qualitative study was conducted through a combination of observations, interviews, and focus groups. The children were randomly selected from first- through fifth-grade classrooms at the elementary schools. Formal research took place in the school libraries with the support of the school media specialists.

Investigation began with an evaluation of the current OPACs. Two systems, NOTIS and CARL, were evaluated for their ease of use by children (see Figure 1). Seventy-seven percent of all transactions performed by children on NOTIS and CARL were not successful due to a number of breakdowns, including problems with spelling, keyboarding, computer procedures, and inaccurate queries or the inability to shift their search strategies (broaden or narrow the search or find an alternate term). Solomon (1991) summarizes these breakdowns into three categories: skill breakdowns, which include spelling, reading, and keyboarding; rule breakdowns, which involve misunderstanding mechanical requirements such as proper spacing, and author, title, and subject queries;

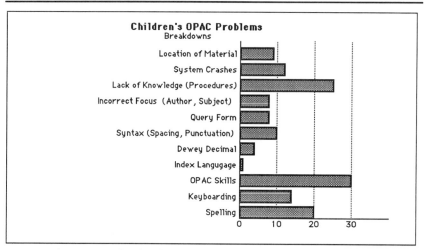

Figure 1. Study of children's use of CARL and NOTIS systems

and knowledge breakdowns, which include lack of content knowledge and inability to revise search strategies.

Interviewing children revealed a range of experiences in libraries. Some children try to find things on the OPAC, locate the author or a general call number, then go browse the shelf. Some children never use the online catalog but go directly to the shelf to browse. Some children successfully manipulate the online catalog but do not utilize any of the bibliographic information. Some children have mastered the OPAC and are quite successful at manipulating the catalog and the system, to the extent that they are even able to retrieve books at other library sites.

THEORETICAL FOUNDATIONS

Observing the repeated difficulties of children with these two OPAC systems provided valuable information for designing an interface for children. This information reinforced my experiences working with children in libraries over the past 15 years. Through observation, independent research, intuition, and thoughtful contemplation, I had been developing a theoretical foundation for the design and implementation of the Kid's Catalog. The following assumptions reflect commonly held views at libraries around the country regarding children as library users, information, and online catalogs. To create a new generation of library catalogs, it became necessary to challenge and rethink these assumptions.

Information

Assumption: More information is always better; the larger the pool of information, the higher the probability that you will find what you are looking for.

Reality: In certain subject areas, the ability to create a subset of information sources allows the researcher to manipulate a richer environment of materials that are specifically applicable to his/her needs. This is particularly true in literature environments for children. While the premise of intellectual freedom is always the overriding goal, allowing children a search option that provides an isolated selection of juvenile titles assists children in decision making. In public library settings, "getting rid" of the adult titles helps alleviate a large amount of noise that confuses children when they are looking for materials. Evaluating appropriate subject matter and reading levels is an added detail that is confusing to children who are trying to find a book about tigers, coyotes, or sharks. In a networked environment, the ability to create an information-rich pool of customized sources is critical to the successful search. The Kid's Catalog interface provides this option for libraries and users.

Assumption: All information is of equal value, and library professionals should not identify certain materials as more valuable than others.

Reality: Democracy of information is a misleading premise of intellectual freedom. All information is not equal, and library professionals are some of the best resources to assist customers in pinpointing the material that best suits their needs. We currently provide this service to the walk-in customer; why not create electronic pathways that re-create this knowledge? The Kid's Catalog design is modeled on the premise of continually adding value to the catalog information.

Online Catalogs

Assumption: Classification systems collocate materials logically by subject.

Reality: Classification systems force materials into single subject areas. Any shelving or placement of materials is a static placement. Information is dynamic; it is always changing or being connected and correlated in new ways. Technology allows us to create multiple collocation schemes by manipulation of the database. The design of the Kid's Catalog allows the information professional the flexibility to create connections throughout the database. The question of how to shelve the material, by subject or format, can be eased by a creative interface design that organizes information in multiple patterns.

Assumption: If you provide information on the screen, the customer will read it.

Reality: Users young and old do not read directions on the screen. The challenge is to design an interface that is so "user friendly" that directions are not needed. The Kid's Catalog design team minimized directions to a few words instead of providing sentences or paragraphs of online instructions. The language used in the directions has been tested with children to insure that it is understandable to them. The layout of the MARC record utilized color, larger fonts, and labels to assist children in deciphering the bibliographic information on the screen. Consistency in the interface design from screen to screen and a combination of intuitive and linear information paths create an online environment that needs few user instructions. This design is further enhanced by the addition of color graphics that communicate information and add a level of inquisitive frivolity and aesthetic appeal. With no coaching, children as young as first grade can independently manipulate the Kid's Catalog within three to five minutes. Preliminary evaluation of the Kid's Catalog reveals a 69% success rate for children in first through fifth grade. Success is defined as an unassisted search that resulted in the child locating the bibliographic record.

Assumption: Only text-based bibliographic information should be available in an online catalog.

Reality: The almost daily advances of microprocessors and telecommunications create a sophisticated technology that provides dimensions of information storage and retrieval that were previously unthinkable. The virtual library is not a dream but a possibility. Information contained in book jacket covers, indexes, and tables of contents, as well as audio capability, are elements that were not included in the first version of the Kid's Catalog due to limited time and resources. Inclusion of these additional data elements in the MARC record would greatly enhance information retrieval in a networked environment. The communication of information should embrace graphics and audio capabilities.

Children as Library Users

Assumption: If children are ever to become successful at using the library and catalogs, they must learn the rules.

Reality: Providing education for library users is an important role for information professionals. The complexity of libraries, bibliographic records, Library of Congress Subject Headings, and search strategies is beyond the cognitive capabilities of most children, especially children younger than fifth grade. Fifth-grade students can begin to combine the information from several sources. This is an appropriate age to learn the Dewey Decimal Classification system, including how the decimal is used to create subdivisions (Kuhlthau, 1988). The Kid's Catalog is designed to introduce children to libraries in a successful, nonstressful manner. Many of the searches are entered "behind the scenes," so children will benefit from the knowledge of library professionals without having to understand complex search strategies or Boolean logic. A prescribed set of subjects and authors is provided for children based on their literature and their subject requests.

Assumption: Children are short adults with simple information needs. Materials don't need to be in order or categorized by subjects—they just go pick out any book.

Reality: Librarians and parents alike will tell you that the questions that come from children equal and often exceed the level of complexity found at an adult reference desk. The Kid's Catalog was developed out of a desire to provide customized access to a very specialized subject area. Adult reference staff shriek when children walk into the library and the children's librarian is not available. In times of staff cutbacks and increased professional generalization, the information needs of children do not get simpler—often they simply go unmet. The Kid's Catalog database has been created to respond to the multiplicity of topics that children request, including information on countries, weapons and wars, monsters, sports, biographies, rocks, planets, crafts, games, trains, planes, cars, riddles, and scary stories.

Assumption: Only nonfiction materials count; fiction is frivolous.

Reality: It doesn't matter how many facts are relayed, people will always remember the story. While there is currently an explosion in the quality and quantity of nonfiction publishing for children, fiction is consistently used to introduce, reinforce, and illustrate significant concepts. Whether children are learning geography, astronomy, or math, an appropriate story communicates additional levels of meaning. On its own, fiction provides recreation, comfort, solace, humor, and escape. Children have sophisticated reading requests that require a new concept in the online catalog: the online reader's advisory. The Kid's Catalog provides capabilities for connecting fiction with nonfiction categories; it also provides a database of recommended children's literature. This customizeable database currently lists award and multicultural categories, as well as children's favorite topics, including animal and scary stories. Recommending good books has always been an important role for librarians, and the computer can help us do it more effectively. Children who may be hesitant to ask a librarian for help can independently browse suggestions for reading in a manner that gives them an added sense of autonomy and privacy. Libraries can encourage children to create their own lists of recommended books for inclusion on the catalog.

Assumption: Only those who can type and spell should have access to an online database.

Reality: These mechanical functions hinder the access of information to a large pre-literate population. While many children have large verbal vocabularies, their writing, spelling, and typing skills lag behind their oral skills. The Kid's Catalog has created multiple access points that require no typing; emphasis has been placed on recognizing rather than correctly spelling their search request, whether it is an author, title, subject, or series request. Another problem, linked to children's cognitive abilities, is their difficulty in shifting search strategies once their initial option fails. In the Kid's Catalog, a database of over 5,000 options has been created that provides alternative relationships and search strategies. Observing children using the Kid's Catalog has demonstrated that they don't stop at one option if they do not find what they want—they continue to explore other avenues to find their desired information.

Assumption: Children work on online catalogs alone.

Reality: Children have a community network of information dissemination. They rely on their peers for information. Observing children working in the library reinforces this premise. Children gather around the online catalog as a group, prodding and assisting the child at the keyboard to help produce a successful search. They recommend favorite topics and titles, looking up the name of the book that their friend just read. The creation of a mechanism that allows networking ideas and information in school and library settings provides an exciting look into the future of global education. While the Kid's Catalog does not currently address the community networking needs of children, it is a perfect environment for creating such a scenario.

Assumption: The Kid's Catalog interface is just for children.

Reality: Nearly all of the problems children have in accessing information are paralleled in the adult information use realm. From physicists in Switzerland to computer scientists in California, adults have little time, patience, or expertise when it comes to successfully manipulating the vast array of information currently available. When demonstrating the Kid's Catalog, one of the most frequently asked questions is, "When are you going to make one for adults?" Information professionals throughout the country have shown interest in adapting this concept for their varying clients and library settings.

Customizing online catalogs for children is a first step in creating successful information users in the future. Figure 2 represents the main menu screen of the Kid's Catalog and should provide a sample of the results of our customization efforts. By creating an interface that encourages children to use and explore information, we can encourage development of the skills necessary to manipulate and retrieve information. Information professionals play an important role in customizing information over the networks and in our libraries.

Figure 2. Main menu of the Kid's Catalog

ACKNOWLEDGMENTS

I would like to gratefully acknowledge the contributions of Tom Doerr and Paula Busey in designing and carrying out the children's research study and development efforts reported upon in this paper. Their contributions of time, energy, and enthusiasm for the Kid's Catalog project have been superhuman. Special thanks for the visionary programming wizardry of John Duanne of CARL Systems, who is also a dreamer. Thank you to the Denver Public Library for trusting and supporting this unconventional but timely idea.

REFERENCES

Edmonds, L.; Moore, P.; & Blacom, K. M. (1990). The effectiveness of an online catalog. *School Library Journal, 36*(10), 28-32.

Kuhlthau, C. C. (1988). Meeting the information needs of children and young adults: Basing library media programs on developmental states. *Journal of Youth Services in Libraries, 2*(1), 51-57.

Sandlian, P., & Walters, S. (1991). A room of their own: Planning the new Denver Children's Library. *School Library Journal, 37*(2), 26-29.

Solomon, P. (1991). Information systems for children: Explorations in information access and interface usability for an online catalog in an elementary school library (Doctoral dissertation, University of Maryland, College Park, 1991). *Dissertation Abstracts International, 52*, 1927-A. (University Microfilms No. DA9133166)

Walter, V. A., & Borgman, C. L. (1991). The Science Library Catalog: A prototype information retrieval system for children. *Journal of Youth Services in Libraries, 4*(2), 159-166.

MICHAEL WAUGH

Associate Professor
Department of Curriculum and Instruction
University of Illinois at Urbana-Champaign

JAMES LEVIN

Associate Professor
Department of Educational Psychology
University of Illinois at Urbana-Champaign

Use of Networking in K-12 Schools: Research Results

INTRODUCTION

Electronic networks are starting to be widely used in K-12 schools. And with the new National Research and Education Network (NREN) legislation and other federal, state, and grass roots efforts, their use will become ever more common. Yet the educational use of these networks in K-12 schools has yet to be closely examined. What are appropriate and effective uses of electronic networks in education? How can classroom activities be structured to support these activities?

Electronic networks make available a wide range of resources for schools. The most obvious of these are the rich variety of online computer-based resources such as online library catalogs, databases, and other electronic information sources. However, networks make available a wide range of human resources as well. Through electronic mail (e-mail), teleconferencing systems, and newsgroups/electronic bulletin boards, students and teachers can work cooperatively on a wide variety of activities with students and teachers and others elsewhere. Our research and the research of others have identified some of the structures and processes of network-based activities. Based on these results, we have started to sketch out the important roles for teachers and librarians as mediators in these instructional activities.

THE STRUCTURE AND PROCESS OF NETWORK-BASED PROJECTS

Based on our analysis of more than 75 network-based project activities during the past five years, we have seen that projects progress through a series of developmental stages:
1. Proposal
2. Refinement

3. Organization
4. Pursuit
5. Wrap-up
6. Publication

The life cycle of network-based activities is the sequence of stages through which the activity progresses from beginning until end (Levin, Waugh, Chung, & Miyake, 1992; Stapleton, 1992). The "life cycle" concept provides a framework that can be used to compare projects and to analyze the different mediator roles employed during specific portions of the activities.

MEDIATOR ROLES FOR TEACHERS AND LIBRARIANS

Teachers and librarians play important mediator roles for network-based projects. We will now describe some of the specific strategies and tactics we have observed teachers and librarians using in electronic network-based projects to facilitate their successful completion. Some of these techniques are useful across multiple stages of the project's life cycle; however, they are introduced and discussed according to the life cycle stages mentioned earlier: proposal, refinement, organization, pursuit, wrap-up, and publication.

Proposal

On many networks, one of the first problems that newcomers face is how to find willing participants for their own project activities. Many newcomers post a description of their projects on a public bulletin board or newsgroup, or respond to someone else's project announcement posted there. However, we have observed teachers employing another tactic with great success: "co-opting pen pals."

One of the first projects that seems to come to the minds of newcomers is "electronic pen pals," a relatively unfocused type of project that calls for having a class of students exchange messages with another class. We have found that this type of project activity is often disappointing for beginners (Levin, Rogers, Waugh, & Smith, 1989). In order to try to avoid the negative effects that can accompany electronic pen pals projects, we recommend that individuals attempt to co-opt a pen pal project by responding to those calls for participation with something like, "I'm glad to hear that you and your class are looking for other classes to communicate with you. My class is studying a unit on pollution [or some specific topic] and we would like to communicate with your students by writing [or some other type of activity] about that topic. Would your class be interested in communicating with us on this topic?" Although at first this may seem a bit sneaky, in reality it is quite an effective strategy for finding activity partners. Generally, those newcomers who propose a pen pals activity are saying something like, "Hello, we are here and we are looking for partners and we are pretty flexible about the topic so long as the students become involved in writing [or in some other way]." As long as your topic is acceptable to them, then you've found an activity partner. If your project is not acceptable to them, then you are no worse off than you were before you contacted them, and you might be much better off in terms of making a contact for possible future collaboration.

A related tactic is one that we refer to as the "back scratching" approach. With this approach, one responds to someone else's project idea and proposes joining their project if they will reciprocate. While it is possible that they might not be interested in your project, it is equally possible that you both will become involved in two good network projects. If you choose well, you will become involved with another related topic and secure involvement in your own project as well. In any event, you are bound to learn something during the experience that you can use in future projects. This tactic is systematically employed in the Learning Circles of the AT&T Learning Network (Riel, 1992). Each participant is required to join each other participant's project in exchange for their reciprocal participation.

A good tactic for finding partners is to be persistent and to approach the problem in an organized way. The most effective calls for participation are those relatively short and concise announcements (approximately a screenful) that describe an activity—but not a grade level or age group—and give a few details about what would be expected of participants. Following this announcement, we recommend that the lengthy details of project planning be exchanged via private e-mail between the project originator and the participants during the refinement and organizational stages of the project. Should the original call for participation go without a reply for two weeks, then we recommend that another call for participation be issued for the same project. This is because beginners (and others) often do not take the time to go back and re-read old postings as often as they read the new postings.

We also recommend that the original posting *not* contain any reference to grade level or age group because we have found that the fact that participants are from different age groups does not generally inhibit their ability to work together—rather it often improves the project. Yet, this fact is not generally appreciated, and the most common tendency is for participants to seek partners at the same age/grade level. Don't limit the group of potential project participants by arbitrarily assuming that the activity will only work with a particular age/grade level group.

Refinement

A powerful strategy for project management is being able to set up conference groups. A conference group is an electronic list of all of the project participants. This list can be established so that electronic messages sent to the list address (a single e-mail address) are then re-sent to each e-mail address on the list. One problem with conference groups is that it is easy for beginners to become confused about groups and how they work. It is often confusing for them to find mail in *their* mailboxes that is addressed to a group (a name that they don't recognize) and often the messages themselves seem as though they were intended to be private messages for some other individual (usually because the person sending the message to the group didn't realize that it was going to a group). This can easily happen because of the way in which a user's e-mail software generates automatic replies to correspondence. A simple rule about groups is to remember that an electronic conference group is *not* a single individual, and so any mail that is sent to the group should contain information of general interest to *all* group members. If that is not the case, then address the correspondence to the individual for whom it is relevant.

Organization

We have seen a number of management strategies used with great success in networking activities. A couple of important ones are the use of a timeline and distributed project ownership.

Timelines

Probably very little needs to be said about the instructional value of using a timeline. Generally, it is highly desirable to be able to publish a scheduled sequence of events concerning any instructional activity. However, while we recommend the use of a timeline when possible, there are a number of instances in electronic networking when timelines are not practical. Thus, our advice would be *not* to think of a timeline as absolutely essential, but rather to use one as it seems appropriate. An example of an instance in which timelines are not as important is when a new instructional activity is being developed and piloted for the first time. In this case, it is often difficult to determine what comes next, much less when it should happen, in relation to the other aspects of the activity, and how long it will take to accomplish each step.

We have also seen that when using a timeline to help organize an electronic network-based instructional activity, it is best to build such a timeline with considerable allowance for changes and unforeseen circumstances. For a wide variety of reasons, it is quite difficult to achieve close coordination when working with large numbers of groups in different parts of the United States and around the world. Ample allowance must be made to accommodate individuals who experience problems and require additional time. If the project must proceed at a specific point in time, then provisions should be made to accommodate the "stragglers" who would like to catch up at a later date and the "newcomers" who wish to join a project in progress.

Distributed Project Ownership

Another management strategy that we have seen put to good use is that of allowing distributed project ownership. This concept is quite alien to many teachers who are used to working from an individually developed plan when conducting classroom activities. Many teachers are even more familiar with collaborative situations where there is a common lesson plan and all participants work through essentially the same sequence of events to arrive at essentially the same outcomes. What we are proposing is that, when possible, a group of people working together on the network determine the key elements and general timeline for the project activity through joint agreement. Even then, individual teachers should be encouraged to adapt the project in unique and individual ways to suit the needs of their particular situations. When this occurs, each participant can come to "own" much more of the project and will experience more identification with and involvement in the project goals and outcomes—even while these goals and outcomes become highly variable because of this strategy. In actuality, the need for an immutable, identical set of activity procedures is relatively rare. In network-based activities that involve data collection, for example, once the data have been obtained and shared, there is no need for teachers to utilize the data in identical ways with their students. Instead, teachers can adapt specific procedures for utilizing the data in ways most appropriate for their students.

In essence, the project activity should grow from the needs and interests and the skills and abilities of the participants; and each participant should feel as though the project ideally suits his or her needs. When this occurs, the group members should become aware that their unique talents have contributed to the development of a valuable project activity and also that the group's collective wisdom can be far greater than their separate contributions.

Pursuit

We have found another strategy to be of help to project organizers—the use of "keeping-things-alive" messages. Network activities typically extend over longer time periods than classroom-based activities. Often there are multiple exchanges of information, and each of these is preceded or succeeded by a classroom-based component, often involving student writing. The net effect of all this is that the activities tend to take place over an extended period, during which network colleagues might wonder what is going on and when or if they will hear from you again. Our solution to this problem is to utilize a variety of short messages that we call "ping," "return receipt," and "cheerleader" messages.

A ping message is one that briefly says that you are making progress and expect to have something to share soon or that you are waiting for some information from your colleagues. The idea is merely to say, "I'm here and will get back to you soon" or "I'm waiting for something from you before I can proceed." Often this simple reassurance or reminder is all that is necessary to maintain the smooth flow of the activity.

The return receipt message has the same basic purpose as the ping message except it is a reply rather than an initiation message. It says, "I got your note and am waiting for further communication." When you don't have anything major to report, don't waste a lot of energy but don't forget that your colleagues often need little reassurances to "keep on hanging in there." There may also be times when you might wish to expend a little more energy and develop and share an interim progress report of some nature. If you can find time for doing this, your personal example can often serve to motivate others to do likewise.

The cheerleader message should be employed when people have invested a lot of time and energy in writing and sharing something. When this occurs, it is a good idea to recognize their efforts, even if you don't want to join their project or elaborate on their comments in any substantive way. Something like this is particularly important to do for members of your immediate project group, but it is also a helpful strategy for those wishing to establish a network presence. And finally, a valuable tactic related to the cheerleader message is the old-fashioned thank-you message. People like knowing that their efforts are appreciated, and our experience has been that a few kind words go a long way.

Wrap-up

Wrap-up communications generally serve to coordinate the completion stages of the activity. This stage becomes very important in projects that have a loose timeline, because with no precise timeline or plan for completion, there is little to ensure closure without this stage. This can easily happen in projects where the participants each plan to modify or adapt the project to uniquely fit their classroom activities and situations. In these instances, we have seen that the participants often feel that their own adaptations would be of little interest to the other participants, and so they don't think about sending anything back to the others participating in the project. However, these local adaptations of projects are *very important* to preserve for the next occasion on which the project is conducted. Thus, this stage is particularly important in helping to ensure that the publication stage is completed and that the local curriculum adaptations are preserved.

Wrap-up communications serve to coordinate the date, time, and format of the publication stage, and they can also serve as a means by which the participants can discuss the question: "Where do we go from here?"

Publication

Another management strategy that we feel contributes significantly to the success of network-based activities is the creation of a post-project publication. This stage is the development of a written description of the project activity upon the completion of the activity, written for a broader audience than the other participants in the project. Our observations have shown us that this stage rarely occurs spontaneously and must be encouraged strongly if it is to occur at all. This publication stage helps the participants place what they've learned from the project into a more public arena so that others can apply the knowledge and procedures successfully.

In addition, since a great many network-based projects are unique curriculum development efforts, they should be preserved and shared with a group that extends beyond the immediate group of project participants. Since much of the actual collaboration might be conducted via private e-mail and not in a public electronic forum like a bulletin board, the activity planning and data exchanges and any summary descriptions might typically be seen by only a few other individuals. The post-project publication stage should be included in the planning of all network-based projects to help facilitate the development and dissemination of these valuable curriculum development efforts.

SUMMARY

We have described the results of our research, which has uncovered structures and processes involved in instructional interactions on electronic networks.

We have described some successful instructional strategies and tactics that we have found in our research. In successful uses of electronic networks, teachers and librarians are crucial mediators of these activities. Some of roles they play on the network are the same as their roles in conventional instruction, but some are new mediating roles required by this new instructional medium.

Librarians and information specialists can play a critically important role both in providing information and guidance during an electronic network activity and also in encouraging and facilitating the publication phase of these innovative curriculum development efforts. In addition, they can also play a critical role in organizing, indexing, and making available the new curriculum materials generated during these online instructional activities.

ACKNOWLEDGMENTS

This material is based upon work supported by the National Science Foundation under grant no. RED-9253423. The U.S. government has certain rights in this material. Any opinions, findings, and conclusions or recommendations expressed in this material are those of the authors and do not necessarily reflect the views of the National Science Foundation.

REFERENCES

Levin, J.; Waugh, M.; Chung, H. K.; & Miyake, N. (1992). Activity cycles in educational electronic networks. *Interactive Learning Environments, 2*(1), 3-13.
Levin, J. A.; Rogers, A.; Waugh, M.; & Smith, K. (1989). Observations on educational electronic networks: Appropriate activities for learning. *Computing Teacher, 16*(8), 17-21.
Riel, M. (1992). A functional analysis of educational telecomputing: A case study of learning circles. *Interactive Learning Environments, 2*(1), 15-29.
Stapleton, C. E. (1992). Network activity stages: Organization of successful electronic collaboration and communication. In S. Gayle (Ed.), *Windows to the world: National Educational Computing Conference: Proceedings* (pp. 241-247). Eugene, OR: International Society for Technology in Education.

JOHN L. HANKINS

Deputy Director
CICNet, Inc.
Ann Arbor, Michigan

The Pioneering Partners Project: Collaboration Among K-12 Educators, Librarians, and Community Leaders

INTRODUCTION

The Pioneering Partners program was developed by GTE North, Inc., in cooperation with the Great Lakes Council of Governors. Broadly stated, the goals of the program were to enhance learning in K-12 classrooms by accelerating the use of educational technology. Specific goals of the program focused on team building, development of innovative ideas, adoption of innovative technology, planning, and development of strategies to secure matching program funds. The specific program goal that resulted in CICNet's involvement was to "telecommunicate regularly with other Pioneering Partners, sharing ideas, products, experiences and support for dissemination of innovative technology practices." CICNet's role extended beyond simply supplying network access; it included providing a network environment that supports collaborative activities and communication. This required the development of the system components, documentation, and end-user support. In addition, the environment was designed to expose participants to the Internet and kindle their interest in using the Internet and its resources in classroom projects.

SELECTION OF PARTICIPANTS

Participants in the Pioneering Partners program included teams of educators from the eight Great Lakes states (New York, Pennsylvania, Michigan, Indiana, Illinois, Ohio, Wisconsin, and Minnesota). Three schools were selected per state through a competition in which participants were judged on their use of innovative technologies. Examples of winning projects included the use of computers to create technical drawings and maintain logs for the development of prototype inventions that solve specific technical problems, a schoolwide network and technology committee supporting teachers using computers to develop learning materials, and use of computers and networking to exchange information with schools in several countries around the world.

Pioneering Partners teams were made up of school personnel including teachers, librarians, vocational-ed teachers, and administrators. However, the program emphasized community involvement and in some cases included school board members, technical personnel and managers from local businesses, and faculty from local universities. Other key participants included the project team, composed of several individuals from the GTE or Great Lakes Council of Governors staffs, an advisory council consisting of representatives appointed by the governors of each of the participating states, and several educational and technical consultants.

The selection process for participating teams was completed in the 1991-1992 academic year with the intent of launching Pioneering Partners at the beginning of the 1992-1993 academic year. A five-day training program for all participants, staff, the advisory council, and consultants was held at the GTE corporate training facilities in August 1992 to launch the program. The training program focused on team building, interpersonal communication, and project planning but also included hands-on sessions on how to use the network. Several computers were made available so the participants could try out the system during breaks and in the evenings. Following the training program, teams returned to their schools ready to begin participation in the program with the start of school in September.

SYSTEM DESIGN AND DEVELOPMENT

CICNet was approached by the Pioneering Partners management team at GTE in June 1992 regarding their interest in building a dial-up network to support the program. The CICNet staff was very interested in participating in the project, primarily because of the experience we would gain in working in a K-12 environment. At the same time, there was some concern within CICNet about our organization's capacity to deliver due to two factors—our lack of experience in supporting dial-up services and the short timeline to get the project launched. CICNet also was concerned that it not become directly involved in extensive end-user support. We wanted our role to be the design, implementation, and operation of a system that would support the goals of the Pioneering Partners program. This could include a "train the trainers" role and the development of documentation, but direct user support would be supplied by GTE or another participant. Following some discussion of these issues, it was agreed that CICNet would provide the networking component of the Pioneering Partners program.

Once design work began, it became immediately clear that the network would have two distinct components—dial-up infrastructure for network access and a suite of services for utilizing the information resources on the network. CICNet staff quickly began to evaluate 9.6 kb/s high-speed modems and terminal servers. After a review, the AT&T Paradyne modem was selected, primarily because of recommendations of peers in the networking community and the Paradyne's network management features. As a terminal server, CICNet selected the Cisco 500CS, primarily because of CICNet's heavy use of Cisco routers in its network. A Sun Sparcstation was chosen as the platform for running the suite of applications software. Approximately 500 megabytes of storage was allocated for the project.

While the hardware infrastructure consisted of a straightforward setup to provide dial-up access, the network applications and software presented a challenge in that there are few standards for building systems specifically for a user population of K-12 teachers. As defined by the program staff, the system had to include several features, including the following:

- electronic mail (e-mail),
- a conferencing system,
- net news,
- menu-driven access to various Internet resources, and
- access to basic Internet tools, such as File Transfer Protocol (FTP).

And, of course, the system had to be easy to use.

The list of features can be applied to two distinct tasks: supporting communication and information sharing among program participants (e-mail and conferencing) and supporting exploration and use of Internet-based resources (e-mail, news, menu-driven access, and FTP). However, given the state of the art in Internet tools and applications, it was challenging to find a suite of tools that would be easy to use, let alone a suite that would provide something that approached a consistent environment for the end-user. Given time constraints and budget, any development work would have to be extremely limited.

With this in mind, CICNet staff selected Pine, an easy-to-use, menu-driven mailer developed at the University of Washington. This mailer came highly recommended by several individuals with experience in the K-12 community. The conferencing system selected was Caucus. CICNet had used it in an earlier project, and based on that experience, we believed it would be well suited for this project.

The primary tool used for providing access to Internet resources was the Gopher service, developed at the University of Minnesota. Gopher is a menu-driven, easily configurable front-end that provides access to an extremely wide array of Internet resources. Gopher can be configured to provide access to a number of resources including online library catalogs, FTP archives, full-text files, e-mail directories, national weather reports, and other Gopher servers. Access to USENET news was provided via the TIN news reader. Users also had access to standard UNIX system commands if they so chose.

Since end-users were going to access the GreatLinks service from a wide variety of desktop platforms, it was decided to confine access technology to terminal emulation only. That is, CICNet would not support SLIP (Serial Line Internet Protocol) or PPP (Point to Point Protocol), two popular but potentially complex Internet access protocols. This immediately raised the issue of standardizing on a terminal emulation package, such as Procomm or Kermit, and caused something of a problem in that CICNet saw itself being drawn into direct support activities. Concern around this issue was particularly keen given the wide array of systems, modems, and levels of expertise.

CICNet also determined that an initial menu screen would be particularly important in creating a user-friendly environment. An initial menu screen was developed using perl and UNIX scripts. The menu choices include the following:

- Electronic Mail
- Network News
- Internet and Pioneering Partners Resources
- File Transfer
- System Commands
- Personal Configuration Options
- Conferencing
- Information About Users

The Electronic Mail selection provides access to the Pine mailer. The Network News selection provides access to net news using the TIN news reader. Internet and Pioneering Partners Resources provides access to Gopher, which in turn provides access to many standard Gopher resources such as the list of all Gopher servers. In addition, this Gopher server provides access to a "Best of the Internet" menu item, a help file for the GreatLinks system, and a description of the Pioneering Partners program. File Transfer is a menu-driven interface for executing Kermit file transfers between the GreatLinks host machine and the user's desktop system. System Commands provides a menu for various UNIX commands. Personal Configuration Options allows the individual user to set options for use of either the Pine or Elm mailer, use of menus or command line at startup, changing passwords, and setting default editor to vi or pico. Conferencing provides access to the Caucus conferencing system. Information About Users provides access to a directory listing the e-mail addresses for all Pioneering Partners participants, information on who is currently logged into the system, and access to the "Chat" facility, which provides for real-time correspondence between participants.

Documentation was the final piece of the system to be put into place. The documentation packet developed by the CICNet staff included approximately 15 pages of documentation developed exclusively for the project and another 40 pages pulled from existing documentation for the various applications, such as Pine and Caucus, being used by the project. A concerted attempt was made to make the system easy to use but to also allow more sophisticated users to explore more advanced applications.

SYSTEM UTILIZATION

The system became available to approximately 120 end-users in October 1992. All users were supplied with documentation and access via an 800 number and e-mail to consultants, GTE staff, and CICNet staff who served as user support specialists. The first problems encountered were with end-users who could not get their desktop systems to access GreatLinks. Because end-users were accessing GreatLinks from numerous platforms with many different types of terminal emulation packages, the support task was more complex. We decided to standardize on the Kermit terminal emulation package, which made the support task much easier.

Initial utilization of the system varied quite widely among users. Tables 1-3 show data for four months (November 1993 through February 1993). Table 1 describes the total hours of connect time and the total number of sessions for each month. The first month of utilization shows much higher utilization than each of the following months even though the number of users remained relatively constant during each month. It is reasonable to attribute this initial high level of usage to users becoming familiar with the system and an initial exploration of the Internet.

TABLE 1
MONTHLY TOTALS
(IN HOURS)

Month	Total Connect Time	Total Sessions	Number of Users
Nov.	416	1,036	55
Dec.	206	731	46
Jan.	255	920	51
Feb.	297	986	49

The data in Table 2 provide details regarding individual participants' average use of the system. These data are consistent with the data in Table 1 in that there is a peak in November and then usage levels off. The data also show that usage after the initial peak is about what would be expected. That is, users are initiating between 16 and 20 sessions per month, and each session lasts between 15 and 25 minutes—about what might be expected for users who are checking mail and doing some amount of network exploration.

TABLE 2
MONTHLY AVERAGES PER USER
(IN HOURS)

Month	Average Total Connect Time	Average Number of Sessions	Average Session Length	Number of Users
Nov.	7.56	19	.40	55
Dec.	4.48	16	.28	46
Jan.	5.01	18	.28	51
Feb.	6.06	20	.30	49

Table 3 shows maximums for individual connect time and number of sessions for each month. When compared with the data in Table 2, it is obvious that some small number of users are using the system very extensively. Unfortunately, no data have yet been collected beyond what appears in these three tables so it is impossible to draw any conclusions regarding what would account for variance in individual usage. At this point, however, it is reasonable to say that such differences are not unexpected and that further research with this group, or with similar groups, would add to our understanding of how the network is used.

TABLE 3
MONTHLY MAXIMUMS
(IN HOURS)

Month	Maximum Total Connect Time	Maximum Number of Sessions	Number of Users
Nov.	147	190	55
Dec.	26	64	46
Jan.	24	108	51
Feb.	56	108	49

We have also measured the use of the Caucus conferencing system. During the development of the GreatLinks system, the project leaders expected that access to a moderated, online conference would add considerable value to the system and become the cornerstone for collaboration and individual interaction. An examination of conferences provides some insight into the success of this plan.

For users unfamiliar with conferencing software, typically, conferences are structured using a hierarchy of conference items and discussion responses, which is the structure used for GreatLinks. It is worth noting, however, that there are a number of other ways in which conferences can be structured.

In the four-month period studied here, three different conferences were set up. All conferences were moderated by a staff member or consultant to the project. The first conference was devoted to providing online help for supporting the GreatLinks system. This conference has 9 items and 20 total discussion responses (2.2 responses per item). The second conference focused on the dissemination of information regarding project participants' activities. This conference, then, is most central to the mission of the Pioneering Partners program. It has 8 items and 16 discussion responses (2.0 responses per item). The third, and final conference, is for the discussion of the structure of the Pioneering Partners program and the application and award process. This conference has 5 items and 4 discussion responses (.8 responses per item).

The conference activity described above shows that, contrary to expectations, the conferences have not served as important a role as was hoped. While it is hard to draw any final conclusions from such a short period of operation, it is worth speculating about why this is true.

While everyone involved in GreatLinks devoted considerable energy to providing structure for the services available on GreatLinks, no particular attention was paid to conferencing beyond making sure it was easily available. More careful consideration of potential topics of interest to participants and ways to get them involved could add to the value of the system. For instance, recruiting a well-known K-12 network person to moderate a conference on K-12 Internet resources would provide more motivation to participate regularly in the conference.

Conference activities might also be increased by widening the scope of the participants. Initially, it was thought that staff from the participating governor's offices and other state agencies would participate in the program.

However, that has not happened. The presence of individuals outside the Pioneering Partners program, especially individuals who are perceived as having influence in state government, could be a strong motivation.

A third barrier to conference utilization could simply be the lack of critical mass. While the number of individuals with access to GreatLinks is about 120, approximately 50 use the system in any given month. It can be argued that 50 end-users is too small a group to sustain a significant level of ongoing conferencing activity. It may be that none of the efforts described above will make any difference until more active users join the system.

Finally, additional end-user support may be required to build the size of the core group of active users. Most of the current user support for GreatLinks is asynchronous in nature. A user can either leave a message on voice mail or pose a question via the conferencing system or e-mail. Increasing the amount of proactive support or outreach through such means as seeking out users who appear to be having problems or who are not using the system, developing tutorials or other training materials, or conducting real-time, network-based workshops could have a positive impact on the number of participants who regularly use GreatLinks.

CONCLUSION

The Pioneering Partners program and the GreatLinks system present us with an opportunity to examine an effort to provide network access to a group of K-12 educators located across several states. This discussion is useful in that it provides a description of the hardware, software, and personnel components of the system for those organizations that may be considering building such a system. We believe the services developed for the GreatLinks network constitute a well-thought-out, high-quality solution to network access, and we encourage others to use the GreatLinks system as a model.

In addition, this paper raises a set of issues regarding use of the system by a fairly naive group of users. While the data presented here are clearly preliminary, it is a first step in understanding what has and has not worked for this group. Hopefully, a follow-up paper will continue the line of analysis begun here with a more robust data set.

Finally, the GreatLinks project raises an important issue in that this type of activity is becoming an increasingly common approach to providing access to the Internet for specific user groups. As the scope of resources on the Internet has grown, much of the Internet community's attention has been focused on the navigational tools and services needed to make Internet resources available to various user communities. While GreatLinks clearly addresses this issue, it goes further in that it forces us to consider the issue of how to build a point of access to the Internet. In the case of GreatLinks, the Internet is imbedded into local systems, and GreatLinks itself becomes the window through which users view the Internet. In developing such systems, we need to give careful consideration to exactly how that window to the Internet is structured and what local structure and resources are necessary to accomplish goals that may be unique to the group or project served by the system.

HOPE N. TILLMAN

Director of Libraries
Horn Library
Babson College
Babson Park, Massachusetts

SHARYN J. LADNER

Associate Professor and Business Librarian
Richter Library
University of Miami
Coral Gables, Florida

Special Librarians and the Internet:
A Descriptive Study

INTRODUCTION

In the summer of 1991, we conducted an exploratory study of special librarians who had access to extraorganizational electronic networks such as BITNET or the Internet to determine their use of these networks. (We are using the term *Internet* in a broad sense to include other networks that transfer electronic mail with the Internet. While our respondents used the Internet, BITNET, CompuServe, and MCImail, the majority by far used the Internet and BITNET. It should be noted, however, that certain functions, such as remote login (Telnet) and File Transfer Protocol are only available on the Internet and not on BITNET, CompuServe, and MCImail.) We asked special librarians to tell us how they used these networks and what value they received from this use. We also asked them how they became aware of the existence of the Internet and how they learned how to use it. Papers based on this research have appeared in a variety of sources (Ladner & Tillman, 1992a, 1992b, 1992c, 1993a; Tillman & Ladner, 1992, in press) and form the basis for a book published by the Special Libraries Association (SLA) (Ladner & Tillman, 1993b).

Our purpose in conducting research on special librarians is to find out how and for what purposes a group of information professionals who are themselves specialists in the retrieval, organization, and dissemination of information use the Internet. Most of the articles appearing in the library literature on the Internet have been written by academic librarians or computer systems professionals. Special librarians, whether in the one-professional environment, as managers of larger industrial libraries, or as academic subject specialists, are more often in public services positions, and they may use the Internet differently from their colleagues in academe.

Even though our 1991 data did not indicate differences in the use of the Internet between special librarians in and outside of academe, because only

35% of the 54 respondents we surveyed in 1991 were nonacademic special librarians, we felt it was important to expand our study to include more nonacademic special librarians. In the fall of 1992, therefore, we surveyed an additional 27 special librarians who worked in nonacademic libraries or information centers.

This paper, then, is an analysis of the data we collected on special librarians in 1991 and 1992 to determine if special librarians working in colleges and universities differ from special librarians in corporations, not-for-profit organizations, and government agencies. In this paper, we will focus on comparing the academic and nonacademic use of the Internet and training issues. Specifically, we will describe:

- how special librarians learn about the Internet;
- how special librarians access and pay for the Internet;
- how special librarians are trained, gain employer support, and provide training;
- how special librarians use the Internet; and
- how training needs are expressed by special librarians.

CHARACTERISTICS OF SPECIAL LIBRARIANSHIP

In this study, we define special librarianship as library and/or information service geared to meet the needs of specialized users or specialized situations. Special librarianship is independent of organizational structure: special librarians work in "information organizations sponsored by private companies, government agencies, not-for-profit organizations, or professional associations" as well as in "specialty units in public and academic libraries" (Mount, 1991, p. 2). Our research focuses on the individual, not the organization, and includes special librarians working in not-for-profit organizations, for-profit corporations, and governmental agencies, as well as academic institutions.

Special libraries in industry differ from those in academe. Industrial libraries tend to be smaller than academic libraries, sharing many of the characteristics of small libraries, such as small staff and limited time spent in technical services functions like original cataloging (Hill, 1985). Industrial libraries have more specialized collections than academic libraries, and even though small, within their specialty these collections are also more comprehensive, often including obscure journals and grey literature such as pamphlets, preprints, and technical reports (Mount, 1985). They also have different security requirements because of the existence of confidential or proprietary materials in their collections.

Special libraries in the private sector are more economically driven than academic or public libraries. Because they are part of a larger organization, managers of these special libraries must justify major expenditures, including capital projects, to a management that often does not understand library operations and needs (Ladner, 1990; Hill, 1985).

Many special librarians in science or technology fields work closely with researchers who have been using Internet precursors such as ARPANET, NSFNET, and MILNET for years. In some cases, these librarians are serving as intermediaries between the network and the end-users to access the network. Stern (1988) describes the use of BITNET by physics, astronomy, and math librarians for electronic mail (e-mail) functions such as obtaining hard-to-find conference proceedings. This informal use of BITNET by members of the SLA Physics-Astronomy-Mathematics Division evolved into the BITNET listserv forum, SLA-PAM@UKCC (Tillman, 1991). In other cases, however, researchers may be using the networks independently of the library and are unaware that their librarians are network users as well.

RESEARCH DESIGN

Because this is an exploratory study of Internet use by special librarians, we employ a qualitative approach to our research. Qualitative researchers strive to understand phenomena and situations as a whole without imposing preexisting expectations on the research setting (Patton, 1980). Hiltz and Turoff (1978) stress the need for a holistic approach in studying the impact of computer conferencing systems; the unanticipated consequences of a new technology are often more important in the long run than the testing of explicit hypotheses. We have tried to approach our investigation of how special librarians use the Internet and what it means to them with a similar lack of preconceived ideas and expectations. We have also used the Internet to collect our data electronically.

Several researchers have compared electronic forms of data collection with other methods for both quantitative and qualitative applications. Electronic surveys are easy to administer to people who are linked by a computer network. The network can locate respondents automatically through distribution lists, deliver the questionnaire to remote locations, and permit respondents to answer questions at their own convenience (Hiltz & Turoff, 1978).

Kiesler and Sproull (1986) found that responses to open-ended questions that could be edited on the computer were more than twice as long as those received from participants using a conventional mail survey. Electronic surveys also had a faster turnaround time and fewer item incompletions. Sproull (1986) determined that e-mail "produced adequate data, response rates, and willingness for further participation, with little expenditure of researcher time or effort and a high degree of convenience for respondents" (p. 167) and for these reasons recommends its use in organizational research.

In both our 1991 and 1992 surveys, we used the Internet as a tool to locate special librarians to participate in this study as well as to administer the survey instrument and collect data.

1991 Survey

Participants were solicited through Call for Participation announcements posted on nine computer conferences (also called listservs or forums) in July 1991. The computer forums, all library-related, were chosen because of their interest to special librarians in various subject specialties. A similar announcement was also placed in the August issue of *SpeciaList*, the monthly newsletter of the SLA, in order to obtain participants who may be users of the Internet but not active on computer forums. We sent a five-page electronic questionnaire to the 113 librarians who responded to this initial announcement; the 54 special librarians who responded to this second survey comprise the 1991 sample.

In the Call for Participation announcement, we included a brief questionnaire that potential respondents were asked to return, either electronically, via fax, or regular mail. Here we asked respondents to list the computer conferences to which they subscribed, the length of time they had been using either BITNET or the Internet, and to "Briefly describe (in a paragraph or less) your use (and/or your patrons' use) of BITNET or the Internet." On the five-page questionnaire, we asked a series of structured questions to find out how and for what purposes our respondents used BITNET or the Internet so that we could flesh out the information we had already received through the preliminary survey. We also included a series of questions about training and costs involved in accessing these systems.

To determine the importance and value of BITNET or the Internet to their work and for special librarians in general, we asked respondents to describe, based on their experience, "the major advantage or opportunity for special librarians in using BITNET/Internet"; "the major disadvantage or barrier for special librarians in using BITNET/Internet"; their "most interesting or memorable experience on BITNET or Internet"; and finally, we asked them for "any other comments [they'd] like to make about the use of BITNET or Internet by special librarians."

1992 Survey

Recognizing that the majority of our 1991 respondents were academic special librarians, we attempted to address this potential bias by selecting only nonacademic special librarians in 1992. We identified nonacademic special librarians through multiple venues. We recruited participants who attended programs on the Internet at the SLA Annual Conference in San Francisco in June 1992, as well as attendees at other conferences attracting special librarians. We also solicited respondents from Internet computer forums of interest to special librarians by sending surveys directly to list subscribers whom we tentatively identified as nonacademic librarians. Finally, we sent e-mail letters to special librarians who had posted messages on other listservs to which we subscribe, asking the poster to participate in our study.

A total of 27 nonacademic special librarians completed the 1992 questionnaire. These 27 respondents plus the 54 special librarians who were surveyed in 1991 are the focus of our study.

In 1992, we combined the questions found in the 1991 preliminary and five-page follow-up questionnaires into one survey instrument. This questionnaire contained 22 questions that were identical to those found on the 1991 questionnaires, plus several new questions dealing with how the Internet is accessed and a series of questions concerning frequency of use by function. Respondents to the 1992 survey were also asked to indicate the importance of five Internet functions (e-mail, Telnet, discussion lists, file transfer, and chat/talk) based on a five-point scale. All results reported in this paper are rounded to the nearest whole number.

Survey Participants

Forty-three percent of the special librarians who participated in this study work in academic institutions; 24% work in for-profit corporations, 15% in not-for-profit organizations, 14% in government or public agencies; and 5% are information specialists who do not work in libraries. Participants represent a wide range of administrative levels: 44% of the academic librarians and 39% of the nonacademic respondents are in management (library directors, assistant directors, or branch or department heads); 56% of the academic and 50% of the nonacademic respondents are librarians, information specialists, or subject specialists (e.g., business librarian, math librarian, or science librarian). Survey respondents from the most technologically advanced institutions to smaller colleges and universities outside the urban, technological mainstream are represented; 94% of respondents are located in the United States. The majority of respondents work in sci-tech disciplines.

Study participants cannot be considered to be representative of special librarians as a whole, mainly because access to the Internet is so heavily skewed toward academic and sci-tech organizations. Although sci-tech and business comprise the two largest subject categories of special libraries (Ladner, 1992), only 7% of the respondents in this study are business librarians. We did not, however, intend our sample to be representative of special librarians as a whole. The purpose of this study is not to generalize our findings to a larger group but to investigate the ways in which a subset of special librarians who are "early adopters" (Rogers, 1986) use the Internet. These librarians can serve as role models for those to come.

FINDINGS

Learning about the Internet

Professional literature and informal contacts were responsible for many respondents learning about the Internet. One difference between 1991 and 1992 has been the availability of programs offered by professional associations, commercial vendors, and individuals (e.g., the very successful series of self-paced exercises offered via the Internet by Richard Smith, of the University of Southwestern Louisiana, that saw enrollment of 800 when first offered and 15,000 the second time). More of the 1992 respondents, in particular recent subscribers, credited conferences and regional or local workshops than the 1991 respondents. We believe that this finding is solely a function of the different time period. In the words of one 1992 respondent, "Internet is a hot conference topic." Therefore, no conclusions can be drawn concerning the higher mention of programs for nonacademics than academics.

One corporate librarian's description of how she learned is echoed by several other respondents as well. She did not see its relevance to her needs at first:

> I heard about it (Internet) at an SLA annual conference two years ago, in a casual discussion with an academic librarian. I might add that she seemed genuinely shocked that I, or any librarian, would not be on the Internet. When I asked why I should be . . . she never really came up with an answer. My own conclusion at the time was that I needed to get access to it just so I wouldn't feel so inadequate the next time I ran into the same type of situation. I have since come to realize that there are better reasons for using the Internet, but I had to do most of the discovery and learning on my own, with precious little time for it given my day-to-day workload.

On the other hand, a very different attitude is also evident by the response of another corporate librarian, who joined as soon as he realized he could. The loosening of the restrictions in the National Science Foundation Acceptable Use Policy is an important factor in the acceptance of the Internet for the special library community (Tillman & Ladner, in press).

Access and Cost

We asked survey respondents whether the library/department or the parent organization paid for access to the Internet and how this compared to the expense for internal e-mail. Slightly more than half of respondents had the cost of both internal e-mail and Internet access paid for by their parent organizations, and about 20% did not know who covered these costs. Only 9% said their library or department was charged for Internet access. There are no differences between academic and nonacademic respondents in how they pay for access to the Internet or internal e-mail.

We also asked our 1992 respondents (all nonacademic special librarians) how they accessed the Internet. About 90% of the special librarians surveyed in 1992 access the Internet through their own organizations. Of these, the majority access the Internet through their organization's own Internet connection. Others report that their organization provides access to the Internet through a university connection or other outside service. Outside sources for Internet access mentioned by respondents include, in addition to universities, a health sciences library consortium, The WELL, Cleveland Free-Net, MCImail, and CLASS. An analysis of cost and access for 1992 respondents reveals that 3 of the 10 respondents who access the Internet through outside sources, rather than through their own organization's Internet connection, pay for this access from departmental funds. By comparison, none of the 14 respondents whose organization provides Internet access have this cost charged back to their departments.

Training and Employer Support

We provided respondents with a list of training methods and asked them to check off all that were applicable. While 63% of the respondents taught themselves, 52% learned informally from a colleague or friend. Formal training from a single one-hour class to a more structured learning experience was mentioned by 35%. That none of them learned in library school could easily be a function of when the respondents attended library school; the Internet is relatively new to library school curricula. Only 30% of nonacademic librarians checked that they had attended a class or other formal training, as compared to over 43% of academic librarians. In general, respondents indicated they were responsible for their own training (25% indicated they read manuals or other guides); this did not vary by time on the net or by type of library.

Interestingly, a growing number of training tools are now available that appeared around the time of our survey but not early enough that survey respondents had time to make use of them. Future respondents are likely to mention the wealth of published print materials, including Krol's (1992) *The Whole Internet: User's Guide and Catalog* and LaQuey and Ryer's (1993) *Internet Companion.*

Both academic and nonacademic respondents described similar types of training that they provide to others in their organizations. Primarily informal, this training includes helping clients learn how to send mail to someone outside the company, creating short handouts or "cheatsheets," archiving and distributing documentation on the Internet, and one-on-one instruction. More formal training was described in terms of providing training to staff and teaching employees to learn to use the various online public access computers (OPACs) available. One respondent commented that recently a librarian had been hired with specific responsibility to teach and help clients use the Internet/BITNET. Interestingly, two of the 1992 respondents described external training ventures in which they offered networking instruction to people outside their own organizations. The question that asked respondents to describe the support provided by their employers elicited comments ranging from minimal to strong encouragement and financial backing, with little differentiation between academic and nonacademic librarians. The issue of lack of time was commonly mentioned. This problem was succinctly expressed by a corporate research and development librarian, who wrote: "Employer is supportive. I don't have time."

Extent and Frequency of Use

Half of the respondents had been using the Internet or its precursors for less than 18 months. More of the nonacademic special librarians were new users of the Internet, compared to those in academe; almost half (44%) had been using the Internet for 12 months or less, compared to 32% of the academic librarians. Our least experienced Internet user signed on to the network just one month before completing the questionnaire. Our most experienced respondent, by contrast, had been using Internet-type networks since 1969 and was involved with ARPANET since it began at Stanford.

A surprisingly large number of respondents (27%) had been using the Internet for more than three years at the time they were surveyed. This is prior to the appearance of most of the articles in the library literature on the Internet. There was virtually no difference between academic librarians (29%) and nonacademic librarians (26%) among these long-time Internet users. The finding that so many of our respondents have been using the Internet for at least two years demonstrates that they can be considered early adopters (Rogers, 1986) of this communications technology. Some characteristics of early adopters, according to Rogers, are higher socioeconomic status, more active seeking of information about technological innovations, and eclectic interests.

Another indicator of experience with electronic networking is the amount of time spent each week on interactive communications technologies. We computed two such measures: number of hours spent each week on the Internet and hours spent per week on e-mail within the organization. These findings are displayed in Table 1.

TABLE 1
ELECTRONIC NETWORKING PATTERNS BY LIBRARY TYPE

Item	Academic (%)	Nonacademic (%)	Total (%)
(number of respondents)	(35)	(46)	(81)
Time Spent on BITNET/Internet			
5 or more hours/week	25.7	28.3	27.2
2.0-4.9 hours/week	57.1	43.5	49.4
1.0-1.9 hours/week	14.3	26.1	21.0
Less than 1 hour/week	2.9	2.2	2.5
Mean*	4.4	3.9	4.1
Median	3.0	2.0	2.5
Length of Time on Internet at Time of Survey (months)			
Mean**	32.9	27.1	29.6
Median	24.0	17.0	18.0

*$t = 0.53$; $p = .597$. Mean and median based on respondents who use internal e-mail (29 academic, 45 nonacademic); $t = -1.36$, $p = .179$.
**$t = 1.02$, $p = .311$.

About half of our respondents spend between 2 and 5 hours each week on the Internet. Frequency of use ranged from less than one hour each week (one respondent) to 15 hours a week on the network (three people). Academic and nonacademic respondents did not differ in their frequency of Internet use. This distribution of Internet use that we observed in these special librarians is similar to those reported by Rogers (1986, p. 125) in his studies of the patterns of use of new communications technologies, where a small percentage of users accounts for a large percentage of use. In our study, 10% of the users accounted for 46% of the total use, measured in hours per week. Table 2 breaks down frequency of use by type of use for the nonacademic special librarians surveyed in 1992. E-mail is by far the most common function, used by all but one respondent. By contrast, FTP is the least used Internet utility: 11 of the 21 who reported they have access to FTP have never used it.

How the Internet Is Used

This section describes how the special librarians we surveyed actually use the Internet and the importance they attach to five Internet functions: e-mail, discussion lists, Telnet, FTP, and Internet Relay Chat (chat/talk).

We organized responses to our unprompted Internet use question—"Briefly describe your use of the Internet or BITNET"—into six umbrella categories based on the constant comparative method (Mellon, 1990). Listed below are the functions and tasks included under each of these Internet use categories:

Internet Use Categories

Work-related communication, e-mail:
   Communicating with colleagues outside the organization
   Communicating with colleagues and patrons within the organization
   Providing electronic reference service to patrons
   Requesting/providing electronic reference to/from other librarians
   Receiving patron requests for new books, journals, media, ILLs
   Requesting/providing ILLs to other libraries
   Requesting/providing missing issues, duplicates exchange
   Conducting professional association business, committee work, program
      planning
   Conducting consortium business
   Providing/receiving technical assistance to/from other e-mail users
   Requesting/ordering library materials, documents
   Identifying document sources
   Getting quick copyright permission
   Exchanging management and other work-related information
   Submitting applications for employment
   Communicating with vendors/customers
   Delivering search results from vendor to corporate e-mail

Discussion lists, bulletin boards, e-journals:
   Monitoring/participating in newsgroups, BBS, and computer forums
   Accessing electronic journals and newsletters
   Obtaining information on courses, conferences, scholarships, jobs
   Participating in subject-specific lists
   Serving as list owner/moderator
   Subscribing to electronic publications

Searching remote databases:
   Searching remote library catalogs and union lists
   Searching online systems, e.g., RLIN, LEXIS, EPIC, MEDLINE
   Scanning journal tables of contents, e.g., BIOSCI, UnCover
   Searching non-OPAC databases outside organization
   Searching databases on mainframes within organization
   Accessing campus computer systems
   Obtaining cataloging information

File transfer, data exchange:
   Retrieving files via FTP, e.g., getting RFCs
   Receiving documents, technical data
   Sending files, e.g., search results, acquisitions lists, articles, technical data
   Creating mailing/distribution lists for sending files

Research and publication:
   Collaborating in research efforts, coauthoring papers
   Contacting editors and publishers
   Writing dissertation, articles for publication
   Working on Project Gutenberg

Engaging in electronic publishing
Submitting drafts of papers for feedback and comment
Engaging in business research and development

Personal communication, leisure activities:
Engaging in non-business-related communication with friends, relatives, and
spouses
Contacting children in college
Playing games

Other uses:
Training others in Internet use
Demonstrating Internet functions to others
Maintaining organization's client/server
Getting Internet access for patrons, clients
Using Internet for technical services support

TABLE 2
FREQUENCY OF INTERNET USE BY FUNCTION
$(n = 27)$*

Function**	Percent
Have access to e-mail on Internet?	100.0
Time spent on e-mail	
5 or more hours/week	7.4
2.0-4.9 hours/week	18.5
1.0-1.9 hours/week	25.9
less than 1 hour/week	44.4
never/don't use	3.7
Have access to Telnet?	85.2
Time spent on Telnet activity	
5 or more hours/week	0.0
2.0-4.9 hours/week	13.0
1.0-1.9 hours/week	21.7
less than 1 hour/week	43.5
never/don't use	21.7
Have access to FTP?	84.0
Time spent in FTP activity	
5 or more hours/week	0.0
2.0-4.9 hours/week	4.5
1.0-1.9 hours/week	13.6
less than 1 hour/week	31.8
never/don't use	50.0
Have access to computer lists?	82.6
Time spent on lists	
5 or more hours/week	5.3
2.0-4.9 hours/week	15.8
1.0-1.9 hours/week	42.1
less than 1 hour/week	21.1
never/don't use	15.8

*Nonacademic special librarians surveyed in 1992.
**Frequencies are based on number of respondents who have access to the function,
not the total number of respondents.

Table 3 shows percentages of academic and nonacademic survey respondents who described or provided examples of Internet use based on the categories we developed. These percentages are not rates of use by function because we did not directly ask respondents if they used features like e-mail, Telnet, FTP, etc. Since these percentages are based on unprompted responses to a general question about use, we suspect that actual rates for specific Internet functions are higher. Responses to unprompted questions like the above can be used to indicate relative importance of system features, since respondents are more likely to list those features that are most important or valuable to them. Caution, however, should be used in detecting trends in Internet use based on the percentages displayed in Table 3. For one thing, academic respondents do not differ statistically from nonacademic respondents in any of the listed categories. One factor, however, that needs to be considered is that all of the academic library respondents were surveyed in 1991—before the appearance of user-friendly front-ends like Gopher, which simplifies the process of searching remote systems through Telnet, and Veronica, a powerful searching tool.

TABLE 3
INTERNET USE BY LIBRARY TYPE*

Category	Academic (%)	Nonacademic (%)	Total (%)
(number of respondents)	(35)	(46)	(81)
Work-related communication, e-mail	91.4	87.0	88.9
Electronic forums, bulletin boards, e-journals	65.7	54.3	59.3
Searching remote databases (Telnet)	34.3	43.5	39.5
FTP and other file transfer	34.3	23.9	28.4
Research and publication	25.7	10.9	17.3
Personal communication, leisure activities	8.6	8.7	8.6
Other	2.9	8.7	6.2

*Source: content analysis of survey question, "Briefly describe your use of the Internet or BITNET." Difference of proportions in dichotomies were evaluated with z-scores (Blalock, 1972).

What the data in Table 3 do show is the overwhelming use of the Internet for e-mail by survey respondents. We first observed the importance of e-mail to the special librarians we surveyed in 1991, the majority of whom were academic librarians. These special librarians use the Internet primarily for communication—with each other, with other librarians, and with their clientele (Ladner & Tillman, 1992a, 1992b, 1992c; 1993b). Increasing the number of nonacademic special librarians in our study does not alter this finding.

In 1992, we asked respondents to indicate the importance of five Internet functions (e-mail, Telnet, discussion lists, file transfer, and chat/talk) based on a five-point scale. The results of this analysis show that e-mail ranks first, followed by Telnet and discussion lists. Three out of four consider e-mail to be essential or important in their work, and two out of three consider Telnet to be essential or important. In comparison, less than half consider discussion lists to be essential or important, and only one out of four feel that way about FTP.

Training Needs

While a few questioned the need for any instruction, most respondents assigned responsibility for training to multiple bases: parent organizations (by both libraries and computer centers), professional associations, library schools, and commercial trainers. Instructional tools desired included manuals, print documentation, tutorials, video, and demonstration disks. Respondents repeatedly expressed their need for easy-to-use packaged information.

Both academic and nonacademic librarians viewed their own organization as prime sites providing facilities, written materials, and staff to conduct workshops. They felt that organizations should offer basic training in FTP, Telnet, e-mail, and USENET news. Respondents in larger organizations described the viability of subdividing the training within the parent organization, with the computing center offering classes on the basics of the Internet and the library offering seminars on available network resources in specialized subject areas.

An academic law librarian also mentioned the need for informal mentor training, providing help when it is needed. Half of the librarians surveyed, in fact, had checked informal training as one of the ways they had been trained to use the Internet. Others cited family members as also playing a role in their training. Several librarians cited the Internet itself as a way they received their training by asking questions of their colleagues or others via the net or by finding online documentation.

Both academic and nonacademic librarians urged library schools to be in the forefront in educating students about the Internet. Library schools should provide accounts to students and probably require at least a minimum amount of usage. Library schools should also offer classes in network access, including not only basic training, but theory, and some information on how the network can be helpful to librarians. Some respondents cautioned library schools against making their Internet instruction too specific or procedural because the technology changes too quickly and varies among institutions and disciplines. One special librarian, using the Internet to facilitate work on her Ph.D. dissertation, felt strongly that the skill "should be expected of library school students (and faculty) and not specifically taught as part of that program for credit."

Respondents said that the role for professional associations is particularly important for experienced librarians and for librarian-specific applications, especially in providing a setting where experienced librarians who did not learn network use in library school could obtain an introduction and hands-on training without embarrassment at "not knowing." A science librarian in a government agency advocated that professional organizations demonstrate their support by adding e-mail addresses to directories. Professional organizations should be providing exposure to what is on the Internet, but they, like library schools, cannot replace the parent organization's local training on how to use that organization's specific system.

The most interesting difference between 1991 and 1992 survey responses was the identification of new sources for trainers. Several respondents surveyed in 1992 reported that their OCLC-affiliated library consortia are getting into the arena of Internet access and training. One librarian saw a role for public libraries to offer classes for the public, because as the network grows and more and more people have access, the bigger the gap will be between those who can afford access, or who have it through their jobs, and those who cannot afford access.

What Training Should be Provided?

In answer to our question on what training should be provided for new users, respondents identified very specific knowledge that should be imparted in the training. The need for coverage of both theory and basic training techniques was frequently mentioned. Training should cover both history and philosophy of the Internet along with what it is, what's out there, and how it works. Useful training sessions would include training in FTP, Telnet, e-mail, USENET news, listservs, addressing algorithms, proper etiquette (netiquette), security rules to safeguard computers/data, how to connect to the Internet, how to keep up with Internet developments and changing resources, how to manage the flow of information, and how this differs and/or complements for-fee online services.

Respondents also mentioned training needs specific to librarians, for example: how networking is helpful to librarians and its potential for libraries, how to identify information nodes to locate and access relevant forums and publishers, how to make the best use of increased connectivity to streamline library procedures, and how to persuade important vendors to provide e-mail access of electronic data interchange (EDI). Respondents to the 1992 survey added the need to cover specific Internet tools, such as Wide Area Information Servers (WAIS) and archie, which were not mentioned in comments of 1991 respondents.

Survey respondents considered that the end result of training should be to impart sufficient knowledge of what is on the Internet and how to use it in order to integrate Internet resources into organizational needs, information technology expertise, and a high comfort level with continuing change. Their responses to our series of questions about how they were trained and training needs of special librarians can be grouped into the following questions:

1. What is the Internet (or more broadly, electronic networking)?
2. Why should I be interested in it? (In particular, what's in it for me and my company? What is out there that will add value to my performance?)
3. How do I get connected? (How do I arrange for access? How do I log on?)
4. What do I need to learn to get started?
5. How do I build my competence and keep up to date?
6. What's coming in the future?

IMPLICATIONS AND CHALLENGES

Our findings indicate that there are no real differences between the way that academic and nonacademic special librarians use the Internet. Responses from the 27 additional nonacademic special librarians we surveyed in 1992 mirror and reinforce those of 1991 respondents and are independent of organizational type.

Training and Trainers

Our analysis of how special librarians learned to use the Internet provides some answers but also raises additional questions. Where are library schools in the training continuum? There was a plethora of training sessions described by the 1992 respondents, but none sponsored by library schools. Respondents, particularly those with less than a year's Internet experience, expressed the need to know more. Their reaction to the quality of training was mixed; some respondents expressed satisfaction, others dissatisfaction with the training they received.

Those surveyed presented specific recommendations to improve present training. How will their expressed needs be addressed? Will Internet training continue to be met by the same providers that respondents mentioned? Most likely not. The introduction of textbooks and commercial trainers brings an added dimension to Internet training that will most likely expand in the future. It will be interesting to observe what types of training will be best addressed by commercial providers. In addition, the widening access to the Internet beyond the research and educational community to the public at large will mean a continued expansion in the need for training for new users. Librarians from all types of organizations can play an important role in this area in the future.

Access

The academic and nonacademic special librarians in our study access the Internet through different means. Generally respondents who access the Internet through consortia or from accounts with external providers are nonacademics, and this type of access may be charged back to the library or department. Having to pay for Internet access from departmental funds requires that special librarians justify its use in order to fund the line, whereas special librarians whose organizations provide access do not have this problem.

The growing number of Internet access providers in the marketplace may herald greater opportunities for nonacademic special librarians to gain access to the Internet at a reasonable price. The addition of some OCLC regional networks offering individual accounts to their members may be of particular value to some smaller libraries because the Internet access fee can be folded into a budget line that already exists for cataloging. Also, the growing market of Internet providers offering user accounts empowers the small or one-person library that may never have been able to justify the need for an Internet node.

Types of Use

The special librarians we surveyed use the Internet to communicate—with each other, with their clientele, with outside experts, with other librarians, and with other professionals they happen to meet on the network. They spend more time in e-mail-related activities, and three out of four consider e-mail essential or important to their work.

We anticipate, however, that relative use may shift away from e-mail as a result of Gopher and WAIS and their successors that make use of Telnet and FTP within a more user-friendly interface. More of the respondents surveyed in 1992 considered Telnet to be important or essential to their work than they did discussion lists. This is not to say that e-mail will diminish in importance, but we predict that Telnet and FTP will increase in use over the next few years.

We observed that respondents surveyed in 1992 rank Telnet higher than discussion lists, second only to e-mail. By comparison, although we did not ask respondents in 1991 to rate Internet functions as to importance, we did find that there were fewer unprompted descriptions of Internet use for remote database searching than for discussion lists among this group. There is the very real possibility that special librarians outside of academe may find the discussion lists too oriented to academic librarianship and consequently less relevant to their needs. The emergence of specific lists relevant to special librarianship may offset this possibility.

As the number of discussion list subscribers increases, will these lists' value as an interactive, human-based source of information decrease? Price (1963, pp. 62-91) postulated 30 years ago, in his essay on the nature of invisible colleges, that it is possible to keep up with a colleague group no larger than a few hundred members; once this size is exceeded, it becomes impossible to monitor the subject area. Will the same hold true for discussion groups, which seem to serve the function of electronic invisible colleges? Will more experienced users drop out of discussion groups, frustrated with seeing the same questions asked over and over again by novice users? Or will the group move from the openness of small lists to become managed by a "moderator" who will handle the messages sent in error to the group as well as inappropriate comments? Or will software enable better management of mail received?

Current Users

The majority of special librarians we surveyed work in scientific, technical, and medical disciplines. Special librarians in other fields, such as business, may use the Internet differently. Ladner (1992) found that more sci-tech than business special librarians are members of resource-sharing networks and use them more frequently. Will a similar pattern be observed for business librarians with the Internet? Our respondents can also be considered early adopters of Internet technology, and as such, may not use the Internet in the same way as special librarians who come on board later.

While this research does not provide a definitive picture of the special librarian on the Internet, we have in this exploratory study created a composite role model for the many special librarians looking for guidance in what the

Internet can do for them. Our research encompasses a wealth of data that is richly descriptive but exploratory. These data must be viewed in the context in which they were collected—we surveyed special librarians who responded to a Call for Participation in a research project—and cannot be generalized to special librarians as a whole. Our findings raise questions that beg to be answered through additional research on other Internet users.

REFERENCES

Blalock, H. M., Jr. (1972). *Social statistics* (2nd ed.). New York: McGraw-Hill.

Hill, L. L. (1985). Issues in network participation for corporate librarians. *Special Libraries, 76*(1), 2-10.

Hiltz, S. R., & Turoff, M. (1978). *The network nation: Human communication via computer.* Reading, MA: Addison-Wesley.

Kiesler, S., & Sproull, L. S. (1986). Response effects in the electronic survey. *Public Opinion Quarterly, 50*(3), 402-413.

Krol, E. (1992). *The whole Internet: User's guide & catalog.* Sebastopol, CA: O'Reilly.

Ladner, S. J. (1990). Networking and special libraries: Impact of technology, economics and human nature. In D. C. Genaway (Comp.), *IOLS '90: Proceedings of the Fifth National Conference on Integrated Online Library Systems* (pp. 129-135). Medford, NJ: Learned Information.

Ladner, S. J. (1992). Resource sharing in sci-tech and business libraries: Formal networking practices. *Special Libraries, 83*(2), 96-112.

Ladner, S. J., & Tillman, H. N. (1992a). How special librarians really use the Internet: Summary of findings and implications for the library of the future. (Report available via anonymous FTP on host hydra.uwo.ca in directory Libsoft, filename SPEC_LIBS.TXT) (ERIC Document Reproduction Service No. ED 345 751)

Ladner, S. J., & Tillman, H. N. (1992b). How special librarians really use the Internet. *Canadian Library Journal, 49*(3), 211-215.

Ladner, S. J., & Tillman, H. N. (1992c). How special librarians really use the Internet. *BF Bulletin: Business and Finance Division, Special Libraries Association,* no. 91, 9-15.

Ladner, S. J., & Tillman, H. N. (1993a). Using the Internet for reference. *Online, 17*(1), 45-51.

Ladner, S. J., & Tillman, H. N. (1993b). *The Internet and special librarians: Use, training and the future.* Washington, DC: Special Libraries Association.

LaQuey, T., & Ryer, J. C. (1993). *Internet companion: A beginner's guide to global networking.* Reading, MA: Addison-Wesley.

Mellon, C. A. (1990). *Naturalistic inquiry for library science: Methods and applications for research, evaluation, and teaching.* New York: Greenwood Press.

Mount, E. (1985). *University science and engineering libraries* (2nd ed.). Westport, CT: Greenwood Press.

Mount, E. (1991). *Special libraries and information centers: An introductory text* (2nd ed.). Washington, DC: Special Libraries Association.

Patton, M. Q. (1980). *Qualitative research methods.* Beverly Hills, CA: Sage.

Price, D. J. de S. (1963). *Little science, big science.* New York: Columbia University Press.

Rogers, E. M. (1986). *Communication technology: The new media in society.* New York: Free Press.

Sproull, L. S. (1986). Using electronic mail for data collection in organizational research. *Academy of Management Journal, 29*(1), 159-169.

Stern, D. (1988). An alternative national electronic mail network for libraries. *Special Libraries, 79*(2), 139-142.

Tillman, H. (1991). SLA programs cover the Internet. *B/ITE: Bulletin of the Information Technology Division, Special Libraries Association, 8*(4), n.p.

Tillman, H. N., & Ladner, S. J. (1992). Special librarians and the Internet. *Special Libraries, 83*(2), 127-131.

Tillman, H. N., & Ladner, S. J. (in press). Special libraries and the NREN. In C. R. McClure, (Ed.). *The role of libraries in the Internet/NREN: Perspectives, issues and challenge.* Westport, CT: Meckler.

DEIRDRE C. STAM

Associate Professor
School of Library and Information Science
Catholic University
Washington, DC

Wiring the Muse:
Problems and Issues of Integrating Networked
Information into Museum Operations

INTRODUCTION

Unlike most writers on the current networking scene, whose difficulty is to compress an enormous amount of networking information into a few readable pages, my problem as a reporter of museum networking is that I have little to describe. Museums, frankly, are not heavily into the networking game. Furthermore, except for a few institutions connected to technologically minded universities, museums show relatively little inclination to move onto the playing field at all. Curiously enough, it was not always so, but it is so now. This is ironic given that it is only now that the real possibilities for effective networking exist, and others are standing in line for the privilege. Museums are firmly on the sidelines.

The skeptic who is immersed in network talk might well wonder whether this assessment can be true. He might think it more likely that I am simply ignorant of activity in the museum community. That, of course, is possible, but frankly unlikely, in view of my recent history. I should describe my connection to the museum information world in order to establish my qualifications to speak.

A dozen years ago, after 15 years of art library and museum curatorial jobs, I began in earnest to investigate museum information with a dissertation at Columbia University in the late lamented School of Library Service on the topic of art historians' information seeking in museums and colleges. This topic became the focus of teaching and research at Syracuse University and Catholic University, with a brief stint spent as executive director of the Museum Computer Network (an organization that, despite its name, does not maintain an electronic network). In the natural course of events, I edited two of the (nonprofit) journals where the largest proportion of discussion on museum information issues has appeared: *Art Documentation* (from the Art Libraries Society of North America) and *Spectra* (from the Museum Computer Network).

I have been visiting museums over the past few years specifically to find out about their information management practices while working on publications on that topic. Additionally, I have organized sessions on the topic of museum information, and specifically its automation, at conferences run by the American Society for Information Science (ASIS) and the American Association of Museums (AAM), and participated in countless other panels at the meetings of the Society of American Archivists, the Visual Resources Association, the (U.K.) Museum Documentation Association, the International Federation of Library Associations and Institutions' (IFLA) Art Section, regional museum associations, and other organizations.

What have I heard there? Promises, promises—and these mostly from consultants, vendors, library school faculty, library network staff (most specifically, the Research Library Group), and the employees of the sui generis J. Paul Getty Trust. From museum professionals themselves, one hears very little. Does that really mean that museum people have little to report? A reasonable question, especially in light of the fact that museum professionals, unlike library and information scientists, have a fairly small professional literature and do not readily report therein their every passing thought or action. Furthermore, their managerial interests, as indicated at conferences and in conversation, include a wide range of other topics more compelling to them, such as display techniques, security, and fund-raising. Information management, although reasonably considered here as fundamental to museum work, is not yet a topic that museum people themselves are particularly aware of or used to addressing. That said, I am convinced that the lack of reportage does indeed reflect lack of networking activity.

Many in library circles are surprised to learn that electronic networking in museums is in a rudimentary stage, indeed, that automation of information generally lags far behind library norms. Librarians see museums as kindred institutions to their own, with largely similar missions (traditionally to collect informational materials and to encourage informal education through making these artifacts available to the public) and similar professional issues (collection development, cataloging, classification, preservation, storage, and access). This characterization, while true for many though not all museums, ignores those elements of museums that make them very different from libraries and help to explain their very different attitude toward automation.

The significant uniqueness of museums, in contrast to libraries, in addition to the different natures of their collections, lies in at least two areas. The first deals with mission. A major responsibility of museums lies in the presentation of their material to their publics. This function involves value judgments, interpretation, and explanation through visual and textual means. Museum people are thus engaged in a teaching function in relation to a body of professional knowledge and material to a degree largely subordinated in libraries. The library-like functions of collecting, cataloging, etc., are only supportive of this scholarly activity and are not fundamental in themselves to the institution's raison d'etre. The second difference, growing out of the first, is the institutional framework in which museum professionals work. A review of this framework, with emphasis upon the tradition of informal (nonelectronic) networking, would help to explain the difference in these institutions.

THE INFORMAL NETWORKING TRADITION IN MUSEUMS

Funding and Governance

Museums in the United States—and in this country the term includes institutions for the exhibition of art objects, historical artifacts, and objects of natural history—are almost entirely self-sufficient entities. Their sources of funding are frequently a mixture of private endowment and public funds, but the policy making of the institution lies firmly in the hands of boards of trustees, often self-perpetuating and more or less representative of community establishment (including, these days, representation of the minority establishment). The expertise of trustees is typically concentrated in banking, real estate, business, and the law—in brief, not in museum matters and certainly not in the museum's information management per se. Though local government funding plays an increasingly large part in museum financing, local government officials play almost no direct role in governing museums. The relationship of museums to funding sources in government contrasts sharply with that of libraries in the public sector where the director typically reports to a local government body, or in academic settings where the library director reports to an academic administrator. Few museums experience oversight of this sort.

Formal Alliances Among Museums

Legal connections of any significance among museums are exceedingly rare, though talk of such alliances has been heard recently. It is true that very loose alliances of institutions in local regions have sprung up in recent decades, such as a newly active alliance centered in Philadelphia or New York State regional affiliations, but the formation of these groups very often represents a transparent attempt to obtain financing from a local trust or state government that professes interest in cooperative action. Such motivation lay, for example, behind the formation of the always optimistic but perennially underfunded Museum Computer Network (Vance, 1986, p. 40). Within the institutions involved in these marriages of convenience, such alliances have almost no presence and even less real effect in the member institutions.

A notable exception of closely allied museums is the largely federally financed Smithsonian Institution (SI), where meaningful managerial connections exist, but these links are not particularly welcomed by the constituent museums (I am telling tales out of school here as a former SI employee), and initiatives at the centralized level are sometimes undermined locally through intentional, mulish adherence to bureaucratic procedure. The SI, though prominent in the public eye by reason of its geography and collections, does not play the leadership role in relation to other American museums that the Library of Congress exerts in relation to American libraries. No U.S. museum has assumed the comparable leadership role for the museum world, despite the renaming in recent years of various institutions as "The National Museum of This-and-That."

It should be noted in passing that a few museums in academic institutions have legal affiliation to other educational entities, but these museums are relatively few in number and considered by museum professionals as somewhat outside the mainstream of the museum profession. Ironically, it is here, in academic settings, that electronic facilities are in relative abundance, and some of the most advanced museum networking is taking place (Besser, 1990).

Professional Associations

Museums have, relative to libraries, few professional associations, and membership in them is uneven and unpredictable. Most museum professionals— curators and administrators alike—come from an academic discipline, such as medieval history or anthropology, and belong to an appropriate scholarly association. Their first allegiance is probably there. Secondarily they might belong to a professional museum organization.

Many administrators and some curators of small museums belong to the American Association of Museums, an organization showing increasing emphasis upon activities of persuasion "on the Hill" and interest in "professionalizing" museum work through such outward signs as accreditation and statistics gathering. The directors of major art museums are more likely to put their energies into the Association of American Art Museum Directors. The staff of small historical societies turn frequently to the American Association for State and Local History, an organization struggling for stability following a few troubled years of overly ambitious expansion. Science and natural history staff, and zookeepers, have comparable professional organizations that deal with the administrative problems of their peculiar collections and publics.

A strong emphasis of all of the professional organizations serving the highly varied museum field is on helping individual members and their institutions increase their support base—often through programmatic activity—so that, ultimately, museums can raise money and manage their affairs effectively, thus ensuring their survival. Program-directed networking as is basic in libraries, designed first of all to meet clients' needs, is not uppermost in the minds of museum association staff or members. That is not to say that members of museums staffs are self-serving but rather to point out that survival of museums is far more precarious than that of any kind of library (except perhaps the Library of the New York Historical Society, which has the misfortune of looking for its support to a museum). The effort to keep afloat must be a preoccupation of museum staff.

Professional Training

Much of the information "networking" that librarians engage in begins with their graduate school experience, where relationships to faculty and to fellow students take root. Despite the vociferousness of the numerous, small, and new academic programs in museum studies operating at the master's level, the truth is they prepare only a small proportion of museum staff. Museum workers, even in what one might think of as professional positions, are likely to come from any and all backgrounds, with preparation ranging from high school to doctoral programs in their disciplines. There is no clear criterion for professional status, and this status is achieved as often through longevity and performance as through formal qualification. It is folklore in this subculture that the most prestigious museums prefer academically trained staff, particularly from the avowedly old-fashioned programs at Harvard and New York University's Institute of Fine Arts, to those who have been trained in museum management in the newer museum training programs. Even in those newer "professional" schools of museum training, the curriculum varies greatly from one program to another, and from year to year. (There is, for example, no standard approach to teaching the cataloging of museum objects.) The most meaningful informal (social) networking that can be gained from these professional museum management programs, many museum professionals believe, comes from the in-museum internship segment of these programs.

Publications

Oddly enough, there are fewer than a handful of publications that deal with managerial issues of museums, and of these almost none recognize information management as pertinent at all to the museum profession. The American Association of Museums (AAM) publishes *Museum News*, which as the major publication of the largest professional organization in the field is roughly comparable to—though slicker than—*American Libraries*. *Museum News* consists of largely invited articles that address a single theme per issue, at a popular level. *History News*, a more modestly produced vehicle from the American Association for State and Local History (AASLH), contains a mixture of subject-oriented articles, "how we do it good" descriptions, and one highly informative and well-researched, brief, detachable centerfold insert per issue devoted to a professional function. This journal is widely and carefully read, as are the practically oriented monograph publications of the AASLH. More theoretical and more fully researched curatorial and to some degree managerial issues are treated in the refereed journal *Curator* published by the American Museum of Natural History. Judging from citations and from conversation with museum people, I would guess that *Curator* is not widely read, though it is known to the museum intelligentsia (if I may be forgiven an elitist characterization). Even more abstract and international in its focus is the little-known *Museum Management and Curatorship* produced in the United Kingdom—the kind of offbeat journal, incidentally, that publishes my sort of contribution.

The topic of electronic information is treated directly in two journals with short histories and always uncertain futures: *Museum and Archives Informatics*, published by David Bearman's basically-one-person consulting firm, and *Spectra*, which is the official journal of the peripatetic Museum Computer Network. Almost all information that exists in the public record relating to electronic networking in museums can be found in the latter two, somewhat irregular, publications. The circulation of the latter two journals is probably in the low hundreds—circulation figures on proprietary publications are not readily available—and relatively few of these subscriptions are maintained by libraries where the potential of a wider readership might exist.

ELECTRONIC NETWORKING IN MUSEUMS

The foregoing review of the tradition of information networking in museums might lead one to conclude that there is no electronic networking in place. That is not the case. A small amount of fairly predictable networking exists. Electronic networking made its way into museums usually first through museum libraries, then—particularly in large historical museums—in archives where these collections are substantial. More recent for many museums is networking in relation to object catalogs (known as collection management systems) and in relation to development office address files, though in both cases networking is in-house at best. The use of networked information for management purposes is almost unknown in actuality, though discussed in some of the more theoretical literature produced by information specialists who advise museums. A few other networking applications have cropped up, but despite the enthusiasm of their proponents, these projects, relating to visual resources for example, should not be interpreted as indicating a ground swell of networking activity. Some specifics would be useful here.

Libraries

The Research Libraries Group (RLG) made a determined and successful effort in the 1980s to enroll art museum libraries as special members, at relatively modest rates. The result has been commitment to RLG among many institutions to develop a rich database of holdings, to develop ancillary tools such as a database of auction catalogs, and more recently to use RLG electronic mail (e-mail) as a communication device. It should be understood that only fairly large museums have been able to avail themselves of this resource, and of these it is primarily art museums that have signed on. OCLC is found in other larger museum libraries, though many museum libraries have no automation at all, not even stand-alone systems. E-mail, except for RLG, is still quite unusual even in museum libraries.

It should also be clearly understood that the appearance of automated information handling in libraries has not had notable influence on the rest of the museums (with a handful of exceptions including the Boston Museum of Fine Arts and Winterthur). Most museum staff, other than librarians, still do not communicate electronically with anybody; indeed the largest number of museum staff do not work with automation at all except perhaps through stand-alone word processors. In larger museums, some staff might work with collection management systems, but access, even where systems exist, is by no means assured to all professional staff even within such a fortunate institution. Collection management systems in many institutions are seen primarily as registrars' tools.

As extensions of libraries, in terms of function if not in organizational structures, visual resource collections should be mentioned. The story is brief. Automation has been slow to take hold here, due in part to lack of standards of description, classification schemes, and vocabulary control, even within single institutions. At least one commercial vendor is offering the potential for communication among his customers, and while enthusiasm for such networking is high among visual resource curators, effective "realization," as the French say, does not yet exist (Roberts, 1985).

Archives

In quite a number of large history museums, and in a very few major art museums (parts of the Smithsonian Institution, the Philadelphia Museum of Art, and the Boston Museum of Fine Arts, for example), archivists are showing interest in the exchange of electronic collections records. Some institutions are actually contributing to the Research Libraries Information Network (RLIN) Archives and Manuscripts Control (AMC) file. This step is quite revolutionary for museums in that it requires adherence to one descriptive standard, that is, the AMC format. The adoption of a national format for communication is quite a new step for museums, one that has not yet occurred in relation to museum objects themselves.

Several museums that have seen the utility of adhering to a nationally recognized format are using the AMC framework to build an in-house archival database using proprietary software that incorporates many aspects of the AMC standard. There is some question as to how many of the records thus built would be truly exportable to a combined national archival database. It should be understood that the AMC standard is itself relatively new, and its application in museums specifically has a history of only a few years where it has been adopted.

RLG has invested several years' work in the development of a full archives and records management system, known as AMIS, that could be used for museum objects as well (Research, 1991). This system would allow communication of data among institutions. It is not at all clear at this point, however, what kind of market exists for the high degree of sophistication and high cost that will be characteristic of this product.

Collection Management Systems

After an ill-fated cooperative attempt on the part of several major New York museums in the early 1970s to build mainframe-based object-cataloging systems with some potential for communication, museums were gun-shy about automation for at least a decade (Stam, 1989). With the appearance of the personal computer in the early 1980s, several museums undertook small-scale, stand-alone cataloging projects, but these often bogged down under the weight of data and inadequacy of technology. The lack of tradition concerning standards of description was an additional problem in these automation attempts, as it still is today. Another serious inhibitor to collection management systems is the lack of acceptable and inexpensive visual-imaging technology, a vital requirement for the museum field. In brief, there is not yet a national database of museum object information, or anything like it.

In-house collection management systems, consisting of something like a library catalog combined with processing and circulation records, exist in quite a significant number of larger museums. In almost all cases, the software has been licensed from a proprietary source, and its code is a carefully guarded secret. (Many of these companies, incidentally, are virtual mom-and-pop shops, with short histories and little capital behind them.) The software comes typically with field labels and processes defined (with some modest tailoring allowed). While the overall needs of museums are somewhat similar, and therefore their record structures for collection management fall into a few clear patterns, there are no recognized standards of description, communication formats, or tools of vocabulary control. Each system is unique, and at this point incapable of communicating with any other—even in some cases with other systems in different departments of the same museum. Meaningful electronic networking relating to collections between the library and the registrar's office is almost unknown in this country, though it does exist occasionally elsewhere (van der Wateren, 1988). The kind of integrated systems that are now commonplace in libraries are hardly dreamt of in the museum context.

A few vendors of collection management systems speak of networking, but what they mean is that two of their users who might configure their products similarly can query one another's files or could theoretically intermingle data. Given the utter lack of standards, this possibility is at best remote.

There is hope for better communication on the distant horizon. Two projects now in early stages (and both lacking firm institutional foundations and funding) might improve this situation. One is the Art Information Task Force, which is working on descriptive standards; the other is the Computerized Interchange of Museum Information (CIMI) Project, which has as its goal the identification of technical standards for the exchange of museum data (Perkins, 1992). Other task forces are emerging to deal with descriptive standards for museum fields other than art. In all cases, official, sanctioned national leadership is, however, conspicuously lacking. Also lacking are standards for the transmission of visual imagery, an absolute necessity to the museum profession given its preeminent visual orientation.

Administration

It is a curiosity in the museum field that the current enthusiasm for improving management practices does not include significant reference (in AAM publications or in the curriculum of the prestigious Museum Management Institute, for example) to the management of information. Almost nothing is said, and even less is done, about using modern information technology to aid in gathering, analyzing, and using information for institutional benefit (Stam, 1992). It is true that some automation occurs in the development office, in the form of donors' address lists, and this information is beginning, in a very few cases, to be shared in-house through local area networks. The sharing of data across the profession is barely conceived of as being desirable. Even the cooperative design of loan forms, so that comparable information is required from one institution to another, has taken years of still uncompleted work; the electronic transmission of such forms—beyond the fax—is almost inconceivable in this community.

The AAM contribution to network development has thus far been to contract with a communications company to provide better telephone rates for AAM member institutions than single museums can negotiate and to start on the path toward providing the technological means for data exchange should that be seen as desirable. Many American information people look admiringly at Canada, where the Canadian Heritage Information Network has all but overcome the "tyranny of distance" affecting Canadian institutions through its shared cataloging and communication links, but it should be recognized that the system is underwritten by the Canadian government (Sutherland, 1992). No such cultural centralization or funding pattern occurs in this country.

What does exist as museum community networking is the scantily subscribed electronic discussion list known as MUSEUM-L. The questions that are posed there indicate an ill-defined need for advice of all kinds and little understanding, at least among the electronically "vocal," of where they should look for professional information relating to management issues. If their librarians read the list, I suspect that answers would be forthcoming from them, but there appears to be little cross-function readership in the subscribers to this list.

Networked Art

Curiously enough, in the museum world it seems to be artists who are most venturesome in using computer networks (Loeffler, 1992). This development is very new and strongly dependent upon the recent development of visual-imaging technology. Artists use electronic networking to create joint art projects, to reach large audiences, and to explore such fundamental questions about art as the functions of time, or space, or art institutions themselves (Shipe, 1990). While their pursuits might be seen as a threat to the central place of the museum itself in the art world, it can also be seen more benignly as a phenomenon of new museology where issues of communication, audience need, and the museum's "aura" and values are being questioned (Stam, in press).

CONCLUSIONS

Why are museums so slow to take to networking? The old explanations—not enough money, not enough expertise, and inadequate technology—no longer hold water. Time and technological developments have solved some of these problems. It is quite obvious, however, that some barriers remain. The inhibitions to museum networking that are relevant today fall into two categories: those internal to the museum profession and those external to it—and, incidentally, central to our concerns as information professionals (Bearman, 1992; Zoeckler, 1991).

First, the internal barriers—they are primarily expressed here as deprivations. Museums still lack an authoritative body and leadership to coordinate efforts toward cooperative use of automation technology and information management. Museums also lack standardization in practice from one museum to another and standards for data formatting and transmission. Museums lack a sense of direction and imagination about how networked information might help fulfill their missions and improve their management practices to that end (Neufeld, 1992). And finally, the museum community lacks opportunity through contact with other pertinent communities to get into the networking loop. These hiatuses the museum world must deal with primarily by itself.

Other barriers to museum networking can best be overcome by professions exterior to the museum world—most specifically information professionals. Museums need, for example, models for the functions of producers, owners, marketplace, and payment in the network environment (Bearman, 1992). They need standards for the transmission of visual information and laws to govern the use of such media. They need help in articulating their needs and making demands of the automation marketplace. They, like other potential network participants, need ongoing education about the power of the networking phenomenon. And they need models for decision making and leadership in networking activities.

Wiring the muse can be done and probably will be done eventually. How soon and how well museums become wired to the national networking scene will depend to some extent on their own efforts as a community. To a larger extent, however, it will depend on the ability of the information community that is designing the "net" to recognize and accommodate the kind of visual and object-oriented cultural information that has been traditionally associated with museums but that in reality should be of interest to us all.

REFERENCES

Bearman, D. (1992). Network advisory committee tackles multimedia. *Archives and Museum Informatics, 6*(4), 7-8.

Besser, H. (1990). Visual access to visual images: The UC Berkeley Image Database Project. *Library Trends, 38*(4), 787-798.

Loeffler, C. (1992). The networked virtual art museum. *Bulletin of the American Society for Information Science, 19*(1), 13-14.

Neufeld, S. (1992). Systems development and the small museum: Recent trends affecting the sharing of information. In D. A. Roberts (Ed.), *Sharing the information resources of museums* (Proceedings of an international conference held in York, England, 14-18 September 1989) (pp. 15-28). Cambridge, England: Museum Documentation Association.

Perkins, J. (1992). CIMI's data movement. *Museum News, 71*(4), 24-26.

Research Libraries Group to develop information management system for museums and archives. (1991). *Technical Services Quarterly, 9*(2), 65-66.

Roberts, H. E. (1985). Visual resources: Proposals for an ideal network. *Art Libraries Journal, 10*(3), 32-41.

Shipe, T. (1990). Art networks and information systems. *Art Documentation, 9*(1), 9-11.

Stam, D. C. (1989). The quest for a code, or a brief history of the computerized cataloging of art objects. *Art Documentation, 8*(1), 7-15.

Stam, D. C. (1992). Taming the beast: Guidance for administrators on managing museum computerization. *Museum Management and Curatorship, 11*(1), 45-60.

Stam, D. C. (in press). The informed muse: The implications of new museology for museum practice. *Museum Management and Curatorship, 12*(4).

Sutherland, I. (1992). Information for Canadian museums: The Canadian Heritage Information Network. *Bulletin of the American Society for Information Science, 18*(2), 16-18.

van der Wateren, J. F. (1988). Achieving the link between art object and documentation: Experiences in the British Architectural Library. *Library Trends, 37*(2), 243-251.

Vance, D. (1986). The Museum Computer Network in context. In R. B. Light, D. A. Roberts, & J. D. Stewart (Eds.), *Museum documentation systems: Developments and applications* (pp. 37-48). London: Butterworths.

Zoeckler, L. K. (1991). Collections management systems & their impact on museum libraries. *Art Documentation, 10*(2), 91-92.

JANET M. VRATNY

Information Scientist
Apple Library
Apple Computer
Cupertino, California

Integrating Networked Information into Corporate Library Services*

ABSTRACT

The author will describe and explore the issues related to the integration of "traditional" library services and networked information in a corporate library setting. The case study of Apple Library's staff and their users will be used to illustrate a number of specific integration issues, such as user expectation, staff training and workload, changing job roles, content development, security, and the growing complexity of user access. The integration of CD-ROM via local area network access versus Internet-based resources will be discussed. Specific applications and prototypes for networked access to information resources that are under development or in use will be demonstrated.

*Editor's Note: We are unable to include the text of this presentation in the Proceedings. For further information on its contents, contact the author: Janet Vratny, Information Scientist, Apple Library, 4 Infinite Loop, 304-2A, Cupertino, CA 95014.

JOHN R. GARRETT

Director, Information Resources
Corporation for National Research Initiatives
Reston, Virginia

The World We Want:
Emerging Communities, Emerging Information

EMERGING DEMOCRATIC COMMUNITIES

In a recent essay, the philosopher Richard Rorty (1992) reflected on a lifetime of engagement with the fundamental ideas of our time and concluded that the historic quest for a single vision that encompasses both the real and the ideal worlds is, sadly, a mistake. Further, Rorty argues that "the main trouble is that you might succeed, and your success might let you imagine that you have something more to rely on than the tolerance and decency of your fellow human beings" (p. 153). Indeed, the search to realize one or another ideal world—through philosophy, religion, national identity—remains a root cause of human suffering, as each day's news broadcasts all too vividly remind us.

Rorty's alternative, building on Dewey, is the always evolving democratic community, which combines a shared understanding of human fragility and mutual dependence with the recognition of individual rights, limited only by the prohibition against causing injury to others:

> It is a community in which everybody thinks that it is human solidarity, rather than knowledge of something not merely human, that really matters. The actually existing approximations to such a fully democratic, fully secular community now seem to me the greatest achievement of our species. (Rorty, 1992, p. 153)

I will argue here that distributed digital information, seamlessly integrated into a comprehensive National Information Infrastructure, is essential to realizing Rorty's secular, communitarian vision: the creation and sharing of knowledge about what it means to be "merely human." But creating the infrastructure will also require creating a version, at least, of Rorty's democratic community. I believe that this will depend, in large measure, on the ability of the many organizations and interest groups in the information universe to transcend their narrow, absolute views of past, present, and future, and create—if only for a little while—the integrated, democratic communities that Rorty envisions: communities of experimentation, communities of trust.

If the integrated, democratic information-rich community is our vision of the future, what of the present? The anthropologist Mary Douglas has devoted her professional life to thinking about, and chronicling, the conceptual and structural underpinnings of cultures. With Aaron Wildavsky, she has written about the assessment of ecological dangers as a canvas to limn the relationship between the "center" and the "border," between conventional and sectarian perspectives on our shared human nature, and the world.

Early on, Douglas and Wildavsky (1982) define knowledge in a manner that would sustain and extend Rorty's vision of an evolving democratic community:

> Instead of the old recurrent imagery of knowledge as a solid thing, bounded or mapped out, we prefer the idea of knowledge as the changing product of social activity. It is not so much like a building, eventually to be finished, but more like an airport, always under construction. It has been compared to an open-ended communal enterprise, to a ship voyaging to an unknown destination but never arriving and never dropping anchor. It is like a many-sided conversation in which being ultimately right or wrong is not at issue. What matters is that the conversation continue with new definitions and solutions and terms made deep enough to hold the meanings being tried. (pp. 192-193)

Evolving, democratic, communal. Change, social activity, always under construction. Unknown destinations. Fragility, mutual dependence, human solidarity. Conversation. Meaning.

Together, these rich ideas create a human tapestry, which may be at odds with the commonly understood goals of information in the information society, and of librarians as creators, with others, of this tapestry. In the next section of this paper, I will look at networked information in the light of Rorty's and Douglas's shared vision, and challenge—or at least revisit—some cherished assumptions about the meaning and purpose of the information enterprise.

A NATIONAL INFORMATION INFRASTRUCTURE

The traditional justification for building the National Information Infrastructure, and creating digital libraries of scientific and technical information, is that

> building an electronic science library will have impact on education, industry, research and the general state of science in the U.S. It will permit people throughout the U.S. to immediately answer scientific questions and keep abreast of new technology more rapidly and with less effort. It will permit U.S. scientists, whether in industry or academia, to deliver their results immediately to educational or commercial users. It will stimulate development of computer-based training systems, informal information circulation, and other new forms of information transfer. And it will provide a base on which the U.S. can maintain a leading position in the international information industry. (Nationwide Electronic Science, 1992, p. 12)

The focus, in statements of purpose such as this, is on immediate answers to straightforward questions, on instantaneous access to new facts. These are worthy aims and represent some of the tasks that a National Information Infrastructure must support. It is interesting to note, however, some of the core ideas from Rorty and Douglas that are absent here—like the social construction of knowledge, change, mutual dependence, meaning, and, perhaps most important, innovation and creativity. No technology is neutral: or, rather, all technologies bear whatever meanings we assign to them. Therefore, we must not only ask whether a technology will work, but what kind of a society is promoted by the meanings it bears.

Choosing to embark on a ship "voyaging to an unknown destination" has profound implications for the choices we make in designing and implementing an infrastructure for a national system of digital libraries. Some of the issues include:

- Who builds it?
- Who runs it?
- What do we want it to do?

Who Builds It? Who Runs It?

Building the computer and network infrastructure for a comprehensive national digital library system is a complicated and expensive enterprise. One recent study (Egan, 1991, p. 118 and supra) estimated that it would cost about $310 billion to provide fiber optic linkages to every American home, without even considering the cost of computing or of creating and distributing content.

Even the telecommunications giants would have trouble producing this level of investment without significant changes in the regulatory environment. Cable companies are even more fragmented, and local monopolies are unlikely to pursue aggressive investment strategies without any competitive threat. And in the current economic environment, the computer companies, suppliers, intellectual property owners, or user organizations would also have a difficult time, alone, putting together the resources required to build and disseminate a national fiber optic infrastructure—or to equip it with knowledge.

Hence, many argue, the federal government must assume leadership in funding and directing this massive effort. This appeared to be the thrust of several of Vice President Gore's comments at the pre-inauguration planning conference in Little Rock and more recently at the February Clinton-Gore infrastructure briefing at Silicon Graphics in California. A major federal role is also contemplated in the High Performance Computing Act of 1991, which created the National Research and Education Network (NREN); further legislation is anticipated, along with a major report from the President's Council on Competitiveness.

In addition, the newly formed Computer Systems Policy Project (CSPP), created by the chief executive officers of 13 leading American computer companies, has proposed the establishment of a federal National Information Infrastructure Council and substantial federal investment in infrastructure research and implementation (CSPP, 1993).

But is a leading federal role appropriate, given Rorty's and Douglas's vision of the role of knowledge in an evolving, democratic community? So far, the results are mixed: the federal government has funded a limited amount of research into the major technical issues impeding large-scale dissemination of digital libraries (mostly through the Defense Advanced Research Project Agency [DARPA] and the National Science Foundation [NSF]). But it has also adopted positions that are inimical to the goals of openness and dialogue, which are fundamental to the vision. The Federal Bureau of Investigation has proposed legislation that would require any network provider to ensure that their system could be tapped by law enforcement agencies. Furthermore, the National Security Agency has supported restrictions on the export of key encryption algorithms: the algorithms are needed to help protect digital libraries against unauthorized intrusion and the information they store against unauthorized distortion or destruction. Bits know no boundaries.

Bringing in the full involvement of the federal government is a little like inviting a 500-pound gorilla to your four-year-old's birthday party: terrific if he behaves himself, not so good if he decides to sit on the cake. And once he's there, it's especially tough to get him back in his cage again.

The analogy suggests that the ideal federal role would involve creating a regulatory and financial climate that supports private investment in a National Information Infrastructure, while also perhaps funding research and development in areas that appear unlikely to provide short-term payoff (see Egan [1991] for specific actions): that is, behaving itself, eating only its own piece of cake, going back in the cage when the party's over. The government's willingness to leave the enterprise to private initiative will depend, in large measure, on the readiness of other key stakeholders to work collaboratively to build it.

Why collaboration? It is evident that no one community—network providers, computer companies, content owners, researchers, government, information specialists, or users—can bring to bear all or even most of the elements required for a successful system. Networks are empty without content; content is inaccessible without networks; networks and content are useless without computer systems, information specialists, and users; research is meaningless without systems for instantiating and disseminating the results; government funds, policies, and regulations have no impact unless they result in innovation; information specialists and users are isolated without systems to satisfy their needs for information. And so it goes.

Therefore, a knowledge-rich information community must grow, in the words of Tennessee Williams, "out of the kindness of strangers": through the complex interworkings of mutually dependent, evolving communities, communities that may come to resemble, if we are very fortunate, Rorty's emerging democracies.

But will we in fact be fortunate? We have already reviewed some of the risks involved in the government assuming primary leadership in designing and building the National Information Infrastructure; there are others to be considered as well. Control of the infrastructure by any one private organization, or industry, could have an equally negative effect. There is widespread agreement that digitized information must generate a profit for those who invest in its creation and dissemination. Narrow control could lead to monopolistic pricing, while competition, both within and across industries, should reduce prices to the lowest profitable level. Look, for instance, at what has happened to the price per unit of computing power since clone competition entered the IBM/ DOS marketplace. There are powerful, well-financed players entering the information infrastructure sweepstakes, and we will all need to maintain vigilance, and build alliances, to ensure that the interests of all parties in this fragile, mutually dependent coalition are satisfied.

What alliances? I believe that there are some important opportunities awaiting key interest groups, as the various parties seek others to reinforce their position. In particular, there is a natural alliance—obscured by old antagonisms and competition for limited resources—bringing together librarians and other information specialists with publishers and other information owners and providers. My friend Paul Peters has led librarians, administrators, computerfolk, and publishers in the Coalition for Networked Information (CNI) to recognize their mutual interests and the value of collaborative effort.

These mutual interests include, for example:

- the need for regular, predictable content and schedules;
- a commitment to maintaining standards of quality in information products;
- the need for standardized systems for identifying and describing information content;
- mutual dependence, at least in the scholarly publishing world, on the same set of creators and end-users;
- a shared recognition of the need for user-centered diversity in content and mode of delivery;
- a recognition of archival responsibilities to future generations;
- the need for confidence in the significance of their own long-term role in any national digital library system;
- the need for strategic alliances, as other organizations and industries assume increasingly significant roles in designing and implementing the infrastructure;
- a fundamental commitment to the importance of thoughtful, accessible information in enriching the work and life of the nation.

I do not need to elaborate on the forces that, historically, have led librarians and publishers into mutual suspicion and occasional conflict. Neither can afford the luxury of these self-satisfying but unproductive sentiments. Nor can the other key stakeholders in the information infrastructure: all will have to hang together, or hang separately.

As we have seen, a number of powerful forces push key stakeholders in the emerging information infrastructure to work together for common goals. One important argument on the other side needs, at least, to be discussed. In his elegant little book *The Logic of Collective Action,* the economics Nobel laureate Mancur Olson (1965) argues that rational individuals (or organizations) will be reluctant to contribute to a common goal, if they can be assured to benefit from the results whether or not they contribute. Take, for example, taxes. Olson argues, persuasively, that we must be coerced into paying our taxes, because we are assured the benefits (if any) whether or not we contribute. Applied to infrastructure, this suggests that collective action would be unlikely *if* the key stakeholders were convinced that the national infrastructure would be built and disseminated without their contribution, *and* that their role in the system would be sustained whether or not they contributed.

A big *if*, and an even larger *and*. For the time being, I believe, cooperation among the stakeholders in building the infrastructure, and in constructing a consensual community around it, is both necessary and inevitable. However, as the process evolves and new working partnerships develop, it is conceivable that this initially fragile consensus may dissolve. It needs to be supported and sustained.

What Do We Want It to Do?

Most discussions of the National Information Infrastructure have focused on wide-ranging visions of new capacities for information dissemination and on the whiz-bang technologies that, we hope, will take us there. At the Silicon Graphics briefing, for instance, Vice President Gore noted that "one of the things that this plan calls for is the rapid completion of a nationwide network of information super highways. . . . We want to make it possible for a school child to come home after class and, instead of just playing Nintendo, to plug into a digital library that has color-moving graphics that respond interactively to that child's curiosity" (Office of the Press Secretary, 1993).

This vision has several powerful elements, from the fashionable dismissal of Nintendo (and the accompanying assumption that "real learning" can and should be even more fun) to the child (potential Einstein?) creating at her home computer. Discussions of the vision generally focus on the formidable technical and economic obstacles that must be surmounted: Where is all that bandwidth going to come from? How will the computer know what information to select? What happens if the child comes home, asks to know everything about dinosaurs, and the overload drags the entire world computer system to a screeching halt? Who pays?

There is much too little said about what we want the system to do for us—about what kind of world we want, and how an information infrastructure can help provide it. I believe that librarians (and information specialists: librarians in computer clothing) are better equipped by skill, commitment, and training to address these questions than anyone. Why? How can this voice be heard?

By choosing their profession, librarians have embraced a unique culture and are especially well suited to provide leadership in the emerging information age. Librarians are among the most computer literate of all professionals, and the most skilled navigators of the Internet/NREN. The value of libraries, and librarians, is defined by the intermingling of information and user/learners, generating new relationships, new knowledge—while preserving older ones. The physical library is simply a contingent means to that end, an information coffeehouse where the necessary linkages—and preservation—can occur. These values may be better sustained in an automated environment, where the physical limitations disappear, allowing learners and their agents—librarians—to focus on information and its use.

The values embraced by Rorty and Douglas—nurturing a fragile democracy while embarking on the ship of knowledge, bound for an unknown destination—are also deeply imbedded in librarians. Librarians have led the fight to ensure that public libraries and resource-poor user communities (e.g., small towns, inner cities) not be further disenfranchised by the information revolution. And librarians understand as well that knowledge is process, not outcome.

But these important factors have not resulted in a powerful librarian voice in the vision, design, and implementation of the National Information Infrastructure and digital libraries. Why is this?

First, librarians have sometimes been reluctant to seek alliances with other parties who share common goals, even if they do not agree about all aspects of the enterprise. Instead, too often, librarians (and their organizations) have expressed their views in isolation, hoping that someone in power will listen.

Second, until recently there have been few opportunities for librarians to talk together about the future of their profession and the role it can and should play in the information age. In the last year or so, however, there have been several encouraging efforts to discuss and present a vision and to provide, in the words of one, a "basis for librarianship in the 21st century."

Its goals include, for instance, "furthering the development of the 'virtual library', a concept of information housed electronically and deliverable without regard to its location or to time," and "taking responsibility for information policy development, information technology application, environmental awareness, and risk-taking in making strategic choices in the information arena" (Strategic Visions, 1992).

Among other things, this effort has generated a draft, by Anne Lipow (a national resource), of a "21st Century Library Position Announcement," a wonderful and challenging description of one possible (quite rosy) information future. For example, Lipow (1992) describes how people have personalized their computer-mediated relationships:

> However, around the turn of the century a practice arose that has become an international convention: staff and client 'touch' forefingers on the screen—especially as a parting gesture. (A recent embellishment by some high school users of the public library teledesk may be spreading in popularity: a rather complicated 'handshake' that involves a sequence of maneuvers using all fingers, the palm, the front and back of the wrist, and the elbow. Parents have begun to protest the inclusion of hip-action in this ritual.)

These are important first steps, but they have not materially increased the power and influence of librarians in the emerging infrastructure. Too often, discussions of a vision for librarians have seemed to descend into credentialing, with too much emphasis on figuring out how to protect the existing turf from incursions by computerfolk and information techies and too little on how to influence the larger equation and build the desired world. Furthermore, the dialogue has been largely restricted to librarians, with little success in involving other key parties: government, private corporations, information providers, university administration, end-users.

But not entirely—with the support of the Research Libraries Group (RLG), Richard M. Dougherty and Carol Hughes (1991) of the University of Michigan have initiated a series of efforts to involve library directors, chief academic officers, computer center directors, other key university personnel, and outside specialists in a collaborative process to discuss and select preferred futures for libraries and to decide how to achieve them. Beginning with university provosts and library directors, the effort is now focused on what Dick Dougherty (1992) calls the "I-Think Project":

> The objective of this project is to build an innovative problem-solving approach that can be used to facilitate the work of information professionals who seek to create a new world of scholarly and technical information for a networked environment. The heart and soul of the project will be a virtual think-tank based on computer-mediated communications tools. The structure of this envisioned capacity will be malleable so that it can be used to serve multiple purposes, e.g., projects that might range from decision support to policy analysis and strategy development activities. (pp. 3-4)

CONCLUSION

In this paper, I have attempted to link several normally disparate elements: ideas about democracy, ideas about information, ideas about infrastructure, ideas about libraries and librarians. In the information ferment that envelops our work and lives, it is all too easy to assume that emerging technologies will somehow "take care of" the issues of goals and purposes I have discussed here. That assumption is correct: they will take care of them. But as Orwell and Huxley understood many years ago, if we want the worlds we seek, we had best take care of them ourselves—in communities of dialogue, communities of purpose, communities where "it is human solidarity . . . that really matters" (Rorty, 1992, p. 153).

REFERENCES

CSPP Press Release. (1993, January 12). Computer industry CEOs provide administration with vision and recommendations for a National Information Infrastructure. Computer Systems Policy Project.

Dougherty, R. M. (1992, November 17). The I-Think Project: A telecommunications-based policy-analysis and decision support system for the information professions.

Dougherty, R. M., and Hughes, C. (1991). *Preferred futures for libraries: A summary of six workshops with university provosts and library directors.* Mountain View, CA: Research Libraries Group.

Douglas, M., & Wildavsky, A. (1982). *Risk and culture: An essay on the selection of technical and environmental dangers.* Berkeley: University of California Press.

Egan, B. L. (1991). *Information superhighways: The economics of advanced public communication networks.* Boston, MA: Artech House.

Lipow, A. (1992, August 7). *21st Century library position announcement.* Electronic mail message, Visions listserv.

A Nationwide Electronic Science, Engineering and Technology Library (Proposal to the National Science Foundation). (1992).

Office of the Press Secretary. The White House. (1993, February 22). Transcript of Clinton-Gore press conference at Silicon Graphics Company. Available through Internet Society, White House Press Release Gopher Service.

Olson, M. (1965). *The logic of collective action: Public goods and the theory of groups.* Cambridge, MA: Harvard University Press.

Rorty, R. (1992). Trotsky and the wild orchids. *Common Knowledge, 1*(3), 140-153.

Strategic Visions Steering Committee. (1992, January 15). *Revised visions statement.* Electronic mail message, Visions listserv.

JAMES P. LOVE

Director, Taxpayer Assets Project
Center for Study of Responsive Law
Washington, DC

Current Issues and Initiatives in the Electronic Dissemination of Government Information

INTRODUCTION

The election of President Bill Clinton and Vice President Albert Gore has given rise to heady optimism among those who long for better access to the federal government's extensive electronic collections of documents, statistics, and technical data. The new administration's interest in the development and use of modern information technologies was a surprisingly common theme on the campaign trail and was given high visibility in the earliest days of governance. Among the memorable images were the verbal sparring between Gore and AT&T officials over the role of the federal government in the development of the National Research and Education Network (NREN) during the first Economic Summit and the symbolism of Apple Computer President John Sculley seated next to Hillary Clinton during President Clinton's first State of the Union Address. These moves, followed by numerous White House statements about new technology policies, seem to signal a new government push to exploit and expand the frontiers of information technologies.

Yet despite this hoopla, the details of the new technology initiatives are still sketchy, and many thorny policy issues have yet to be resolved. This paper will examine several interrelated issues:

- Who will own and control the information resources and systems that are created with federal funds?
- What types of value-added services will federal agencies be authorized or encouraged to provide?
- What will be the role of ordinary citizens in shaping federal information policies?
- How will federal electronic information products and services be priced?
- Will the federal government provide centralized access to its information products and services?
- Which federal agencies will be responsible for providing expanded public access to federal information resources?

OWNERSHIP AND CONTROL OF FEDERAL INFORMATION
RESOURCES AND SYSTEMS

Through a wide range of policy initiatives, Congress and the executive branch have systematically reduced the public's ownership and control over vast federal information resources (Love, 1992a, 1992b; Claybrook, 1991). The procedures for privatizing ownership or control over publicly funded data or information systems are often complex and technical.

SEC's EDGAR System

The Securities and Exchange Commission's (SEC) Electronic Data Gathering, Analysis and Retrieval (EDGAR) system will modernize its paper and microfiche-based "full disclosure" program. Beginning this April, publicly held corporations will be required to electronically file dozens of disclosure reports, including such items as 10k and 10q reports, proxy statements, and registrations for new securities.

The EDGAR filings will constitute the world's most important and valuable financial database. While the principal beneficiaries of this program are investors, the filings are used by government regulators, journalists, private investigators, citizen groups, academic researchers, and many others, to study, monitor, and investigate a wide range of corporate activities.

EDGAR, which has been under development since 1983 and will cost the taxpayers about $100 million through 1997, is of interest for two reasons. First, EDGAR is often promoted by the Information Industry Association (IIA) as a model that should be emulated by other agencies. Second, it illustrates how the management of electronic records can be manipulated to force most users to rely upon private vendors for access to public records stored on a government system, even when the system itself is funded by public appropriations and there is a nonexclusive method of dissemination without restrictions on the resale or redissemination of the records (Love, 1993b; Love & Nader, 1992).

The filings comprising the EDGAR database are public documents, which are not subject to copyright. Under a contract negotiated with private contractors in 1989, the federal government agreed to a complex arrangement that greatly diminished its control over its own records. Under this scheme, the SEC will receive incoming filings in electronic formats but will retain only a nonpublic "history log" of the filings in an electronic format, while the contractor will create a microfiche copy of the accepted filings for the SEC's official public record.

Mead Data Central, one of the private contractors for the EDGAR system, was given control over the management of the electronic records, both to disseminate "bulk" filings to the "public" and to maintain an online full-text search and retrieval system for the SEC's own use. The "bulk" dissemination program is extremely limited in terms of the services it provides. Mead will only sell records from the *current* day's filings—there will be no access to historical records (except for limited online access to filings that are no older than 72 hours). According to SEC staff, the initial cost of these services is now estimated at $36,000 to $183,000 per year (depending upon the level of service and scope of filings). Since the data will be expensive to receive *and* process, the customers of the dissemination program will be limited to a handful of commercial data vendors and large financial concerns. While Mead and the SEC have extolled the workings of the free market in meeting user needs, the lack of access to historical or cumulative records is a conscious attempt to create entry barriers in the market for EDGAR data—a move that will benefit large incumbent firms such as Mead at the expense of late entrants and the consumers who would benefit from more private sector competition (Love, 1993c).

Mead will also provide the SEC with online full-text search and retrieval to the EDGAR database, but only for 650 government terminals, including a handful of public terminals in a few states (which can only print output to paper formats). On paper, the government will retain ownership of the EDGAR database, which the SEC staff often refers to as the "Mead Database," but it does not plan to take possession of the records until 1997 or later, depending upon when and if the Mead contract is terminated. Since the data will reside on computers owned by Mead, the SEC says the database will not be subject to disclosure under the federal Freedom of Information Act (FOIA).

The limited public access to the EDGAR data has become controversial, even before the system becomes operational, and the SEC has taken a few steps to make things better, but even here the approach is revealing. Over the past two years, a large number of citizen, library, journalist, and business groups have asked the SEC to modify its dissemination program by

1. modifying the "bulk" dissemination program to include historical and cumulative records,
2. providing direct online public access to the full-text search and retrieval service, and
3. publishing selected subsets of EDGAR filings on CD-ROMs.

The SEC was asked to price the online and CD-ROM service at the "incremental cost" of dissemination for use in homes and offices and to provide free access to the 1,400-member federal Depository Library Program (DLP).

The SEC staff has tentatively agreed to provide a system of CD-ROM dissemination to the federal DLP, but it has hesitated to allow the CD-ROMs to be disseminated through the Government Printing Office (GPO) sales program and has also resisted all efforts to provide direct online access to EDGAR. The SEC staff has made it clear that it is anxious to prevent "leakage"— an erosion of Mead's retail sales of EDGAR information. Dissemination of filings on CD-ROM to the DLP was perceived to be the option that would cost Mead the least in terms of reduced demand for its LEXIS services.

Congress is finally becoming interested in the issue of public access to EDGAR, and we believe that much broader public access is attainable. But the immense problems with the current system and the enormous difficulties in modifying the current contract illustrate the need to address public access issues when federal information systems are first designed. Particularly troublesome are the conflict-of-interest issues that arise when the private contractors for such systems have incentives to restrict public access in order to protect profits from their sales of public records as commercial data vendors.

Department of Justice JURIS System

The Department of Justice JURIS system is a large online database of federal legal information. The JURIS database is extremely broad, including such items as

- published and unpublished federal judicial opinions;
- the U.S. Code, public laws, Indian law, immigration and naturalization law, tax law, the code of federal regulations, federal acquisition regulations, federal executive orders, foreign treaties, and legislative histories;
- extensive administrative law on topics such as EPA enforcement, equal employment opportunity, government ethics, contracts, and published and unpublished Comptroller General decisions; and
- Department of Justice monographs, briefs, and manuals.

The JURIS system is run by the Justice Department on government-owned software and computers. The system was originally developed as an in-house service, but Executive Order 12146 (July 18, 1979) directed the Justice Department to provide the service to other government agencies. JURIS currently provides online access to about 15,000 government officials. The Justice Department charges JURIS users a flat rate of $68 per hour, which is far less than the cost of WESTLAW or LEXIS, the two commercial vendors who dominate the market for online legal information. The JURIS fee structure is designed to cover the average unit costs of the system, including the costs of support, development, and administration. The incremental cost of adding new users is quite low, perhaps a few dollars per hour, since most of the budget covers the system's fixed costs.

While there is wide public interest in JURIS, neither the online service nor the underlying database are available to the public. The barrier to public access is a contract with West Publishing, the company that sells the WESTLAW online service. In the early 1980s, the Justice Department entered into a contract with West to supply the government with case law and other legal information in digital formats. West, which obtained the contract through a competitive bid, "licenses" the data to DOJ for a limited time, with a provision which reportedly prohibits DOJ from providing public access to the data. Thus, West is able to frustrate public access to such items as federal judicial opinions, even though these documents are not subject to copyright. DOJ claims that its contract with West alienates the public's right to JURIS data, even under FOIA.

The West contract provides vast commercial benefits to West and Mead, which owns LEXIS. Indeed, the West contract benefits Mead almost as much as it does West. As a result of the West restrictions on public access to JURIS, both companies are protected in two ways. First, the Department of Justice will not provide public access to the online system, thus eliminating a low-cost alternative to the WESTLAW and LEXIS services. Second, other data vendors, including specialty CD-ROM publishers, cannot obtain copies of the JURIS database in order to create products and services that would compete with WESTLAW or LEXIS.

The Taxpayer Assets Project asked the Department of Justice to take steps to provide public access in 1991. We plan to mount a grass roots campaign to persuade the new attorney general, Janet Reno, to pursue this matter and to provide public online access through the new GPO Access program, as well as CD-ROM products that are based on selected subsets of the JURIS database.

Federal Acquisition Regulations (FAR)

On October 15, 1990, the Department of Defense (DOD), the Department of Energy (DOE), and the General Services Administration (GSA) issued an Advanced Notice of Proposed Rulemaking (ANPR) that would dramatically change the rules of ownership of all information products that are developed with federal funds. The rulemaking is directed at the parts of the Defense Federal Acquisition Regulations (DFAR) and Federal Acquisition Regulations (FAR) that govern the allocation of property rights to data that are created with federal funding.

The proposed rules, which will affect virtually all federal agencies, define "data" as "recorded information regardless of form, the media on which it may be recorded, or the method of recording." Among the types of information products that will be covered are reports or memoranda printed on paper or microfiche, computer databases, audio or video recordings, and software. The information covered by the rules could be consulting reports, statistics, bibliographic materials, research abstracts, or countless other items (Love & Dushoff, 1991a, 1991b).

The ANPR stated four policy objectives in its overview and policy summary:

1. The federal government should obtain only those rights in data that it needs.
2. The federal government should assure the protection of contractors' rights in proprietary interest in data.
3. The federal government should assure that a contractor does not have to relinquish legitimate rights it has in data as a condition for obtaining a government contract.
4. The federal government should provide rights in data as incentives to contractors to commercialize the results of government funding.

Of the four policy objectives, the first and the fourth are the most controversial, since agency judgments about the "rights in data that it needs," are often different from the public's, who finance the information products and want access without having to purchase the data from a contractor that has been given exclusive marketing rights.

The ANPR defined four categories for the government's rights in data:

1. *Unlimited Rights.* Under unlimited rights, the federal government can use or disseminate information in any way it sees fit. The government obtains these rights when the data "result" directly from government funding and when the contractor is not permitted or *does not choose* to copyright data or claim exclusive commercial rights.
2. *Limited Purpose Rights.* Under limited purpose rights, the federal government can only use data for uses allowed by the contractor. It may

only be released outside the government for limited purposes if the government designates prohibitions against further disclosure and use.

3. *Restricted Rights.* Restricted rights apply to software "developed at private expense." The government would only be allowed to exercise the rights to use such software for internal purposes, subject to restrictions on duplication and disclosure.

4. *Government Purpose Rights.* When a contractor declares an "intention to commercialize the items, components, or processes" to which data or software pertain, the government can grant all commercial rights in the data or software to the contractor, except for government purpose rights, which allow government agencies to use the data for internal purposes, subject to disclosure prohibitions. The ANPR proposed that government purpose rights be "normally" granted to the contractor, unless they are found to conflict with agency statutory or programmatic needs.

Under the ANPR, vast amounts of information created by federal contractors would no longer be considered public records.

The proposed changes in the FAR will have broad impact on every aspect of federal information policy. For example, the Department of Education recently referred to the proposed changes in the FAR in justifying its attempts to allow a private contractor to copyright the government-funded ERIC database. Consider also a recent study on recycling performed by the Tellus Institute of Boston. Tellus received substantial Environmental Protection Agency (EPA) funding for a three-year report on the environmental impact of various plastic, paper, steel, glass, and aluminum packaging materials. Tellus obtained the commercial rights to the final report. Thus, while EPA has a copy of the Tellus report in its possession, the public is not allowed to make copies. Tellus sells the complete study for $495 or an executive summary for $55.

The changes in the FAR are likely to be as important as other better known federal policy initiatives such as the revisions of the Office of Management and Budget (OMB) Circular A-130 discussed later. Many federal agencies are using outside contractors to do substantial research and policy analysis. The EPA, for example, has been plagued with staff cuts, while its responsibilities have grown. Other federal agencies are faced with increasing demands that they contract out important work.

The growing emphasis on the privatization of publicly funded research and information resources is part of a larger shift of public policy that is found in such measures as the Stevenson-Wydler Technology Innovation Act (PL 96-480) and the Bayh-Dole University and Small Business Patent Procedures Act (PL 96-517), which were passed in 1980, and the Federal Technology Transfer Act of 1986 (PL 99-502). The Bayh-Dole Act and subsequent amendments and executive orders grant universities and other contractors automatic titles to wide ranges of property rights on research and development (R&D) and information resources developed with federal funds. The Stevenson-Wydler Act, the Federal Technology Transfer Act, and other federal initiatives direct agencies to enter into Cooperative Research and Development Agreements (CRADAs) and other agreements to transfer exclusive commercial rights to many types of federally funded R&D and information resources to private firms (Nader & Love, 1993).

For example, a recent National Cancer Institution's (NCI) CRADA with Bristol-Myers Squibb gives that firm commercial rights to all federal research on the cancer drug Taxol, including research that was performed years before the CRADA was signed and *all* research that will be funded in the *future,* including research funded through universities.

While the Clinton/Gore administration has signaled a more open policy toward public access to government information stored in electronic formats, they have also announced plans to expand the use of CRADAs and other public/private partnerships in a wide range of cases, including the development of computer software and information technologies. Few details of these plans are available, but government officials working on the FAR revisions believe that the new administration is in step with the prior Bush administration on these topics. Moreover, President Clinton's recent announcements concerning across-the-board staff reductions at federal agencies suggest that private contractors will continue to play an important role in the creation of federally funded information resources. It is also important to note that in many cases Congressional Democrats were even more aggressive than the Bush administration in proposing broader and broader transfers of property rights on software and data to the private sector. Indeed, in the case of the proposed FAR revisions, Congress has taken positions that are decidedly more generous to industry than under the Bush administration.

VALUE-ADDED SERVICES

One of the most pernicious aspects of the Reagan and Bush administrations' approach to federal information policy was the attempt to discourage federal agencies from providing value-added services to disseminate information in electronic formats. Although the "value-added" debate surfaces in a wide range of instances, the best known case involves the OMB Circular A-130, which is an agency advisory concerning the management of federal information resources.

OMB Circular A-130

The first version of the circular was published on December 24, 1985 (*Federal Register, 50,* 52730-52751). This circular, which is still in effect, requires agencies to ensure that "existing and planned major information systems do not unnecessarily duplicate information systems available . . . from the private sector." The most widely quoted phrase was the directive that agencies place "maximum feasible reliance upon the private sector" for the dissemination of federal information resources.

The 1985 circular, however, was not a strict prohibition against government value-added services, and indeed it could have been interpreted much differently. One provision which has been rarely quoted, stated:

> For example, before an agency establishes a service for electronic dissemination of government information via an online computer system the agency should compare the cost of contracting for operation of the service versus in-house performance *and determine whether in-house*

> *performance is less costly both for the government and for the public who*
> *will receive the service* [emphasis added]. (*Federal Register*, 52748)

In another passage, the 1985 circular cautioned agencies against uncritical reliance upon the private sector and suggested that agencies that rely upon the private sector consider contractual provisions that would protect data users:

> When agencies use private sector contractors to accomplish dissemination,
> *they must take care that they do not permit contractors to exercise*
> *monopolistic controls in ways that defeat the agencies' information*
> *dissemination obligations, for example, by setting unreasonably high prices*
> [emphasis added]. (*Federal Register*, 52748)

In January 1989, OMB attempted a major revision of A-130 that would have imposed far stricter restrictions on agency value-added services:

> While electronic dissemination is generally desirable, agencies must observe
> certain boundaries on such activities. As a rule of thumb, Federal agencies
> should take it as a rebuttable presumption that they are to concentrate
> dissemination activities on supplying basic information, the provision of
> which is unique to the government, and to avoid offering value-added
> products to end users. That is, given a choice between expending resources
> on disseminating more government information in forms that are useable
> for general purposes and expending resources on tailoring fewer information
> dissemination products to specific user needs, agencies should presume they
> are to choose the former. In effect, agencies should prefer to "wholesale"
> government information and leave "retail" value-added functions to the
> private sector, especially when they know that the private sector is ready
> and able to perform the value-added functions. (*Federal Register*, 54(2), 217)

On June 9, 1989, OMB withdrew the January 1989 notice, citing public concern that the January 1989 notice and OMB Circular A-130 "were heavily biased, concentrating so much on private sector prerogatives that OMB had failed to elaborate a positive role for Federal agencies in the dissemination of government information, even in situations where dissemination of such information was basic to agencies' missions" (*Federal Register*, 54(114), 25554-25559). On April 29, 1992, OMB issued yet another proposed revision to A-130. When this revision is finally issued, it is expected to give a far broader mandate to federal agencies to embrace value-added services.

Despite the welcome changes in A-130, important debates remain over the degree to which federal agencies should provide value-added services to individuals. The "wholesale/retail" dichotomy referred to in the 1989 proposed revisions remains highly relevant. The battles over the SEC's EDGAR system are precisely over the appropriateness of value-added services for individuals, as opposed to a "wholesale" dissemination system that relies upon the private sector to deliver records to individuals. Agencies such as the National Agriculture Library have yet to seriously consider online services or CD-ROM products for AGRICOLA. Moreover, many agencies operate under laws that contain special barriers to value-added services. The Department of Commerce, for example, believes that it cannot provide online access to its widely used National Trade Data Bank due to the original authorizing legislation.

What has changed is that there are no longer government-wide policies that discourage such innovations, and it is now necessary to work with individual agencies to expand their dissemination services to include new value-added products that serve individuals.

THE PUBLIC ROLE IN SHAPING
FEDERAL INFORMATION POLICIES

Agencies have very limited responsibilities to consult with the public over the development of information policies. Often requirements for public consultation are "filtered" through advisory boards or focus groups that are highly selective in terms of their membership.

While well known and politically powerful interest groups sometimes have input, agencies rarely are in touch with grass roots data users, and they can punish their critics by limiting their access to the consultation process. The single most important failures of federal agencies are errors of omission. Agencies do not revisit important policy issues long after the state of technology has radically changed from that which existed when the original policies were adopted. Moreover, agencies often do not consider broad dissemination of information from agency information systems to be essential to the agency's mission.

While there are a multitude of important policy issues relating to the management of federal information resources, it is exceedingly difficult for citizens to raise these issues with agencies. We have argued that it is necessary to force federal agencies to create annual opportunities for public comment on a wide range of agency practices and policies. This proposal was endorsed in a report by the House Subcommittee on Printing and Procurement in 1990:

> One of the most useful suggestions put forward is to make it easier for citizens to comment on the adequacy for agency information dissemination programs. This is particularly difficult for data users, who are often confused by the complexity of federal laws and jurisdiction disputes, and who are rarely heard in debates over important changes in federal information dissemination programs. Certainly GPO could benefit from a better dialogue with the public over its service, product line, and prices. (Bates, 1991, p. 645)

The report recommends that GPO prepare an annual report that describes its information dissemination policies and practices, including plans to introduce or discontinue information products, efforts to use standardized record formats, progress in creating and disseminating comprehensive bibliographies of information products and services, and the methods for accessing information, including the modes and outlets available to the public. GPO should alert the public about the annual report and solicit comments on the types of information GPO disseminates, the methods and outlets that GPO uses to store and disseminate information, the prices charged for information, and the validity, reliability, timeliness, and usefulness of the information disseminated. The comments received from this notice should be placed in a public file; GPO's response to the comments should also be available (Bates, 1991, p. 645).

In 1991, Representative Major Owens introduced legislation (H.R. 3459) that would have required every federal agency to issue similar annual reports and to accept and consider public comments. These requirements were also included in the GPO WINDO/Gateway (H.R. 2772, S. 2813) bills introduced in the last Congress. However, these requirements were eliminated in this year's GPO Access legislation in favor of a more general requirement that GPO "consult" with affected parties, despite a determined effort to have them included, along with a suggestion that GPO be required to disseminate the report and accept public comments by electronic mail. Congressional staff who worked on the GPO Access legislation were not persuaded that mandatory requirements for regular public were important.

We believe that public notice and comment mechanisms are not trivial issues. The most significant development in federal information policy is the manner in which debates over policy are now facilitated by Internet discussion groups. Lists such as GOVDOC-L, PACS-L, COM-PRIV, CPSR, and hundreds of others devoted to a wide range of issues regularly disseminate information and ideas about new federal policy initiatives. Issues that were once debated by a handful of specialists are now accessible to thousands of data users, many of whom are eager to shape federal policy. This rapid democratization of the debate will have profound consequences.

Many of the best ideas about information technologies come from librarians, small businesses, software developers, and data users who are not well plugged into the Washington influence scene. Lobbyist and interest groups organizations are often not as savvy or creative as the people at the grass roots who use (and create) information technologies every day in their jobs and businesses. Moreover, grass roots data users often have higher expectations about the rate at which federal agencies should embrace new technologies, and they are less likely to accept as constraints the corrupting influence of industry expenditures on lobbying and campaign contributions. Broader public notice and comment mechanisms are essential to empower grass roots data users to become informed and organized on crucial federal information policy issues.

PRICING OF FEDERAL ELECTRONIC
INFORMATION PRODUCTS AND SERVICES

The pricing of government information in electronic formats by federal agencies is a policy matter that has been set adrift over the past decade. Some agencies provide public access to data in electronic formats at the costs of dissemination, while other agencies charge prices that are based upon willingness-to-pay criteria. While it is doubtful that federal agencies will ever realize significant revenues from the sale of information products and services, there is nonetheless a wide range of cases where agencies use revenues from these high prices to supplement appropriated funds, creating an enormous threat to the public's right to know. It is always important to note that the rules used by many federal agencies to price data in electronic formats bear little resemblance to the policies used for information published in paper formats. The dangers of these changes were addressed by Joan Claybrook, president of Public Citizen, in testimony before the Joint Committee on Printing on April 25, 1991:

Computer technology is new to many of us, but it is important that we do not lose sight of principles which are the foundation for the public's right-to-know. If a Federal agency decided to use single spacing instead of double spacing on its documents, you would not expect it to double its prices because twice as much information was printed on each page. If a million words or numbers of Federal information can be stored on a diskette that costs 20 cents to duplicate, then it should be sold to the public for no more than 20 cents, regardless of the amount of information on the diskette. . . . Any other policy promotes to accept the principle that the Government can earn profits from the dissemination of information. If this principle is established, Government officials will ration information to the most affluent, or will use the price to manipulate public access to Government information. (Claybrook, 1991, p. 98)

Many of the current jurisdictional disputes concerning federal information policy are directly related to pricing issues. The strictest pricing rules are found at GPO and under the federal Freedom of Information Act (FOIA). GPO is bound by title 44 to price most information products at 150% of the "rider" cost of the publication. Under the GPO Access legislation, GPO user fees for online access must not exceed the "incremental cost" of dissemination. Under the FOIA, citizens pay no more than the agencies' costs of locating and disseminating records. The National Archives and Records Administration (NARA) also prices electronic records at dissemination costs. For a database on magnetic tape, NARA charges $70 for the first reel of tape and only $17 for each additional reel.

In contrast, agencies that sell electronic information products themselves are given broad discretion in setting prices. The Bureau of the Census claims that the $250 per CD-ROM that it charges for its TIGER files reflect only dissemination costs, while USGS prices its CD-ROM products at about $30. The Bureau of Labor Statistics generally offers low prices on most of its datasets but also charges about $700 for a single reel of tape containing county-level ES-202 employment data. EPA disseminates its Toxic Release Inventory at low prices but charges thousands of dollars for other datasets.

Among the worst problems are electronic records disseminated by the National Technical Information Service (NTIS), a federal agency that is funded largely through user fees. While NTIS is expected to break even on its overall product line, it has no bounds on the prices that it charges for particular datasets. NTIS uses its electronic records to subsidize its low-volume microfiche products, which lose money. Moreover, NTIS revenue-sharing agreements with agencies encourage agencies to use NTIS rather than GPO or NARA to disseminate records or to avoid releasing the records under FOIA (see Love, 1993a, for examples).

The use of electronic formats should lower the public's cost of receiving government information. For example, GPO sells the entire U.S. Code on CD-ROM for $30, compared to $1,200 for the paper version. The OMB position on the pricing of federal information is decidedly enlightened. In the June 1989 notice withdrawing the January 1989 proposed revisions in Circular A-130, OMB stated that prices would not be raised above the costs of dissemination and that agencies would be precluded from using information products as a profit center or budgeting mechanism (*Federal Register, 54*[114]). OMB retained this position on the most recent proposed revision of A-130, but it declined to provide any mechanisms to enforce the pricing provisions and has ignored completely the enormously important issue of the NTIS pricing structure.

The Clinton/Gore administration has indicated that it will ensure that public information is available at reasonable prices to the taxpayers who paid for the information, but there are no details on how this policy objective will be met.

CENTRALIZED PUBLIC ACCESS

Today, data users are confronted with a highly decentralized and fragmented system of access to federal information. It is difficult to find, purchase, and use federal information resources. The solution to many user problems will involve centralized forms of access (Nader & Love, 1991; Love, 1992a, 1992b). A well-integrated system of centralized access should provide three benefits:

1. Information should be easier to locate. The system should provide user manuals, online locators, and other user support to identify the scope of information resources that are available.
2. The system should have standardized user interfaces. Query command structures and downloading procedures should be consistent across different databases, making it easier to use the system.
3. The system should offer centralized subscription and billing services. Users should not have to obtain and maintain hundreds of different subscriptions and invoices for each database they want access to.

The benefits of centralized access are important to most data users but particularly to users who are not technically sophisticated in computer technologies. Anyone who has provided research support services to a staff that is only marginally comfortable with computers will recognize the importance of integrated online systems, and anyone who has eclectic research interests will recognize the frustrations of using fragmented services with multiple billing and subscription requirements.

Of course, virtually all successful commercial vendors offer precisely these types of integrated environments. CompuServe, Dow Jones, LEXIS, DIALOG, WEFA, and Data Resources, Inc. (DRI) are examples of integrated systems. Indeed, the recent cooperative agreement between WESTLAW and DIALOG that allows users of either service to access the joint offerings of both services is an attempt to make their offerings more attractive to data users. Much of the competition among online vendors today concerns the scope of services rather than the prices for access.

The Information Industry Association (IIA) believes that it is extremely important to prevent the federal government from doing what each of its members does. The federal government's current highly fragmented approach is, in fact, a product of the IIA lobbying efforts. The vendors have skillfully enlisted the support of some academic policy analysts and computer specialists to oppose a more integrated federal government approach. The preferred euphemism for the present chaos in the federal system is "diversity." This term is a useful polemic against a more centralized federal system, although in practice it is often used in ways that have little to do with the issues at hand.

In some cases, the vendors argue that a more centralized federal system will prevent a diversity of dissemination strategies at the agency level or will encourage "monopolist" practices. However, while a more centralized federal system could lead to monopolist control by federal agencies, or inhibit innovation, that need not be the case, nor are user groups asking for such controls. The ALA, the Taxpayer Assets Project, Computer Professionals for Social Responsibility, and other groups who support centralized systems such as the GPO WINDO/Gateway/Access legislation also oppose government copyrighting of data and exclusive dissemination contracts. These groups are strong defenders of the rights of agencies to use alternative methods of dissemination to meet other user needs, as well as the rights of data vendors to obtain the underlying records of databases to compete directly with the government.

In our view, the vendors' manipulation of the "diversity" debate is really an attempt to limit an important element of diversity. A government that cannot provide users centralized access to its databases is denied one of the most useful options that should be available, leading to less diversity, not more. Moreover, today it is possible to design centralized systems that allow broader diversity in terms of the software for end-users. Standards such as Z39.50 will lead to servers that connect databases to competitively marketed user interfaces and searching engines. The central system will be integrated in terms of billing and access but decentralized in terms of innovations that address different users' needs.

AGENCY JURISDICTION

While many agency officials now recognize that there is substantial public interest in centralized online access to the federal government's extensive information resources, there is still considerable debate over which agencies should provide such services. The first serious Congressional effort to provide a centralized system for online access to federal information was H.R. 2772, the GPO Wide Information Network for Data Online (GPO WINDO), introduced by Representative Charlie Rose on June 26, 1991, in the 102nd Congress. The findings of H.R. 2772 stated "access to public electronic information will be greatly enhanced by a single point of online public access." The bill stated that the GPO was "the appropriate federal office to establish, coordinate, and maintain, single-point [online] access to a wide range of government electronic databases."

On June 4, 1992, Senator Gore and others introduced S. 2813, the GPO Gateway to Government Act, which was largely based upon the H.R. 2772, with a few changes. The term "single-point" access was dropped to avoid the inference that the GPO online service would preclude other agency options for providing online services, including in-house systems or systems run by NTIS or other federal agencies.

On March 11, 1993, the House and Senate introduced identical versions of the legislation that were based upon the WINDO/Gateway bills. The bills (S. 564, H.R. 1328), which were officially referred to as the "GPO Electronic

Information Access Enhancement Act of 1993," and unofficially referred to as "GPO Access," were a scaled down version of the earlier bills. The principal changes were a weaker mandate, which the Republican minority said was designed to make the bill a more "incremental" approach than the WINDO/Gateway bills. GPO was required to consolidate all its online programs through the new GPO Access program, but the bill and the report language made it clear that executive branch agencies would participate in the program on a voluntary basis. The legislation and the report language require that GPO provide online access to the *Congressional Record,* the *Federal Register,* a locator system, the GPO's online dissemination of Supreme Court decisions, the GPO Federal Bulletin Board, "other publications distributed by the Superintendent of Documents," and information published at the request of other federal agencies.

NTIS, which declined requests from the Taxpayer Assets Project that it provide online access to its collections in 1990, has recently expressed considerable interest in providing online services and is expected to "compete" with GPO. The NTIS FedWorld was NTIS's initial effort, but the service was little more than a dial-in service to a number of government bulletin boards with limited offerings. At present, FedWorld does not offer any integration of billing or authorization for use for the connected bulletin boards. NTIS officials are reportedly investigating methods of providing gateway access to a larger number of online services. This would include more sophisticated full-text and numeric data systems, with an online system for authorization of use and consolidated billing through a single account at NTIS. GPO is expected to investigate similar value-added services.

Agencies may either participate in both online systems or operate their own system. The GPO Access program will provide free access to the federal Depository Library Program and price its online service for other users at the "incremental cost" of dissemination, while NTIS has no bounds on its prices. It is unclear how and if GPO can compensate agencies for costs they incur in participating in the GPO Access program. A provision in the GPO Gateway to Government Act that specifically provided for such compensation was deleted from the GPO Access bill. NTIS routinely provides for sharing of revenues with agencies.

GPO and NTIS are expected to proceed with separate systems. It is unclear if major federal online systems such as the Department of Justice JURIS, National Library of Medicine MEDLARS, Congressional LEGIS, the Patent and Trademark Office Automated Patent System (APS), Securities and Exchange Commission EDGAR, CIA Foreign Broadcast Information Service (FBIS), Department of Labor LABSTAT, Bureau of the Census CENDATA, or Department of Agriculture CIDS will be available through either system in the short run. Some agencies may decide to continue to use private vendors as their sole outlet for online access or to operate their own in-house services, independent of either agency. NTIS may ask for excessive fees to integrate services, and GPO may not sanction the types of high fees or restrictions on the redissemination of information that increase agency sales revenues.

The Clinton/Gore administration is just beginning to focus on dissemination issues, having been preoccupied by major policy questions concerning the development of national telecommunications infrastructure—much of which is concerned with interactive communications and development of commercial services, including the sale of both government and privately copyrighted works. Vice President Gore is also expected to review larger questions concerning the appropriateness of current agency responsibilities for federal information policy, including a possible transfer of OMB's information policy functions to a White House office.

REFERENCES

Bates, J. (1991). Report on the General Sales Program of the United States Government Printing Office. In U.S. House Committee on House Administration, Subcommittee on Printing and Procurement, *Oversight on the U.S. Government Printing Office General Sales Program, Hearings, 26-27 July 1990* (Y4.H81/3:5a1) (pp. 644-645). Washington, DC: U.S. Government Printing Office.

Claybrook, J. (1991). Prepared statement of Joan Claybrook. In U.S. Congress, Joint Committee on Printing, *Government information as a public asset, Hearings, 25 April 1991* (S. Hrg. 102-114) (Y4.P93/1:G74/12) (pp. 93-100). Washington, DC: U.S. Government Printing Office.

Love, J. P. (1992a). Democratizing the data banks: Getting government online. *American Prospect, 9*(Spring), 48-50.

Love, J. P. (1992b). The marketplace and electronic government information. *Government Publications Review, 19*(4), 397-412.

Love, J. P. (1993a, March). Knowledge for the rich. *Dollars and Sense*, pp. 16-22.

Love, J. P. (1993b). The ownership and control of the U.S. Securities and Exchange Commission's EDGAR system. *Government Publications Review, 20*(1), 61-71.

Love, J. P. (1993c, March 12). Letter to Representative Edward Markey, Chair, U.S. House of Representatives, Committee on Energy and Commerce, Subcommittee on Telecommunications and Finance.

Love, J. P., & Dushoff, J. (1991a, January 31). Comments Regarding FAR/DAR Case 90-438 submitted to Linda W. Neilson, Procurement Analyst, ODASD(P)/DARS, Pentagon.

Love, J. P., & Dushoff, J. (1991b, January 25). Statement of James Love and Jonathan Dushoff (Testimony before the Patents, Data and Copyrights Committee).

Love, J. P., & Nader, R. (1992, August 24). SEC's EDGAR information system: You paid for it, but don't expect to use it. *MacWEEK*, p. 18.

Nader, R., & Love, J. P. (1991, November 11). Public deserves access to federal databases. *Computerworld*, p. 25.

Nader, R., & Love, J. P. (1993, February 24). Federally funded pharmaceutical inventions. Prepared statement included in U.S. Senate, Special Committee on Aging, *The federal government's investment in new drug research and development: Are we getting our money's worth, Hearings* (serial no. 103-1, pp. 26-71). Washington, DC: U.S. Government Printing Office.

U.S. Senate. (1993, March 18). Government Printing Office Electronic Access Enhancement Act of 1993, Senate Report 103-127. Washington, DC: U.S. Government Printing Office.

PAUL EVAN PETERS

Director
Coalition for Networked Information
Washington, DC

Progress Toward and Prospects for a Global Digital Information Infrastructure in Support of Research and Education*

INTRODUCTION

I want to do several things in this presentation. The first is provide some basic information about what is being called the information superhighways measures already proposed by the Clinton administration and already acted on by the 103rd Congress. It was only in February 1993 that two major proposals responsive to the theme of this conference were put forth, and they were acted on by the 103rd Congress when it passed the president's budget. Some things remain to be reconciled, but these provisions of the president's budget were not controversial in the House and Senate debates in late March. So, they've already found their way pretty far down the road of this new administration's policy. There are a lot of new policy initiatives in the realm of global networking, but I'm going to focus on just a very small part of it.

The second thing I want to do is to call attention to the characteristics of four of the constituencies that are the most active and influential in shaping how issues are defined and how public policies are formulated in the areas of networks and networked information. I really think these four constituencies have been competing for public attention for quite a while now. It is important to reflect upon what each of these four constituencies has to offer because my opinion is that there has to be something that comes out of this process for each of these constituencies, otherwise we won't get what we all want—a universally better world as a result of all this.

CURRENT POLICY INITIATIVES

The basic characteristics of the new administration's approach to all of this are evident in the budget statement that President Clinton presented to the Congress on February 17. The title of this document is "A Vision of Change

---

*This paper is an edited transcript of the author's presentation at the Clinic.
©1993 Paul Evan Peters

for America." It's not just a tax proposal as the media would like us to believe, and I think all of us need to help not only ourselves but people who rely upon us to stay oriented in a very busy world to understand the concept of the relationship between government and the people that is so thoroughly different and refreshing in this document.

But, even more to the point, on February 22, a statement describing the initial economic program of the president was separated out and articulated by Clinton and Gore when they made a visit to Silicon Valley. This document is now available from the Office of the President, and it is titled "Technology for America's Growth: A New Direction to Build Economic Strength." Before I focus in on just one part of that, the measures pertaining to information superhighways, I'd like to say that ever since June of last year it's been clear that Bill Clinton views information infrastructure as a strategic asset.

There is a tendency among those of us who have known first Senator Gore and now Vice President Gore to feel that the influence on Clinton's thinking in this area arises solely from this person who's been so important in helping us find our vision and having it expressed in public law. But when candidate Clinton's economic plan was announced in June of 1992, the second measure of the economic plan was federal government investment in information infrastructure, and I wondered where that came from. And where it came from, to name a single source, is a book written by now labor secretary Robert Reich entitled *The Work of Nations*, which is a book I'd recommend to you. It's rather heavy going—you know how much economists love numbers and so forth—but the basic public policy argument advanced by Reich is that the appropriate targets of government investment in the 21st century are people in infrastructure because they are relatively immobile, national assets. This sort of resonated with me because I knew we might be coming out of 24 years where the appropriate focus of government investment was thought to be capital formation. It's very clear from the economic statistics based on those 24 years of experience (I'm holding the Carter years aside for reasons I expect you understand) that if you focus on capital formation, then the capital will flee the country to labor markets that leverage the capital. In contemporary manufacturing that means labor markets that are low wage. We would expect that as time goes by capital will seek labor markets that are highly skilled rather than labor markets that are just low wage, thus reflecting the transition from a predominantly manufacturing economy to a predominantly information or service economy. In any case, Robert Reich and that book in particular have had a very important impact on Bill Clinton's thinking. And the argument is that if government builds infrastructure and focuses on an educated population, it's very unlikely that the infrastructure will pick up and go to Mexico or Singapore or someplace else. Generally speaking, population is relatively immobile, so the government investment continues to circulate within the nation and is a sure target of generating overall wealth.

So, Bill Clinton was exposed to these ideas, and I think we need to think of his selection of Vice President Gore as a kindred spirit selection. It is really a partnership and a quite heady partnership. When Bill Clinton selected Al Gore as his running mate, the favorite joke of the Washington wags was: "Bill Clinton is so intellectually secure he selected an intellectual equal as his running mate. Come to think of it, so did George Bush." So I think we have plenty of reason to believe that President Clinton selected Gore to *act* on these things, not because he wanted Gore to *run* them.

So this dynamic duo has brought forth a document, with the able assistance of a number of people, called "Technology for America's Growth: A New Direction to Build Economic Strength," and about one quarter of the way through it, they articulate five measures pertaining to information super-highways.

The first measure may appear obvious, but it's very carefully worded: implementation of the High Performance Computing and Communications Program established by the High Performance Computing Act of 1991. That was the Act that brought the NREN vision into public laws—Public Law 102 194. That may appear to be an unqualified victory, but one of the problems with implementing the NREN provisions of PL 102 194 last year was that there was a continuing disagreement about whether the *administration's* concept of the networking enterprise as a federal network and the *Congress's* concept of the networking enterprise as a national network would be resolved. We had difficulty resolving that last year, and, in fact, a key report that the Science Advisor of the President was charged by the legislation to produce by December 1992 articulated the notion that what this NREN was supposed to do was to be a collaboration of federal networks, a consolidation of federal networking activities. There are plenty of provisions of PL 102 194, in particular its NREN provisions, that show that what the Congress wanted was not just a harmonization of federal activity. It wanted a networking program that was progressively more responsible to the national needs of the research and education communities. So the fact that this initiative is linked to the High Performance Computing Act of 1991 is one of those signals that the Congressional concept of this networking program will be the ascendent one in this administration. And, more to that point, it continues to be the case that the Office of Science and Technology Policy of the Executive Office of the President has a key role in developing this NREN program. The deputy director of that office is Mike Nelson, who was Gore's staffer on this when the legislation proceeded through the Senate. So, that's still one more signal— not a surprising signal but a welcome signal—that the Congress's conception of this network as a national asset rather than a federal program is going to prevail in this new administration.

The second initiative articulated in this document is the creation of a task force on information infrastructure, a high-level interagency task force within the National Economic Council that will work with Congress and the private sector to find consensus on, and implement policy changes needed to accelerate deployment of, the National Information Infrastructure. This is "ramping up" in a positive way, as it indicates the administration's recognition that global networking is one of those things you have to send people out to talk to other people about. It hasn't become exactly clear, but it's thought that Vice President Gore will chair this task force, which will be staffed by people like Mike Nelson and people who are assigned to the Office of Science and Technology Policy. It will function very like the Council of Competitiveness, which was an agency that Vice President Quayle chaired in the previous administration. It will have a lot of interagency power, and it will have the ability to relieve regulatory constraints that are thought to be inhibiting useful progress, which, of course, can be both good and bad. But it's nice to have Cabinet officers or their delegates sitting in a room with the vice president on an ongoing basis with a staff of right-thinking people saying, "What needs to be done to move as quickly as possible toward a favorable vision of a National Information Infrastructure?" So although a lot of the details of how it will work and so forth remain to be revealed, the attention of the new administration is clearly being allocated, at the highest level, to these issues.

The program's third proposal is to create an information infrastructure technology program to assist industry in the development of the hardware and software needed to fully apply advanced computing and networking technology in health care, in life-long learning, and in libraries. The third and fourth provisions of this program have a tendency to make people like (he's not here so I can say this) Chuck McClure swoon because they felt, and had good reason during the last 24 years to believe, that they would never read a federal policy document, let alone a presidential policy document, that would single out libraries in this context, for this kind of attention. So if we have any doubts about whether there have been people listening the last three to four years, and coming to wrap themselves around the library part of this equation of useful social progress, statements like this give us reason to stay engaged. But, of course, we have more work to do now that they are seriously interested.

It's widely thought that the National Institute of Standards and Technology will be asked to be the lead agency on this program, and they will be asked to develop a civilian technology program that will function in some measure— this may not be an entirely favorable analogy—but will function in some measure as the Advanced Research Projects Agency or the Department of the Army have functioned in the transfer of defense technology into the private sector.

The fourth element of this program is to provide funding for networking pilot projects through the National Telecommunication and Information Administration (NTIA) of the Department of Commerce. NTIA will provide matching grants to states, school districts, libraries, and other nonprofit entities so that they can purchase connections needed for distance learning and for hooking into computer networks like the Internet. These pilot projects will demonstrate the benefits of networking to the educational library communities. In the budget that was passed by the two Houses of Congress at the end of March, $64 million was targeted for this matching grant program. Now, the people on the ground, as it were, i.e., those in NTIA right now, say that they would like to spend that $64 million on programs that are already "in their pipeline," involved in what is generally known as the Public Telecommunications Facilities Programs. This might mean that we have to wait until this time next year to have a clearer slate for which to put pilot project proposals before NTIA for this new funding stream. Or maybe, when the new appointments to the Department of Commerce are confirmed, there will be a change in the thinking of NTIA on how this money should be spent this year. In any case, it is tremendously encouraging to read this kind of statement in a presidential policy document.

The fifth element of the program is to promote dissemination of federal information. Again, it's very nice to have a presidential policy document that's not only linking technology with the promotion of dissemination of federal information but is very clearly indicating that they regard the promotion of the dissemination of federal information as a very important national agenda item.

This is just one slice from these two policy documents. Reading the rhetoric, the social philosophy, the concept of government that surround these things is a very heady experience, at least for me. I think those of us who are involved in the information enterprise, broadly conceived, can see here a serious attempt by this new administration to try to move the nation forward in this regard.

IMPORTANT NETWORKING
CONSTITUENCIES AND THEIR VISIONS

Now, I think that how all of this will play out depends a great deal on the activities of four particular constituencies. I don't really want to call them four different visions, and you shouldn't think of these constituencies as necessarily orthogonal. But I think there are four quite different and quite active constituencies that will be very influential in determining how things go from here.

I would characterize the first constituency by its core belief that networking is an appropriate national agenda item because it increases returns on research and education, meaning that government investments in networking are important because they leverage government investments in research and education. This is the constituency that formed around the National Research and Education Networking initiative. It argued, eventually successfully, to the Congress and the Bush administration that government at all levels is the primary funder of research and education in the United States, and that if some of those investments are spent on networking, then the investments that are spent on the directly productive activities of the research and education enterprise go farther.

Sad to say, there is very little new money that's been spent on networking. In general, the research and education community has been playing a zero sum game with itself, taking money that would otherwise go to grants for doing specific research and education activities and investing it in one or another research or education network, with the NREN being the most recent initiative of that type. Nonetheless, we have been able to demonstrate that government expenditures on research and education result in more productive activities if some of those expenditures go to research and education networking.

So, my point is that this is the constituency that built the support that led to the passage of the High Performance Computing Act of 1991 and its enactment as PL 102 194. The NREN is not a proposal before Congress; it's U.S. public law. What we're working on now is to make sure that this opportunity is actually realized and that the national attention generated to support this opportunity yields tremendous national fruit.

There's a second public policy constituency that I think was as active during the NREN period as this first public policy constituency; it's the one to which Vice President Gore has been very clear that he belongs. As *Senator* Gore, he was willing to declare a common cause with this first constituency, but now that he's *Vice President* Gore, he's clearly pushing what I think has always been his family's vision of how government should interact with the nation. I would summarize the interest of this second public policy constituency by saying that its members believe that government activity is required in this area because networks can lay a foundation for 21st-century life and enterprise. These are the people who have coined the term "the National Information Infrastructure." I'm a card-carrying member of this community, too. I wouldn't want you to think I wasn't. In fact, I feel I have some allegiance with all four of these communities. What is meant by the National Information Infrastructure is still up for grabs. But it is clear that what a lot of us mean is some sort of national, digital information enterprise or architecture that's subject to principles like those that were articulated for the telephone and broadcasting systems in the Communications Act of 1934. The NREN was not required to be responsive to those kinds of equal access, universal service conditions because the public policy needs addressed by the NREN legislation were quite different from that. Now we have a vice president, indeed a president and an entire federal government, that is pushing government activity and networking to try to lay a foundation for 21st-century life and enterprise.

It's very important, as far as I'm concerned, to make sure that this opportunity actually materializes. It's going to be tough because the administration has chosen the Department of Commerce as the agent of change in this regard, and there are two problems with that. First, the Department of Commerce does not have a reputation in the federal government as a particularly agile or focused agency, so they are going to have to reform the Department of Commerce to make it relevant to 21st-century life and enterprise before it can pursue the promise of networks in that regard. Second, the fact that it's the Department of Commerce rather than the Department of Education or some other more "public interested" agency that is more popular with those of us in the not-for-profit community is a worry for some people. So, there will be a lot of work and a lot of support that we'll have to offer to make sure that this second public policy constituency is successful during the early days of the Clinton administration without supplanting the others that I'm mentioning—the first one and the third one.

Just at this moment, wind is being caught in the sail of the ships of the people in the third public policy constituency. I'm afraid my way of summarizing their interests may be regarded as unsympathetic, and I don't mean it as such: their interest is that networks should create a retail paradise for couch potatoes. One way of describing their vision is to remind you all that you're receiving a lot of catalogs every year, particularly around the holiday period. Some of these come to you from L. L. Bean; some of them come to you from other companies. It's very clear to me that this constituency is imagining a future where, let's say, it's 1997, and Paul Peters is sitting in his living room. He's got his information remote in his hand. He dials 1-900-LLBean, and on his high-definition television suddenly the L. L. Bean catalog appears. And, just to get really crazy, let's assume it's voice activated. I say I want slacks. I want men's slacks. I want Dockers. I want blue . . . now show me those Dockers on a bigger guy. Now, this is something I feel you need to know about because, personally, as I have hoped you have sensed, I would really *like* to be able to interact with these catalogs in this way. And you can see the money that's being spent to bring these retail opportunities to you by paper mail right now, so the people who focus on these business plans will soon see how one thing might lead to another.

Just so you know that this is not all just speculation, I'd like to point out that fascinating stories have recently appeared about a character named Barry Diller. For those of you who haven't heard of Diller, I refer you to the February 22 *New Yorker* and the cover article of the February 28 *New York Times Magazine*. After I read these two articles and considered what it meant for this fellow to be covered in these two locations in the same week, I was led to make some entries in my personal diary. The one entry I would like to read for you is one that I wrote after reading the *New York Times Magazine:* "What does it mean that a former head of prime time television for ABC Entertainment (this is Barry Diller), former chief of Paramount Pictures and chairman of Fox, has just become the CEO of QVC (Quality Value and Convenience) Network, the home shopping division of Telecommunications, Inc. (TCI), the nation's largest cable company, less than a year after he had what is widely reported to be a rhapsodic encounter with an Apple Power Book?" And what these articles will tell you is that he wanted to buy a controlling interest in Fox from Rupert Murdoch, but they couldn't agree on terms. Barry Diller took a one-year sabbatical and is now reentering commerce, and, believe me, Barry Diller doesn't have to work now with home shopping. The article also reports that Vanna White makes $50,000 a minute on QVC when her, I almost said narcotics, but I think the word is cosmetics, are being sold.

It's also the case, as the March 16 *Wall Street Journal* reports, that Alfred Sikes, the chairman of the FCC during the Bush administration, has just been named head of the new media and technology division of Hearst Corporation, and that when the CEO of Hearst, Frank A. Bennack, Jr., announced this appointment, he said that his company was interested in finding partners to form a high-capacity, interactive electronic superhighway similar to that recently proposed by Time-Warner.

Now, consumer activity alone is not enough to generate the investment to build this infrastructure, but it's interesting to note that consumer-driven interests are now beginning to take a role in advocating certain futures for what we call the National Information Infrastructure.

Finally, let me call attention to the fourth constituency, which is a constituency that I think is extremely important. In fact, I think it's a constituency that has generated a large measure of the intellectual capital and the positive excitement that we associate with the contemporary Internet. However, for reasons I'll spend a minute on in a moment, I don't think it's a constituency that's ever had a very strong role in the public policy process. It would be interesting to see the interests of this constituency played out at the national level, but I think it will also have a very strong influence on the public policy process at the local level. This is the constituency that believes that networks provide an opportunity for the emergence of a new social order. This is, in many respects, a vision of networking that national interests cannot really embrace because, obviously, national interests are where the establishment is placing the greatest emphasis, and the establishment has shown that it resists utopian visions quite effectively. Progress on visions like this has always happened at the local, not the national, level in both this country and in other countries around the world, and I think that for some time to come, the linkage of local networking visions to these national networking visions will require the dedicated efforts of people who see the entire picture. People like yourselves.

THE POWER OF METAPHOR

I'd like to close my presentation by mentioning what I feel is an important philosophical issue: the power of metaphor in determining the shape of national networking. I'd like to end on something that has interested me a lot lately, a sort of private correspondence project I have with a couple of people that came out of a listserv that CNI has been operating a while, called CNI Big Ideas, which basically I would describe as a discussion reflecting a new way to think about the Internet. This is sort of a linguistic excursion . . . we started to talk among ourselves about how certain metaphors for our networked information future place control with, and encourage the participation of, only certain types of people. The whole language of thinking of this, as with language in general, may be creating barriers. This is the sort of philosophical issue that GraceAnne DeCandido from the *Wilson Library Bulletin* calls the "little boy metaphor problem." Thinking of the Internet as an erector set just does not do it for everyone. This is an important issue because the metaphors used have some power in shaping the future of national networking. I invite you all to think about this and enter into the discussion.

RONALD L. LARSEN

Associate Director for Information Technology
University of Maryland Libraries
College Park, Maryland

The Role of Networks in Achieving Academic Library Goals

INTRODUCTION

The term "networks" is prominent in the proceedings of this conference and maintains its prominence in the title of this paper. For those whose background involves a heavy dose of computer networks, the term immediately conjures up the vast and continually growing infrastructure of computer networks now spanning the globe and the technologies that contribute to the spread of the network tendrils throughout our personal and professional communities. Indeed, even our definition and understanding of the term "communities" have been forever changed through network technologies, now including the notion of a "virtual community" linking us to individuals of like mind or spirit wherever they may be. To an increasing extent, we find members of our community with whom we establish a lasting relationship to be individuals whose personae are known to us only through the messages we exchange over a computer network.

But library colleagues are quick to broaden this perspective through reminders of the long tradition networking enjoys among libraries—networks growing out of a history of cooperation and coordination intended to cost-share resources and operations throughout the library community, thereby reducing local costs of operation and providing patrons with enhanced access to materials not held locally. I'm referring here, clearly, to the formation of the bibliographic utilities OCLC and Research Libraries Group (RLG), to interlibrary loan, and related services. Just as libraries provide patron access to information in a variety of forms, library networks are also found in many forms, but all are designed to move information. Extant networks serving this function utilize physical delivery networks such as the mail system, UPS, and couriers, as well as electronic delivery systems such as telefacsimile, commercial networks, and the Internet.

Just as new media types augment before they supplant old media types (if they ever supplant), new network technologies tend also to augment. The University of Maryland's use of the Internet has not reduced its use of UPS. Quite the opposite—remote patrons now use the Internet to identify and request materials they wish to borrow; available materials are then shipped by UPS to the University of Maryland library of their choice.

In this paper, I will look more closely at computer networks and, in particular, at how networks are affecting academic libraries' ability to meet their goals. I will consider a typical set of academic library goals, and then explore the interactions between network technology and meeting goals such as these, and the implications that follow. The apparently inevitable conclusion is that the tradition of sharing that already exists among libraries will become much more fundamental to the success of libraries. Indeed, even the notion of a library as a stand-alone physical entity may be in question as libraries become inextricably linked with each other in the pursuit of their goals. The virtual library concept evolves from this line of thought.

A MODEL FOR CONSIDERING ACADEMIC LIBRARY PLANS

Review of several noteworthy plans for academic libraries (Mosher, 1990, pp. 2-6; Strategic Directions, 1990, pp. 7-14; Commitment to Renewal, 1992) and reflection on planning activities in Maryland (Wellford et al., 1992; Larsen, 1993; Seymour Plan, 1992) suggest a common theme underlying current academic library plans. One can consider the goals and objectives expressed in these plans as products of an exploration of a three-dimensional abstract space whose dimensions are collections, services, and management. More specifically, planning activities can be viewed as exploring the three planes formed by the axes of this space: collection services, collection management, and services management. Full exploration of the three-dimensional space is a rigorous venture requiring measures that are at best uncertain and the consideration of a fourth dimension, time. Time is certainly not ignored in these plans but is embodied in analysis of, reflections on, and extrapolations of trends.

Simple measures along the axes are difficult to find. Certainly any measure that sufficiently characterizes the dimension for a modern academic library will be quite complex. But let us not be discouraged. This is a very simple model of a very complex world, after all. A suitable collections metric reflects breadth and depth of materials accessible to the patron. The services metric reflects search and access time and relevance of materials secured for the patron. The management metric is a utility measure perhaps analogous to return on investment. It includes the difficult optimization of resources across and beyond the campus libraries, including investment in collections, facilities, and people, while maintaining a management agility and adaptability to change. Without attempting to be more precise, let us continue, for these plans rely on experience and intuition more than mathematical rigor. The proposed model merely normalizes them to recognize common directions.

Imprecise as such a model may be, its power is in its ability to foster consideration of library goals and objectives in an abstract setting free of the conceptual blocks that frequently accompany tradition.

TYPICAL ACADEMIC LIBRARY GOALS

Libraries everywhere are wrestling with the same four forces: first, the number of published titles continues to increase geometrically; second, the cost per title rises year after year, typically at a rate substantially greater than inflation; third, the cost of delivering services with human labor continues to rise; and, fourth, library budgets rarely keep up with inflation and are more frequently falling behind. The ability of academic libraries to meet the comprehensive needs of their local scholarly community with locally held resources is no longer in question. It is simply impossible. Partnerships that have historically been instrumental in improving library services are now vital to meeting the scholar's basic needs. Networks that once augmented library services now enable them.

It is perhaps ironic, but fortuitous nonetheless, that computing and communications costs have followed trends quite the opposite of those outlined above. For more than 40 years, the price/performance ratios for computing and communications technologies have typically fallen an order of magnitude each five years—that is a factor of 100 million since 1950! And this trend is expected to continue for at least another 15 years. So a useful, if not absolutely valid, question to raise is how academic libraries would change if computing and communications were absolutely free. The answer to this question would provide a major clue as to the nature of the library in the 21st century.

The goals espoused by contemporary academic libraries attempt to come to terms with these issues. How can the problems besetting libraries from the publishing community and the economy at large be offset by innovative and creative approaches that attempt to recast the traditions of academic librarianship in a world where affordable computing and communications technology is widely available? Let us now consider these plans.

Collection Services

The overarching goal of collection services is to provide effective and timely access to the full depth and breadth of relevant scholarly publication, regardless of medium. Collection decisions are increasingly driven by content rather than form, and networked information services are increasingly cited as a delivery mechanism of choice. In this view, the notion of a library that is electronically accessible at any time from any place begins to take on a seriousness that transforms an otherwise desperate prognosis into an opportunity to revitalize through collaborative interdependence.

Typical Goals

Three goals recur in academic library plans for their collection services. The first is a call to complete retrospective conversion and to keep ongoing cataloging up to date. This is an absolute requirement in an environment in which the public access catalog is the primary access tool for the collection. The second is to build online access to certain primary materials that are locally held. Whereas many people fantasize about the capability to access any and all materials electronically, it is clear that this will not be seen in our lifetimes. Existing print collections are simply too vast to anticipate providing online access to their content within the foreseeable future. There are portions of those collections, however, for which online access is appropriate in the near term. These include the unique or special collections that set each of our libraries apart, deteriorating materials for which electronic scanning is an appropriate preservation alternative, and newly published materials that already exist in electronic form. These materials, in particular, are of interest, since they include multimedia, hypertext documents, and other electronic representations— materials that represent the leading edge of publication technology. The third common goal is to establish the interdependencies among networked libraries that render the electronic online collections of each library accessible and usable throughout the network. These three goals form the enabling foundation for the development of a network-based electronic virtual library.

Network Role

Networks play a fundamental, enabling role for collection services, and have done so for a considerable time. The best example of this is probably cataloging, which depends on network services from the bibliographic utilities. Many of these services have been delivered over dedicated, specialized networks but now are evolving toward Internet- and NREN-compatible facilities. This evolution is essential. We must move toward a common, ubiquitous network infrastructure in which competition and discrimination of services occur at the application level rather than at the lower levels of connectivity.

The burgeoning ability to link bibliographic records directly to primary content in network-deliverable form is clearly a network-enabled capability. It presents the potential for providing a major extension to the services available through libraries and opens the door to 24-hour-a-day access. It also raises protocol and policy issues regarding how to identify uniquely and access primary materials in a standard and generalized way. A satisfactory solution to these problems is essential, as this capability is the basic building block of the local electronic library.

Given local linkage from the bibliographic record to primary content accessible across the network, and given the ability to link bibliographic catalogs through the National Information Standards Organization (NISO) Z39.50 protocol, we now have two of the essential building blocks for the electronic virtual library—a network-based information infrastructure among libraries and other information sources that provides online patron access to organized information without regard for the relative location of the patron and the information. The third building block, yet to be addressed effectively, eliminates the need for the patron explicitly to select information sources based on their geographic location. The Internet metaphor is still largely one of navigation among information resources. I believe this metaphor is inappropriate to the electronic virtual library and will succumb eventually to a more versatile metaphor, more akin to union search of distributed library catalogs.

Internet-based projects such as the Wide Area Information Servers (WAIS) and Gopher begin to tackle the problem of finding and using information resources in a distributed environment. These are extremely valuable efforts through which we can hope to understand more about organizing and using networked information. Efforts such as these deserve aggressive support and informed leadership from the library community.

Collection Management

Collection management strives to acquire and ensure the local availability of information resources of greatest potential value to the immediate community of scholars and researchers, while maintaining an integrity to the collection that transcends temporary fluctuations in funding and disciplinary priorities.

Typical Goals

Library planning documents reflect a growing concern for life cycle collection management, in which collection decisions consider not only immediate needs and sources but also the long-term impact of these decisions on the library and its constituency. An investment model hardly seems out of place here. The collection management job is fundamentally one of maximizing the return on investment in library materials by making the right choices early. The life cycle includes selection, acquisition, cataloging, circulation, maintenance, security, and preservation. Ironically, constrained budgets force libraries to invest more heavily in labor-intensive management in an effort to ensure that collection decisions are congruous with academic priorities. The difficulty of this process should be apparent to anyone who has attempted to sort out the academic priorities of a large university, let alone balance the competing interests of research (where breadth and depth is valued), instruction (where alignment with curriculum is required), and service (where broad-based access and ease of use are necessary).

Network Role

Networks play supportive roles for collection management. Electronic linkages to brokers and vendors support routine activities such as ordering of materials, paying of invoices, and filing of claims for missing materials. Dedicated lines and special-purpose networks have been put to this use with reasonable success in terms of internal library productivity. These services, as well, are migrating to the more general purpose, widely accessible Internet, but not just to serve back room interests of libraries and vendors. Catalogs and databases of available materials maintained by vendors and brokers are also of value to the patron interested in either finding materials inaccessible locally or influencing acquisitions decisions of the library.

Collection management is enhanced by linkage to interdependent libraries and information servers. As libraries scale back their acquisitions in light of decreasing budgets and increasing costs, cooperative collection analysis and development take on increased importance. Networks facilitate cooperative collection analysis among interdependent libraries, enabling optimization of acquisition strategies across a larger base, fostering cooperative collection development, and supporting the basic infrastructure for resource sharing.

Services Management

The goal of services management in academic libraries can be viewed as maximizing the return on investment in the people and facilities mediating between the patron and the collection, including the tools by which a patron finds relevant materials, accesses them, and uses them.

Typical Goals

Library plans typically include goals such as improving library infrastructure, empowering the patron, leveraging library expertise, and responding to institutional directions in efforts to improve a library's services to its community.

The technological components of plans to improve the utility of the library typically incorporate a recognition of the need for an integrated electronic information infrastructure, including hardware, software, data, and services. The importance of a consistent and intuitive online user interface is perhaps better understood by the library than by those more traditionally involved in technology-based development activities on campus.

A literate, self-sufficient patron improves the library's productivity by reducing the need to provide basic assistance. Library plans recognize the value of investment in bibliographic instruction and information literacy programs as a means of both empowering patrons and reducing professional staff hours in individual patron assistance. In addition, careful system design includes design goals supporting patron self-sufficiency.

Academic libraries invest heavily in highly educated, highly capable professionals who are masters in organizing information for subsequent access and use. More often than not, these information professionals also have discipline expertise required for organizing subject materials and communicating effectively with those creating and using them. These skills are important for providing subject-specific reference services but can also be used in an outreach capacity to assist scholars, academic departments, and administrative units in organizing their collections. The magnitude of this problem (and opportunity) only gets larger as the creation and use of networked information spreads.

Libraries are service organizations on campus. As such, they must be sensitive and responsive to institutional directions and priorities. Libraries on the campuses of state institutions must also be sensitive and responsive to the expressed needs and directions of the state. Academic library goals typically reflect this reality explicitly in such aims as supporting distance education, invigorating teaching and learning, and supporting state extension services.

Network Role

Services management provides one of the richest opportunities for the application of networks. Modernization of traditional services given a network infrastructure provides the starting point, followed shortly thereafter by innovation in outreach services, and ultimately by the transformation of patron services through the adaptation of modern network-based architectural concepts. Traditional personal services of the library, typified by reference desk activities, need to be generalized to the network environment. Existing electronic mail, bulletin board systems, and "chat" facilities provide the primitive platform on which to initiate such services. In addition, libraries can extend their value as service organizations by assisting in the organization of institutional electronic materials and then providing online access, through the library's catalog, to nonlibrary databases.

Public institutions, in particular, are encountering increasing pressures to extend their outreach and service activities to the public sector. This is evidenced by the growth in distance education, in economic development initiatives based on information access, and in broad-based, publicly sponsored network initiatives such as the Seymour Plan (1992), which strive to provide unmetered online access to public information for every resident of the state. For these programs to succeed, online systems must be self-instructing and self-documenting. Few users will abide complex user manuals; most will sit impatiently through even the best online tutorials. Few institutions can afford the help desk that would otherwise be required to assist such a massive constituency. Network-based information systems must be intuitively usable at the entry level, yet sufficiently rich to meet the needs of the demanding user.

Most of today's online library systems are based on a primitive master/slave architecture for online systems. In this model, the user is perceived to be entering the system from a dumb terminal, and all of the information processing is performed centrally on a mainframe processor. Even though most remote users now access information systems from personal computers that have more power than the mainframes that existed when this model was devised, they run emulation programs that convert these powerful networked processors back into primitive dumb terminals. This model must be discarded as obsolete.

Contemporary network architectures are based on a client/server notion in which client and server are viewed as peer systems, both with substantial computational sophistication. In this model, the patron enters from a client system, accessing the library information server. The client manages the local patron interface, customizes it to the user's desires, and negotiates with the server system for the delivery of information and services that will meet the needs of the customer. The NISO Z39.50 protocol, for example, is based on this architecture, as is WAIS. (WAIS is actually based on an early version of the Z39.50 protocol.) This architecture is important in that it distributes the computational workload to machines specialized to specific functions. Valuable centralized mainframes designed for large-scale information management are no longer echoing characters to dumb terminals, and sophisticated end-users can tailor their local access facilities to their individual needs, desires, and interests. Valuable network resources can also be optimized to make more efficient use of communications capacity.

The client/server architecture is based on a one-to-one (client-to-server) model. It is not hard conceptually to extend it to a one-to-many (client-to-multiserver) model, but the model does not seem extensible to a many-to-many (multiserver-to-multiserver) interpretation. Yet, if our institutional trends are a credible guide, the need for collaboration among systems in a fairly general sense is not far away. This need may force the extension of the client/server model to a team model, in which the discrimination between user and provider becomes muted, to be replaced by a model based on cooperating distributed processes.

CONCLUSION: VIRTUALIZATION IS INEVITABLE

Economic forces and technological opportunities appear to point towards an unavoidable conclusion: fundamental change in academic libraries is inevitable, assured by economic forces and predestined by emerging technological alternatives. Academic libraries that aspire to meet the comprehensive needs of the 21st-century scholar will also recognize the impossibility of the task, if using only traditional approaches. Absolute comprehensiveness will be replaced by virtual comprehensiveness, which ultimately relies on a robust, fast, demand-access acquisition strategy. A significant proportion of local collections will be built strictly on the basis of patron demand, supported by comprehensive access to bibliographic citations to the available literature. Not unlike the basic strategies governing the management of virtual memory in computer systems, libraries will implement a local collection management strategy that attempts to meet a substantial proportion of immediate, local needs with local collections, while providing virtual access to the entire corpus of published literature on a demand basis. This will be accomplished with a distribution system that delivers any scholarly publication anywhere within a reasonable period of time (24 hours seems reasonable in 1993, but this, also, may be subject to downward pressures).

REFERENCES

Commitment to renewal: A strategic plan for the Harvard College Library. (1992, February). Cambridge, MA: Harvard College Library.

Larsen, R. L. (1993, January). *Computing in the libraries.* College Park: University of Maryland Libraries.

Mosher, P. H. (1990, February). *Information at Penn in the year 2000: A conceptual planning document. Almanac Supplement.* Philadelphia: University of Pennsylvania Libraries.

The Seymour Plan: Electronically connecting Maryland's libraries. (1992, December). Baltimore: Maryland State Library Network Coordinating Council, Division of Library Development and Services, Maryland State Department of Education.

Strategic directions for information systems and computing at the University of Pennsylvania. Almanac Supplement. (1990, February). Philadelphia: Office of the Vice Provost for Information Systems and Computing.

Wellford, C.; Gentile, J.; Gilbert, G.; Larsen, R.; Munn, R.; Ricart, G.; Scheraga, C.; & Tripathi, S. (1992, December). *Strategic plan for information technology.* College Park: Computer Science Center, University of Maryland at College Park.

WILLIAM V. GARRISON

Interface Designer
Albert R. Mann Library
Cornell University
Ithaca, New York

Integrating Networked Information into Library Services: Philosophy, Strategy, and Implementation at Mann Library

INTRODUCTION

Until the relatively recent introduction of computer networks into the academic community, the records of scholarship and the collection of the academic library have consisted primarily of physical materials in print-based formats. The publication, distribution, and use of scholarly works are being transformed by the application of computer networking and information technologies. As Hirshon (1993) observes, "since the invention of the printing press, there has been no change so fundamental to the publishing industry as the advent of electronic and networked information" (p. 1). Advances in computing technology have made it possible for digital formats to subsume nearly all previous formats of publication. Text, still and moving images, sounds, music, computer programs, and statistical data—all can be published in a digital format and stored on a computer's magnetic disk. Wide-reaching computer networks make it possible to distribute those digitally formatted materials to thousands of people within just a few minutes. This transformation from printed to networked information is so profound that we are now considered in the midst of a revolution and paradigm shift, in which the very nature of libraries and librarianship is being challenged (Hirshon, 1993; Lynch, 1992; Malinconico, 1992; Olsen, 1990).

PHILOSOPHY

Mann Library believes that the academic library has a central and critical role to play with regard to networked information in the academic community. Our philosophy is founded on two primary beliefs: first, that the mission of the academic library remains unchanged in the face of changes in publication formats; and, second, that the role of the academic library in the process of scholarship becomes increasingly critical with the emergence of networked scholarly information. The academic library maintains the unique responsibility for providing the academic community with fair and equitable access to an unbiased collection of intellectual works. The importance of this role to the pursuit of scholarship is without question. "Ideas are the currency of the academy. The free exchange, open criticism, and independent exploration of ideas constitute basic activities of academics" (Duncan, 1993, p. 50). Without fair and equitable access to a complete record of scholarship, there can be no scholarly inquiry and no viable pursuit of truth. The transformation of scholarly publishing from print to digital formats does not change the purpose or mission of the library in the academy.

The traditional mission of the academic library has been to support the activities of research and instruction by providing scholars with access to the records of scholarship. Librarians build collections of scholarly works by identifying, selecting, and preserving items from various disciplines, by organizing and presenting the collection to facilitate its use, and by providing equitable access, assistance, and instruction. These fundamental functions continue in the face of changes in either the formats of publication or the technologies required to accommodate those formats. We believe that networked information resources of relevance to scholarship should be integrated into the collection and services of the academic library.

As Saunders (1992) notes, "technological change is an inherent part of the evolving virtual library" (p. 71). Sophisticated computing and networking technologies are needed for the storage, access, and delivery of networked information resources. Computers have certainly become a more prominent element in academic libraries over the past decade, but the technologies and expertise needed to support networked information resources are not yet commonplace in most. Consequently, many in the academic and library communities have considered what role can be played by campus computing organizations in bringing both informal and scholarly networked information to the academic community (Malinconico, 1992; Martin, 1992; Weber, 1988; Woodsworth, 1988; Post & Sessions, 1986; Neff, 1985). Campus computing organizations have the requisite technical expertise, facilities, and access to the networks and computing technologies necessary to deliver networked information, whereas most libraries currently do not.

Although technology is an important and highly visible component, the infrastructure required to support a collection of networked information resources is comprised of much more. In comparing the library and the campus computing centers, Martin (1992), paraphrasing Moran, observes that "libraries are struggling to incorporate the computer within their long tradition of consistency, while computer centers struggle to develop some consistency in a climate of constant change" (p. 80). Weber also comments that "the academic computer center . . . exists in a volatile entrepreneurial environment with rapidly changing generations of operational technology" (cited in Martin, 1992, p. 78). The entrepreneurial nature of today's academic computing organizations is at odds with that of the library. Any shift away from the library's traditional emphasis on service and public good should raise serious concerns among librarians, administrators, and faculty alike for the provision of fair and equitable access to networked information. The need for technological evolution in the academic library should not be confused with a need to redefine its role in the academic community. That role remains to support and ensure intellectual freedom in scholarship.

Mann Library believes that the academic library must retain leadership in providing scholars with access to networked information. We have taken the approach that networked information of relevance to scholarship should be integrated into the collection of the academic library. The library must retool its procedures and operations to accommodate this new format of scholarly publication and distribution. Our approach has been guided by the following underlying assumptions (Olsen, 1990, pp. 221-222):

- The fundamental purpose of the campus library remains unique; it continues to be the library's responsibility to connect the scholar with the records of scholarship.
- The records of scholarship will increasingly be stored electronically rather than in print.
- Scholars' microcomputers will become more central to their professional work, which includes the access, use, and retrieval of scholarly information.
- Libraries have a critical stake in the nature of scholars' workstations, as well as the campus, national, and international telecommunications systems that link these machines.
- There is a fundamental difference in the way in which scholars approach and interact with electronic information as opposed to print, which has serious implications for the design of user interfaces to that information.
- Scholars' access to information is not limited by their ability to pay nor by varying degrees of "rights" to access.
- Libraries will continue to share resources even in electronic form.

STRATEGY

In developing a strategy for integrating networked information into library services, Mann Library has, conceptually, approached these information resources as we would scholarly materials published in any nonprint format. While this may seem an oversimplification of an obviously challenging task, this approach has given us a useful framework within which to analyze and address the issues that arise from integrating these resources into the collection. There are five areas of concern that must be addressed when integrating any material in nonprint format into a collection.

Technological Requirements for Storage and Use

Nearly all types of nonprint materials require some technology for their effective use. Videocassettes require a videocassette player and a television set to be viewed; microfiche requires a specialized microfiche reader. To access and retrieve networked information, a person needs a computer, specialized communication software, and a network connection. Specialized software may also be needed to manipulate and manage the information once retrieved (e.g., personal reference managers, spreadsheets, image-processing software). On a networked campus, many members of the community may already possess the necessary technology to use networked information from their own homes, offices, and laboratories. However, to ensure equitable access for all in the community to the networked information in its collection, a library must provide or otherwise secure public access to networked computers configured with appropriate hardware, software, and peripheral devices.

Unlike other nonprint formats which exist in a physical form, networked information relies on a variety of computer technologies to facilitate its storage. To locally store a digitally formatted information resource for network access, a library would need networked computer, high-capacity disk storage devices, and specialized access and retrieval software. For physical storage of the digitally formatted information, the computer must be equipped with magnetic or optical disks that can range in capacity from a few megabytes to several gigabytes, depending on the size and nature of the resource. The networked computer could range in size from a small personal computer to a large mainframe, depending on the number of patrons for which the library would like to afford simultaneous use of the locally stored information resource. The computer will also need specialized software that can efficiently regulate networked access and provide a user interface with which patrons can interact with the networked information.

Facilities for Storage and Access

Few libraries store their nonprint materials in the stacks along with their books and journals. More often a special facility or area of the library is established where the collection of nonprint materials can be stored near the devices needed to use them. With regard to networked information, its virtual nature obviates the need for access workstations to be housed near the collection. In fact, neither the access workstations nor the collection need be housed in the library at all. A library's collection of networked information can be defined as a virtual one of *accessible* resources that includes information stored locally at the library or remotely at other institutions around the world. Patrons can interact with this collection through any networked computer. It makes little difference to the patron where the networked information resources are actually stored or from where they are accessed—all resources appear equally accessible. Conceptually, the virtual library facility exists wherever a patron has access to a networked computer.

In practice, a library will probably not want the existence of its virtual library to depend on the availability of networked public access computers outside the library or remotely stored information resources from other institutions. To provide in-house access to its collection of networked information, a facility will be needed in a public area of the library to house a collection of networked computer workstations and necessary peripherals. As a library begins to establish a collection of locally stored networked information, facilities for archiving those digitally formatted materials will be needed. Given the complexity and cost of the computing technology needed for storage of networked information, this facility will need to be located in a secure and environmentally controlled area of the library. Unfortunately, the facilities used for archiving a primarily print-based collection are not adequate for this purpose. A library's archive of digitally formatted materials will need physical facilities that are designed specifically to support the operating requirements of the requisite computing technologies.

Staff Knowledge and Skills

The integration of materials in a new publication format into a library's collection invariably requires changes in staff knowledge and skills. With nonprint formats, new expertise must be acquired to handle both the materials and the devices required to use them. Maintaining and supporting a collection of networked information resources present a particularly challenging demand on staff. To provide a minimal level of assistance to the broadest spectrum of networked patrons, staff must be knowledgeable about the networks, facile in the use of several computing environments (e.g., Macintosh, DOS, and Windows), and comfortable with a wide variety of access software. In addition, staff may need familiarity with a variety of post-processing and information management applications such as spreadsheets, image-processing/graphics software, database programs, and word processors. There must also be staff with technical expertise for managing local networked computer servers and maintaining locally stored information resources.

Changes in Practices of Librarianship

Nonprint materials typically require changes to the manner in which items are collected, cataloged, organized, and presented for access. Existing methods and procedures are modified or new ones developed to accommodate the nonprint format. The selection of nonprint materials for a collection requires the consideration of additional factors not relevant for printed matter, such as compatibility with the library's existing access technology. Nonprint materials often do not contain the "clues" present in print materials, like a title page, table of contents, or an index, and it can be difficult to examine their contents. The presentation of the nonprint collection for public access can also exhibit a problematic fit with existing print-oriented models of circulation. Networked information presents even more challenges to the practices of librarianship.

Many, if not most, users of a library's collection of networked information will not be physically present in the library building. They will be using the library's networked information resources from their homes, offices, classrooms, and laboratories. Reference and instruction librarians must find ways of remaining in contact with these networked patrons to provide assistance, instruction, and information about changes in the collection.

Collection development of networked information is difficult and time-consuming. There does not yet exist a reliable mechanism of communication between publishers of networked information and librarians responsible for selecting those resources for their library's collections. Many of the information resources published on the Internet are announced through networked channels of communication, like online newsgroups and electronic mail discussion lists, that are not usually monitored by collection development staff. Many publications of networked information are often not announced at all—they just spontaneously appear at the neighborhood archive. Announcements of updates, new versions, or discontinuations are infrequent. Since little descriptive information typically accompanies networked information resources, one must examine them closely to determine if they are of interest and of good quality.

The cataloging and presentation of a collection of networked information resources are also uniquely challenging. It is difficult to create and maintain the accuracy of cataloging records for networked information, particularly those resources that are not stored locally by the library. The same problems faced by collection development librarians—lack of adequate descriptions and unreliability of communication with network publishers—also present challenges to the cataloger. Maintaining accurate records can be time-consuming and labor intensive when the title, content, and even storage location of a networked information resource can change with relatively high frequency and little warning. Adding to this challenge is the fact that the current definitions of cataloging standards such as USMARC and AACR2, and consequently many library cataloging systems, do not readily accommodate the bibliographic description of networked information.

The virtual nature of networked information also has implications for change in the nature of a collection's catalog and in patrons' use of that catalog. In speaking to the use of the traditional collection of physical materials, Hirshon (1993) notes that "access to information was a two-step process, physically represented between the presence of the book on the shelf and the library catalog to help find that book" (p. 2). In contrast, networked information, once located, can be instantly accessed and retrieved. In addition to helping locate an item in the collection, the functionality of an online catalog of a library's collection of networked information will also need to include means of providing direct access to those information resources.

User Instruction

Patrons often require specific instruction from library staff in the handling of nonprint materials. The introduction of networked information and its associated access technologies into the library's collection present the same challenges for user instruction as for staff instruction, except on a larger scale. There will always be more patrons inexperienced with computing technology and networked information than staff. While the basic knowledge and skills of computer use are on the rise, there will be many patrons who will get their first exposure to computers and networks in the library. The need for computer literacy as well as information literacy has serious implications for the content of any library instruction program that supports the use of a collection of networked information.

IMPLEMENTATION

Since May 1991, Mann Library has been providing our community of Cornell University students, faculty, and staff with campus network access to a collection of networked information resources stored locally at the library and remotely at other institutions connected to the Internet. The integration of networked information into library services has been a measured process of systematic research and strategic planning. Over the past decade, Mann Library has pursued an aggressive program of automation to introduce computing technologies into all aspects of library operation and services. These efforts have resulted in the development of new facilities, services, and staff expertise that formed a crucial foundation for the integration of networked information resources into the library's collection.

Changes in Organization, Facilities, and Services

In 1984, the Mann Library opened the first microcomputer center on the Cornell campus (Curtis, 1987). Its purpose was to provide a comprehensive information literacy program as well as public access to information technologies and electronic information resources. While at the library, patrons can make use of word processing, spreadsheet, and database management software. The microcenter's workstations are connected to a local network that has access to the campus network and the Internet. Faculty, staff, and students can access a variety of networked information resources and services from the microcomputer center including electronic mail, Gopher, File Transfer Protocol (FTP), terminal-based information services on the Internet, and local information resources such as the Cornell Libraries Online Catalog and Mann Library's collection of bibliographic and numeric databases.

In conjunction with the development of the microcomputer center, the library added two full-time staff dedicated to computing support and operation of the microcomputer center. In 1986, these staff formed the basis of a new unit in Mann Library known as the Information Technology Section (ITS) (Curtis, 1987, p. 13). The ITS serves as Mann Library's computing systems group, analogous in organizational function to the management information systems (MIS) departments found in corporations whose operations have become highly automated. The role of the ITS includes introduction and support of information technology throughout the library, staff and patron instruction, and participation in library research projects. Since its formation, the ITS has expanded in size to a staff of six full-time computer professionals, with expertise in microcomputer hardware and software support, local area networking, software development, UNIX computer systems management, and user interface design.

With the opening of our microcomputer facility, Mann Library expanded its instruction program beyond traditional bibliographic instruction into areas related to the handling of digitally formatted, electronically stored information. Today, the library's instruction program includes workshops in basic microcomputer skills, end-user searching of bibliographic and numeric databases accessible online and on compact disk, and the use of specific software applications for managing and manipulating information retrieved using a computer. An extensive treatment of our approach can be found in chapters 8-12 in Curtis (1987).

In 1987, Mann Library began integrating compact disk databases of bibliographic, statistical, and textual data into the library services (Barnes &

Spragg, 1990; Coons & Stewart, 1988). Today, a second microcomputer facility of dedicated compact disk workstations has been established in the reference area of the library.

Experimentation with Networked Information

In 1987, Mann Library also began a series of research projects to investigate the issues surrounding the integration of network-accessible, scholarly information resources into the library's collection and services. The underlying theme of this research program was the development of the scholarly information system (Olsen, 1990, p. 222), which was envisioned to consist of four components: first, scholars at workstations in their homes, laboratories, classrooms, or offices; second, computer networks of campus, regional, national, and global scope; third, electronic information resources located on computers throughout the world and accessible via the networks; and, fourth, the campus library, providing scholars with organized access to and assistance with the growing collection of scholarly networked information.

The broad goals of these projects have been to identify and assess the organizational, technical, service, and marketing issues that arise in support of a collection of networked information resources. Individually, the projects focused on research and experimentation with local storage of networked bibliographic, numeric, and textual information, and with mechanisms for providing scholars with access to a collection of these genres of information.

Mann Library's initial research project involved maintaining locally stored bibliographic databases for network access. In collaboration with Cornell Information Technologies (CIT) and with contributions from the National Agriculture Library, Biosciences Information Service (BIOSIS), and BRS Information Technologies, Mann Library developed the "Scholars' Information System." Using a campus minicomputer maintained by CIT, we acquired the BRS/Search database management software and mounted four bibliographic databases in the disciplines of agriculture and biological sciences. Access to the Scholars' Information System was offered as an experimental service for two years to a group of approximately 200 Cornell faculty and staff who had agreed to participate in the project. Workshops in bibliographic database searching were developed by library staff and offered to all participants. Reference and technical support was provided via telephone and electronic mail by library staff members of the project team. We gained valuable experience in the acquisition of files from database producers and techniques for locally loading databases for network access. We began to identify the desirable hardware and software configurations of the remote users' microcomputer and their instructional needs in using networked bibliographic databases. We also learned that our community of scholars was eager for network access to the library's information resources.

In 1989, Mann Library received a grant from the U.S. Department of Education to investigate the local mounting of numeric databases for network access. Two large datasets produced by the federal government were loaded on a networked minicomputer acquired by the library using Informix/SQL database software. To investigate functional requirements of a system for interacting with numeric data and user interface design issues, library staff on the project developed a custom information retrieval program for the two locally mounted datasets. The library gained experience from this project in large-scale software development, user interface design, and the identification of the unique requirements of database design for numeric datasets.

We are currently engaged in a research project to investigate the provision of networked access to digitally stored full text. This project is known as the Chemistry Online Retrieval Experiment (CORE). Mann Library is collaborating with the American Chemical Society, OCLC, and Bell Communications Research (Bellcore) to test a variety of prototype information systems for the search, retrieval, and delivery of the full-text and page images of core journals in the discipline of chemistry. Within this collaborative project, a primary objective of Mann Library is to investigate the manner in which scholars will make use of full-text journal literature that is readily accessible from networked computers on their desktops.

Building on previous experiences, our next research project was directed at determining the requirements for presenting, maintaining, and supporting a collection of networked information resources. In 1989, Mann Library received a three-year grant from Cornell University's President's Fund for Educational Initiatives to integrate the use of information technology and networked information resources into the curriculum of undergraduate students in the biological sciences. In collaboration with faculty in Cornell's Division of Biological Sciences, we pursued four objectives: first, to mount locally a collection of networked information resources relevant to scholarship in the biological sciences; second, to upgrade selected campus microcomputer centers with connections to the campus network in order to provide students with public access to appropriate information technologies; third, to develop a gateway system to provide organized and convenient access to the library's collection of networked information; and, fourth, to establish a working relationship between library staff and teaching faculty in order to provide students in the biological sciences with integrated instruction in computer and information literacy skills.

With regard to integrating networked information into library services, the creation of the gateway system was a critical element in Mann Library's effort. Known simply as the Mann Library Gateway, this system provided the library with a vehicle for presenting and providing organized access to its heterogeneous collection of networked information resources, regardless of what kind of information they contained, or whether they were stored locally or at other institutions. For our networked patrons, the Mann Library Gateway represents a virtual extension of the library into the milieu of information services that give definition to the local cyberspace of Cornell's campus network.

The design of the Mann Library Gateway was guided by four criteria. First, the system had to be accessible from Macintosh and IBM-compatible computers. At the time of development, a survey of patrons revealed a nearly 50-50 split between use of the two microcomputer platforms and that nearly all were using telecommunications software that emulated the ubiquitous character-based DEC VT100 terminal to connect to remote computer systems. Second, the Gateway had to present the library's collection of networked information in a clearly organized and convenient manner. We wanted our networked patrons to be able to quickly locate and use a database in our collection without the need to remember the arbitrary logon protocols typically required to access networked computer systems. Third, the Gateway had to provide descriptive information about each database in the collection to permit the networked patron to select the items relevant to his or her information need. Many gateway systems present only a list of titles. With names like AGRICOLA, BIOSIS Previews, or RLIN, it can be difficult for patrons to decide which information resource will be relevant and useful. Finally, the Gateway had to clearly communicate how and from where the networked patron could get assistance in using databases in the library's networked collection. It was important to convey to the users of the Gateway that they had network access not only to the library's collection of databases but also to its staff for questions and problems. Figures 1 and 2 depict the catalog and closing screens developed for the Gateway system.

```
                                            Mann Library Gateway

 Databases _____     Description _____

   1. ABI/Inform                 AGRICOLA is a database of citations and
   2. AGRICOLA                    abstracts to literature in agriculture
   3. BIOSIS                      and related subjects.
   4. CARL Uncover
   5. Cornell Online Catalog      Articles are indexed from 5000 journals
   6. Crop Estimates-County File  and other serials.  Books, conference
   7. ERIC                        proceedings, research reports, theses,
   8. Nat'l Resources Inventory   patents, software, and government
   9. RLIN                        documents are also indexed.

                                  Source: National Agriculture Library
                                  Coverage: 1982-present
                                  Updated: Monthly
 Directions _____

   To:  Highlight a resource   -  type its number or use arrow keys.
        Connect to a resource   -  highlight it and press RETURN.
        Change your password    -  type P.
        Quit the Gateway        -  type q.
```

Figure 1. Catalog screen from the Mann Library Gateway

With the successful development of the Gateway, Mann Library had made significant progress toward realizing an integrated collection of networked information resources. It had established an initial collection of networked information resources, had developed a mechanism for presenting and providing access to that networked collection, and had identified the reference and technical support services that networked patrons considered important. This project also provided the library with a valuable opportunity to consider a number of models for mainstreaming the support of networked information into our existing library organization. By the end of the project in 1992, Mann Library was ready to begin the formal integration of its collection of networked information resources into library services.

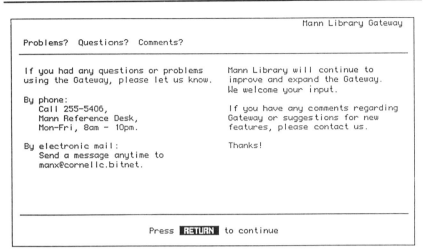

Figure 2. Closing screen from the Mann Library Gateway

INTEGRATING NETWORKED
INFORMATION INTO LIBRARY SERVICES

In our approach to this challenge, Mann Library has considered it important to have participation from staff in all units of the library. We have emphasized participation through group discussions of the issues surrounding networked information and through projects in which library units have been encouraged to experiment to find ways to accommodate this new medium. Our success with providing the community with access to a collection of networked information has been the direct result of a team effort by the entire library organization to absorb and apply the knowledge, skills, and experiences gained from its research projects.

Technological Requirements for Networked Information

Our current collection of networked information consists of 11 resources comprised of bibliographic, statistical, and textual databases, and a table of contents service. At present, the majority of Mann Library's collection of networked information is stored locally on computers at the library: ABI/ Inform, AGRICOLA, BIOSIS Previews, Census of Population and Housing, ERIC, National Resources Inventory, and USDA Crop Estimates. CARL UnCover and RLIN (Research Libraries Information Network) are examples of networked information resources for which access for the Cornell community has been obtained through contracts with other institutions on the network. The Cornell Libraries Online Catalog and CLIMOD are examples of networked information resources that are locally maintained by other organizations at Cornell for which we provide access through the library's Gateway.

To support our locally stored networked information resources, Mann Library currently manages four UNIX-based multiuser computers. One computer supports the Gateway system and serves as the main entry point for patrons to our collection of networked information. A second computer is used as a server for three numeric databases. Informix/SQL and the University of Minnesota's Gopher software are used as the access software. Four bibliographic databases are split across the remaining two servers. BRS/Search full-text search and retrieval software is used as the access software. Each of the library's four server computers has several gigabytes of hard disk storage and is connected through a local area Ethernet network in the library to the Cornell campus network and, subsequently, to the global Internet. Access to the remotely stored information resources in the collection is provided through the Gateway system using the UNIX Telnet and tn3270 programs. In addition to the local database servers, all Mann Library staff have a networked microcomputer at their desk or work area through which they can access the library's collection of networked information and provide services in support of it. Management and maintenance of the database servers and staff computers is performed by the library's Information Technology Section.

Facilities for Storage and Access of Networked Information

To house the library's database servers and associated storage devices, a room within the Mann Library building has been converted for use as a "machine room." The machine room is secured from public access and is environmentally controlled for electrical power supply, temperature, and humidity. As our locally stored collection of networked information grows, this facility will likely be expanded.

Mann Library's microcomputer center serves our patrons with public access to networked microcomputers. Additional networked microcomputers have been placed in the CD-ROM access microcomputer facility within the library's reference area. Cornell's campus computing organization and several individual colleges and departments also maintain public access microcomputer facilities in various locations around the campus. Campus network access in dormitory rooms, offices, and laboratories and dial-in access from off-campus residences also permit private access to our collection of networked information.

Staff Knowledge and Skills for Networked Information

Maintaining and supporting the library's collection of networked information resources has had the most impact to date on our public services and computing systems staff. Reference librarians, information assistants, and technical support staff have had to acquire a great deal of technical knowledge regarding communications software in a variety of microcomputer environments. As Sally Kalin has noted, "telecommunications set-up and troubleshooting is the most heavily demanded service requested by remote access users" (cited in Peters, 1991, p. 164). Staff in the library's Public Services Division have learned to operate eight communications software programs for Macintosh and IBM-compatible computers that are commonly used with Cornell's campus computer networks. Knowledge of local campus networking and the Internet has also been necessary to assist patrons in troubleshooting problems in connecting to the library's Gateway computer.

Training in the technical knowledge needed to support the collection of networked information was provided by the library's ITS and by members of the various project teams through a series of workshops. These workshops covered campus networking and the Internet, introductions to the variety of networked information resources available, and the communications programs and other tools used to locate and access them.

The development of Mann Library's Gateway and its collection of networked information resources required changes in library staffing. In addition to training existing staff, the library has acquired new personnel and reoriented existing positions with a focus on digitally formatted information resources. Staff expertise in user interface design, the development of networked information systems, and the handling of electronically published information was considered critical by the library's director in pursuing the integration of networked information into the collection. Four new staff have been added to the library's computing systems unit, bringing skills in user interface design, network management, large-scale software development, and administration of UNIX-based computer systems. Staff have also been added to the public services and technical services units, including a specialist in numeric information, an electronic resources cataloger, and a coordinator of public access computing facilities. A more complete discussion of administrative and staffing issues can be found in Olsen (1990, pp. 238-240).

User Instruction for Networked Information

Instruction in the access and use of the library's collection of networked information has been integrated into our regular instruction program. A series of workshops is given every semester and during intersessions by staff instructors in the basic use of a microcomputer, communications software, specific networked information resources in the collection, and information processing and management applications such as spreadsheets, word processors, and personal reference managers. Schedules of our workshops are mailed to faculty in our constituent colleges before each semester begins to allow them time to consider integrating our instruction into their courses.

We have found that our patrons work in a variety of personal computing environments and with a range of levels of computer and information literacy. To accommodate this, we have expanded our instruction program to include hands-on workshops on both Macintosh and IBM-compatible computers. To assist the self-directed patron who avoids formal workshops, a selection of short documentation and reference sheets has been created by library staff. These include guides to searching the databases in the collection, "quick guides" to configuring the selection of library-supported communications packages, and a comparative guide to assist patrons in selecting an appropriate communications program for their personal computing environment.

As an adjunct to our regular instruction program, Mann Library staff have also conducted a series of marketing presentations at college and departmental faculty meetings. These presentations have been designed to introduce the faculty in the community to the library's collection of networked information and to encourage them to consider how its use could be integrated into their own research and instruction. These presentations, which have included a hands-on introduction to the Gateway and databases in the collection, have been instrumental in getting many faculty "back into the library" through personal use of the library's electronic resources.

Adapting the Practices of Librarianship to Networked Information

Public Services

For providing assistance and reference service for the collection of networked information, our Public Services staff use a mix of old and new techniques. The reference interview is most often conducted over the phone or through electronic mail. Conducting the interview, with regard to a networked information resource in the collection, is complicated by the need to determine the context of a patron's local computing environment as well as the context of the information need. Staff increasingly answer questions revolving around technical support such as reports of forgotten passwords on personal Gateway accounts, procedures for connecting to the Gateway, and methods for downloading information retrieved from a database search.

Our patrons have also been looking to library staff for advice and assistance in selecting software for use with our networked collection. Two common questions concern evaluating which communications and personal reference management software packages are the best for use with our collection of networked information resources. With personal computers becoming more integral to the use of scholarly information retrieved from the library, patrons will naturally come to expect this kind of consulting service from library staff. This situation has presented us with a dilemma. On one hand, public services librarians have traditionally been wary of providing any potentially biasing opinion regarding information sources and this naturally extends towards the evaluation of particular software programs. On the other hand, to encourage and facilitate the use of information technology and networked information resources, it is in the best interests of the library to recommend the use of software that is known to work well with its collection of networked information. In the case of communications software, which is a critical component of any scholars' information system, a program that is difficult to use or lacking in relevant features can negatively taint a patron's experience with the library's collection. It is good service and good marketing to recommend the use of particular software programs that work effectively and will leave the networked patron with a positive impression of the library's services. We are presently experimenting with a limited form of this consulting service by conducting demonstrations of communications and reference management software available to the local Cornell community and by providing comparative evaluations of the programs based on the features available in each. As we have gained working experience with several of the available programs, we have become more confident in being able to recommend some over the others. However, the scope to which this kind of consulting service should be implemented by the library remains to be explored.

Collection Development

The identification and selection of networked information resources at Mann Library is performed by an internal collection development body known as the Electronic Resources Council (ERC). The ERC is chaired by the library's head of collection development and is comprised of representatives from acquisitions, public services, and the computing systems group, as well as selectors from all units in the library with expertise in particular genres of electronic information (e.g., bibliographic, numeric, textual, and government documents). The ERC evaluates electronic information resources for acquisition using traditional selection criteria, such as subject coverage and currency, as well as additional attributes that are unique to digital formats, such as medium of publication (e.g., network or compact disk), technologies required for storage and access, contractual or licensing restrictions on access, and desired level of reference support.

Mann Library's Collection Development Division has also formed a group known as the "Internet Prospectors" who are surveying the Internet for networked information of relevance to the library's subject areas of collection. This group has identified locations of networked archives and servers with information in the library's subject areas and developed a working knowledge of the various tools used for accessing and retrieving Internet resources.

Technical Services

The acquisition of networked information resources is handled by the acquisitions staff in the library's Technical Services Division. At this time, acquiring the data files for a database to be locally mounted or obtaining accounts and passwords for access to remotely stored information resources requires much negotiation. Commercial producers of databases are still in the process of developing suitable policies for the licensing of data files to libraries. Providers of networked information services are also in a transitional period in which they are developing new policies and pricing schemes for allowing remote access to their information resources. We have found that much individual negotiation has been required with each database producer or access provider to acquire a networked information resource for the collection. "Standard terms" under which libraries can acquire data files for local storage or access to networked information services are still evolving, which makes this task a continual challenge for the acquisitions staff. As the acquisition of networked information becomes a more common activity in libraries, we are confident that standard terms will be established that accommodate the library's traditional mission of collection, preservation, and access to information.

The cataloging of our growing collection of networked information resources has presented us with a particularly vexing problem. Our present collection is so small that a virtual analog to the traditional book catalog has been sufficient to facilitate access for our networked patrons. Mann Library's Gateway system presents an alphabetical list of titles accompanied by short descriptions of each of the networked databases in the collection. Over the next year, we anticipate that our collection will grow into the hundreds. The book catalog model will quickly become unworkable.

A logical place to catalog the virtual holdings of a university library's networked information collection would appear to be its current online catalog. However, the procedures and policies surrounding the construction of the online library catalog have been based upon the existence of scholarly information resources as physical objects with physical library locations. Networked information resources are not easily accommodated in the existing systems. As illustrated by the OCLC Internet Resources study (Dillon, Jul, Burge, & Hickey, 1993), the USMARC record also presents some challenges for accommodating the description of networked information resources.

Staff from the library's cataloging, reference, and computing systems units are currently engaged in a project to develop a network-accessible catalog of the Mann Library's collection of electronic information resources that addresses the unique features of these new formats. This catalog will include not only networked information but also resources in our collection that are stored and accessed on compact disks, diskettes, and magnetic tapes. We are exploring several questions regarding the cataloging of networked and other electronic information resources, including how public services and cataloging staff can work together to provide descriptions of resources, what data elements are important to include in those descriptions for patron use and the library staff needs, and how the accuracy of cataloging records can be maintained for networked information resources whose content can change dynamically and without warning.

FUTURE PLANS

Our future plans for development of our virtual library include expanding our collection of network-accessible information resources, refining the user interfaces to those resources, and making more of the library's traditional services accessible via the campus network. Since the original design of the Mann Library Gateway, a number of developments have occurred in Cornell's computing and networking environment and in the world of networked information. Over the past two years, use of the campus network has become more pervasive among Cornell's faculty, staff, and students. The university's central computing organization has been actively moving its campus information services such as electronic mail and the campus-wide information system from its two campus mainframe computers to smaller UNIX-based computers. The use of terminal emulation programs to access networked information services has given way to other microcomputer-based programs providing user interfaces that take better advantage of the microcomputer's display, processing, and storage capabilities. In the world of the Internet, information publication and retrieval systems based on the client-server computing model, such as Gopher, Wide Area Information Servers (WAIS), and World Wide Web, are widening the possibilities for providing the networked community with digitally formatted information. The continuing development and acceptance of the Z39.50 standard information retrieval protocol will make it possible for people to access a wide variety of different types of networked information resources through a few consistently designed user interfaces.

Over the next two years, Mann Library will be reengineering its Gateway system to follow the recent developments in client-server software and standardized information retrieval protocols. We intend to develop microcomputer-based software following the client-server model that provides direct access to a catalog of our networked information collection, and to the networked resources themselves, using the Z39.50 protocol.

We will also explore other standardized networked information services such as Gopher, WAIS, FTP, and Network News to translate other library services into the networked environment. In particular, we will experiment with providing access through the campus network to documentation, instructional materials, and reference and technical support staff. Interlibrary loan, current awareness services, document delivery, and reserve services are also targets for transition to networked library services.

We intend to expand our collection with the addition of more locally and remotely stored networked information resources. An upcoming project will be exploring ways in which networked information can be provided to the Cornell community in a convenient and cost-effective manner through commercial information providers such as DIALOG and BRS. In addition, we will begin identifying and selecting networked information published on the Internet via Gopher, WAIS, and FTP for inclusion in our virtual collection. The library has recently begun experimenting with these network publishing tools for our own local loading of information resources. We currently have mounted datasets from the 1990 U.S. Census of Population and Housing for campus network access using a locally maintained Gopher server. We are also exploring the use of Gopher, WAIS, and BRS/Search to mount selected electronic journals.

CONCLUSION

Just as use of a large collection of books is made possible by a building and shelves in which to put them, a cataloguing system, borrowing policies, and reference librarians to assist users, so the use of a collection of computers and computer networks is supported by the existence of institutions, services, policies, and experts—in short, by an infrastructure. (Panel on Information Technology and the Conduct of Research, cited in Duncan, 1993, p. 54)

The emergence over the last decade of powerful personal computers, computer networks, and networked information has triggered a revolution and an evolution in the academic community. The infrastructure supporting the pursuit of scholarship, once a stable and well-established system, is now in a state of transformation. Visibility and technical competence are identified by Post and Sessions as two factors of importance for the academic library in maintaining its role in the changing information environment of the academic community (cited in Martin, 1992, p. 79). Visibility is defined as "the extent to which the library is perceived as an information facility." Technical competence is defined as "the extent to which the library is prepared, and

is perceived to be prepared, to provide current and future information services."
Through the pursuit of research projects and the provision of innovative services
in the use of microcomputers and networked information, Mann Library has
attempted to address these factors in a positive way. We hope that our successful
efforts and those of other institutions to integrate networked information into
library services will serve as evidence that the academic library can continue
to play its critical and unique role in the academic community.

REFERENCES

Barnes, S., & Spragg, E. (1990). CD-ROMs for public access: Integral components of
    collections and services in an academic research library. In L. Stewart, K. S. Chiang,
    & B. Coons (Eds.), *Public access CD-ROMs in libraries: Case studies* (pp. 89-100).
    Westport, CT: Meckler.
Coons, B., & Stewart, L. (1988). Mainstreaming CD-ROM into library operations.
    Laserdisk Professional, 1(3), 29-40.
Curtis, H. (Ed.). (1987). *Public access microcomputer centers in academic libraries.*
    Chicago, IL: American Library Association.
Dillon, M.; Jul, E.; Burge, M.; & Hickey, C. (1993). *Assessing information on the Internet:
    Toward providing library services for computer-mediated communication* (Research
    Report No. OCLC/OR/RR-93/1). Dublin, OH: OCLC Online Computer Library
    Center.
Duncan, T. (1993). Implementation of electronic information systems in universities and
    the implications for change in scholarly research. In A. Hirshon (Ed.), *After the
    electronic revolution, will you be the first to go?* (pp. 50-59). Chicago, IL: American
    Library Association.
Hirshon, A. (1993). The convergence of publishing and bibliographic access. In A. Hirshon
    (Eds.), *After the electronic revolution, will you be the first to go?* (pp. 1-8). Chicago,
    IL: American Library Association.
Lynch, C. A. (1992). Networked information: A revolution in progress. In B. Sutton
    & C. H. Davis (Eds.), *Networks, open access, and virtual libraries: Implications for
    research libraries* (Papers presented at the 1991 Clinic on Library Applications of
    Data Processing, 7-9 April 1991) (pp. 12-39). Urbana-Champaign: University of Illinois,
    Graduate School of Library and Information Science.
Malinconico, S. M. (1992). Information's brave new world. *Library Journal, 117*(8), 36-40.
Martin, M. J. (1992). Academic libraries and computing centers: Opportunities for
    leadership. *Library Administration and Management, 6*(2), 77-81.
Neff, R. K. (1985). Merging libraries and computer centers: Manifest destiny or manifestly
    deranged? An academic services perspective. *EDUCOM Bulletin, 20*(4), 8-12, 16.
Olsen, J. K. (1990). Cornell University, Mann Library. In C. Arms (Ed.), *Campus strategies
    for libraries and electronic information* (pp. 218-242). Bedford, MA: Digital Press.
Peters, T. A. (1991). *The online catalog: A critical examination of public use.* Jefferson,
    NC: McFarland.
Post, W., & Sessions, J. A. (1986). Academic institutions and information services: The
    position of the library. *Library Hi Tech News, 29*(July/August), 7-9.
Saunders, L. (1992). The virtual library: Computers in libraries Canada. *Computers in
    Libraries, 12*(11), 71-74.
Weber, D. C. (1988). University libraries and campus information technology organizations:
    Who is in charge here? *Journal of Library Administration, 9*(4), 5-19.
Woodsworth, A. (1988). Computing centers and libraries as cohorts: Exploiting mutual
    strengths. *Journal of Library Administration, 9*(4), 21-34.

RICHARD ENTLICH

Technical Project Manager
Albert R. Mann Library
Cornell University
Ithaca, New York

Networked Delivery of Full-Text Electronic Journals: Diverse Options, Shared Limitations

INTRODUCTION

The term "electronic library" does not yet have a widely accepted meaning in the academic world. Online catalogs, online searching, CD-ROM (Compact Disk-Read Only Memory) stations, and electronic mail, all of which have become familiar (though not quite ubiquitous) in the academic world, herald the arrival of the electronic library to some. To others, the concept of the scholarly electronic library implies a decentralized information distribution system that provides faculty and students with access to the materials and services they require, free from the space and time constraints of the physical library. This has yet to be achieved anywhere in academia.

Scholarly journals play a central role in research and education, so the degree to which they have been freed from the bounds of the print medium is an important measure of progress toward the realization of the "full-service" electronic library. In fact, numerous services claim to deliver full-text electronic journals today, including the following:

- commercial online services such as DIALOG, BRS, and STN;
- CD-ROM collections such as ADONIS and UMI's Business Periodicals OnDisc and individual titles from scholarly societies and other publishers;
- electronic-mail-based journals such as *Psycoloquy* and *Bryn Mawr Classical Review;*
- locally mounted files, obtained on tape or other media and made accessible with full-text search systems, such as BRS/Search, Verity's Topic, Fulcrum's Ful/Text, and others;
- unique services and experimental projects such as the OCLC/AAAS *Online Journal of Current Clinical Trials,* the CORE (Chemistry Online Retrieval Experiment) project at Cornell, Red Sage at University of California at San Francisco, Project Mercury at Carnegie-Mellon, and Elsevier's TULIP project.

A variety of software tools (e.g., Gopher, Wide Area Information Servers [WAIS], World Wide Web [WWW], and File Transfer Protocol [FTP]) permit archives of network-based electronic journals to be browsed, searched, and copied—all from the comfort of one's own home, lab, or office. Each service and access mechanism has something different to offer in terms of cost, accessibility, timeliness, accuracy, faithfulness to the original (if there is a print equivalent), functionality, ease of use, comprehensiveness, performance, and other characteristics.

Yet despite the seeming diversity of options, the great interest that the topic has generated, and the enthusiastic response to many of the services, when one scratches the surface, all is not well with today's electronic journals. Electronic journals available today do not compete favorably on many points when compared to their print counterparts. Problems with readability, portability, user comfort, browsability, flexibility of format and content, navigability, access mechanisms, etc., are commonplace and make clear that the electronic journal is far from being a mature form.

Although point-by-point comparisons between electronic and print journals may seem inappropriate, the rationale for making them is understandable. The long history of scholars' reliance on print journals for current awareness, sharing results, evaluating the quality and legitimacy of new research, establishing credibility, and providing a permanent scholarly record places a heavy burden on any new medium that attempts to supersede them. Alternative communication and publishing mechanisms that fail to provide equal or superior functionality in these and other critical areas will not readily be accepted by the scholarly community.

Much work remains to be done before electronic journals can reproduce many of the best features of print journals. Given the demands that electronic capture and dissemination of journal content make on computing systems, and the fact that affordable equipment, appropriate software tools, and a sufficient networking infrastructure have only appeared recently, it is not surprising that print, which has had several centuries to be polished and refined, still holds an advantage in some areas.

A great deal has already been written about possible new models for the distribution of scholarly publications in electronic form and the financial impact they may have on libraries, publishers, authors, and end-users. Popularizers of network electronic journals have emphasized the push side of the push-pull dynamic in scholarly communication (Harnad, 1992). That is, they have touted the value of nearly instantaneous and wide-scale distribution along with the possibility of immediate feedback, without giving serious consideration to how the format and content of such publications will affect their reception. More exploration is needed of the implications of the technical underpinnings of electronic journal systems for libraries, librarians, and end-users.

This paper will explore some of the difficulties and limitations facing the current generation of electronic journal initiatives, as well as some potential solutions. Many of the examples will be drawn from endeavors underway at Cornell University's Mann Library, where an electronic library has been "under construction" for over a decade, and where a variety of electronic journal efforts are being conducted.

THE RESPONSIBILITIES OF THE LIBRARY IN A VIRTUAL WORLD

Having myriad choices for obtaining the same kind of information can be seen as an embarrassment of riches or a confusing jumble. Collection development librarians are used to making hard choices about what resources to purchase with limited acquisitions funds. But they have not previously faced the complexities imposed by the nature of primary information resources in electronic form. In fact, there has not been much opportunity for libraries to influence the format or presentation of materials in the past. Academic librarians have become accustomed to identifying what materials to buy, organizing them and providing access to them, aiding in their use, and preserving them in usable condition. The question, "Does ink on paper serve the needs of our clients?" has not generally been asked, because there hasn't been an alternative.

On the other hand, machine-readable data are almost infinitely flexible, but there are precious few standards for display, searching, or interchange. More options are thus coupled with far greater responsibility. Although electronic catalogs and indexes of library holdings and scholarly publications are commonplace now, the manner in which primary publications in electronic form support the pursuit of scholarship remains largely untested. We must now ask whether this material really serves the needs of users, and if not, what should we do about it?

Some data on how well electronic systems serve the needs of scholarship were gathered in a large-scale study of the uses of the journal literature by faculty members in the chemistry, sociology, and English departments at Cornell University and the University of Pennsylvania (Olsen, 1993). The study revealed numerous perceived weaknesses in the design of electronic information systems, both in terms of the manner in which they support intellectual activities and their ergonomics. A few of the conclusions of this study include the following:

- In some disciplines, the absence of graphics and/or special characters and symbols dramatically reduces the utility of a resource.
- Users are uncomfortable reading computer screens for any length of time.
- Navigational tools of existing electronic information systems are weak. Scrolling in particular was criticized as a poor substitute for page turning. Poor mechanisms for browsing were seen as inhibitors to serendipitous discovery and creative thinking.
- Electronic searching capabilities were generally praised as a major advantage over print. However, much of the random or less-directed activity that scholars described as typical of their interaction with journals is not well supported in the electronic environment.
- The portability of print is a major advantage over electronic information systems.

In the next section, I will examine some of the underlying causes of the aforementioned complaints, and I will discuss some of the work being conducted at Mann Library to overcome the obstacles to providing network access to electronic journals.

DESIGN PROBLEMS OF ELECTRONIC INFORMATION SYSTEMS

Missing Graphics and Special Symbols

The fact that many electronic journals consist of nothing but ASCII text reflects two problems. The first is the predominance of VT100 terminal emulation as a network telecommunications standard. Character-based terminals used to be the only way of communicating with a remote computer. Yet today, with powerful desktop personal computers, graphical user interfaces, and high-speed local and wide area networks (LANs and WANs), VT100 emulation still dominates the telecommunications landscape. In today's heterogeneous computing environment, this is less a technological than a standards issue.

The second problem is at least partially a derivative of the first. VT100 emulation enforces use of unadorned ASCII text, which does not permit, for example, the transmission of graphics. Thus, use of ASCII makes meaningful communication in many fields of scholarship nearly impossible. It is no accident that most of the early network-distributed electronic journals are in fields that can manage pretty well with ASCII. Yet even in disciplines where graphics and non-ASCII characters are essential for publication (e.g., most science and engineering fields, music, and art history), there is a paucity of machine-readable text and graphics, and much of what is available is simple ASCII text. This situation prevails despite the fact that most publishers converted to electronic composition systems quite a few years ago, and such systems require the creation of machine-readable text prior to publication.

Unusual amongst publishers, the American Chemical Society (ACS) began to retain the input files for its phototypesetting system in 1975 and began exploring uses for them other than the production of print journals. These files contain all the information necessary to produce the textual portion of ACS journals on paper, including references to the many special symbols used in chemistry. For many years, these full-text files (largely stripped down to plain ASCII) have been available for searching over STN (Science and Technology Network) as part of the CJO (Chemical Journals Online) datafiles. With these same files as the foundation, ACS is now participating in the creation of a full-fledged networked electronic journal system—including the complete special chemistry character set and all original graphics—as a collaborator in the CORE (Chemistry Online Retrieval Experiment) project.

The CORE project, a collaboration involving Cornell's Mann Library, Bellcore, OCLC, and ACS and its Chemical Abstracts Service division, is using SGML (for a discussion of SGML applications for personal computers, see Flynn [1993] and Karney [1993]) to tag the full text of 20 ACS journals going back to 1975. SGML is substituted for the original ACS proprietary markup by a translation program. SGML permits and/or facilitates (a) customized restructuring of the text on a display or hard-copy device; (b) fine level fielded searching of text from all elements of the original document; (c) references to nontext objects such as graphs, equations, and bitmapped figures; (d) references to characters outside of the ASCII set; and (e) some hypertext features.

SGML is a powerful tool, but it alone does not solve the VT100 problem. An alternative to VT100 emulation, which is becoming more widely used with improvements in hardware, software, and networks, is the X Window System (hereafter just "X"). X has the potential to address several of the criticisms of electronic journals mentioned by scholars, but especially those concerning the absence of important content features. X is being used for development of all user interfaces in the CORE project.

Like many disciplines, chemistry relies heavily on nontextual material in its publications. ACS did not have any of the graphics from its journals available in machine-readable form, so these had to be captured by scanning from paper and microfilm. The files resulting from scanning are bitmapped page images.

A bitmapped image of a page from a print journal can offer much that is missing from an ASCII representation. All the elements that are impossible to represent with an ASCII display are present—all the illustrative matter, all the unusual characters and symbols, all the text attributes and structure that give the printed page much of its readability.

Unfortunately, bitmaps have several major drawbacks. One has to do with the nature of bitmapped page images. Since bitmaps are just streams of data representing dots, it is not possible to do much more than display them unless further processing is undertaken. The text represented cannot be searched, and there is no positional association between the dots and the content they represent. Thus, features such as highlighting and hypertext links, which can easily be accomplished with electronic text, are difficult to achieve.

Another drawback is storage size. Experience has shown that bitmaps scanned at less than 300 dots per inch (dpi) capture insufficient detail. A typical 300-dpi scan of an 8.5 × 11 inch page in monochrome (i.e., each dot is either black or white, no color and no shades of gray) from one of the ACS journals takes up about a megabyte before compression. (The use of monochrome bitmaps was considered acceptable in the CORE project since ACS journals contain little color or halftone material, but would be more difficult to justify in fields where journals have heavy photographic content.) Compression (using the CCITT Group 4 fax standard) can reduce this to about 100 kilobytes per page. This is at least 10 times the size of even a heavily marked up page of ASCII representing the same text (minus the images, of course).

The large size of bitmap files has influenced the kind of hardware used to store them. Most projects and products utilizing large collections of bitmaps employ optical storage media, such as CD-ROM and WORM (Write Once Read Many), since they provide the most economical large-capacity storage solutions available today. But consider that even with 600 megabytes of available storage, a single CD-ROM can only hold about 6,000 pages of compressed monochrome images. The ACS alone produces about 100,000 new journal pages each year. The cost advantage of optical media is quickly lost if one drive is provided for each disk, so mechanical jukeboxes, in which a robot arm manages the insertion and removal of a large number of disks in and out of a small number of drives, are used.

Optical drives result in access times and data transfer rates on the order of 10-20 times slower than magnetic drives. Jukeboxes can have anywhere from a few to hundreds of shelves, but usually only two or three drives. Thus in a heavily used system, there is considerable competition for the few drives, and substantial retrieval delays can result. Add to this the time required to decompress the image before display, and the period between request and ultimate display can be quite lengthy.

The CORE project is taking steps to deal with some of these problems. The most obvious remedy is to take advantage of faster technology as it becomes available. Servers with faster CPUs cut down on decompression time. CORE is also utilizing an optimized Group IV fax decompression algorithm in order to lessen the time required for image decompression. New networking technologies such as FDDI (Fiber Distributed Data Interface) and ATM (Asynchronous Transfer Mode) cut down on data transmission times. Mann Library took advantage of the installation of a fiber optic backbone at Cornell and connected the CORE servers to it shortly after they became available.

We are also making the bitmapped page images available in two resolutions. In addition to the original 300-dpi images, we are offering a scaled down image at 100 dpi that has been enhanced for readability. The lower resolution images can be transmitted more rapidly across the network (they are about one-fifth the size of the high-resolution files), and we are able to store the most recent couple of years on magnetic drives for rapid retrieval.

A more unusual approach is to combine the best of the ASCII world and the bitmapped world. CORE is experimenting with two interfaces (Scepter from OCLC and SuperBook from Bellcore) that combine SGML machine-readable text with bitmaps of just the graphical portion of each page. The resulting file (including indexes) is small enough to store the complete contents of nearly three quarters of a million pages on fast magnetic drives.

However, speed of retrieval is only one aspect of total system performance. By exploring multiple techniques for presenting the same data, we have an opportunity to compare and contrast various functional parameters as well as important user preferences.

Others are working on overcoming some of the other limitations of bitmaps. The RightPages application from Bell Laboratories has focused on how to extract more information from bitmaps (Story, O'Gorman, Fox, Schaper, & Jagadish, 1992). They have developed algorithms for cleaning up bitmap images (to improve the accuracy and reliability of other post-processing activities), for identifying important structural components of certain critical journal pages (e.g., the table of contents) and for improved display of scaled down bitmaps. RightPages is a component of a new experimental electronic journal collaboration called Red Sage, involving Springer-Verlag, AT&T Bell Labs, and the University of California at San Francisco (Jacobs, Lucier, & Badger, 1992).

Reading from Computer Displays

Lack of comfort reading from computer displays stems largely from limitations in computer display technology. The resolution of displays sold even with high-priced engineering workstations rarely exceeds 100 dpi, much less than what can be achieved on the printed page. Other problems derive from low refresh rates (which causes subtle flicker) and glare.

Within the CORE project, we are trying to make due with the limitations of current technology. Only a small portion of a 300-dpi bitmap of an 8.5 × 11 inch page can be viewed at any one time on a 19-inch display with 75-dpi resolution (common specifications for a workstation monitor). By scaling the image down, it is possible to fit much more of the page on smaller displays, which provides improved browsability on displays costing substantially less than those normally found on engineering workstations.

Use of machine-readable text circumvents some of the problems of readability of scanned text. The fonts used are designed for use on 75- or 100-dpi displays, and text displayed with these fonts does not suffer from the size or clarity problems that can plague bitmaps.

Navigational Tools of Existing Electronic Journal Systems

Because existing tools are weak, we have tried to include features in the CORE interfaces that provide reasonable support for browsing. In addition to browsing by page, article, and issue, we also expect to supply a mechanism to browse the graphics. This may prove to be of more value to some chemists than others, since the graphics vary in significance between chemical subdisciplines.

The CORE interfaces utilize some hypertext features. One interface permits a new search to be initiated by clicking on any term in the text. Another makes it possible to move directly from a citation in the bibliography of one article to the cited article (assuming it's also in the database). We have not found a substitute for scrolling, but we are exploring a number of different navigational techniques in the hope of learning what works best for different types of users.

Searching Capabilities

The first widely available Boolean search systems were designed around bibliographic databases. Such systems have been refined over several decades into what are thought of today as state-of-the-art search capabilities represented by DIALOG, BRS, Silver Platter, and many others. As full-text material became available, new features such as more flexible proximity searching were added.

What has not changed, and what remains as a holdover from the days of "bibliographic-only" searching, is the notion that the user approaches the system because he/she has a specific information need and expects to be lead to specific citations that address that need. The ability to support less-directed information needs (i.e., anything from browsing for current awareness to idle curiosity) is not nearly as well supported in these environments.

One might expect that the CORE interfaces, having been designed from the beginning as vehicles for the primary literature, would incorporate a profoundly different approach to the information underlying them. Yet the text-searching capabilities provided in CORE are mostly quite conventional. Facilities for browsing are more accessible and more complete than what is typically found in bibliographic search systems, but it is unlikely that they provide for as wide a range of undirected interaction as do print journals. More work needs to be done to understand the subtleties of these interactions and how they may be transferred to and enhanced in an electronic environment.

Lack of Portability

True portability of electronic journals in a manner approaching that of print journals will have to await improvements in storage technology, display technology, wireless LANs, and batteries. Nevertheless, bringing electronic journals that more closely resemble their print equivalent in content and function to the labs and offices of those who rely on them most heavily is an important step toward breaking the physical and temporal bounds of the library building.

EQUITABLE ACCESS CONCERNS

CORE is a research project that may help shape the direction that future initiatives in electronic journal publishing take. But how realistic is it as a model for what is possible in most academic libraries today and in the near future? After all, CORE is, in some respects, a "best of all possible worlds" project. The data we are working with are very likely unique in terms of their depth and breadth within a discipline. The collaborative nature of the project has made resources available that are not typically found in libraries.

On the other hand, if libraries wait to get involved until better quality data are ubiquitous and most users have high-end workstations and high-speed network connections, it will be too late to have much of a say in resolving the critical issues that the transition from paper to electronic media present. The dilemma that arises is how to uphold a commitment to the provision of free, equitable access to information resources without becoming a slave to lowest common denominator standards in hardware, software, data, telecommunications, and networks.

I would suggest that this question arises, at least in part, because of the self-delusion that librarians have indulged in since the introduction of remotely accessible electronic resources. Providing electronic resources via "lowest common denominator" standards does not guarantee equitable access any more than having an entirely print-based collection did (e.g., we have not made our print collections readily accessible to visually impaired or wheelchair-bound patrons). Even today, not everyone has a computer or network connection in his/her home or office, so universal remote access is a myth. We attempt to make up for this by providing public access computers, but some users are inevitably better off than others.

I believe that we need to experiment with systems that are closer to the state of the art than are those we use to deliver our mainstream resources. In many cases, by the time that experimentation is complete, the bulk of users will have caught up with the level of technology used during the experiment. Such experimentation may, in fact, be the only practical way to keep up with the seemingly unending rise in the computing price/performance curve.

In the meantime, we must draw the line somewhere in deciding what facilities to utilize in providing remote access services. A single standard for all institutions will not do, but regular surveys could go a long way toward providing a rational basis for deciding when the local user community is ready to take advantage of new technologies. I am not prepared to recommend at which level of technology saturation a new service based on that technology should be offered. But if the library expects to continue having a major role in information management, it must either adopt new technologies or be displaced by other service providers who will.

There are ways to do this without shutting out users with less-sophisticated systems. For instance, SGML-tagged text could be stripped of its markup and sent as plain ASCII, or even formatted especially for use with character-based terminal emulators, while still allowing users of more sophisticated display devices to take full advantage of it (Weibel, 1993). In addition, we should maintain a commitment to providing high-quality access from within the library building, and elsewhere on campus, as may be appropriate.

MAKING THE BEST OF ASCII DATA IN A VT100 ENVIRONMENT

As limited as ASCII data in a VT100 environment seem, they are much more representative of what is "out there" than the richly marked-up data of the CORE project. In fact, most of the electronic journals being passed around the network are ASCII only (Strangelove, 1993). At present, all of Mann Library's production networked electronic resources (as opposed to research projects) are in this form. We are currently working on two projects exploring ways to enhance the utility of available ASCII files.

On a much smaller scale than the CORE project, Mann Library is experimenting with the markup of several networked-based ASCII journals, including *New Horizons in Adult Education* and *Psycoloquy*. The goal of this project has been to try to automate to whatever degree possible the processing of these titles into BRS load format. This will allow us to make them available to patrons for search and display using BRS/Search, a multiuser, full-text, search-and-retrieval package that we currently use to provide networked access to four bibliographic files.

One of the more interesting observations from this work to date is that ASCII may not be such an intractable form after all. With a well-structured, consistently formatted ASCII journal, it is possible to make a one-time effort to write a reformatting program and completely automate the process of formatting future issues. Journals that lack consistency require considerably more manual processing labor. It is not clear whether the absence of consistent structure is an expression of editorial creativity or, rather, of unconcern. It would certainly be worth the effort of the library community to raise this issue with editors, since in many cases a small additional effort toward consistent layout could result in substantial benefits for libraries and their patrons.

Mann Library has gotten additional experience with ASCII electronic journals through its participation in the Cornell University Library Task Force on Electronic Journals. The task force has mounted the full text of several network-based electronic journals under WAIS, Gopher, and CUINFO (Cornell's campus-wide information system). The purpose of this pilot project is to examine a variety of library-wide concerns related to network-based electronic resources. Some of these are patron access, staff training, investment in technology infrastructure, archiving, and copyright. Other institutions have already investigated these issues on their campuses and reported their findings (Dougherty et al., 1991; Manoff, Dorschner, Geller, Morgan, & Snowden, 1992).

Mann Library is responsible for the Gopher portion of the task force installation. Some of the steps we have taken in order to maximize the utility of the installation include the following:

1. making as much use as possible of meaningful file names in the menu hierarchy (primarily through the heavy use of ".cap" files);
2. installing a version of WAIS behind the Gopher server that permits the use of Boolean operators, partial string matches, and literal phrases in searching;
3. creating multiple indexes (at the issue and volume level) to permit searches restricted by time;
4. installing the UNIX Gopher client on the same machine as the server so that users without direct Internet access and/or those without a locally mounted Gopher client may still use the system; and
5. installing an intelligent pager that provides easier navigation, better searching within files, and customizable help (for users running the client described in point 4).

We are also planning to install an improved help system and to experiment with the creation of indexes to support fielded searching, a feature not normally found under Gopher.

The point is that working with ASCII need not be thought of as second rate, if we are willing to explore enhancements that increase the utility of such data. Though we may be working with ASCII data for many years to come, we can do more than just bemoan its limitations.

In the meantime, successors to ASCII are already waiting in the wings. There is an 8-bit (256-character) standard called Latin1, which comfortably accommodates all the European languages. There are also two more ambitious coding systems in the works—Unicode and ISO 10646—which are 16-bit and 32-bit codes, respectively. Each would be able to represent the characters of all the known alphabets of the world, as well as numerous punctuation marks and symbols, but at a cost of fatter text files and more network traffic (Sheldon, 1991).

CONCLUSION

The question of how to cope with the coming transition of primary scholarly publications from print to electronic-based media is undoubtedly one of the most significant issues facing academic libraries today. Some libraries that are studying the question have concluded that materials in electronic form should be dealt with according to the same time-honored traditions that have guided our approach to print-based materials for so many years. That is, we should be guided by existing policies for selection, acquisitions, cataloging, etc.

This approach may be fine, but it is rarely taken far enough. For example, many libraries still have poor or nonexistent network connections. Many libraries have little or no experience with multiuser computing systems. Allowing others, be they academic computing centers, publishers, or cable companies, to provide the computing expertise (as well as the computers and networking infrastructure) means abandoning control of the management of electronic resources. Strategic alliances with outside organizations may be desirable but not at the cost of complete abrogation of responsibility.

In order for libraries to have a voice and a role in the transition from print to digital media, we must have knowledge and experience. There is still time to gain both, but that time is rapidly running out. Now is an excellent time to start experimenting. Electronic journals are in their infancy. Publishers and technology firms are interested in joint ventures with libraries. Such collaborations give libraries an important opportunity to make their partners aware of the difficulties they face and of the issues that are most critical to them and their patrons. As licensing begins to replace subscription as the predominant mechanism for marketing scholarly information, libraries need as strong a voice as possible to keep licensing agreements that are contrary to the library's mission, and the best interests of its patrons, from becoming the industry standard.

Libraries that do not feel prepared to enter as equal partners into projects with major publishers or computing companies, or who are not financially positioned to do so, may still benefit from joint projects with other libraries. There is still much work to be done regarding issues such as cooperative collection and dissemination of electronic resources, as well as cooperative processing and archiving. There is freely available full-text data available on the nets as well as free software for providing network access.

Multiuser computer systems are not free, nor are the trained staff needed to operate them. However, the cost of the former has dropped dramatically in the past few years, and the cost of the latter, though still high, will very likely be less, in the long run, than the cost of always having to depend on outside expertise.

Libraries cannot afford to look at the limitations in the current generation of electronic journals as "somebody else's problem." The process of overcoming those limitations may well embody the future of scholarly communication and, quite possibly, the future of academic librarianship.

ACKNOWLEDGMENTS

The CORE project is a collaboration led by Cornell University and includes, in addition to Cornell, Bellcore, the American Chemical Society, Chemical Abstracts Service, and OCLC. Among the people who direct this project and contribute most of the work to it are Jan Olsen, Richard Entlich, and John Udall of the Albert R. Mann Library, Cornell University; Lorrin Garson of the American Chemical Society; Lorraine Normore of Chemical Abstracts Service; Michael Lesk, Dennis Egan, Dan Ketchum, Joel Remde, and Carol Lochbaum of Bellcore; and Stu Weibel, Mark Bendig, Jean Godby, Eric Miller, and Will Ray of OCLC. The collaborators are grateful for the support of Digital Equipment Corporation, Sony Corporation of America, Springer-Verlag, Sun Microsystems, Inc., and Thinking Machines, Inc.

REFERENCES

Dougherty, W.; Hanson, B.; Litchfield, C.; McMillan, G.; Metz, P.; Nicol, J.; & Queijo, K. (1991). *Report of the Task Force on the Electronic Journal*. Blacksburg, VA: University Libraries, Virginia Polytechnic Institute and State University.
Flynn, M. K. (1993). Documents under control. *PC Magazine, 12*(7), 31-32.

Harnad, S. (1992). What scholars want and need from electronic journals [Summary]. In D. Shaw (Ed.), *Celebrating change: Information management on the move* (Proceedings of the 55th ASIS Annual Meeting) (Vol. 29, pp. 342-343). Medford, NJ: Learned Information.

Jacobs, M.; Lucier, R.; & Badger, R. (1992). Press release on the Red Sage project.

Karney, J. (1993). SGML: The quiet revolution. *PC Magazine, 12*(3), 246.

Manoff, M.; Dorschner, E.; Geller; M.; Morgan, K.; & Snowden, C. (1992). Report of the Electronic Journals Task Force, MIT Libraries. *Serials Review, 18*(1-2), 113-129.

Olsen, J. (1993). Implications of electronic journal literature for scholars (Doctoral dissertation, Cornell University, 1992). *Dissertation Abstracts International, 53*, 2267A.

Sheldon, K. M. (1991). ASCII goes global. *Byte, 16*(7), 108-112, 114, 116.

Story, G. A.; O'Gorman, L.; Fox, D.; Schaper, L. L.; & Jagadish, H. V. (1992). The RightPages image-based electronic library for alerting and browsing. *Computer, 25*(9), 17-26.

Strangelove, M. (1993). Reflections on developments draft RFC. Message on the VPIEJ-L listserv dated 2/15/93.

Weibel, S. (1993). Re: Reflections on developments draft RFC. Message on the VPIEJ-L listserv dated 2/16/93.

DIANE K. KOVACS

Humanities Reference Librarian
Kent State University
Kent, Ohio

MARTHA FLEMING

Graduate Reference Assistant
Kent State University
Kent, Ohio

Internet Resources and Humanities Reference Service

INTRODUCTION

We are beginning a great format shift from print and paper format to the electronic format. Evidence of this shift appears in the physical space of our libraries in the form of CD-ROM databases and online catalogs. But the shift is also changing libraries from places that own or hold informational materials to places where researchers can access information. While dial-up database services like DIALOG and BRS are familiar to all of us, the global computer networks gaining popularity in academia are adding a new dimension to the electronic format shift.

Information resources produced by scholars and distributed via the Internet infrastructure, outside of the traditional print publication mechanisms, are being created to support humanities research; and the means to meet the challenges posed by these resources are also emerging from the Internet infrastructure itself. Electronic-mail-based conferences (e-conferences) form the core of the scholarly communities on the Internet and are the central mechanism for the exchange of information on network-accessible resources. By using Internet navigation software such as HYTELNET, Gopher, Veronica, archie, Wide Area Information Servers (WAIS), World Wide Web, and the new applications that will follow, librarians can mediate between the user and electronic information resources, just as they have with print resources. Traditionally, the librarian's professional role has been to identify appropriate resources and enhance patrons' access to and use of them. Today, identifying and enhancing access to Internet resources for humanities scholars has become a vital facet of humanities reference service (Kovacs, Schloman, & McDaniel, in press; Stover, 1992).

This paper discusses the information needs of humanities scholars and how humanities reference librarians can use Internet or BITNET resources to fulfil those information needs. Computer networks encompass a vast array of information resources. Because BITNET is linked to the Internet—albeit with some different functionality—when the term Internet is used in this paper, it refers to both networks.

It is outside the scope of this paper to provide instruction on the basic use of computers and the Internet. Throughout this paper, some instructions for accessing networked resources are given. It is assumed, however, that readers are familiar with basic FTP and Telnet commands; actual command sequences are not provided in all cases. Further information is available in several recent publications, including those by Kehoe (1993), Krol (1992), and Quarterman (1990). For the purpose of this paper, however, some basic concepts that are important in understanding the nature of the resources will be discussed. Computer networks are groups of linked computers. These groups of computers can be relatively small, as in a local area network (LAN), or as large as the global Internet. The software used to connect computers on a LAN might be Ethernet and Appleshare or Novell. The software used to connect computers on the Internet is called TCP/IP (Transfer Control Protocol/Internet Protocol). It allows two basic functions called FTP (File Transfer Protocol) and Telnet that are important in accessing and using network information resources. FTP allows computer files to be transferred over the network. Telnet allows people to use their computers and the network to log into other computers in remote locations.

INFORMATION NEEDS OF HUMANITIES SCHOLARS

Information Needs in the Humanities: An Assessment (Gould, 1988) analyzes information needs in eight humanities disciplines: classical studies, history, art history, literature, philosophy, religion, music, and linguistics. In all eight fields, access to primary resources such as manuscripts, rare books, and unpublished material was identified as important to the research process. Finding aids—indexes, abstracts, bibliographies, and catalogs—were important to researchers looking for primary resources as well as secondary materials such as articles and recent monographs. Locating materials at other libraries and archives, which the scholar could then travel to, was identified as an immediate need. The next step is full-text online access to the primary materials. The scholars surveyed stated a desire for computerized versions of the finding aids in their disciplines as well as full-text versions of the primary documents used in their research. In addition to these general needs, each discipline has specific needs:

- Classical studies scholars stated a need to identify and locate primary texts in Greek and Latin as well as Bible texts.
- Historical scholarship can encompass any time period and includes the use of resources in political science, economics, sociology, and anthropology. In addition, access to unpublished manuscripts and other primary historical sources is critical to history research.
- Art historians need exhibit catalogs, museum bulletins, artists' books, and art newspapers.
- Literature scholars need access to primary and secondary sources in all modern languages, and they often use unpublished material such as diaries and letters

of authors in their research. Literature research sometimes draws on the literature of psychology, anthropology, or other disciplines.

- Philosophy is a field that has changed radically in the 20th century. Recently, scholars in this discipline have been focusing more on the history of philosophy to shape their interpretations. In addition, international bibliographies of philosophical texts are important resources for retrospective research. Unpublished materials such as the original drafts of philosophers' writings have gained more importance because of the new emphasis being placed on the history of philosophy; therefore, catalogs detailing the location and content of the manuscript collections of these philosophers are extremely valuable tools for research in philosophy.

- Religious studies has an expanding focus that includes any human encounter with divinity. Since this field is broadening at such a rapid rate, current bibliographic resources are particularly important. Primary and secondary material in all modern languages are essential resources as are ancient holy texts and unpublished materials such as church histories.

- Music encompasses many subfields such as performance, composition, theory, and the history of music. Naturally, bibliographic resources are important for following the trends in the literature in all these subfields. Music scholars often need access to musical scores, and they are beginning to rely more upon unpublished materials because interest in the history of music has increased. In addition, comprehensive catalogs listing the locations of manuscripts concerning musical history are in much demand.

- Linguistics is a highly interdisciplinary field. Unpublished materials are especially important because this field is changing so rapidly and journal articles are often outdated by the time they are published. Other materials such as dissertations, recordings of speech, videotapes, and language data in machine-readable forms are also important resources.

Gould's findings are supported by other studies. Pankake (1991) reviews several citation studies designed to highlight the types of resources that were most useful to humanities researchers. Overall, the findings reveal that information needs in the humanities cover a broad spectrum ranging from the latest trends in popular culture to texts of ancient Greek manuscripts. Given this diversity, it is difficult to discern a consistent pattern of information use among humanities scholars, except that most require both primary and secondary materials. After identifying the needed material, the researcher must then be able to locate these resources in as efficient a manner as possible. General reference sources also prove invaluable by quickly confirming facts and providing information about grants and foundations.

Wiberley (1991) also emphasizes the diversity of information needs in humanities disciplines while calling attention to some unique behavioral traits humanists display while seeking to meet their information needs. Communication among scholars in the humanities is of vital importance to research in these fields. Since research in the humanities is becoming more specialized, scholars tend to rely upon their private collections of research materials and correspondence with peers to meet most of their information needs—often overlooking the resources available to them at the university library. Academic librarians should be aware of these unique characteristics and specific information needs of humanists in order to provide more efficient and relevant reference service. By mediating between humanities scholars and Internet resources, librarians can function as part of the humanities scholar's information network.

LOCATING AND IDENTIFYING INTERNET RESOURCES

Humanities reference librarians must make themselves aware of Internet resources. This paper describes five types of Internet resources commonly used by humanities scholars: full-text and bibliographic databases, electronic books and other texts, electronic journals, e-conferences, and online library catalogs. The growth of these resources has led to the development of new distribution mechanisms for them that take advantage of the capabilities of FTP, Telnet, and electronic mail. Network-based storage and distribution mechanisms include the following:

- *E-conferences:* Subscription mechanisms vary with the type of software used to maintain the e-conference. The most common form of e-conference is a discussion maintained via electronic mailing lists software (e.g., listserv). USENET news uses a specific file format and subscribers use "News Reader" software to participate in USENET news e-conference discussions.
- *E-conference archives:* These are databases of all the transactions that have taken place on a given e-conference during pre-established intervals. With the listserv software written by Eric Thomas, the e-conference archives are interactively and batch searchable. Listserv e-conference archives are also retrievable via an e-mail message sent to listserv@<site> that reads GET Filename Filetype. E-conference archives may also be stored at FTP sites, Internet bulletin boards, Gopher servers, or WAIS servers.
- *Fileservers:* Researchers can also retrieve other kinds of texts stored on fileservers via an e-mail message sent to listserv@<site> GET Filename Filetype.
- *Internet-accessible electronic bulletin boards:* These can be accessed using the Telnet command in addition to or instead of the traditional dial-up with modem access.
- *FTP sites:* These are the locations of electronic texts stored in a directory on a computer on the Internet. Researchers use an FTP command to connect to the site and retrieve the texts back to their own computer.
- *Gopher servers:* Gopher servers can store electronic texts and provide links to Internet resources at other sites as well. Researchers use a Gopher client to connect to a Gopher server where they can browse resources stored there or connect to yet other Internet resources. Resources appear as items in hierarchies of lists.
- *WAIS servers:* Electronic texts stored on a server. Researchers use a WAIS client to connect to the WAIS server, identifying and browsing electronic texts and other resources.

Librarians maintain awareness of print resources by reading reviews in journals and from publishers' flyers in the mail. Awareness of Internet resources can be started via a parallel mechanism. It is essential to subscribe to an e-conference where information on electronic resources in the humanities is exchanged (Kovacs & Kovacs, 1991). The Humanist e-conference, moderated by Allen Renear and Ellen Brennan, is a general clearinghouse for information in the humanities and the use of computers in the humanities. (For more information, contact editors@brownvm or editors@brownvm.brown.edu.)

The Directory of Scholarly E-conferences (Kovacs et al., 1993) provides a classified and indexed list of e-conferences in the humanities as well as other disciplines. It also provides subscription instructions for all the different types of e-conferences. E-conferences are also excellent sources of information about resources *not* available over the Internet. They have been used to answer many types of humanities reference questions concerning, for example, other scholars doing research on the Greek translation of the Epistles of St. Paul, specialized translation instruction, or use of VHS movies in teaching literature.

There are also a number of Internet tools that can be used to locate Internet resources:

- *HYTELNET:* Hypertext front-end software developed by Peter Scott (scott@sklib.usask.ca) and Earl Fogel (fogel@jester.usask.ca) of the University of Saskatchewan used to access a directory of Internet-accessible resources compiled by Billy Barron (billy@vaxb.acs.unt.edu) of the University of North Texas (PC, UNIX, and VMS versions are available via anonymous FTP from access.usask.ca or 128.233.3.1 in the /pub/hytelnet directory).
- *LIBS:* Front-end software developed by Mark Resmer of Sonoma State University to access the directory of Internet-accessible resources compiled by Art St. George of the University of New Mexico.
- *Gopher:* Interface software for an Internet-distributed database developed at the University of Minnesota, which allows the storage of electronic texts for interactive searching, viewing, and retrieval via nested lists (for more information, address an e-mail message to boombox.micro.umn.edu).
- *Veronica:* A part of the Gopher server that allows keyword and Boolean searching through the universe of Gopher servers to identify and connect to Internet resources that are stored in or linked to Gopher servers.
- *WAIS and archie:* Tools for locating electronic resources via keyword searches.
- *World Wide Web:* A project to develop a searchable hypertext Internet-distributed database on a global scale.

The HYTELNET hypertext directory of Internet resources and the Gopher software with the Veronica finding tool are particularly valuable and easy to use.

ESTABLISHING THE USE OF INTERNET
RESOURCES IN REFERENCE SERVICE

In order to use Internet resources in reference services, three basic needs must be met: equipment, awareness, and time. Librarians must have access to a microcomputer or dumb terminal that has a connection to the Internet. This could be a microcomputer running TCP/IP that is networked into a campus, state, or regional network; or it could be a microcomputer with telecommunications software such as Kermit or Procomm dialed up to a mainframe, minicomputer, or workstation that is running TCP/IP and networked into a campus, state, or regional network. Dumb terminals that are directly cabled to a mainframe, minicomputer, or workstation that is running TCP/IP and networked into a campus, state, or regional network are also usable.

Ready reference or referral uses of Internet resources require that the equipment be located at the reference desk or in an adjacent area. Having the appropriate equipment in the librarian's office makes it much easier and more likely that Internet resources can be integrated into reference work by appointment, allowing the librarian to provide in-depth Internet reference assistance to patrons.

Imagine the Internet as a new library reference center. The first thing to do is to look over the center, identify the familiar sources, and get a general idea of what is available, what "color" it is, and approximately where it is located. Also become aware of the tools for finding the sources in the reference center.

In order to select and use Internet resources to answer reference questions, librarians must have directories and catalogs of Internet resources, or tools such as HYTELNET, readily accessible at the reference desk. Many libraries have access to a campus or library Gopher server on which selected resources have been linked.

Awareness of the resources means more than just knowing they exist. Librarians need to have some knowledge of how stable and available a given resource is to be able to decide whether a question can be answered immediately or whether it will require an appointment with the library user. For example, most Internet-accessible libraries are reliably stable and available, so it would be appropriate to use them to answer a question immediately or to instruct the library user in using them. Several of the Internet databases have unpredictable down times and might be unavailable, thus making it necessary to make an appointment when the librarian is off the busy desk in order to conduct the search. E-conference archives are reliably available but may take more time to search than is possible at the desk and should be searched by appointment. The key is to make decisions based on experience and knowledge of the resources.

Time is a premium. It requires time for librarians to develop awareness of Internet resources and more time to introduce and instruct library users. Currently, the reference desk is not the most suitable place to do this. Rather, Internet resources are more efficiently introduced where time has been formally allotted to do so, such as specially arranged orientation sessions, workshops, or tutorials.

Ideally, librarians would establish their own local menu, using Gopher or World Wide Web or similar software, of Internet resources suitable for their library users. This saves time for everyone. Library users may even be able to explore without assistance if guides are provided.

Using Internet resources as part of reference services is logical and very possible when done with appropriate equipment, awareness, and sufficient time.

INTERNET RESOURCES IN THE HUMANITIES

This section describes selected Internet resources of interest to humanities scholars in each of the eight disciplines described earlier. These examples show that there are Internet resources available that fulfil the kinds of information needs identified by Gould (1988) for humanities scholars.

Classical Studies

Although classical studies scholars will find useful Internet resources among those described in all the following disciplines, the Philosophy E-texts Project and the *Electric Mystics Guide to the Internet* provide details about Internet resources that will be of particular interest to classical studies scholars. There is also one classical studies e-conference listed in Kovacs et al. (1993); however, many e-conferences in the other disciplines listed would be of interest to classical studies scholars as well.

History

Historians rival literature scholars as some of the most active users and creators of Internet resources. There are 28 history e-conferences listed in Kovacs et al. (1993). Don Mabry at Mississippi State University (djml@ra.msstate.edu) brought to the authors' attention the HISTOWNR e-conference's History Network project. The participating historians are setting up FTP sites in the United States and Europe to provide access to primary historical documents in electronic format. Among the electronic texts already available via FTP to ftp.msstate.edu are primary historical documents (e.g., diaries of the Gulf War), databases and bibliographies of historical resources, the texts of historical documents (e.g., Articles of Confederation, Bill of Rights, Mayflower Compact, Iroquois Constitution), and software (free- or shareware).

Another interesting history resource is the Martin Luther King, Jr. Bibliography at Stanford University. The MLK Bibliography lists approximately 2,700 bibliographic citations to works by or about Martin Luther King, Jr. and the civil rights movement. This bibliography was compiled by staff of the Martin Luther King, Jr., Papers Project as a first step in preparing to publish King's works. It is intended to help both the student and the scholar traverse the rich and varied terrain of primary and secondary historical, sociological, and journalistic sources on King and the Black freedom struggle. (This information was taken from the HYTELNET directory.) The Martin Luther King Archives are available via Telnet to forsythetn.stanford.edu or 36.54.0.12; account: socrates; terminal: VT100; response: MLK.

RLIN makes available the AMC (Archives and Manuscripts) database. The AMC is progressing towards a union catalog of archives and manuscript collections. Once you are telnetted to rlg.stanford.edu and logged in, type CALL RLIN—Activity CAT—select file AMC.

Art History

Because of its emphasis on visual and plastic resources, art is a discipline that is very difficult to work with in the current technological state of the Internet. In the future, when high-speed transmission connections are the norm, art images will be more freely exchanged across the Internet. Currently, researchers in art are discussing mechanisms for making art available over the networks through a variety of formats that encode the images for transmission. There are 27 e-conferences on different art-related topics listed in Kovacs et al. (1993).

The staff of the Carnegie-Mellon Libraries have developed a database called Archpics (Pisciotta, 1993). Archpics is a finding tool for architectural drawings, photographs, and other art images available in archival storage and in books in Carnegie-Mellon Libraries collections. (Details for Internet access to Archpics may be obtained from Henry A. Pisciotta, Head, Fine Arts and Special Collections at Carnegie Mellon University Libraries, Frew Street, Pittsburgh, PA 15213.)

Literature

Literature scholars are very active on the Internet. Kovacs et al. (1993) list 33 literature e-conferences. In addition, the Gutenberg Project founded by Michael Hart (hart@vmd.cso.uiuc.edu) has been putting electronic texts of public domain books on the Internet. The locations of these electronic books can be identified through the HYTELNET software and many Gopher servers. Other typical resources include the American and French Research on the Treasury of the French Language (ARTFL) database and Dartmouth's Dante Project and Shakespeare databases.

ARTFL is located at the University of Chicago. It is a searchable full-text database of the works of major French authors and is useful to scholars doing textual analysis of French literature. Users of ARTFL pay an annual subscription fee. The database is accessible to researchers or libraries by telnetting to artfl.uchicago.edu and logging in with their assigned user id and password. ARTFL can be browsed by using the user id GUEST and the password SUGGEST. (For more information, contact Mark Olson, Department of Romance Languages and Literatures, University of Chicago [mark@gide.uchicago.edu].)

The Dante and Shakespeare full-text databases are located at Dartmouth College. Researchers can telnet to lib.dartmouth.edu or 129.170.16.11 to search either database as well as other full-text databases. (For more information, contact Katharina Klemperer [kathy.klemperer@dartmouth.edu].) SHAKSPER: The Global Electronic Shakespeare Conference is an international electronic conference for Shakespearean researchers, instructors, students, and those who share their interests and concerns. Like the national and international Shakespeare Association conferences, SHAKSPER offers announcements and bulletins, scholarly papers, and the formal exchange of ideas, but SHAKSPER also offers ongoing opportunities for spontaneous informal discussion, eavesdropping, peer review, and a fresh sense of worldwide scholarly community. The SHAKSPER fileserver offers conference papers and abstracts, an international directory of Shakespeare institutes, biographies of conference members, and a variety of announcements and bibliographies. Members of a number of seminars at the upcoming Shakespeare Association of America Conference will find their colleagues ready to share papers, comments, and strategies in advance. The participants in SHAKSPER are collaborating to place other authoritative versions of Shakespeare's works on the Internet. SHAKSPER (shaksper@utoronto) is edited by Dr. Hardy M. Cook (hmcook@boe00.minc.umd.edu).

Hundreds of other electronic full-text projects are listed in the Georgetown E-Text Catalog available through Georgetown University's Gopher server or via FTP to guvax.georgetown.edu or 141.161.1.2 in the directory cpet—projects—in—electronic—textvia. Also available (through RLIN) is the Eighteenth Century Short Title Catalog. Researchers can telnet to rlg.stanford.edu, and once logged in, type CALL RLIN (ESTC).

Philosophy

The *Electronic Texts in Philosophy* bibliography, compiled by Leslie Burkholder, CDEC, Carnegie Mellon University, for the APA Subcommittee on Electronic Texts in Philosophy, contains hundreds of projects. The bibliography is available by addressing an e-mail message to listserv@brownvm (on BITNET) or listserv@brownvm.brown.edu (on Internet), leaving the subject line blank. The text of the e-mail message must read get philosfy etexts. (For more information, contact David Owen [owen@arizrvax].)

Religion

The *Electric Mystic's Guide to the Internet: A Complete Bibliography of Networked Electronic Documents Online Conferences, Serials, Software and Archives Relevant to Religious Studies,* compiled by Michael Strangelove, Department of Religious Studies, University of Ottawa (441495@uottawa or 441495@acadvm1.uottawa.ca) is a very comprehensive source of information about Internet resources for religious studies and philosophy scholars. The *Electric Mystics Guide* is available via FTP to panda1.uottawa.ca or 137.122.6.16 in the directory pub/religion. It is also available from the listserv fileserver for the contents: Religious Studies Publication Electronic Journal, at listserv@uottawa or listserv@acadvm1.uottawa.

Music

Music scholars are making active use of the Internet. There are 24 music-related e-conferences listed in Kovacs et al. (1993) through which music researchers are sharing research and resources. (Kara Robinson [krobinso@kentvm or krobinso@kentvm.kent.edu] is compiler of the music section of the *Directory of Scholarly E-Conferences.*) For example, the TML-L (Thesaurus Musicarum Latinarum database for Latin music theory) e-conference edited by Thomas J. Mathiesen (mathiese@iubacs) is working on and discussing the TML database.

Linguistics

Linguists are also a presence on the Internet. The e-conference LINGUIST moderated by Anthony Aristar (aristar@tamuts.tamu.edu) and Helen Dry (hdry@emunix.emich.edu) is an international discussion of linguistics. Conference members share linguistics analysis software and information. There is also a Linguists nameserver, which serves as a directory of linguists on the Internet. Norval Smith (linguist-request@uniwa.uwa.oz.au) is the contact for the Linguist nameserver.

General

Internet-accessible library catalogs have immediate uses for scholars in all eight areas. There are Internet-accessible library catalogs all over the world that have been used to answer many reference questions, including those related to, for example, archival cataloging of correspondence in the Wisconsin Historical Archives; bibliographic verification of French, Spanish, German, and Lithuanian titles; and publications for French, German, and Slavic literature scholars. These scholars had already checked the standard reference books, and in the case of the literature scholars, had checked OCLC and RLIN.

RLIN has some special databases for humanities resources. It is of interest to humanities scholars because it provides access to primary documents, rare books, and archival collections. Although it is a fee-based service, the pricing structure is very reasonable. RLIN is available via Telnet to rlg.stanford.edu; log in with the account number and password that is used in the traditional dial-up process. LEXIS/NEXIS, DIALOG, and OCLC's FirstSearch and Epic services are also accessible over the Internet.

CONCLUSIONS

There are many resources available for humanities research on the Internet, and new tools and resources will be added in the future. Librarians have the opportunity to provide service to scholars in this area by identifying and referring scholars to appropriate and useful Internet resources. In a survey of 58 library and information science e-conferences conducted in spring 1992, 37.5% of those surveyed had used Internet resources in providing reference services (Kovacs & Robinson, in press). As Internet resources become part of the mainstream of reference service, librarians are faced with a new challenge. Humanities reference librarians are demonstrating that they will meet this challenge.

REFERENCES

Gould, C. C. (1988). *Information needs in the humanities: An assessment.* Palo Alto, CA: Research Libraries Group.

Kehoe, B. P. (1993). *Zen and the art of the Internet: A beginner's guide to the Internet.* Englewood Cliffs, NJ: Prentice-Hall.

Kovacs, D. K.; Bell, G. S.; Fehrmann, P.; Haas, L.; Holmes, G.; Kovacs, M.; Langendorfer, J.; Park, A.; & Robinson, K. (1993). *Directory of scholarly electronic conferences* (6th rev.). Kent, OH: Kent State University Libraries—Internet Resource (ftp ksuvxa.kent.edu; directory: library; files: acadlist.file1, acadlist.file2, acadlist.file3, acadlist.file4, acadlist.file5, acadlist.file6, acadlist file7, acadlist.file8; also available as a HyperCard stack acadstac.hqx and in print format from the Association of Research Libraries).

Kovacs, D. K., & Robinson, K. (in press). Scholarly e-conferences on the academic networks: How library and information science scholars use them. *Journal of the American Society for Information Science.*

Kovacs, D. K.; Schloman, B. F.; & McDaniel, J. A. (in press). A model for planning and providing reference services using Internet resources. In D. Brunning & G. Machovec (Eds.), *Information highways.* Phoenix, AZ: Oryx Press.

Kovacs, M. J.; & Kovacs, D. K. (1991). The state of scholarly electronic conferencing. *Electronic Networking: Research, Applications, and Policy, 1*(2), 29-36.

Krol, E. (1992). *The whole Internet: User's guide & catalog.* Sebastopol, CA: O'Reilly.

Pankake, M. (1991). Humanities research in the 90's: What scholars need; What librarians can do. *Library Hi Tech, 9*(1), 9-16.

Pisciotta, H. A. (1993). An index to reproductions of modern architecture: The shoe box card file in a networked environment. *Art Reference Services Quarterly, 1*(1), 3-17.

Quarterman, J. S. (1990). *The matrix: Computer networks and conferencing systems worldwide.* Bedford, MA: Digital Press.

Stover, M. (Ed.). (1992). Electronic information for the humanities. *Library Trends, 40*(4).

Wiberley, S. E., Jr. (1991). Habits of humanists: Scholarly behavior and new information technologies. *Library Hi Tech, 9*(1), 17-22.

BRUCE R. SCHATZ

Associate Professor
Graduate School of Library and Information Science

Research Scientist
National Center for Supercomputing Applications
University of Illinois at Urbana-Champaign

Electronic Libraries and Electronic Librarians: Who Does What in a National Electronic Community*

INTRODUCTION

I'm an information systems architect who worked at Bell Labs and Bellcore and IBM for many years, so it's my great privilege to be talking about electronic libraries at this Clinic. Actually, starting in the fall, I'll be a professor in the School of Library and Information Science here at the University of Illinois, and you'll see why that is potentially a very good match, although many of the things I talk about might seem very odd. I hope you'll realize that a lot of things I'm talking about are, in fact, mainline topics for library and information science. I'm honored to be giving this talk, and I hope I can give you a practical taste of "what the future will be like" and also what the information professional's role might actually be in this.

This talk will have two parts: First, I'm going to describe very briefly what this new kind of library technology is like through a discussion of the Worm Community System (WCS), why it is going to be very important, and why it will involve a lot of money. What I want to emphasize at the start is that while WCS may seem like an esoteric research project, in fact it is one of the flagship information projects funded by the National Science Foundation. In addition, the National Information Infrastructure Act looms in the immediate future, authorizing an enormous amount of money to be spent in the development of digital libraries in specialized areas. Digital libraries will require information systems like WCS. This project has become a national model of this new kind of information system, but its primary content is really just a special collection, in the same sense you already know. It is an important national effort, but there will be lots of other efforts like this in many different subject areas.

---

*This paper is an edited transcript of the author's presentation at the Clinic.

Second, I'm going to discuss in more detail what kinds of people are required to do this kind of activity. The roles range from traditional librarians all the way to systems architects. Similarly, the roles range from those that involve no computer knowledge at all to those that involve very intensive computing. My expectation is that people who call themselves "librarians" in the foreseeable future will actually span this entire range, even though now they are significantly skewed towards the traditional end.

ELECTRONIC LIBRARIES

What is a digital or electronic library? It's something like a physical library except that it's got different materials in it. It's dynamic so that people are not only navigating archival collections, but they are publishing their own materials as well. It's a repository of all sorts of things—different levels of quality and different types of information. Finally, all the items are linked together, and it's knowledge in some very profound sense. In effect, you get what I usually call an *electronic community*. The particular ones that I will discuss are in science, but you could imagine very similar communities in other subject domains.

In an electronic community, you have both formal and informal information, from both literature and data. The formal literature is a traditional domain of librarians, e.g., abstracts and full text. But, in science, large data collections are also important. For example, scientific databases are a very big area in genome projects and physics projects. The people who manage these collections are called librarians, but often they are actually trained first in a science and then in library schools. The informal literature and data include the communications services across the networks, such as electronic mail and bulletin boards; however, in an electronic community, the generated messages do not exist in isolation but are interlinked together back to the formal archives they discuss. This all is like a hypertext system, except that there is a whole library of items from many sources spread across the network. Therefore, it is really more like a hyperlibrary, where related items are linked together and references can be followed back to the source. This moves towards one system that lets you sit at your computer and navigate through all these different kinds of knowledge.

In order to see what such an interconnected space would be like and to understand what's involved in building the collection and writing the software, I've been concentrating on specialized collections in a subdomain of science in molecular biology. In particular, the library is for the "worm community," the molecular biologists who study the nematode worm *C. elegans*, and the project is called the Worm Community System (WCS).

This particular worm is a major organism in molecular biology. It has become the model for the human genome project because it's sort of bite sized— it's only got a thousand cells. It's big enough to be a real animal but small enough so you can learn everything about it. Its community is similarly appropriate for building a library, because it's big enough to be interesting but small enough to be doable. The knowledge base is fairly small in amount (about 30,000 total units of information) and in size (mostly text and line graphics). The people are mostly at big universities that are hooked up to the Internet, so you can think seriously about building an interactive electronic library across national networks.

There are about 500 people in the United States and Europe who participate in the worm community. It's big enough so if you say, "Is this really a model of a national library?" the answer is, "Yes, it's sort of like a national library." It isn't really a full one, since it's small enough so that a modest research project can build it and do all the steps. And we've actually built the library, gathered the collection, and implemented the technology, so that we can study the social and organizational needs for effective system use. Remember that before the country spends 100 billion dollars to build a national information infrastructure and make a universal library, it might be prudent to build a large-scale model to understand what this would actually involve and which things would work and which things wouldn't work. I'm not going to tell you now which things would work and which wouldn't work (although I do have a little bit of information about that); I'm just going to indicate what the problems are, so you can understand what kind of people are needed to solve them.

The kind of knowledge in WCS covers both data and literature. There is a wide range of biology data, which is very specialized, genomic data (like genes and maps and sequences), and cellular data (like lineages). Then there are things that look like traditional literature, not just journals, but also newsletters and conferences. In biology communities, this latter informal literature is a very important source of information. For this community, we took the primary newsletter—about 10 back years of one-page articles—scanned it to get searchable text and figures, and proofread it so we could build automatic links from the references in the text. It turned out that this was one of the main activities that sold the system. The people who did this literature encoding are now calling themselves data librarians, although they needed a little bit of specialized biology knowledge. Lastly, there are informal materials, both data (like methods) and literature (like notes), that complement the formal archives.

Next I'm going to give you just a brief taste of the system functionality. WCS is a custom-written piece of software. It's running in 25 worm labs across the United States and a few in Europe. The system has an internal representation called an *information space*—not any of the traditional data representations but little pieces of information that could be text or pictures or graphics are all interconnected. The user can point to one piece and display it, then hop to the next one and display it, even though the first might be text and the second might be a picture, and the first might be in one physical location and the second might be in another. Internally, the system has something like a "federated distributed heterogeneous object-oriented database," that keeps track of where the information objects are and what type they are, so that different software can be invoked at the appropriate time. If you have seen demonstrations of WCS and other network-based information software, you know that the Internet is now fast enough for transparent access to be practical for the types of data needed for biologists.

The basic stages of system functionality within the information space are browsing, filtering, and sharing. In browsing, you locate items using information retrieval techniques like keyword searching and by navigation through interconnection links. In filtering, you examine the returned items to select those of current interest. In this domain, with biology data, it's not like text where you can look at it and say, "Yes, that's interesting." It's often something long and dense like a sequence that you want to feed into an analysis program. So this kind of scientific environment has to let you pass objects into other programs without much effort. Finally, in sharing, there's what could be called a publishing system to let you compose new items and propagate them to other people. For a more complete description of the system and how it's used, see Schatz (1991/92). For a general portrayal of the role of information technology in the context of science, see the National Research Council (1993).

Though we've built this nationwide information space in a specialized area, our goal is to work on building the Interspace, which is the information manipulation analogue of the Internet for data transmission. You build an information space for worms and then expand through molecular biology into another one for flies and another one for humans. Then you do neuroscience (which we've already started on), then physics, then humanities, and so on. What you get is all these specialized communities, special libraries that together across the national network will make up the grand national library. And so, if you keep connecting information spaces into the Interspace, finally you get the WorldNet. Thus the electronic community strategy is, "Today the Worm. Tomorrow the World."

ELECTRONIC LIBRARIANS

Well, the WorldNet is a great thing, but where is it going to come from? It's going to come from lots and lots of hard work and smart people who have a wide range of interests and skills. So what I really want to discuss is, "Where do those people come from?" The answer will explain why someone like me, who is in some sense only a systems designer, is a professor in a library school. It's because there is an important set of people who already exist, called "librarians," who don't quite have the right orientation yet to do this kind of project, and there's another important set of people who don't exist at all, namely those who design these kind of systems. These latter people, called "architects," aren't getting trained anywhere despite the crying need in significant national efforts. As part of their training, these systems architects need to understand traditional library and information science in order to be able to build the kinds of systems that are very much needed in the future. This is why systems architects and systems architecture belong in their natural home—library schools—to prepare people for these new roles.

Now that you know that there's a need for new librarians and that there's money in it and that it might be interesting to you, what do you have to do to be an *electronic librarian?* Well, here are the parts of the electronic library the way I've been defining it. There are users (who are the people who use the library), there's knowledge, and then there are things called systems that are supposed to connect users to knowledge without getting in the way. Knowledge is the material coming from the community, and the question is, "How do you get it into the system, how do you encode it, how do you interconnect it?" The users don't care at all about that—the encoded representation. They care about the interactive navigation, or "How do I find what I'm looking for?" The systems designers, conversely, care mostly about building the information environments, or "How do I make everything transparent?" Transparency is a technical term that means that when I point to something, the system finds and displays it—I don't care where it is in the network or what type of data it is. There might be a lot going on in order to accomplish transparency, and the design represents very hard questions in information systems and computer science. Let me emphasize that you need to address all these (users—systems—knowledge) to have a complete and functional electronic library.

Before discussing roles per se, let's view the functions of electronic libraries in a slightly different way. There are three pieces: data—environment—programs. Each of these pieces is critical to a complete library, and each requires appropriate librarians to support the desired functionality. The "data librarian" is involved with supporting the electronic materials, i.e., "Where does the data come from? How is it gathered and connected?" The "program librarian" is involved with supporting the semantic relationships, i.e., "What are all the ways these data can or should be related? How are the relationships recorded?" This person must evaluate both the situation, e.g., standard places or exhaustive search, and the user, e.g., casual or serious interest, to be prepared to match the users to the knowledge. In some cases, there may be analysis programs that will help with this process, whereas in others, only personal experience will help. Finally, the "environment librarian" is involved with supporting the uniform interaction for the data and the programs, i.e., "What system is necessary to provide appropriate transparency?" This person is like an architect. If you only have books, you want somebody who builds a building for books. If you have a computer system, you have to have someone who builds the software, lays the networks, worries about the data.

All of these kinds of librarians are necessary to build electronic libraries in the future. As I discuss the roles of each in more detail, please note that all of these roles already exist in traditional physical libraries. What is different is the degree of programming needs and computer expertise required. In the discussion, I try to lay out a range of different levels of programming activity, to emphasize that there are important roles requiring very little computer expertise and important roles demanding very much computer expertise—that there is a role for everyone.

The problem with the future is that it's different from the past so it seems scary. But, on the other hand, it rarely is fundamentally different. In some significant sense, the same problems exist now as when the Greeks were trying to build the library in Alexandria. What happens is that the technology changes. Whether there are scrolls or books or disks, you have to worry about how to collect the materials, how to locate desired items, and how to retrieve the located items. So the same topics in library science, information science, and information systems recur in each generation of technology.

The title of the school here at Illinois—the Graduate School of Library and Information Science—is very nice because it includes both library science and information science as integral parts that are actually very closely related but that also have their own domains. The third domain—information systems— is beginning to come into its own as a separate entity with the current proliferation of computers and communications technology. I'm going to emphasize this third domain a bit more heavily because it's the one you are least familiar with and because it's the one that is my particular specialty.

Traditionally, librarians have simply bought information systems, primarily for automating circulation and card catalogs. Everybody knows that online card catalogs are really bad, and even if they weren't, they certainly do not do this community systems stuff. You need new, custom software to perform this new functionality, and it's got to be developed by somebody. Those somebodies are not people in computer science who are only interested in the technology itself. Those somebodies will be people in library and information science who are interested in building libraries to serve traditional needs with the new technologies.

To summarize the roles for electronic librarians, I propose that these new people provide new solutions for old problems. Those in "library science" are like "collection librarians," who perform the encoding and classification for electronic materials. Those in "information science" are like "reference librarians," who provide paths and analysis for electronic navigation. Those in "information systems" are like "systems architects," who design plugs and transparency for electronic environments. All these together are needed to build and maintain electronic libraries. Remember that for each role, there is a whole spectrum of people ranging from those who don't know anything about computing but now happen to deal with data instead of books to people who are expert programmers.

What I want to do now is go through each one of these roles and describe a range of sample tasks and real-life jobs that are going to be important in the future. I hope to give a concrete impression so that you can decide for yourselves if you would like to do this kind of activity or where you'd like to position yourself. The old activities will still exist, but they will become decreasingly important, and these new activities will become increasingly important. So you should think about how much training you need in order to be ready for the future. I've chosen stereotyped ways of discussing each one of these roles, which I know aren't the only ways, and I'm not a professional librarian, so I hope you'll bear with me if they seem narrow-minded. However, they should be illustrative of what kind of activities might be possible.

Library Science

A library scientist deals with these collections of interconnected knowledge; the corresponding role might be termed a data librarian. Library scientists have three primary tasks in dealing with the knowledge: collecting the materials, transforming the formats, and connecting related items within the materials.

The collecting task is very much like that performed by librarians in relation to traditional collections. For example, there are people in genome centers, more than 20 in the United States, who maintain electronic collections of biological data without the need to know much about computing. They are database administrators, who basically know how to enter files and do word processing. But what they do for a living is just what librarians do. They locate a lot of sources, they figure out which ones are reasonable quality and which ones aren't, they classify the items, they make sure the items all have a name, and they update the collection periodically. It's just like maintaining a collection except that it is a database, and it involves a little bit of computing knowledge but no programming at all. It's really just getting a file from somebody, putting it in a specified place, and running a program on it that somebody else wrote. The skill here is making sure it's current, and if there are 10 possible sources for this piece of material, choosing the one that best meets your users' needs. There's a lot of people skills here, which librarians have, and a lot of economics, too, which is very important.

Transforming data, the middle stage of collection management in the electronic library, approaches territory that is new for most librarians. The problem is that almost none of the collected databases are in the right format for this grand universal system, and they have to be changed. Now, typically, these transformation programs are very simple to write and execute. They are like two-page C or awk programs that change the formats of data by changing the names of the fields and a little bit of the values. This is the sort of program that someone who has taken a single programming course in a library school can write. These are very easy programs—if you are at all facile with writing programs, you can write one of these in an hour or two. This makes you enormously more valuable because once you can do that, every time you want to change or add a database, you don't have to run over to the programmers and bother them and say, "I don't know how to change the names of the fields." That's so easy for them, they don't even want to talk to you. On the other hand, if you can take a programming course and write a few of these very simple programs, you now have an immensely valuable skill. It means you can traverse the network, grab these sources, and start adding them to the databases all by yourself. That's a very reasonable thing to want to learn, even for people who swear that they are not electronic librarians. Such a skill means you can move right into one of the big science projects, for example, and be the data librarian as a stand-alone, independent person. My guess is that while most of the current positions are at the collecting level, most of the future positions are going to be at this transforming level. Therefore, in the future, the data librarians are going to have to learn some programming and do their own database transformations.

Connecting, the final level for collections, is much harder and involves more extensive programming skills. It requires writing software to automatically build links between related items, by parsing out embedded names of objects and standard syntax for names. For example, in molecular biology, the programs parse text from many sources for gene names and connect them to referencing sources. These are somewhat harder programs than the transformation ones, though still within the reach of someone with a programming course or two, and require some biology knowledge to implement properly. But, again, it's not terribly hard, so the more sophisticated people who know programming will tend to operate at this even more valuable level.

Information Science

An information scientist deals with the navigation of interconnected knowledge; the corresponding role might be termed a user coordinator (program librarian). Information scientists have three primary tasks in dealing with navigation: assisting the user in operating the system, scripting standard paths through the materials, and analyzing significant patterns between related items in the information space.

The assisting function is very much like the function performed by traditional reference librarians. Their primary task is helping people use the system to find desired items within the available sources. So they must understand the system as well as the knowledge, from a usage standpoint rather than from a system standpoint. Since the users typically run the system from their own computers, these librarians have the additional role of community systems administrators, ensuring that the users' sites have correctly operating machines and systems. These librarians answer questions such as, "How do I install the system? What software do I need? I want to do this search, how do I do it? What kind of words do I use?" They also write the online help and the tutorials by working with the users and the programmers. So, they understand how to listen to people, but they don't actually have much computing knowledge.

Every project that succeeds has a number of people who essentially provide user assistance and training. It's computer assistance, but their knowledge of programming isn't very great. When they get a little more knowledgeable, they can find standard paths. One of the problems with having this grand interconnected space is that you can't find anything. Anyone who has used Gopher, for example, knows that this is a real problem if there are hundreds of thousands of sources. It's like having a library without a card catalog, and you have to read a book then jump to all the things that some person who didn't know what he was doing and didn't understand the subject very well connected to it. Well, there are facilities in these community systems for recording navigation, so if you have found a valuable path through the space, you can record it by either recording an actual session or by doing a sort of meta-classification by specifying a set of useful items about, say, molecular biology, even though some of them are in a physics database.

Scripting is thus like the work of a reference librarian, who can write programs available to users to satisfy simple requests. So, if you can do a little programming, really just specifying sequences of commands, then you can be a more effective reference librarian because you provide scripts that can automatically handle some common user queries. This mechanism is not as good as a person, but it serves more users. In slightly more general implementations, such scripts become an encoding of reference works about basic information sources. This type of program is becoming popular on the

Internet as a solution to the resource discovery problem of "knowing where to look."

Analyzing is the final level for navigating the information space. This consists of writing interactive software to perform sophisticated pattern finding and real semantic matching. Finding nontrivial patterns of related items will likely require both deep semantic parsing and flexible contextual display of the resulting connection graphs. For example, in the worm space, you might say, "I've done this traversal through genes and maps and literature, and I think this uncovers the mechanism for fertilization of eggs in worms. Find me some other navigation graph that's very similar in biology space, which represents some similar pattern in some higher organism, so I can compare the mechanisms." Then the analysis software suggests related hyperbooks or related subcollections, which is very sophisticated programming that doesn't work very well at present. On the other hand, my guess is that a lot of people who at one time might have been reference librarians, and who are now sailing around the Internet and the information spaces, will want to write sophisticated programs to help them find patterns more efficiently so that they can become real trailblazers.

Information Systems

An information systems designer deals with environments for inter-connected knowledge; the corresponding role might be termed an information specialist (environment librarian) at the low level and a systems architect at the high level. Information systems designers have three primary tasks in dealing with the environments: customizing existing systems, designing new systems to match user needs, and implementing new designs to provide functional electronic libraries.

Customizing is very much like what is done by a traditional information specialist. Such a person is a technical staff member in a library, who interviews vendors of existing information systems and chooses the most suitable system for the needs of the users. If the specialists are lucky, they can customize the system a little bit and change the data to their taste. Usually, however, the system does what it does, and the library must cope with the functionality provided. The specialists have to know a little computing, but mostly they just select from given choices.

The problem is that existing information systems do a poor job of satisfying the needs of many users. For example, all the big science projects that have tried to use commercial databases find they just don't suffice. The systems don't lose the data, but they don't provide any help in navigating and analyzing, in finding out what really is connected to what. That is, existing systems don't really allow the scientists to ask the kind of questions that they want to ask in order to make good use of databases. To have an effective system, you really need an architect.

Designing is what an architect does. A building architect designs buildings (physical structures), and a systems architect designs systems (logical structures). An architect finds out from the users such vital sociological specifications as what kind of searching they want to do, what kind of navigation they need, what kind of sharing they want to do, and what kind of analysis they need. Given these specifications, the architect lays out the entire functionality of the system, then knows enough about the technology to estimate what can be implemented, what cannot be implemented, how much it costs, how long it's going to take to build, and so on, through the entire process of creating an electronic library.

Implementing, on the other hand, is what a builder does—the realization of a design into an actual structure. In established fields of architecture, such as those for physical structures, there are formal disciplines for architects and builders with different organizations specialized to the different tasks. For less-established fields of architecture, such as that involving logical structures like systems design, the tasks merge. Typically, there is a small architecture team formed at the beginning of the project, which then expands to become the complete development team. The original architects then become the supervisors of the programmers doing the implementation. Some organization must stay in place to maintain the system and help it evolve until it stabilizes to fulfill the needs of the users.

Information Systems Architect

What emerges from these observations is that there must be a true profession of information systems architects. Just as the world needs people who create buildings, namely, architects who design buildings for particular needs, the world needs people who create systems, namely, architects who design systems for particular needs. Architects have to understand a little bit about everything. They are really artists, if you think about it, but also like engineers. What they do is match user needs to feasible technology. Or, restated, an architect matches a set of knowledge and navigation needs to what environments you can actually build now. And what you can do now varies dramatically over time. The computer industry is growing very fast, while the users' needs are relatively static. An information systems architect designs and implements electronic libraries, in this case, for specialized communities that have a particular set of knowledge, a particular set of needs. They are special librarians, who can create all of the components necessary to build and maintain an electronic community library.

Professors in library school can't actually build large commercial systems; they build models of future systems. In that sense, I'm no longer a commercial systems architect. Instead, I do research in information systems architecture by designing and implementing large-scale models in scientific domains. What I try to do is to design protocols for information manipulation and to build frameworks of underlying software to increase the technological understanding and sociological analysis of electronic community systems. This might be thought of as constructing toolkits for knowledge environments, to learn how to effectively construct complete community library toolkits by implementing model community library systems in the sciences. To be successful at architectural design of toolkits, you have to design a lot of real systems and see how they play in the living world—at least small ones, if not huge commercial ones.

The conclusion is that if you want to construct these large-scale electronic libraries that are special collections for particular communities, you need the magic triangle of users—systems—knowledge. This is actually the same triangle that appears in library school brochures as the core of the subject. And everybody likes triangles because they look complete. What is at the apex—I am immodestly putting myself at the apex—is the environment, the system actually running, but in order to make it work at the base, on one hand you need to have all the knowledge stuff, the real data, and on the other hand you need to have all the user stuff, the real people. So to make electronic libraries happen, you need systems architects, data librarians, and reference librarians.

The problem is, and the reason I'm at a library school now, is that there are people who train data librarians that are sort of like library scientists, although they need to be pushed more to higher levels of more electronic and computing skills. And there are people who train reference librarians who are sort of like information scientists, but, again, if you're really going to search around these huge information spaces, you need people with higher levels of skills in computing and information analysis programs. But right now, there's a large hole in the training of the requisite systems architects.

Where do new information systems come from? The answer is that right now they really don't come from anywhere. The hardware is growing on an almost infinite upwards curve, and the software is sort of sneaking along but getting increasingly more sophisticated. But the information systems, not just fancy displays but what people can really do, are very little changed from what they were 25 years ago. There's a big national crisis here. If you have lots of people who live in cities, you really need architects or you can't have a functional city. Well, if you have lots of people who are going to live in information spaces and live in these electronic worlds, then you really need information systems architects or you can't have functional systems. The revolution of the WorldNet will never reach its genuine potential without fundamentally new information systems, which must be designed by these missing architects. All of you can see that the revolution should and must come, or you wouldn't be at this conference on networked communities. Systems architects must be trained, like other architects, through an apprenticeship, where they build increasingly larger systems and learn the complexities required to design functioning electronic libraries.

So, if anyone in the audience would like to learn to be a systems architect, I'd be very pleased to talk with you afterwards. Thank you for your patience and attention—it is you who will invent the future.

REFERENCES

Schatz, B. R. (1991/92). Building an electronic community system. *Journal of Management Information Systems, 8*(Winter), 87-107. (Reprinted in R. Baecker (Ed.), *Readings in groupware and computer supported cooperative work.* Los Altos, CA: Morgan Kaufmann.)

National Research Council. Committee on a National Collaboratory. (1993). *National collaboratories: Applying information technology for scientific research* (Computer Science and Telecommunications Board study report). Washington, DC: National Academy Press.

PAT MOLHOLT

Assistant Vice President for Scholarly Resources
Columbia University Health Sciences
New York, New York

Integrating Libraries into the Curriculum: The CHIPS Project

INTRODUCTION

Libraries have played a role in support of teaching, but only in rare instances have they had a key role. Of course the faculty use library resources in preparing lectures, and there are often substantial collections of reserve materials drawn from the library, but these represent passive roles. At Columbia University Health Sciences, we are creating a pivotal role for the library with the Columbia Health Information PerspectiveS project (CHIPS). The objectives of the project are to promote the development of the curriculum as an integrated whole; to create an electronic curriculum that enables students to move through the learning process with a significant degree of control over how and when, where, and in what sequence they learn; and to track the progress of students against individual objectives, course requirements, and learning timelines while providing tutor-like assistance.

A HISTORY OF FOLLOWING

Libraries have been called the heart of a university, an appellation we librarians would like to believe is true. Various aspects of reality, including fiscal constraints, paint a somewhat different picture. In the area of curriculum support, perhaps we see most clearly the supportive, secondary role libraries play. I am referring to the traditional reserve room operation where faculty call for a variety of materials, some from the collections, some not, to be put aside for students' use. We have, in some enlightened libraries, allowed students open access to reserve materials. In other cases, we have invested in methods of providing some of the information online. Yet by and large we have played a passive role.

Another intersection of libraries and the curriculum occurs in classroom lectures on library use and library resources with occasional collaboration between a faculty member and a librarian in the design of an assignment emphasizing library skills. However, professional education in medicine tends to be intensive and highly structured, so that faculty often prepare extensive syllabi for students' use. There is little time in the curriculum for students to do research, browse, or explore topics until the end when, in some cases, a minor "thesis" is assigned to justify the D after the M or J.

While librarians worry about the cost of publications, the lack of standards in CD-ROM products, teaching Internet skills, and a host of other issues, our parent institutions are facing major problems in the delivery of education. It is certainly true that library budgets represent competition for resources with hard-pressed instructional needs, yet I contend that librarians have skills and resources that can be an important part of the cost-effective delivery of instruction.

MANDATES FOR CHANGE

Several compelling reasons argue for a reexamination of the delivery of education. While each of our institutions stands apart from its peers in some ways, all of them stand with their toes up against the same line in two notable areas: the constant need to incorporate new information into the curriculum and the concern over the cost of education. Though the "I lecture, you listen" method has been used for centuries (millennia?), its shortcomings have become ever more glaring over time.

Knowledge Expansion

One can trot out any of the hundreds of studies that show the unparalleled rate of growth in information today. We have all read those studies, and, more importantly, we personally feel the effects as we ourselves work to stay current. The information impacting on a science-based curriculum is not incidental— it is fundamental and complex. How do we decide what to include in a course, and how do we incorporate it with as little effort as possible?

Pressure on Faculty

Many of you know first hand the pressure on faculty for research, publishing, finding outside support, participating in the broader community as reviewers and panelists, and participating in the more immediate community on committees and task forces. These comprise the typical path to promotion and tenure, where value is measured in research dollars and numbers of articles published. Teaching, on the other hand, is like the weather—we talk about it a lot, we believe in it, but just as we are lousy at predicting the weather, we are terrible at applying quantitative (or even qualitative) measures to teaching. Partly as a result, excellence in and dedication to teaching do not carry much weight outside the home institution (however well they may play within). The rational faculty member allocating effort cannot fail to realize that teaching and counseling reduce mobility, while scholarly and professional accomplishments increase it. It is also true that college teachers, having never been taught to teach, are seldom good at the nuts and bolts of organization and curriculum development, the craft skills provided to our K-12 teachers by the much-maligned education schools. In addition, many good intentions in higher education run aground on the shoals of photocopying, copyright, and other sources of minor frustration and delay. Is there a way to provide faculty with meaningful support as they go about creating new courses, revising old ones, and making choices about what to include and what to leave aside? Can we offer meaningful alternatives for the delivery of information to supplement the lecture environment?

Curriculum Revision

As I mentioned, there is a constant need to incorporate new information and to rethink existing information in the curriculum, particularly in professional education. Among medical schools, there is currently a major effort across the country to get students out of the large lecture hall environment and into problem-solving groups. It is amazing to realize how rare collaborative work is for students in higher education, especially college where it tends to be labeled "cheating," when one considers how vital teamwork is in the world of professional practice. Except for professional schools, it is uncommon to have massive revisions of an entire curriculum, but in those instances, we need to consider how we make such revisions rational, interwoven, connected, and continuous.

Varied Learning Styles

We are not all alike. Some of us learn better from seeing an idea written out; some prefer images and graphics; some do best hearing an idea explained. In the mainstream of the curriculum, we do not—cannot—take heed of that. It is left to the initiative of the individual student to seek augmenting materials that support his or her learning style. Just as we have broken away from the notion of a uniform look to a catalog entry in an online public access catalog (OPAC), can we be more attuned to learning styles and provide information in more forms in order to facilitate and individualize students' interaction with the curriculum?

Variety of Media

The original medium for instruction was the spoken word, and the oral tradition included elaborate systems for memorization; then came writing—slow and laborious; then the printing press; then typing and telephonic devices. The computer era—begun not so long ago—has generated vast changes in how we store, transmit, and access information. Videotape, audiotape, CDs—both video and audio—laser disks, camcorders, laptops, palmtops that are more powerful than some early mainframes, and so forth. How do we effectively, and in an integrated way, direct this array of media and technology toward helping students learn?

Structure of Information

We can look with genuine pleasure at the beauty and simplicity of the printed text—particularly as manifested in the earliest books. Today, though, information is commonly found as molecular diagrams, chemical structures, dynamic wave formations on a CRT screen, MRI scans, or microscopic camera images from inside the knee. The alphanumeric keyboard symbols no longer suffice. Again, how do we effectively utilize these new kinds of information and the accompanying technology to the benefit of the student?

Continuing Education

The "half-life" of a bachelor's degree in engineering is five years; that of a librarian's master's degree is, in my estimation, even less, considering the change in media and technology and the explosion of knowledge to be acquired, organized, and made accessible. The medical profession and, interestingly enough, medical librarianship as well have recognized the need for continuing education in their certification or credentialing processes. If, as will be the case for Columbia, we train health science professionals in a different way, that is by using more technology and reassessing the role of memorization, can we not also provide graduates with continuous updates to their knowledge? The learning process does not stop at graduation, but our information-based relationship with the student does. With the Internet and increasing connectivity from every part of the globe, might we not have options for a longer term relationship and a more extended/protracted role of the alma mater in lifelong learning?

Cost of Education

Our current health care crisis mandates that the cost of education be the first consideration, and I would have put it at the top of this list save for the fact that we know so little about the costs of education. We do know that a massive study conducted by the Institute of Medicine in 1974, *Costs of Education in the Health Professions,* yielded figures that ranged from $6,900 to $21,000 per student for four years of education. Extrapolating *only* for inflation and not counting for increased use of technology, the cost moves up to a range of $21,000 to $56,000. Can the use of information technology in the curriculum save money in the delivery of education? We sincerely hope the answer is yes.

ENABLING FACTORS

Three critical elements are converging to facilitate the kind of change in curriculum delivery for which I have argued. The first is the proliferation of reliable, high-speed networks—local, regional, national, and international. These electronic highways, as they are so frequently called, make it possible to share information resources, collaborate interactively with colleagues, and redefine the boundaries around the user populations we serve.

The second enabling element is the availability of powerful portable computers with excellent screen resolution, fast processors, and large amounts of memory. These increasingly affordable devices will make it possible for students to create individualized learning materials—notes from one course, images from another—blended together in a way that makes sense to the individual student.

Third is the availability of information in electronic form. While not a new phenomenon, it is finally reaching a critical mass, making worthwhile the efforts needed to create systems that rely on such information. It would appear that available tools such as Wide Area Information Servers (WAIS) and Gopher can be used in accessing text and images in reasonably standard ways. If that is true and we no longer have to worry about building fundamental tools, we can, instead, concentrate on individualized user interfaces that will make the difference in whether a system is used or ignored. It is the interface and application areas that are the focus of our project.

MEETING THE CHALLENGE

Many schools have undertaken highly visible efforts focusing on technology in the classroom. Multimedia computer aided instruction (CAI) programs are often used to teach concepts. Hypertext network-based textbooks allow students to follow a variety of paths, check what they have learned with simple quizzes, and move on to the next section. Some medical and dental schools have developed databases of curriculum information to track the amount of lecture time devoted to particular topics, maintain a record of which faculty member is responsible for particular segments of the curriculum, and aid in scheduling classes.

All of these efforts are important, in good measure for what they teach us about how to design better systems, but they tend to remain disjointed, lacking an overall plan or vision for exactly how they work together and how they fit into the curriculum.

The project at Columbia approaches the matter from a fundamentally different point of view. We are creating an "electronic curriculum" that will accompany students through their professional training and into their practice. We are formulating a student-centered, networked-based curriculum environment that functions from an underlying knowledge model linking information resources unique to Columbia with those developed and resident elsewhere in the world. The project is called CHIPS, the Columbia Health Information PerspectiveS project. The user will have the ability to view the curriculum from many perspectives—the perspective of a student of nursing, medicine, public health, dentistry; a perspective attuned to a student's learning style; a perspective that threads an idea across various "courses" and across years and disciplines; the perspective of a faculty member wanting to augment a lecture or an administrator compiling a report for an accrediting agency, and so forth. The vision we have for the educational environment reverses the usual learning model in which it is assumed that the writer of texts, or the individual giving the lecture, knows what the student needs and in what order. We take the view that students are capable of directing much of their learning and that they can learn more effectively and efficiently when self-directed.

The CHIPS project, encompassing the schools of medicine, dentistry, nursing, and public health, will become a medium or mechanism for the exchange of information within the various components of the curriculum. It will foster a highly collaborative environment among faculty as they engage in developing aspects of the electronic curriculum. The vision of CHIPS is to create for the student a learning resource that combines aspects of the library with aspects of tutoring and testing, and includes the added benefit of 24-hour accessibility, from any location.

COLUMBIA HEALTH INFORMATION PERSPECTIVES

Figure 1 is a high-level schematic of the elements of this project. The drawing can be read in several ways: the upper portion represents work that we anticipate will be done locally (develop a knowledge map, analyze course material, create image files, standardize concepts), while the bottom portion suggests the numerous projects and products external to Columbia to which we want to link. Reading left to right, one sees information resources on the left and a mapping or linking device on the right. The shaded areas dividing sections are interfaces which are pierced by dotted lines representing queries or pathways. As the figure suggests, we will be assembling a variety of existing curriculum materials from course notes, bibliographies, syllabi, images, and graphics, and we will be mapping them into a structure that is loosely represented on the right side of the figure. This knowledge map or concept space is intended as a mechanism for browsing the intellectual content of the system, as well as a mechanism for providing directed pathways through required material.

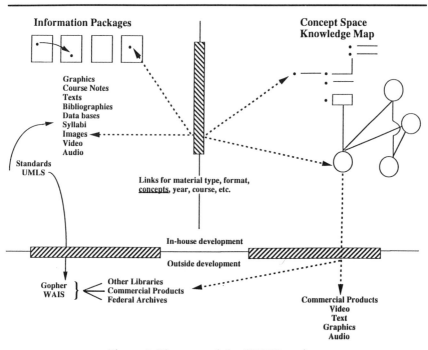

Figure 1. Elements of the CHIPS project

The work of implementation will be divided into at least three stages. The first is under way. We are gathering existing paper-based curriculum materials and analyzing them for content, structure, and overlap, and we are building a prototype of a segment of the knowledge map. Because I have participated in most of the curriculum revision meetings held in the medical school since July 1992, course directors are aware of our intention to build CHIPS and they are actively making suggestions on what to include—in particular what to off-load from the lecture environment into the electronic environment.

In this first stage, we are, in effect, building the electronic counterpart to the library's collection of books and journals. As much of the book and journal collection as we are able to acquire in electronic form will be part of the knowledge base, along with materials such as still images, digitized videos of surgical and dental procedures, and audio materials.

The second stage is building the curriculum model. We are beginning with medicine but will eventually encompass the schools of dentistry, nursing, and some aspects of public health. The job involves building a generic skeleton of health sciences knowledge to which will be attached the various information resources. We will use the Unified Medical Language System (UMLS) of the National Library of Medicine as a mapping device to link not only resources at Columbia but those that will be developed across the country. The stability and adequacy of UMLS is only one of many questions that face us in this project.

In the third stage, we will develop and then build the links that bind the information resources—the images, the animation, the full-motion video—to the skeleton that is the curriculum model. It is our intention to create only those information resources that we cannot acquire from others, whether commercially or on an exchange basis. As a result, there is considerable room for collaboration across schools. The linking will encompass the various "library" information resources as well as the clinical information system already in place at Columbia Presbyterian Medical Center.

This last stage also includes building the pathways for the students to use in moving about the resources, perusing new knowledge, taking tests on material, or being tutored. Some pathways will be prescribed, and traversing them can be monitored on a student-by-student basis to be sure that all students have completed required segments of the curriculum. Other pathways will be developed by discipline experts to help students learn how to think about a problem and how to ask the right questions in analyzing a patient case. In addition, students will be able to wander, pursue ideas, or create their own pathways, eventually to be either kept or erased.

BACK PLANE ISSUES

At least five issues present major challenges to the realization of this project—and that leaves aside politics. First, how will the system look and work from the user's perspective? This is one of the most critical elements in any system. We have enlisted the active participation of a group of medical students in the building process, and it is our intention to listen to them, particularly on the topic of the user interface. Ultimately the users must be able to configure the interface to meet their needs rather than be forced into a single approach to the system.

Second are issues related to the programming environment. We hope to use as many publicly available tools as possible in order to facilitate connecting to external resources and, of course, to cut down on tool development and concentrate on the knowledge base. We know there are good search engines out there, and work external to Columbia is underway to identify and organize information resources on the network. The work being done by the Clearinghouse for Networked Information Discovery and Retrieval (CNIDR) is critical to this project and others like it. We are pleased to be affiliated with CNIDR and support the efforts of George Brett and his colleagues.

Third, how will we model the knowledge to take advantage of its properties, its complexities, in a way that will elucidate and not obfuscate the learning process? While many knowledge-structuring schemes are available, the rules for applying them are highly interpretive, and the issue of compatibility between our project and work that may be done elsewhere presents itself. The same may be said for the interconcept links that will create the pathways. No agreed-upon set exists—most are ad hoc and often unique to a project's needs.

Fourth, there is an overriding need to make the system operate across multiple platforms—DOS, UNIX, and Apple being the major ones. This problem may be resolved by separating the access mechanism from the user interface/display mechanism and closely adhering to a standard structure within the access mechanism. There was a time when one would, for reasons of programming necessity, choose a hardware/software environment, IBM and DOS for example, and build a system in that environment. The choice was necessary because the various environments were independent of each other, with few communication options across platforms and virtually no collaboration between hardware or software vendors. By 1990, we began to realize the need for interoperability and the notion of closed shops went the way of centralized computing. Unfortunately, we are not yet very far along the road to having a software environment shared by, for example, IBM and Apple. This presents the CHIPS project with a major challenge.

The fifth issue concerns the need for faster network connections. When we start moving full-motion video around the network or still images that are 1,000 × 1,000 pixels, we need gigabit network speeds. Like shared operating environments, gigabit speeds are out there; the question is when will they be on our campuses?

PAYBACK

Now let us leap over all the difficulties and ask: if we manage this—if we create this extensible, interdisciplinary tool, a tool that fosters learning and collaboration—how will it address the educational issues I raised earlier?

The first payback will come from off-loading some information from the classroom to the system, resulting in a better use of the classroom experience and opening up time for more small-group learning and problem-solving sessions.

The second will be easy integration of new information. In order to accommodate the expanding information base, the system will have to remodel itself, that is, as much as possible the structure of this system has to support dynamic links between information and structure. We cannot possibly either hard-link or hand-link the information resources to the appropriate parts of the knowledge model and accommodate the necessary and frequent influx of new information. An interesting question that arises here is how to maintain a dynamic system that is stable enough that the user can be comfortable with it. It would be exasperating to walk into the library and find it arranged differently from one week to the next, even if the changes were being made to improve service or incorporate new material. Where is the right compromise between stability and flexibility?

Once implemented, the system should be tuned to integrate new information and greatly facilitate eventual changes to the curriculum. This will include providing tools for examining the curriculum, growing it here, pruning it there. The curriculum becomes an entity in its own right—an asset like the library, the laboratories, and other capital investments of the university.

Although CHIPS is student focused, it is also intended to be a tool for faculty—to find appropriate information resources, to update lecture materials, or to incorporate visual material into the lecture. In addition, course directors should be able to use the system to orient new faculty—that is, it should be easy to get an overview of a course in which a new faculty member has been asked to participate; it should be easy to see what has been covered, what is planned, and how it fits with other lectures.

The system will use as one of its advantages the incorporation of a variety of media and ways of presenting information. It will accommodate differences in learning styles and variations in the pace of learning to the advantage of the student. In addition, by being network based, it will be time- and place-independent. These are major paybacks for students.

The potential value of the CHIPS project as a link between health sciences graduates and their need for continuing education is enormous. Because such a system is globally accessible, we can consider forming long-term information-based relationships with graduates. In fact, it strikes me that there may be an obligation to do so. If we are successful with the project, we not only will have made changes in the way education is delivered, but we may be changing the premise of what an education in health care is. Faculty in curriculum revision meetings are already deliberating questions of what needs to be taught face-to-face in the classroom and what might be off-loaded to CHIPS; the next step is to question what the role of the information in CHIPS is. Some information will clearly be there to be learned and memorized, and will come out in test scores. But clearly other segments or layers of information are there as resources to be used when needed, not memorized.

The last item is the cost of education—we don't know with any certainty how CHIPS will affect costs, but it is on the agenda as an item to be watched and studied as we proceed with this project. Efficiency in the use of faculty time, convenience to students, and tapping national information resources all come into play, and all are hard to quantify.

CHANGES TO THE LIBRARY

What does CHIPS bode for the library? You might ask whether the library is getting closer to the curriculum or farther away. It is my belief that the more transparent/invisible we can make the boundaries of the library, and the more we can anticipate the user's needs and match our resources to them, the better off we are. Our job should not be to stand between the user and the information if there is a better way for him/her to gain access to what is needed. The role of the library in this scenario is to assist in the design of the system, to accumulate the electronic counterpart of the library that will support this curriculum, and to work with users in navigating the system. All of our traditional skills come into play—understanding the structure of information, acquiring and organizing information, and assisting users. They are simply transferred to a different arena.

This project has the potential to affect a cultural change within Columbia Health Sciences—to transform the way we think about education and how we engage each other regarding our responsibilities as teachers/educators. We have an opportunity to reasses our educational methodology and to make some fundamental changes. Conversely, we may confirm with resolve that change is not needed in some areas, but it will be a decision made knowingly, not by default. Finally, we hope to create a system that will stimulate the imagination of students as well as accommodate their intuition, and at the other end of the spectrum, one that will contribute to more effective and efficient delivery of health care education without compounding costs.

ELLEN I. WATSON

Library Director
Bradley University
Peoria, Illinois

JOEL L. HARTMAN

Associate Provost for Information Technologies and Resources
Bradley University
Peoria, Illinois

Views versus Visions: Implementing the Library's Vision in the Real World

INTRODUCTION

Throughout institutions of higher education, the view of the library takes on many forms: the president may be inclined to see the library as a money pit; the faculty view of their library allocation approaches that of entitlement; some undergraduates view the library as a neat place for an inexpensive date; and the librarians as the place where "My Collection" is kept.

While these stereotypes may appear all too familiar to some, they bear an element of truth. These, and other stereotypical views of the library, derive from the past; libraries and librarians are now in a period of substantial transformation, transition, and opportunity.

This paper speaks to both the evolving role of libraries and to a process for changing the library's institutional position. If you want to be somewhere else, don't stay where you are. But, how do you manage the transition?

THE CHANGING ROLE OF THE LIBRARY

Change is never easy. It can be exciting and energizing to reenvision one's role. However, when change involves the abandonment of comfortable paradigms and assumptions and the actual implementation of the new vision, we all may stumble and fumble. The first step toward implementing the new vision is the transition from our old assumptions to acceptance of the reality of the information age. In particular, there are three dangerous assumptions to be overcome in making the transition to the "real world":

1. the library as the "heart of the institution" versus the library as part of a mix of information services;
2. the concept of mastery of information versus the proliferation and fragmentation of information;

3. the conviction that "there'll always be a library" versus user-based information services.

It has been clear for some time that, despite our protestations and the high-flown language of our accrediting agencies, the library is not at the center of scholarship in many institutions. This is particularly true in the sciences, where high-speed, nearly universal network access provides researchers with the capability of sharing work in progress long before the work reaches publication. It is becoming increasingly true as well in other disciplines—not just the social sciences and business, but the traditionally "library intensive" humanities. As the medium in which information is encapsulated becomes less important, and as more information becomes available in digital form, scholars expect to be able to access information from their desktops, instantaneously. Delivery of that information is provided by a variety of sources—both subsidized campus services and a range of commercial services. While the library may mediate some of the resources and services, the mix increasingly requires librarians to cooperate with a broad range of new colleagues, including computing specialists, commercial information vendors, information developers, and information users.

We have been accustomed to considering ourselves capable of mastering "the universe of information," even though we've been commenting on the "information explosion" for the past 20 years or more. We have been attempting to fit the new information—exploded, fragmented, and proliferated—into our old patterns. We had some limited success when we were attempting to deal only with print resources; when we attempt to impose our old patterns on the new forms of information—digital data, audio, video, multimedia—we are finding the old patterns increasingly inadequate. We have to be able and willing to provide our institutions with both access to and training in the full range of information resources, replacing the concept of "mastery" with an acceptance of adequacy in an environment of lifelong learning and change.

One of our most cherished assumptions, even though we seldom articulate it, is that there will always—must always—be a library. But our institutions and users have no vested interest in libraries per se. Instead, each user is looking for the quickest, easiest, cheapest access to exactly the information he or she needs. Our users, and our institutions, expect responsive, cost-effective information delivery from whatever source. Unless the library is able to develop a range of user-based services, we will become an increasingly irrelevant warehouse, out of the mainstream of academic life and funding.

If we accept these realities—the library as part of a mix of information services, the continuing fragmentation and proliferation of information, and the user as the basis for services—then how do we use this acceptance and understanding to survive in the reality in which we find ourselves? We see—and have begun acting upon—three essential components for survival:

1. grounding the library in the particular institution;
2. involving the library and librarians in the sociopolitical matrix of the institution;
3. making proactive use of new technologies and services.

THE LIBRARY AND ITS PARENT INSTITUTION

Institutions—even the largest or most prestigious ones—are increasingly conscious of their "market niche" and target their programs to maximize their advantage. Libraries, likewise, cannot afford to be generic but must increasingly become identified with the specific goals and expectations of the parent institution. At Bradley, for example, the university has made a specific commitment to maximizing technology for pedagogy and the curriculum. For the library to maintain its significance to faculty and students at Bradley, then, we have used technology to increase access to our resources and services, pushing out the walls of the library to deliver information and services to student and faculty desktops. The particular mix of resources and services—the vision of the library—must be rooted in the dynamics of the particular institution.

The understanding of the dynamics of the institution does not come from librarians holding themselves "above" or aloof from the politics and sociology of the institution. Instead, we have to accept new roles within the decision-making environment of our institutions. We need to develop as "movers and shakers" within the institution—roles with which we have not traditionally been comfortable and which our institutions have not traditionally allocated to us in other than pro forma ways. In the same way that we've developed access tools to maximize the use of our collections, we need to develop our political skills to maximize the library's participation in institutional decisions, from research to curriculum to budget allocation.

If we have shaped the library to the particular institution, and if we have integrated the library and librarians into the political and sociological fabric of the institution, we can develop and deliver services that anticipate the needs of our users. It isn't enough to react to the expressed needs of our patrons. As the information experts, we need to be constantly looking ahead at new technologies and new services that can contribute to the success of our patrons and our institutions.

NEW ROLES FOR LIBRARIANS

In the new reality that we've described, with the required survival skills outlined above, there are formidable expectations of the "new" librarian. These characteristics include the following:

1. expanded collegiality within the information community;
2. expanded collegiality within the institution;
3. visionary as well as pragmatic administrative acumen;
4. proactive and adaptive skills.

We have long prided ourselves on our interlibrary cooperation. We must expand that concept and stretch our abilities so that we can effectively cooperate with our colleagues in the broader information community of which libraries are a part. We need to understand and speak the language of telecommunications, networks, database development, publishing, information marketing, multimedia—all of the broad range of information services and media. If the library is to remain an integral part of the information mix, librarians must participate in the development and implementation of the full range of technologies.

To complement this broader collegiality, librarians must also develop collegial relationships within the institution. This may take the form of working with a biologist to develop a database of local fungi, with a nurse practitioner to develop a demographic profile of a service area, with a journalist to develop a policy on privacy and freedom of information, or with the Art Department to develop a curriculum in the book arts. If we are to retain and enhance our value to the institution, we need to help our colleagues understand that the library and librarians can contribute directly to their success in their own fields.

And all this collegiality will go for naught if we do not have the necessary administrative skills. It is not enough to be able to balance this year's budget (although that skill is becoming increasingly challenging). We have to be able to develop a vision of the future, to institutionalize that vision, to implement the vision within the local environment, and to change the vision and implementation to accommodate changing technological and institutional variables. We must be able to articulate and defend our role in the educational process, as well as to account for the resources that we manage. It is as important that we be able to negotiate the political and sociological shoals of our institutions as that we be able to manage the technology.

Frank Lloyd Wright's architectural dictum holds true in libraries as well: "Form follows function." There is a temptation to focus on the format or medium of information, rather than on the function that we provide. We must be proactive and adaptive in all areas: information access and management, organizational structure, programming and services, and collections and resources.

IMPLEMENTING THE VISION

The vision that we've outlined for the "new" library and librarians is a daunting one. While we recognize that implementing this vision will be stressful for all involved—institutions, libraries, and individual librarians— we can propose some strategies to mitigate the stresses involved in making the transition to the new roles: professional development, team work, developing an explicit statement of expectations, excising the "deadwood," and maintaining an emphasis on quality service.

Professional Development

There is much discussion in the profession about the future, and the "visions" group supported by the Council on Library Resources has done a good job of focusing the issues and fostering discussion. Part of that discussion has focused on the education necessary for the "new" librarian. We all feel comfortable with formal education as a tool for changing the profession. We recognize the role of workshops and training that focus on the use of particular tools, techniques, and resources. There is another type of professional development, however, that we need to begin using more effectively—the development that occurs when a library staff discusses a substantive issue and develops its own sense of the issue and approach to the situation. Although many of us feel uncomfortable in setting ourselves up as "experts" among our peers, at Bradley we've adopted a program of in-house professional development. Periodically, each member of the library faculty leads a discussion on an issue of his or her choice, first with the library faculty and then with the full library staff. Using these regular opportunities to move beyond day-to-day limitations has been very effective in building a common vision of where we are, where we plan to go, and how we plan to reach our goal.

Team Work

We've also used outside facilitators to help us develop a sense of ourselves as a team. In developing a set of "team norms" at a workshop two years ago, we found a remarkable unanimity in our perceived need to "share the load." This is particularly important in dealing with changes. It is less threatening to take the risk of assuming a new role when that risk is shared by others, and when the new role is broadly accepted and understood. It also makes it more difficult for a single individual or a small group to undermine progress toward the new role when the whole group has made a commitment to the new vision.

Explicit Statement of Expectations

Once a vision has been discussed and adopted, there is a tendency to assume that everyone is proceeding identically or equally toward implementation of that vision. This assumption is seldom warranted. Instead, it is critical that the new expectations—the new role—be explicitly incorporated in the goals and objectives of each member of the library staff. The new expectations should be included—with room for flexibility and allowance for failure—in the evaluation process both within the library and within the tenure and promotion guidelines of the institution. Unless the new roles are recognized in the institutions reward structure—salary, job security, and status—it is easy to pay lip service only to the new vision, while effectively reinforcing the status quo.

Excising the Deadwood

Even when we have concentrated on professional development, built effective teams, and developed reward systems for change, there will be situations and individuals that do not adapt to the new roles. It's threatening to the whole organization when a supervisor begins to excise organizational deadwood, whether programmatic or personnel. However, if we are to move forward to implementation of the vision, we have to be willing to accept the responsibility for making those decisions and carrying through with them. The excision may be organizational, like eliminating the pet program or service of a particular member of the faculty or staff. It may be preemptive, like not writing a recommendation to library school for someone we don't believe has the ability to fully participate as a "new" librarian. Most painfully, it may be the dismissal of a member of the library staff who has not been able or willing to accept and participate in the new vision. As administrators, we like to believe that we can build consensus and commitment to the new vision, and we tend to view it as a personal failure when an individual fails to make the transition. It is essential, however, that the whole library—programs, services, resources, and personnel—be committed to participation in the new vision and roles. Terminating employees is never easy, but we must recognize those situations where it is required and be prepared to act on our judgment.

Emphasis on Quality Service

Throughout all of the planning and implementation, an emphasis on the reason for the change—on quality service that meets the needs of library users— helps to focus library staff on the end, rather than on the changes that are bringing about that end. At Bradley, we're in our second year of a "service excellence" program. All members of the library staff and a number of students and teaching faculty are involved in activities focused on improving the quality of the services the library provides. While some of the improvements implemented as part of this program are small, the total program is making a significant impact on the way the library operates. Perhaps even more importantly, the service excellence concept is helping staff to concentrate on the outcomes of changing roles and expectations, rather than on the stresses of actually implementing the changes.

FUTURE OF THE LIBRARY

Neither envisioning new roles nor implementing them will be easy. However, if libraries and librarians are to maintain their value within higher education, we must begin to take action. Unless we plan for the future and then take steps to make that future a reality, we may be locked into the past, with no future at all.

The future view of the library, then, is one of a range of activities and services—not necessarily a place—that is central to the academic and research missions of the institution. In this vision, the library and its employees are capable of participating at least as peers, if not as visionaries, of the information age. That means guaranteeing the availability and developing a mastery of the tools and techniques of tomorrow: computers, high-capacity storage media, networks, multiple information formats and information access tools, as well as the traditional print forms. It also means developing a mastery of our social and political environment: proactive leadership, service emphasis, and integration into the institution. The transformation required for fulfillment of our new visions need not be completely realized to achieve results; rather, we will see the institution's view of us change even as we begin the transformation.

BRADLEY'S EXPERIENCE

The last half decade has been one of significant activity and change at our institution. Within the span of six years, we completed a major capital campaign, constructed six major buildings, created a new administrative unit housing the library and all other information units, and went through a strategic planning process and North Central institutional accreditation. We've about planned and studied ourselves to death. However, these processes have presented us with a singular opportunity to put into practice the philosophies and theories described earlier, with the result that we have begun to transform our library fundamentally and reshape the campus vision of the library and its institutional role.

During the period 1984 through 1988, Bradley conducted the largest capital campaign in its history, with a focus on brick and mortar expansion and renovation. Among the projects included in the campaign was one to renovate the library and double its size. Then, in the spring of 1986, an administrative restructuring took place at Bradley. Among the changes made was the creation of a new unit named Information Technologies and Resources. The library, computing services, telecommunications, AV services, instructional television services, and the campus public radio station were all placed within this unit. This administrative structure has helped to place the library at the center of information services, both in planning and in current practice.

As planning for the new building unfolded, the new administrative structure—and the arrival of Ellen Watson as library director—led to a dual planning strategy of enhanced access to traditional library materials, with a greatly expanded emphasis on electronic information resources. The new library building was conceived as a fully networked facility, designed to accommodate both current and future information technologies; the building was dedicated in 1990. The library has become the campus centerpiece and a showplace for campus information technology. The library's exterior is inviting, and its interior comfortable. All of the librarians and staff have networked personal computers, and access stations for network resources and the online catalog are located throughout the building.

The focal point of the library's system of electronic resources is a local area network consisting of approximately 30 IBM and Macintosh workstations connected via Ethernet to a cluster of application servers. The facility is named the Microcomputer Information Center or MIC. The MIC is designed to provide transparent access to personal productivity software, campus and Internet information resources, electronic mail, CD-ROM databases, and ILLINET Online, our online catalog. The network also supports delivery of fax documents and is being enhanced to include an image database of the 14,000 rare photographs in our Special Collections Center. High-speed laser printing and downloading of information to floppy disks are supported from any workstation.

The MIC's information resources are also made available outside the library; for example, the CD-ROM database server, online catalog, and Internet resources can be accessed from faculty offices, residence hall computers, and the Department of English's writing lab. Librarians conduct, and download information from, online database searches; they use electronic and voice mail to communicate with faculty; they receive requests for materials through electronic mail; and they conduct training for faculty and students on a wide range of subjects dealing with academic applications of information technology.

A second major event that has shaped the development of the library was the university's strategic planning process. This multiyear effort got underway in 1987 and involved the entire campus. This presented an opportunity for our fledgling Information Technologies and Resources unit to develop a long-range plan encompassing elements from all of our constituent units and to embed that plan in the institution's own master plan. The library was one of the major contributors to the information technologies strategic plan. The recently completed building and its technology were a source of inspiration, as well as of credibility, for the concepts embodied in our plan. Throughout the planning process, the information technologies executive committee met with planning committees from each of the colleges to exchange ideas and to stimulate thinking. This collaboration resulted in a final university plan that embodied many of our ideas in the plans of the academic units and reflected their needs in our plan.

The strategic plan places the library at the academic heart of the institution, providing traditional services and resources as well as new ones based on modern technology. The library also provides a wide range of "high touch" services, such as information literacy training, online database searching, and delivery of documents to faculty offices.

Since the university's plan was published in 1991, we have been vigorously pursuing its implementation. Having gained campus-wide consensus through the planning process has made it much easier to implement many of the campus improvements we sought. It is not enough to change institutional expectations; we must also address performance expectations within the library as well. Thus, we have implemented programs to increase staff awareness and abilities to deal with electronic information resources—both their own as well as those used by patrons. We have also begun a quality assessment and improvement program to become more attuned to user needs and to increase the library's ability to meet user expectations.

However, we, like many other libraries, are struggling in the battle between budget growth and acquisitions cost increases. Although we have managed to keep up over the past several years, simply maintaining our current acquisitions has prevented us from making needed basic improvements in the scope of our collection. This year, we will have to cancel some journal subscriptions. And prospects for the immediate future are not much brighter. Thus, we have now begun a project to formally replace some journal acquisitions with online information access, a process that will be made somewhat easier because of the earlier planning process. This will occur only in selective areas where the needed online information is actually available, where the cost of online information usage will be lower than the equivalent journal subscription, and where our faculty will agree to the transition. Unfortunately, this combination is, at present, somewhat rare.

CONCLUSION

Within the current range of opportunities and limitations, our goal has been to develop a new, dynamic vision for the library, based on basic institutional needs and supported by all campus information units. By coordinating this vision with campus academic units and embedding it in the institution's strategic plan, we have made the library's plan de facto institutional policy. That is not to say that a cornucopia of funding has as yet appeared; however, we now find the campus and administration generally receptive—and in some cases demanding—regarding the library's emerging involvement with electronic information services. The impressive new building has also helped.

However, the most important achievement has been to reposition the library as a modern, dynamic enterprise—one that is a leader of campus planning, not a follower. This, we believe, will serve the library well, helping us to face both the challenges and opportunities to come.

INDEX